The Author

ROBERT D. CULVER is professor and chairman of the division of biblical and systematic theology at Trinity Evangelical Divinity School in Deerfield, Illinois. He has previously taught at Grace Theological Seminary, Wheaton College and Graduate School, and Northwestern College.

His extensive pastoral experience includes several pastorates and numerous revival and evangelistic meetings in the United States and in several foreign countries. He has also served as annual director of the Near East School of Archaeology in Jerusalem and as visiting professor at Evangelical Theological College in Hong Kong.

He holds degrees from Grace Theological Seminary (B.D., Th.M., Th.D.) and Heidelberg College (A.B.) and has also studied at Chicago Lutheran Theological Seminary, Ashland College, Central Washington College, and the University of Minnesota.

His published work includes numerous articles for the *Wycliffe Bible Commentary* and *Wycliffe Bible Encyclopedia* as well as a major commentary on the millennial themes of the book of Daniel, *Daniel and the Latter Days*. He has also contributed to the volume *Can I Trust the Bible?*

Toward a
Biblical View
of Civil
Government

Toward a Biblical View of Civil Government

Robert Duncan Culver

moody press
chicago

ISBN: 0-8024-8796-3

Printed in the United States of America

CONTENTS

CHAPTER   PAGE

Introduction   7

Part I: General Doctrinal Background

1. The Grandeur and the Misery of Man   11
2. Human Life Under the Condition of Sin   20
3. The Ambiguity of Biblical Statements About the World   30
4. The Manifoldness of the World in Biblical Thought   40
5. The Nations of Earth and Their Governments as Part of
   a Satanic Kingdom   49

Part II Interpretation of the Essential Biblical Data

6. Civil Government in Biblical History   61
7. Civil Government in Old Testament Biblical Prophecy   84
8. Civil Government in Old Testament Messianic Expectation   102
9. Civil Government in Old Testament Legislation   116
10. Religious Foundations of the Mosaic Commonwealth
    of Israel   126
11. Political Structure and Characteristics of the Mosaic
    Commonwealth of Israel   134
12. Property and Slavery in the Mosaic Commonwealth
    of Israel   151
13. Civil Government in Biblical Wisdom   165
14. The Practice and Example of Jesus with Regard to
    Civil Government   182
15. The Teachings of Jesus with Regard to Civil Government   197
16. The Practice and Example of Paul with Regard to Civil
    Government—Before Jewish Authorities and
    Illegal Mobs   208
17. The Practice and Example of Paul with Regard to Civil
    Government—Before Lawful Civil Magistrates   220

18. The Teachings of Paul with Regard to Civil Government   241
19. The Teachings of Paul and Peter with Regard to Civil
    Government   257
20. New Testament Warnings and Predictions with Regard
    to Civil Government   269
    Epilogue   274
    Notes   291
    General Index   299
    Scripture Index   303

INTRODUCTION

WHAT RECOGNITION AND AUTHORITY does the Christian Bible assign to civil government; and in that connection, what benefits does it claim, and what duties are required from Christians? This question is important because of its bearing upon the conduct of the individual Christian in the civil community and upon the world mission of the church.

If our pursuit of an answer is to be successful, some preliminary matters must be investigated. Since it is *human* civil government which is under consideration, and since government is an aspect of the larger entity called society, we cannot avoid two prior investigations.

The pursuit leads first to the doctrine of man. "What is man, that thou art mindful of him?" (Ps 8:4). Is he good or bad? If bad, is he perfectible or incorrigible? How does the condition of man as individual affect man collectively in society and state?

It leads next to the doctrine of the world: How are we to regard the creation of which man is a part? What does the Bible say about its origin, nature, present control, and future?*

Certain aspects of the biblical doctrine of the world and its present condition render desirable some exposition of the scriptural teaching about suprahuman personal evil—that arcane area where some scoff while others tremble—the doctrine of Satan. Does he exist? Does he have associates and servants evil like himself, that is, demons and fallen angels? Does he have anything to do with civil governments? This is discussed next.

---

*"In order to answer the question what is good for men . . . we must first answer the question: what is man? what ought men to be? . . . If we would penetrate beyond the technique . . . if we would look behind the institutions to the ideas and purposes that they embody and seek to realize in practical affairs we must concern ourselves not only with such problems as the nature of good but with such problems as the nature of man and of the universe he inhabits" (John H. Hallowell, *Main Currents in Modern Political Thought* [1950], p. 000).

7

Civil government (or "the state," as modern men tend to think and speak) is then explored against this general doctrinal background. It will be understood as an important aspect of God's general providence, and it is examined as a fact of biblical history, a subject of biblical prophecy, an area of extensive legislation in the Pentateuch, a topic of comment in biblical wisdom, a matter of practice and teaching by Jesus and His apostles. A chapter of theological and practical conclusions brings the study to a close.

PART

I

General Doctrinal Background

1

THE GRANDEUR AND THE MISERY OF MAN

THE INTEREST of this investigation is government of men in civil relations by men. The field of investigation is the Christian Scriptures, Old Testament and New. Hence, the study must start where mankind first appears in the Scriptures, where man's physical, moral, spiritual, and societal elements are laid out, and wherein the basic elements of his situation in the world are set forth. That portion is the first four chapters of Genesis.

Without reflecting on the mode of revelation employed by the author of Genesis, let us examine what man is by creation. The first movement of the narrative includes the verses through Genesis 2:3.[1] It delineates at least seven features of man himself and his place in the created order:

(1) He is the crown of God's creative art, the pièce de résistance, the final and best item coming at the very end of the creative epoch.

(2) Man is like God in a unique way, not merely in his physical nature reflecting some unnamed divine perfections, but especially in his moral and spiritual constitution wherein he is not even a part of the natural order.

(3) Man is male and female, no distinction being drawn as to the degree in which each sex shares in the excellencies of the divine image, for it may be that the two in aggregate or even in union are so designated.

(4) Perhaps as a feature of the divine image, men are to have the privilege of dominion over the rest of God's earthly creatures.

(5) Man has been given the duty to subdue the earth.

11

(6) Man is to multiply his kind by natural reproduction.

(7) He is privileged to use other creatures—specifically for food, and presumably for other purposes also.

The story summarized by the previous statements has been compared a pyramid with man being the capstone. The story beginning with 2:4 is, so to speak, a series of concentric circles with the different creatures of God forming the circles and man the male at the center, the female being the nearest of the circles. A number of supplemental details about man appear. The first is only a slight advance on two of the items noted above—that creatures of earth are for man, *for* his use and pleasure. But second, man is earthbound, earth from earth, unless God does something more for him (see Ps 115:16). This, however, is balanced by a third emphasis, that though he is, in part, of the earth and will be subject to nature's laws, he has his breath from God (another way of emphasizing spiritual likeness to Him.) This God-likeness is something which is not a part of the world of determined things ruled by natural laws. Important to the doctrine of sin is the fourth item, the organic vital unity of the human race, the woman being derived from the man, and they two being the progenitors of all mankind in subsequent generations. Fifth, man has been from his beginning the possessor of a high degree of intelligence, sufficient to assess the quality of the other sentient creatures and to give them appropriate names. Apparently there are no so-called anthropoids or hominids in the Bible. Hence, sixth, culture emerges spontaneously and *ab origine.* The joyful, relaxed relation of the sexes in monogamous marriage is emphasized—they do not even wear clothing. The duty of labor and its correlate, the keeping of a weekly sabbath, is announced.

The duty of labor, barely suggested in chapter one (v. 28) and rendered explicit herein, calls for some further notice. God "put him in the garden of Eden to dress it and to keep it" (2:15). Many inferences may be drawn: man is *homo faciens,* tool-maker and user from the beginning. The ethic of work is not a Calvinist ethic, but one of the creation ordinances, a clear biblical teaching.[2] Not only so, but man the laborer, given the normal condition of non-sin, is fully capable of developing the arts—in the absence of abundant leisure time. Sad is the fact that a low level of moral attainment has all too frequently accompanied artistic excellence. Is it possibly because artistic expression is (at least in recent times) on the part of those who make an exclusive profession of art, be it literature, painting, sculpture, dance, or drama? In his excellent discussion of the creation ordinances, John Murray has well stated the connection between manual labor on the one hand and true art and culture on the other—a connection largely unnoticed at present. A few lines will impart a bit of the flavor of his remarks.

> There is warrant for the judgment that economics, culture, morality and piety have suffered grave havoc by failure to appreciate the nobility of manual labor. Multitudes of men and women, if they had thought in terms of this principle and had been taught in the home, in the church, and in the school to think in these terms, would have been saved from the catastrophe of economic, moral, and religious ruin because they would have been preserved from the vain ambition of pursuing vocations for which they were not equipped and which, on sober and enlightened reflection, they would not have sought. It is a fallacy to think, and it is one that has greatly impoverished the life of society, that culture cannot exist and flourish among manual toilers.[3]

After the fall of man, the duty of labor is made even more explicit. The New Testament treats voluntary idleness as a sin serious enough to be rebuked with the kind of strong language often directed toward fornication, idolatry, drunkenness, and similar sins. Said Paul, "If any would not work, neither should he eat" (2 Th 3:10, cf. vv. 6-10; 1 Ti 5:8-16; 2 Jn 10-11).

As to a weekly Sabbath, it appears correct to see here a command to man to observe the Sabbath of God in connection with His work in Eden.[4] "The Sabbath was made for man," said Jesus in Mark 2:27. There is no reason to suppose that "was made" has reference to Exodus 20 rather than to Genesis 2. (See also Ex 16:23-30 and Neh 9:13 which indicate that the Sabbath long antedated the Mosaic ordinance.)

The third great biblical passage treating the state of man at creation is Psalm 8. Actually, the passage does not contemplate the fall at all. It treats the Genesis revelation as if the facts about man's creation reported there relate to postlapsarian man quite as much as prelapsarian man. Such is, indeed, the case in general. Adjustments were made, yet man remained man. Only such adjustments as were made necessary by sin are introduced. This is the beginning of the story of coercive civil government.

Several questions about man's nature and original state are aroused by reflecting upon these revelations in the light of later biblical statements. People want to know if man's nature was morally free or determined; if he was able not to sin or not able to sin; if soul is the same as spirit in man, and if the souls of human offspring are procreated by parents, as are their bodies, or if God creates the souls in some other manner and infuses them into the bodies, and, in either case, when and how? A further question is what constitutes the image of God in which He created man (Gen 1:27)?

The significance, difficulty, and importance of these questions are indicated by the number and sizes of the books that have been written, sometimes on only one of the above questions. An older work, for example, on the question of whether soul and spirit are the same, runs to nearly 400 pages.[5] Volume One ("Human Nature") of Reinhold Niebuhr's *The Nature and Destiny of Man* runs to over 300 pages,[6] while G. C. Berkouwer's *Man: The Image of God* runs to 375 pages.[7] The anthropology sections of standard works of systematic or dogmatic theology for over fifteen centuries (if we include Augustine's *Anti-Pelagian Writings)* have been about the most ponderous of all sections of those works.

Yet we cannot here pursue a solution to these problems. They must not be allowed to obscure the essential feature of our study and what ought really to be very plain: Man's original state was one of happiness wherein personal and community fulfillment were possible. This is the normal state of man. Sadly, it was not a permanent state. We can speculate as to why God allowed sin to enter, but our best answers fall short of certainty. This is true not only because God has not revealed the answer; but also because in such an area of investigation, the reasoning powers of fallen men are not fully to be trusted. It is too easy to let erroneous or sinful presuppositions get in the way.

If man were today such as mankind were then, the social organization of men would be completely effective for beauty, truth, happiness, fulfillment, freedom, and all other possible goods. Such social organization would not need to be coercive, for men would respond joyfully to such organization without constraint. So-called social control would not exist.

Not only is the man of paradise normal man, but he is essential man. That is to say, just to the degree that man is perverted, degraded, or alienated from his original nature, he is variant from essential man. The adage, "To err is human," could not be farther from reality. The truth is that to err, or to sin, is inhuman.

None has ever seen this more plainly or put it more vividly in words than Blaise Pascal, French mathematician, philosopher, and Christian apologist (1633-1662). He wrote: "The greatness of man is so evident that it is even proved by his wretchedness. For what in animals is called nature we call wretchedness in man; by which we recognize that, his nature now being like that of animals, he has fallen from a better nature which once was his. For who is unhappy at not being a king except a deposed king? . . .Who is unhappy at having one mouth? And who is not unhappy at having only one eye? Probably no man ever ventured to mourn at not having three eyes. But anyone is inconsolable at having none."[8]

Few have been more precise in addressing this truth to the present world than Reinhold Niebuhr. Though not quite the sensation today that they were when published thirty-five years ago, his words are still impressive: "No man, however deeply involved in sin, is able to regard the misery of sin as normal. Some memory of a previous condition of blessedness seems to linger in his soul; some echo of the law which he has violated seems to resound in his conscience. Every effort to give the habits of sin the appearance of normality betrays something of the frenzy of an uneasy conscience. The contrast between what man is truly and essentially and what he has become is apparent."[9] Though Niebuhr's views of the previous condition of blessedness take some liberty with the proper sense of Scripture—for he rejects out of hand the idea of a historical fall of mankind—he is right again when he writes: "The reason why there is a heightened sense of sin in Christianity is that the vision of Christ heightens the contrast between what man is truly and what he has become; and destroys the prestige of normality which sinful forms of life periodically achieve in the world."[10]

A man born blind and deaf would naturally suppose that all men, known to him only by the other three senses, were blind and deaf, except that he would have no concept of blindness or deafness. Sin, disorder, and violence—manifest signs of human moral squalor—appear everywhere among manifest signs of man's magnificence. Viewed either as an individual or as a society, man is magnificent—a magnificent ruin! Seen in full perspective, he is more similar to the ruins of the Parthenon atop the acropolis of Athens than to the Washington monument or the Taj Mahal.

The focus of the present investigation does not require an extensive analysis of the complete story of the fall of Genesis 3 or of its theological interpretation in the New Testament. Yet nothing is more important to an understanding of why civil government is necessary, what social purposes it properly serves, and how men ought to respond to it, than an understanding of results of the fall of man.

There were results to the entire race of men, affecting both sexes in all ages to follow. As formulated by theologians, they were guilt, that is, blameworthiness and obligation to suffer the penalties of broken divine law; corruption of nature; and the penalty of death.

Mainly on the basis of Romans 5:12-20, wherein Paul says so in various ways at least seven times, biblically-informed Christians have always believed that when Adam became an apostate from God, all mankind—yet unborn—became apostate with him, so that what Adam lost by sin, he lost for us all. The crucial portions read: "Through one man sin entered into the world, and death through sin; and so death passed unto all men, for that all sinned. . . . By the trespass of the one the many died . . . for the judgment came of one unto condemnation . . . by the trespass of the one, death reigned through the one . . . so then as through one trespass the judgment came unto all men to condemnation . . . . For as through the one man's disobedience the many were made sinners" (Ro 5:12, 15-19). Christian theologians, as they have sought to explain this universal participation in the sin and its results, have not always agreed, and there is an enormous literature on the subject. But historically, every genuinely loyal formulation of biblical doctrine, as witnessed by all the great historic creeds and confessions, agrees that mankind is a fallen race, that men are so from birth, that the origin of this tragic condition is traceable through the procreative process of conception and birth back to our first parents in whom the fall took place. Some propose a mediate imputation of guilt rather than immediate, holding that only Adam's corruption, not his guilt, is directly ours. Yet no informed orthodox Christian has held that man ever at any moment from the moment of birth was either innocent or righteous, but rather a guilty sinner. John (or is it Jesus? The context does not clarify), commenting on the significance of Jesus, says in this regard, "He that believeth on the Son hath eternal life; but he that obeyeth not the Son shall not see life, but the wrath of God abideth on him" (Jn 3:36). Paul, referring to the present state of every man apart from divine redemption, observes that he is so without effort, for, "we all once lived in the lusts of our flesh, doing the desires of the flesh and of the mind, and were by nature children of wrath" (Eph 2:3). This is what is meant by the accepted, if commonly misunderstood expression, "original sin."

It has been only after convictions of the historical nature of the Genesis narrative have been almost completely eroded that the doctrine of original sin set forth here has been rejected by those who would be Christian theologians. Thus, for example, though he largely ignores or misrepresents his own Calvinist exegetical tradition, Emil Brunner acknowledges that the doctrine defended here has been "standard . . . for the Christian doctrine of man, from the time of St. Augustine." Yet he asserts that it is "completely foreign to the thought of the Bible."[11] He thus sets aside his own Calvinist traditions, the evangelical Protestant theology in general, and historic Catholic orthodoxy as well. He employs a rather gay cavalier treatment of Romans 5:12, ignoring the weighty matters relating to the tense and meaning of "all sinned" in the passage, pounces on a supposed mistake of Augustine, and turns in a treatment of which any freshman in theology could be proud.[12] But Brunner would never do this, we suspect, if he did not already feel released from the "history" of Genesis three—having accepted myth as the revelatory mode in the Genesis story of the fall.[13] The myth is "wholly timeless . . . a symbol clothed in the form of an event."[14] These remarks of this most influential theologian are pre-Bultmanian and were important in preparing the ground for acceptance of Bultman's *Demythologieserung*. A similar situation in certain quarters of Roman Catholic theology is the near rejection of original sin in the new Dutch Catechism. A few words from the English translation will give the flavor: "Chapters 1-11 of Genesis describe the basic elements of all human encounter with God. It is only with chapter 12, where Abraham appears, that we begin to make out historical figures in the past."[15] With reference to Paul in Romans 5:12-21: "At first it seems that his intention is to stress the fact that it was through one man that sin came into the world. But the repetition of the word 'one,' *occasioned by the view of the world history as it existed in Paul's time,* is only part of the dress, not the message."[16]

Yet strangely enough, on other than strictly biblical grounds, both those of Brunner's type of Protestant neoorthodoxy and the new Roman Catholic liberalism take a dim view of man's moral character, believing him to be much the same sinner as do orthodox Christians, on biblical grounds.

This doctrine has always offended men who are unprepared to accept a mystery known only by revelation. There are few indeed of the wise of this world, ecclesiastically, academically, or otherwise, who truly accept it, however much they may inwardly fear it may be be true. It is one of those mysteries that no one can know except the Father teach him. It is too offensive to human pride.

To quote Pascal once more, after writing, "The mystery, the most profound of all in the whole circle of our experience is namely, the transmission of original sin," he refers to the offensiveness of the biblical doctrine as follows: "Nothing, assuredly, is more repugnant to us than this doctrine; yet, without this mystery, of all the most incomprehensible, we are incomprehensible to ourselves. Through this abyss it is, that the whole tangled thread of our moral condition takes its mazy and devious way; and man is actually more inconceivable apart from this mystery, than the mystery itself is inconceivable by man."[17]

A Christian view of civil government must always steadily and consistently hold to the fact that human society is a society of fallen beings, under the just judgment of God. The perfection of society cannot be either promised or attained, and it is not the purpose of civil government to do so. The Christian religion, on the basis of Scripture, is committed to the doctrine that under the condition of sin man is non-perfectable, either individually or collectively. Any other view is utopian. Certain improvements of relationship are possible. They are indeed, prescribed by Scripture. But the possibilities are not unlimited. This fact, introduced early in Holy Scripture is of paramount importance to any interpretation of civil government in the Bible.

2

HUMAN LIFE UNDER THE CONDITION OF SIN

THE DYNAMICS of the human race, whereby it goes limping but vigorously on its way through the generations, inhere in certain changes wrought by the fall and in God's gracious provisions in view of them.

The results of the fall peculiar to womankind are important to our subject. It is here, in the gracious provision of God for woman, that we begin to see the adjustments made in certain aspects of human behavior and the conditions of family life, how the race can continue in relative civil peace and social well-being, even given the facts of guilt, corruption, and death. What life might have been if our first parents had successfully passed their probation and a holy society had developed we cannot know; it certainly would have been different from what it is!

A very important facet of the new situation for womankind is multiplied conception: "I will greatly multiply . . . thy conception" (Gen 3:16). Woman must now bear more children to perpetuate the race, since death has entered the social equation. If death had not entered, then every baby born would have become a permanent inhabitant of the earth. Countless generations would have become contemporary. Now since death soon removes every generation within a few decades, every couple on the average must produce at least three to fulfill the command to "multiply and replenish the earth" (Gen 1:28); two to replace themselves, one for the increase.

Closely related, but of wider reference than to the mere act of motherhood, is: "I will greatly multiply thy pain" (v. 16). Woman surely does experience more sorrow and pain than man does. From adolescence onward, there is the recurring menstrual cycle with all its familiar inconveniences. Motherhood is her vocation, while fatherhood can be, and frequently is, only an avocation. No man who has sympathized with his wife in her pregnancy, who has stood by her side and listened to her cries in the travail of childbirth, and who has been her stay through the vicissitudes of child-rearing can doubt that God did greatly increase her pain.

If these provisions were not balanced by the two now to follow, the human race would have died out at the beginning. Why should any woman marry under conditions of increased conception and increased pain—given also a fallen self-serving disposition as well? And granting she did marry, why should she continue to sleep with her husband when childbirth has become a burden?

Comes, then, the third adjustment in woman nature, a natural attraction to her husband: "Thy desire shall be to thy husband" (v. 16). This means *she* desires her *husband,* not the other way around. The whole world is abundantly familiar with the aggressive male desire for and interest in the female. It is pervasive. And because men know this passion so well in themselves, they suppose they understand it in their women. Understanding of the mystery of womanhood on this score will not come to a man by projecting his own feelings. Woman is dispositioned to desire and to need a husband in the whole range of living. Desire is not initially focused on coitus as in the male. Adult maidenhood has well-known drawbacks and is rarely deliberately chosen as a way of life. This interest in a husband appears in childhood and is therein directed toward the child's father; it changes direction and grows in adolescence; hopefully flowers in courtship and wedding; bears fruit and matures in marriage-relation and home. This interest lasts as long as life. God has sanctified it. But let there be no mistake: It has drawbacks, as every married woman knows. Great harm, through unrealistic and unbiblical romantic expectation, has been done in this regard also. Marriage, as it took shape under the condition of the fall, was never intended to be bliss. That is reserved for heaven. Its very perpetuation has required built-in tensions. The racial dynamic is built on them. It is unhistorical, unrealistic, and actually cruel to romanticize it out of the true shape of reality. It is important to a happy and peaceful life on this planet to understand some of the limits of expectation. Nothing causes quite such bitter disappointment and resultant frustration and rebellion as the failure of unjustified expectation.

This leads to one final adjustment, subjection of wife to husband: "He shall rule over thee." This is the first mention of what has been called coercive power in the Bible. The same Hebrew word, meaning "rule," is used of the reign of kings, of the power of sin, of the subjection of peoples and even of the providential rule of God over the universe. This was and is a necessary element in the family, under the conditions of sin. Unless there is authority and obedience, there is chaos. It is, indeed, not strange to womanly nature to accept this role in her home. She seems to prefer it that way. Feminism and legal emancipation have not been able to persuade her out of it.

The Bible amplifies many details of this submissive role, chiefly to demonstrate that it is not a repressive role under the conditions of a civilization whose basic ethic has been of biblical origin. The universal effect of paganism has been the degrading of womanhood, while the effect of Christianity has been uniformly a proper emancipation of women. It is not hard to discern signs of the return of woman to the drudgery of work for which she was not made, and under conditions for which she is hardly fitted in the progressive paganizing of Western society. The post-Christian era, now in early stages, seems already to be moving backward rapidly, as the enslavement of woman to men's work progresses. Many women will regret the loss of their reign as queen in the home.

No one can say whether the present movement en masse of womanhood from the home is permanent. If it is, then her external interests must be protected from interests which would exploit her without either loving her (as is presumably the case with husband or father) or justly compensating her. The laborer is worthy of his hire, to say nothing of appreciation. Hence women should be compensated fully—just as men are. Her sex must not be held against her at the pay window. Likewise, if modern society is going to force her out of her immemorial domestic roles, then society must open the doors of the vocations and professions to her.

This aspect of the changes wrought by God in the human estate to preserve the race and to prevent unnecessary degradation is not simply a matter of commands to be obeyed or disobeyed—any more than the prediction of multiplied conception. Womanhood may sometimes resent her dependence on the man, but she cannot wipe it out like a dusty smudge on the tile of her kitchen floor. Though it does not take the same form in all the world, the dependence of women on men and the preeminence of men over women in positions of authority—in home, industry, education, and civil life—are prevalent everywhere.

A Golda Meir or a Senator Margaret Chase Smith here and there do not reverse the rule, any more than the fact that where men for cultural, economic, moral, or other reasons give up their natural responsibilities, their more conscientious female counterparts strive valiantly to carry them on. Understandable as it is in light of the exploitation of women, recurring opposition to the divine-natural arrangement is futile, and effort might better be directed to understanding it and adjusting to it.

The Bible affirms the propriety of obedience of wives to husbands as well as of virgin daughters of the male head of the parental home (Num 30:1-16; 1 Co 7:25, 36; 11:3; 14:34; Eph 5:24-25; Titus 2:3-5;1 Pe 3:1, 5-6). Paul connects his own doctrine in this regard to Genesis 3:16 (see 1 Co 14:34). Peter declares violation of the relationship will prevent desired answers to prayer (1 Pe 3:6), and Paul that it even leads to blasphemy of God's Word (Titus 2:5).

Yet Scripture also conditions the doctrine in such a way as to remove most, if not all, feminist objections. As noted above, the Bible authors understand the familiar lovable difference of woman's nature as something to be cherished and protected. "Can a virgin forget her ornaments, or a bride her attire?" (Jer. 2:32). God Himself, in an Old Testament parable, is represented as adorning a virgin with jewels, beads, and rings—even including a nose ring! (Eze 16:1-14). The Mosaic laws protected her rights against unjust fathers, slavemasters, brothers, or husbands. She is represented, in spite of some misunderstanding of Paul's dictum ("workers at home," Titus 2:5), as having legitimate and profitable interests outside her husband's home ("She considereth a field, and buyeth it . . . her merchandise is profitable" Pr 31:16, 18, cf. 10-31). The public service of gifted women is reported with high approval (e.g., Miriam, Ex 15:20; Deborah, Judg 4:4-24; wise woman of Tekoah, 2 Sa 14:2-20; Huldah, 2 Ch 34:22-28; Philip's daughters, Ac 18:2, 26; 1 Co 16:19; Priscilla, Ac 18:2, 26; Phoebe, Ro 16:1).

All of this is interesting in itself; it is a part of the whole counsel of God, to be taught to believers; but extended treatment here is due to the fact that the role assigned by Scripture, confirmed in numerous ways by history and general behavior, has important consequences for civil government. It means inevitably that in the main, civil government, the exercise of coercive authority of man over man, ordinarily will be a male function. This, however, calls for no special Christian doctrinal emphasis. The feminists notwithstanding, this is the way the matter always has stood and likely will remain. More important is that if it lives up to its duties, civil government must protect womanhood from unnecessary drudgery, from being degraded, exploited, abused, or corrupted by society in general or by any of its members. This apparently will be possible only if the non-equality of male and female, written in their respective natures as well as in the Bible, is recognized in civil law. There is accumulating evidence that otherwise she not only must go to war along with her brothers, but must be placed in all kinds of situations where she must live and serve without protection from overwork and mistreatment—to say nothing of physical abuse.

Results of the fall special to the male are threefold: the ground was cursed, he was condemned to hard labor, and he would ultimately have to die (3:17-24). Extended treatment of these is reserved for later paragraphs of this chapter. It is significant at this juncture, in explaining the human situation under the condition of sin, that all three are heavy restraints upon the excesses of that ambitious aggressor, the male of our species. Though earth challenges his effort and may even inspire him to work, she very reluctantly yields her fruits. He must work very hard to gather them. Ultimately he must give them all back to the earth and return to her himself. Yet, again, under the conditions of sin, this is how life must be if he is to be the loving husband and father. His wife is relieved of the excesses of his interest in and pursuit of his sexual passions, simply because toil has stolen from him the strength to pursue them. If he is to be fit to live with, let him not have too many days off!

Both the feminist movement and the labor interests could learn much from this chapter of Genesis.

The Genesis story of the fall and its immediate consequences is immediately followed by a striking report of the initial development of human civilization under the conditions of sin. Some theological systems begin at this point to talk about covenants—of works and of grace, or of nature and grace—still others of dispensations. All have a certain limited validity as rubrics under which a systematic arrangement may be accomplished—and they should not be discouraged except to observe that each has sometimes been too rigorously applied. The biblical record never speaks of any comprehensive category under which to subsume these developments. What we do see in chapter four of Genesis is the beginnings of civilization in a fallen race. We shall not attempt technically to defiine *civilization,* though we are using the word as a comprehensive name for the activities and institutions (informally defined) of man in society.

First appears the family—father, mother, and children, three of whose names we know (Cain, Abel, and Seth), though there were many more whose names we do not know (Gen 4:1-2,cf. 5:3-4).

One of the very first activities of the family is the exercise of religion, each of the two sons engaging in formal worship of God the Creator. Some, especially those who like to employ the rubric of "covenants," would like to call this the church. Yet, however much validity the concept of covenant has in this connection, it is unhistorical to apply it here and equally so to apply the name "church." An activity is described, for which no English words except religion and worship seem to fit.

One brother's activity represents worship of God as it was intended to be under the condition of sin (see Heb 11:4), the other's is represented as false, as being essentially an anti-worship form of religion (see 1 Jn 3:11-12)—a "way," rather than simply an incident (Jude 11). Civilized life has supported both of these religions ever since, both competing for man the sinner's allegiance throughout his journey through life toward death, the one with legitimate vivifying hope, the other essentially a hopeless ministry of death unto death. Here is the biblical answer to the philosophers' and anthropologists' quest for the origin of religion. A generic something called religion, however, does not exist in the Bible or elsewhere. There are only *religions,* and basically two of them. They arise out of man's need to return to God—out of alienation from God to sin. One is the revealed religion of grace; the other is that pervasive natural religion of supposed human merit.

The revealed religion of grace is seen in Abel's worship. It had its outward visible side: rituals, forms, observances, ordinances or sacraments—at least three of them. The first was a known visible basis of approach to God in worship—sacrifice of the precious commodity of life. Abel likely did not know why God had ordered sacrifice, but he believed God and brought a firstling of the flock. Abel's incipient theology of atonement waited long for explication, but it was nonetheless present (see Jn 1:29; Heb. 9:22).

Some discern also a set time of worship. It was "at the end of days" (Hebrew; English translation usually, "in the process of time"). How many days? A comparison of the relevant Scripture texts suggests seven (see Ex 16:22-30; Neh 9:13-14). At any rate, a regular gathering of worshiping people, in addition to the individual approach to God, has always been a distinctive mark of biblical religion (Heb 10:25).

Finally, there was what appears to have been a set place of worship. This is, of course, essential to any gathering of worshipers. Genesis 4:3 specifies only that the worshiper brought his gift unto the Lord. Verse 16, however, adds that "Cain went out from the presence of the Lord, and dwelt in the land of Nod, on the east of Eden." This sounds like leaving one specified locality for another— the former being some relatively permanently located altar of sacrifice.

These three ordinances are still with all who heed the voice of Abel (Heb 11:4)—a means or basis of worship in God's specified sacrifice, the body and blood of Christ; a time which will vary but will be regular; a place which is known to others and to which we loyally return regularly.

Doctrine features, if we may use the word *doctrine* in this connection, are not missing. There is a doctrine of God which seems to have been simply the recognition of His claim for worship as Creator. If He is, God must be worshiped (compare Ro 1:21-23). There is an incipient doctrine of sacrifice, atonement, or reconciliation. There is a doctrine of salvation by faith—believing God (cf. Heb 11:4). This presupposes a doctrine of revelation, for saving faith in God is always in God as revealed by His Word (Ro 10:17; 1 Pe 1:23-25). Was it primeval revelation, passed on to Abel by his parents? There is no better explanation. A doctrine of good works, of obedience to God, or of the good life, also appears. God worked in Abel not only to will but to do (Eph 2:8-9; Phil 2:12-13; Heb. 11:4).

These forms and doctrines were destined ever to be the heart of true worship of God in the biblical sense—in other words, true religion.

Natural folk religion is displayed in vulgar detail in Cain's story. The differences in the two religions do not spring from differences in essential character of the worshipers, for both were sinners. Furthermore, they had the same family background. The differences cannot, humanly speaking, really be explained at all, for God's grace is just that—grace. Except for special grace—and it cannot be omitted in a true evaluation—there would have been no true worship at all. In that case, Abel would have been another Cain.

Whereas Abel received divine revelation in faith, Cain rejected it in unfaith. Cain had religious forms, perhaps the same as Abel's, but they were just that—forms without heart religion. Cain brought his offering—the fruit of his own effort—singing, so to speak, "Something in my hand I bring." As it turned out, his false religion was one of hatred for the true worshipers and their faith as well (cf. 1 Jn 3:10-11). So he slew his believing brother. The results for Cain were all disastrous: disappointment (5-6), slavery to sin (v. 7), deeper depravity (vv. 8-9), further condemnation by God (vv. 10-12), misery in this life (vv. 13-14) and ultimately alienation from God forever. There is a condition, though, a possibility for a better end to Cain's story. God's last recorded act on Cain's behalf was to put a mark on him, lest any recognizing him should kill him (vv. 13-15). He was given space to repent. There is no hint that he did repent, though the possibility of it cannot be ruled out.

The last part of the chapter presents further development of civilization and advancement of culture: urban development (vv. 16-17), art and industry (vv. 20-22), and philosophical reflection in artistic expression (vv. 19, 23-24). This all occurs in a climate of spiritual apostasy. The developments of chapters five to nine, concluding with a universal judgment, which in turn was followed by a new world order among fallen men, is not surprising at all.

This is the human situation, in part, wherein civil government came to be set up. The basic elements in the situation have not

changed to the present hour. They have only grown old and customary.

Let us summarize some of our findings and relate them to the
subject of civil government. The human race is by creation composed of rational beings who have capacity and divine mandate to
rule the earth on which they are placed, and lawfully to exploit
it for their own benefit. The need for self-government—in the absence of sin, non-coercive government—is apparent in this mandate.
The command to fill the earth with their own kind through monogamous marriage and procreation is another fact calling for the
growth of some form of organized social direction, for since man
as bearing God's image is a rational free being rather than a pre-
determined and instinctively controlled one, there would be need of
cooperative direction as the race grew in numbers and spread out.
The forms this social direction might have taken are unknown. It
would have been some form consistent with man's likeness to God,
conditioned by the difference of the sexes in function and aptitude.
It would have operated in a manner, under God, to promote man's
improvement as a magnificent yet earthbound creature, sharing with
God a spiritual nature, providing expression for the talent, ability,
and aspirations of every member of the human family in honest
work. God would have been worshiped and glorified. "For though
it be admitted that even without sin the need would have asserted
itself of combining the many families in a higher unity, this unity
would have internally been bound up in the Kingship of God, which
would have ruled regularly, directly and harmoniously in the hearts
of all men, and would have externally incorporated itself in a patriarchal hierarchy. Thus no States would have existed, but only one
organic world empire, with God as its king, exactly what it prophesied
for the future which awaits us, when all sin shall have disappeared."[1]

But this never took place. A fall took place. Sin, with resulting
guilt, corruption, and condemnation became the invariable rule. The
evenness and balance of existence on earth were broken up, requir-
ing changes in man himself and in his environment if life was to
go on. A metabolic and systemic cycle ending in death became inherent in every man. Life among men became limited by contrary
competing passions. Changes in family life brought necessary coercive authority. For a while, with the restraints of a revealed religion,

culture and civilization continued to grow. Perhaps some form of patriarchal government existed. But an increasing weight of violence and corruption made necessary something stronger than mere voluntary cooperation. This is the meaning, for our search, of Genesis chapters six to nine.

The doctrine of sin informs us that civil government will never provide social perfection. Man the sinner is an incorrigible rebel. It is not surprising, as many competent historians remind us, that periods of prolonged social peace and economic prosperity frequently dissolve in civil disorder. Man is capable of ruling his fellows by force, but not by love. Love is strong, but only God's love is strong enough to perfect man, and then only by divine redemption. Our hope for the future, however much we may approve of good government, does not lie in man at all. Our hope is in God. "Behold, your God will come" (Is 35:4).

3

THE AMBIGUITY OF BIBLICAL STATEMENTS
ABOUT THE WORLD

IF THE BIBLE has a doctrine of society, it will be unnecessary to prove that it is important to a study of civil government in the Bible. Transform "society," a secular, nonbiblical term, into "world," the commonest biblical term for society, and the matter is clarified at once. Though the complexity of the subject forbids a detailed definition of the world or of society, the subject is briefly outlined here.

The Christian doctrine of the world is the precise area which seems most frequently to be overlooked in current theological debate over two related critical issues—the church's mission to the world, and the place of civil government in the social structure. There is a prevalent assumption that the world is a neutral entity in which there are both good and evil influences at work. If sufficient effort is deployed toward its betterment, it may be assumed that justice, if not holiness, ultimately will prevail. Biblical teachings do not support this assumption. Some religious people, on the other hand, have supposed the world to be evil without qualification and have drawn the unwarranted conclusion that the only thing for good people to do is to withdraw from it—some to monasteries, others to what might be termed evangelical ghettos, pietistical cloisters, or religious clubs.

Three related concepts connected with the biblical teaching arise from examination of the materials involved: first, the apparent ambiguity of the biblical statements about the world; second, the manifoldness of the concept and the injunctions connected therewith; third, the satanic character of the world's present organic processes.

If an interested person, initially ignorant of the Scriptures, were to begin serious Bible study by reading carefully from Genesis through Revelation, the ambiguity of which we speak would not seem acute, for he would be partially prepared for each facet of the problem before arriving at it. But one who comes to the subject directly from the world of ordinary discourse to read Scripture texts on the various aspects of the world as they appear in a topical index or concordance, will find them more than a little confusing.

For example, it is said in one place, "Love not the world, neither the things that are in the world. If any man love the world, the love of the Father is not in him" (1 Jn 2: 15). Yet in another book ascribed to the same author, it is said, "For God so loved the world, that he gave his only begotten Son" (Jn 3:16). In still another place, it is commanded, "Be ye therefore followers of God, as dear children" (Eph 5:1). Does God love the world, then command us not to love it, yet all the while asking us to imitate Him? It would appear that the signals have been mixed and that perhaps another huddle might be necessary! For other examples compare Psalm 24:1-2; 103:19; Daniel 4:35; Ephesians 1:11 with 1 Chronicles 21:1 (contrast 2 Sa 24:1); John 14:30; Daniel 10:2, 11-13.

This ambiguity of the biblical affirmations regarding the world roots in four facts of divine revelation. In the first place, God created the world perfectly good. With whatever sort of hermeneutical approach one reads the Genesis account, this is the resounding doctrinal affirmation of chapter one (see vv. 4, 31). Whatever good is, the original creation was in perfection to the superlative degree.*

---

*Christians have always pondered the question, If God is infinitely good, infinitely wise and powerful, why is there sin, suffering, stupidity, and anxiety in God's created world? Why do these moral, physical, intellectual and psychological evils exist? Certain ancient and modern religions have denied the existence of evil, though almost invariably in declaiming against error or illusion, they have really only acknowledged the existence of evil under a more pleasing name. Some very ancient forms of thought in various ways have declared evil to be, along with good, part of the primal stuff of the universe. Not uncommonly, nontheists and even some non-Christian theists, have represented evil as merely limitation or creatureliness, or even as good in the process of becoming. And there are many other views of evil. But whether he knows the name for his view or not, every biblically informed Christian takes a theistic view—that is, he knows the world to be created, sustained, and controlled by a personal God who is holy, wise, and powerful in infinite degree. He may have moments of doubt when, like the patriarch Job, he may be tempted to reproach God for allowing pain or sin; he may reflect upon the hypothetical possibility that God cannot do better; and he may even question God's benevolence asking, "Does Jesus care?" Yet his faith always recovers, as did Job's; for his basic convictions, drawn from Scripture and experience by the Spirit of God, allow him no recourse but to leave the questions with God whom he knows he can personally trust. He accepts the partial answer he has, with faith, and awaits further knowledge in the day when he no longer walks by faith alone, but by immediate vision of God. He does not really suspend judgment on the question. He makes a judgment on what he knows of God, postponing rational explanations for the time when he has sufficient knowledge.

This doctrine is joyfully proclaimed in all its glory throughout the Bible for the happiness of the human race and all God's lesser creatures.

Attention is now directed to the second fact of revelation in which ambiguity finds root: The highest part of God's creation fell, and somehow all the world fell with him. Those unfamiliar with the Genesis story may read it. The reader's predilections may incline him to interpret it literally, parabolically, metaphorically, typically, by a mixture of these methods, or even mythologically. In any case, treated fairly and taken seriously as a revelation of truth, his interpretation must conclude that man has evil at his heart, that nature has disorder, but that man and nature have not always been so. No one needs a book of special divine revelation to know that there is something perverse about man and something askew in his environment. But one must take recourse to special divine revelation to be informed that such was not the case originally. Sin and evil are not original. They are perversions of original good.

We shall shortly return to relate these facts to the theme of civil government, but at this stage we must give them attention in the interest of steady confidence in the correctness of the assertion that nature as well as mankind was affected by the events of Genesis chapter three. Of special significance is 3:17-19: "And unto Adam he said, Because thou hast hearkened unto the voice of thy wife, and hast eaten of the tree, of which I commanded thee, saying, Thou shalt not eat of it: cursed is the ground for thy sake; in toil shalt thou eat of it all the days of thy life; thorns also and thistles shall it bring forth to thee; and thou shalt eat the herb of the field; in the sweat of thy face shalt thou eat bread, till thou return unto the ground; for out of it wast thou taken: for dust thou art, and unto dust shalt thou return."†

Many commentators have noted that postlapsarian man was to find

---

†An important fine point connected with a play on words and derivation is present in the Hebrew. Among the several available terms for man, the one used in verse 7 (rendered Adam, but meaning man) is *adham*. The word for ground, used later in the verse, is *adhamah*, the same as the word for man, except that ground is feminine gender. Hence we understand that in calling him Adam (*adham*), God is calling attention to his physical origin from the ground: "The Lord God made the *adham* dust from the *adhamah*" (Gen 2:7). Thus the derivation of man's name designates his groundly origin and provides a key to why, once he was cursed for sinning, the ground from which he was taken had to be cursed also. It is apparently neither possible nor proper for a cursed man to gain his living from blessed ground.

nature perverse, unresponsive, and only reluctantly fruitful. This was to be true of nature in her unkept state as the roving bedouin finds her, and likewise as modified by the efforts of the tiller of the soil. In the former case, she gives not only grass, but also thorns and thistles in the field; in the latter the hard ground compels endless grinding toil. [1]

Before commenting further on the passage, attention must be directed to a New Testament explanation of the connection of the fall of man with the present condition of the world. "For the earnest expectation of the creation waiteth for the revealing of the sons of God. For the creation was subjected to vanity [i.e., fruitlessness, failure of effort], not of its own will [creation is unconscious and nonrational as such], but by reason of him [i.e., God] who subjected it [cf. Gen 3:17-19], in hope that the creation itself also shall be delivered from the bondage of corruption [whether this be death in nature or perhaps defilement by man's sin and death is debatable] into the liberty of the glory of the children of God. For we know that the whole creation groaneth and travaileth in pain together until now" (Ro 8:19-22).

In the present-day "ecological crisis," this corruption is said to be approaching its climax. Robert Haldane, in a justly famous old commentary on Romans has written: "The creatures by their nature were appointed for the service of the friends of their Creator, but since the entrance of sin they have become subservient to his enemies. Instead of the sun and the heavens being honored to give light to those who obey God, and the earth to support the righteous, they now minister to rebels. The sun shines upon the wicked; the earth nourishes those who blaspheme their Maker, while its various products, instead of being employed for the glory of God, are used as instruments of ambition, of avarice, of intemperance, of cruelty, of idolatry, and are often employed for the destruction of his children. All these are subjected to vanity when applied by men for vain purposes." [2]

Human evil has, in some sense, polluted the whole natural order. The prevalence of evil and misery witness to the dishonor done creation's Author. It would be degrading the name of God to suppose that the present state of His works, wherein disorder and destruction are prevalent, is the same as that in which they were originally made, or that they shall continue forever as they now are.

Nature includes no moral agents. God stands above nature. Man also, though he shares biological life with nature, is, in the biblical perspective and in very truth, above nature. This is commonly denied today. Yet biblically informed men and even many others not convinced of materialistic humanism insist that at the deepest level of his existence, man is not really a part of nature. "The God of nature is no-God. Nature is God's creation, but he is beyond it, as the Hebrews have been taught. Nature is the kingdom of necessity, bound to unvarying laws, but God is eternally free. God exists outside nature and so does man, for although man is a child of nature, he is also a child of God. If he does not know himself as a child of God, he must eventually consider himself an animal, and has no rights except those he says he has."[3] It is therefore entirely in harmony with the Scriptures that in modern times, those areas of man's habitation where man's likeness to the living God is officially and dogmatically denied (i.e., where Marxian materialistic socialism prevails) are the precise areas wherein human rights and freedoms have been most systematically suppressed.

So there is good reason why, if the life of man was to continue at all on earth after man's failure in his first probation, the world of nature in which his life must be set had to be adjusted downward with him. Man's connection with nature made this necessary, as did also his relationship to God.

Care must be taken to keep strictly before one's attention that there is no moral quality whatsoever in inanimate and irrational things. Jesus took considerable pains to correct a contrary opinion which his disciples had derived from contemporary Judaism (Mk 7:1-4, cf. Mt 15:1-8). Paul likewise emphasized that there is nothing unclean of itself, as the most influential and most deeply morally earnest of the Protestant reformers insisted.[4]

So we are taught by Scripture that, even though, in some not quite clear sense, the world of things is a fallen world and is in bondage to corruption, it is not defiling as such. It is all to be used and received with thanks (1 Ti 4:3). Defilement proceeds from within ("uncontrolled desire . . . immoderate prodigality . . . vanity . . . arrogance"—Calvin). Jesus' words are to the same effect (cf. Mt 15:16-20).

Having said this, we must observe further that we should not eliminate the possibility that the life of fallen but moral man—as it develops in the world of nature which is somehow in bondage to corruption, producing thorns, thistles, and clods as well as fruits, vegetables, and flowers—will be something less than ideal. The society of man will be a scene of both joy and despair.

The consequences of these important facts for a biblical view of civil government are more fully assessed later in this study. A rigorous realism, together with a vivid idealism, will be necessary to attain a proper balance of view. The magnificence of man by creation and the goodness of earth by virtue of the same creation render praiseworthy every effort of government to promote order and harmony in man's attempts to utilize the bounties of earth. Yet, on the contrary, there must be limits of expectation. Man will not cease to be sinful, and the soil will not cease to produce thorns and thistles to keep him toiling. This is for man's good. To date, government has taken mankind but a short way on the road to Utopia. For example, the goals of added leisure for overworked toilers in the early decades of the industrial revolution, advocated by reformers and secured by civil laws, are fully justified. But free man entirely from the curse of toil, and both his moral character and his essential manhood will be destroyed.

It is equally clear that those features of society involved in the preservation of human life and its betterment—education, industry, art, government, police, and so forth—are not, as such, beyond the border where Christians may, with obedience to God, participate in them. Some forms of their development may be evil. These very features of society are the precise areas wherein Christians must work out their own destinies and bear their witness.

Now a third aspect of the ambiguity of biblical representation of the world's condition appears: the Bible presents the world of mankind as evil. One New Testament author speaks of it as "this present evil world." (Gal 1:4). Jesus Himself, after being dared by the members of His own family to perform His works openly in Jerusalem and to show Himself to the world (Jn. 7:3-4), said to his unbelieving brethren: "My time is not yet come; but your time is always ready. The world cannot hate you; but me it hateth, because I testify of it, that its works are evil" (Jn 7:6-7). Jesus testifies that the world's deeds (presumably, in some sense all of the world's deeds) are evil.

It is not important at this point to elaborate on or qualify the affirmation that the present world system of man is evil. We cannot—indeed, we dare not—forget that the present world-system occupies a world of nature created good by God. Even though fallen, the natural order is without moral taint; it is still God's good gift, serving man in opposite ways. If its showers nourish, its floods chasten; if its zephyrs and breezes cool the land, its tornadoes and hurricanes judge us. This is the Christian and biblical point of view.

But mankind and his humanly created systems are evil. The observed facts support the biblical assertions. As man's civilization increases in refinement and complexity, his sins expand; they multiply and intensify in proportion to the square of the increase.

The fourth aspect of the ambiguity of the world's description in the Bible is that the world has already been redeemed by Christ.

This is not the place for extended discussion of the vexing theological question of the extent of the atonement. This author is among many who, holding that the Scriptures plainly teach a special reference of the redemptive ministry of our Lord to the elect, hold there is also a general reference of that work to all men. This is no more nor less than orthodox advocates of both limited atonement and universal atonement acknowledge.

The apostle Paul is acutely aware of this fact of world redemption, devoting an especially exalted peroration to it (Col 1:19-23). He is deeply convinced of the special benefit for believers of Christ's work as is indicated by the words "in whom we have our redemption, the forgiveness of our sins" (Col 1:14). This is followed by declarations that nevertheless all that is, God expected, was created by Jesus Christ and for Him, being Himself the very image of God. The church is His special body (v. 18). Then comes the great text:

> For it was the good pleasure of the Father that in him should all the fulness dwell; and through him to reconcile all things unto himself, having made peace through the blood of his cross; through him, I say, whether things upon the earth, or things in the heavens. And you, being in time past alienated and enemies in your mind in your evil works, yet now hath he reconciled in the body of his flesh through

death, to present you holy and without blemish and unreprovable before him; if so be that ye continue in the faith, grounded and stedfast, and not moved away from the hope of the gospel which ye heard, which was preached in all creation under heaven; whereof I Paul was made a minister" (Col 1:19-23).

Our present interest focuses on verse 20, where reference is made to Christ's work "to reconcile all things unto Himself . . . through the blood of his cross."

In what sense has Christ accomplished this? It must be stated initially that the doctrine of universal salvation, including demons, fallen angels, and the devil, is eliminated as inconsistent with the doctrine of eternal punishment of the unrepentant that is distinctly sounded elsewhere in the New Testament. It is also inconsistent with the fervent zeal of the early church and the apostolic witnesses to win men out of the world.

Observe that here, though Paul uses the expression "to reconcile all things," employing *ta panta,* the ordinary expression for the whole universe, when the writer particularizes, he omits "things under the earth." The latter is the expression Paul uses elsewhere for the unseen evil powers (demons, fallen angels, Satan) in such enumerations, though he does mention "things upon the earth" and "things in the heavens" in this passage (contrast Phil 2:10-11). So we need not suppose that Paul referred to any reconciliation with Satan and his hosts as effected by Christ's redemption. Certain authors (notably Oscar Cullman and Karl Barth) have asserted and sought to prove that reference is here made to a victory by Christ in his redemption over the devil and his hosts which has compelled their obedient, if unwilling, service. It seems more likely that Paul is thinking in the terms of ultimate restoration of the nonrational creation which will take place with the glorification of God's regenerate sons (Ro 8:19-25) at the consummation. Since man's fall brought the curse, his restoration and consummated glorification presages nature's "redemption." Thus a connection between the "reconciliation" wrought through Christ's atonement and the reconciliation and redemption of all things is established. The holy heavenly beings and things, since they have never been alienated from God, are not included in the reconciliation. This much only needs to be affirmed: Whatever effects of human sin have been and wherever they have reached, there peace through the blood of Christ's cross has gone. One may walk into a saloon, a brothel, a vice den, or the godless emporiums of Wall Street and say to the thoughtless and godless, "God now holds nothing against you. 'The Spirit and the bride says, Come . . . take the water of life freely' " (Rev 22:17).

This then means that though he lives on a cursed earth and in the midst of a fallen race, being himself a sinner saved only by grace, the Christian can view the world with compassion. However repelled by what falls in the line of his spiritual vision, he can see, as God sees, a world doomed but presently approachable. Rescue of individuals is possible. It also means that he may feel admitted to the company of the world, if not quite at home in it. Though the world is still an enemy of God, a truce has been effected. Judgment has been reserved for a while.

So the world appears in Scripture somewhat ambiguously as created superlatively good yet fallen on account of man's fall—in bondage to corruption and in moral perspective, as somehow a "present evil world," nevertheless reconciled to God by the death of His Son.

These ambiguities of the biblical picture of the world—good but fallen, evil yet reconciled to God—present a pair of paradoxes. These in turn represent that condition which the Reformers, especially Luther, saw as such that, except for the presence of civil government, the world would have quickly destroyed itself. In the language of Luther, the state belongs to the order of preservation, not of creation. According to Luther, though the fall set loose centrifugal forces that drive men apart and which send them toward destruction, through the civil government inaugurated by the Noahic covenant (Gen 9), God gives an institutional instrument for preservation of the race from violent self-destruction.[5] As Helmut Thielicke has said, "Hence the state is simply the institutional form of God's call to order . . . for Luther the state is the gracious intervention of God which puts a stop to the self-destruction of the fallen world with a view to giving men a *kairos* [season] and bringing them to the last day."[6]

Accordingly, the state must be seen as a work of God whereby it becomes possible for the effects of redemption to be distributed to the elect of all the nations and of all the ages. That is, it is a force holding men in relatively peaceful check while the messengers of the gospel are free to preach and to persuade men to be reconciled to the God who has already provided the reconciliation by the death of His Son. Hence, although it is of the order of preservation rather than creation, in light of what we have seen of the present condition of the world and the need for civil tranquility as a condition of evangelism and Christian nurture, the state is, in a manner of speaking, also of the order of salvation. For that reason, Christians should most certainly pray for their city and for their officials. To the Israelites in captivity, God commanded Jeremiah to write that they should "seek the peace of the city whither I have caused you to be carried away captive, and pray unto the Lord for it; for in the peace thereof shall ye have peace" (Jer 29:7). Much later, Paul directly connected godly prayers for domestic tranquility with the desire of God, "who would have all men to be saved, and to come to the knowledge of the truth" (1 Ti 2:4 cf. vv. 1-5).

4

THE MANIFOLDNESS OF THE WORLD IN
BIBLICAL THOUGHT

FROM THE FIRST REFERENCE to the world in the first sentence of the Bible, and on to the very close of the Old Testament, "the heavens and the earth" is a standard expression, appearing many times.

The ancient Hebrews, at least a few of the gifted men who wrote inspired Scripture, had glimpsed some of the immensity of the world of creation. The author of the book of Job may be cited as example. He did not know about galaxies, Doppler effect, or red shift, nor did he measure anything in terms of light years, yet he understood something of the immensity of created reality (see chaps. 38-39). The authors of the Psalms may also be cited. Reinhold Niebuhr has written with telling irony: "But periodically man is advised and advises himself to moderate his pretensions and admit that he is only a little animal living a precarious existence on a second-rate planet, attached to a second-rate sun. There are modern astronomers who believe that this modesty is the characteristic genius of modern man and the fruit of his discovery of the vastness of interstellar spaces;but it was no modern astronomer who confessed, 'When I consider thy heavens, the work of thy fingers, the moon and the stars, which thou hast ordained; What is man that thou art mindful of him?' (Psa. 8:4)."[1]

While we must reserve for another occasion any extensive technical discussion of the biblical words rendered "world" in the Bible, a limited tour through the territory is necessary. We will eliminate for now the several Old Testament terms and come immediately to the New Testament. The Greek words rendered "world" in the King James Version number four. In addition, there are two other expressions which, though never translated "world," convey that thought. These two expressions may helpfully be considered together. They are *ta panta*, "the all things," with its variant, *panta*, "all things;" and *ktisis*, meaning "creation," once *pasa he ktisis* "the whole creation."

The first, "the all things," becomes in the New Testament a name for all that is, God excepted. This word *panta* (neut. pl. of *pas*) is the common word for "all," including all persons and things of any gender—masculine, feminine, or neuter. The neuter plural word *panta* already had this sense in prebiblical Greek.[2] In the Bible, this "all things" is God's creation. The Christian community and those informed by it have always had this conception, but the pagan world did not in Bible times, and does not now, whether the pagan be a learned scientist or a naked savage. Once paganism becomes reflective, it almost invariably adopts a pantheistic metaphysics, wherein the world of things is God. In the biblical view, not only is the universe (or all things) created by God, but as being made for His glory, it is preserved in existence and order by Him. Paul writes rapturously of these facts: "For of him, and through him, and unto him, are all things" (Ro 11:36).

Because God has created all things (*ta panta*, Eph 3:9), another name for "the all things" is "the creation" (Gr. *ktisis*, with or without the article). "Creation" is used about nine times in the New Testament in this sense (Mk 10:6; 13:19; Ro 1:20; 8:19, 20, 21, 22; 2 Pe 3:4; Rev 3:14).

In the biblical view, the world is wholly the creation of the transcendent, self-existent God. It is also sustained and governed by Him. The "all things" are His creation. From this, certain facts follow which are basic to a Christian view of history itself; hence of the details of the rise and fall of nations, of the powers that be, and of man's relation to all civil powers.

That God sustains the world of created things is the theological doctrine of preservation. That He governs it is the doctrine of providence. The Bible specifically rejects the notion that God in creation placed the creation under such full control of laws and secondary causes that it operates completely without Him. Rather, though God ceased from His works of creation (Gen 2:3, cf. Heb 4:10), His power continues to go forth uninterruptedly to keep it in existence and operation (Neh 9:6; Ps 36:6; 104; Ac 17:28; Col 1:17; Heb 1:1-2).

What are the implications of these scriptural teachings for a Christian understanding of the world in general and civil government in particular?

Negatively, the doctrine of creation implied in the words "all things" and "creation," delivers men who truly understand and believe them from many false and inadequate explanations of men and things, and from false views of their inter-relations and their relation to God. Because God is transcendent, that is, prior to and still above the world, there is no confusion of creation with God. God is not to be identified in any sense whatsoever with created matter, created mind, or created spirit. We can be delivered, thereby, from all the corruptions of idolatry—idolatry of graven images, idolatry of human thoughts and thrones, idolatry of human ideals and spiritual inventions. We do not look within ourselves or in anything we see to find God, Himself, His ways, His glory, His power, and many other things about Him as may be seen in the things which are made, as numerous biblical texts, especially in the Psalms, declare. But God Himself cannot be met in personal encounter in the creation per se. God is transcendent. Thus, although there may be traffic with created things, there should be no worship of them; and though we may be temporarily involved with the world, we have no ultimate concern with present time and space. The things which are seen are temporal and are passing away. Those things which are not seen are eternal and shall never pass away (2 Co 4:18; 1 Jn 2:17).

We are delivered from ancient myths and modern philosophies about cosmology and cosmogony—the processes of and origin of the world. Whatever science may discover or surmise about how the world began, the ultimate cause of the world is not a process, not a principle; it is a person—the God and Father of our Lord Jesus Christ. However it operates, the plan according to which the world proceeds and the power that impells it both are God's. The Christian need not commit himself to any theory of cosmology and cosmogony. He trusts in the living God. It is enough to know that God created the world, that He has plans for it, that He sustains and governs it and will bring it to His own appointed consummation. The cultivated pagan, fresh from crass heathen myths (be he ancient Greek or modern Japanese), may, in Christ, at once experience the relief of such deliverance more deeply than the Christian American who has been educated half in scientism and half in creationism.

Reinhold Niebuhr, in reference to the philosophical advantage of creationism, has written to good effect: "In the same manner the doctrine of creation corrects mistakes in rationalistic and idealistic cosmologies. These cosmologies are forced to presuppose some un-formed stuff, some realm of chaos, which *nous* (mind, intelligence) fashions into order, and to identify this forming process with cre-ation. The Biblical doctrine of creation derives both the formless stuff and the forming principle from a more ultimate source, which it defines as both *logos* and as creative will, as both the principle of form and the principle of vitality."[3] Niebuhr goes on to observe that such a doctrine is not derived strictly from reason, and though he prefers not to refer the source of the idea to special revelation in an orthodox sense, he does observe: "The supra-rational character of this doctrine is proved by the fact that, when pressed logically, it leads to the assertion that God creates *ex nihilo* [out of nothing], the idea at which all logical concepts of derivation must begin and end."[4]

Where these views prevail, a few evils at least, will not appear. Rats will not be protected to eat the corn while people starve, for God is not of the stuff of rats as in Hindu thought. The rat may in good conscience be exterminated. The processes of nature (sexual reproduction, the cycle of seasons, etc.), although created and sus-tained by God, are not a part of Him. There will therefore be no cult of fertility or of astrology. There is no fear of wizards which "peep and mutter" (Is 8:19). God will speak through nature, but not particularly. If He speaks particularly, then God will reveal His Word to prophets in a rational and communicable manner (Num 12:6; Dan 2:19-23).

But if God is transcendent, He is also immanent. He is not nature, but His power and glory are in nature, both seen and active there. Furthermore, it is not as some mere *logos, nous, elan,* or vital prin-ciple that God is in nature. It is as person, especially as the third person of the Godhead. Psalm 104 and 19:1-7 are among the most striking biblical proclamations of the divine presence in nature.

Biblical religion delivers men from unreasonable fear of nature's powers. The tempest may be fierce, but God controls it. Biblical faith, likewise, delivers men from fear of nature spirits and all the hobgoblins of superstitious religion, from simple animism to Bishop Pike's sad spiritism, "For though there be that are called gods, whether in heaven or on earth; as there are gods many and lords many; yet to us there is one God, the Father, of whom are all things, and we unto him; and one Lord, Jesus Christ, through whom are all things, and we through him" (1 Co 8:5-6). The spirits of the dead do not join a shadowy underworld of demonic spirits. The Old Testament people of God who knew of this doctrine among their heathen neighbors did not endorse it. "And when they shall say unto you. Seek unto them that have familiar spirits and unto the wizards, that chirp and that mutter: should not a people seek unto their God? on behalf of the living should they seek unto the dead? To the law and to the testimony! if they speak not according to this word, *it is* because *there is* no light in them." (Is 8:19-20).

The progressive repaganizing of society in Christendom has seen, together with many moral disasters, a startling revival of interest in the occult. Many daily newspapers now regularly publish astrological horoscopes, for example. And this is not done as a matter of humorous entertainment, but with awareness that a significant section of the readership is being served, as by the Saturday church page or the racing sheet. Witches and warlocks are now frequently featured in social gatherings. The sad part is not that the sons and daughters of godly Christian forebears seek a wisdom greater than their own as they face a perilous future, but that they have neglected the Holy Scriptures and the triune God while they turn to the no-gods of hoary-headed heathenism. The people of today are not unlike the Israelites of the time of Moses or of the Judges, as a brief extract from a Song of Moses exhibits: "But Jeshurun waxed fat, and kicked: . . . Then he forsook God who made him, And lightly esteemed the Rock of his salvation. They moved him to jealousy with strange gods; with abominations provoked they him to anger. They sacrificed unto demons, which were no God, To gods that they knew not, To new gods that came up of late, Which your fathers dreaded not. Of the Rock that begat thee thou art unmindful, And hast forgotten God that gave thee birth" (Deu 32:15-18). "They chose new gods" (Judg 5:8).

Likewise the biblical doctrine of creation, affirming both God's transcendence and immanence, has freed those who know and believe the doctrine from that debilitating submission to fate which has killed true joy while it destroyed progress in many parts of the world. The pagans of classical antiquity conceived even of their gods as beneath the sway of an impersonal fate. The gods, like the world, were thought to be of derived being. No loving personal Father was in charge. Only a man who, like Job, knows that God "laid the foundations of the earth" (38:4); that he is above all nature, "upon earth there is not his like" (41:33), can say, "Though he slay me, yet will I trust in him" (13:15, KJV), and "I know that my Redeemer liveth" (19:25). Fate and chance for a biblical Christian are no more than a pagan manner of speaking, existing as orphan children in an alien atmosphere whenever accepted in Christian conversation.

Gē, rendered country twice, earth 18 times, ground 18 times, land (as opposed to sea) 42 times, and world only once, is also of some importance to the biblical concept of the world but has small bearing on the topic of civil government.

Another of the four New Testament words is *oikoumenē,* appearing 15 times. It is rendered world 14 times but earth only once. This word is not really a noun, but a participle meaning "inhabited"; and it is to be understood that *ge* (earth) is to be supplied, hence, "inhabited part of the earth."[5] First, among Greeks it was applied to themselves and their country, as opposed to barbarians and their lands. With the conquest of the east by Alexander in the fourth century B.C., the Greeks came to equate it with civilization, which to a Greek meant Greek civilization. Later, when the Roman Empire absorbed the Grecian one and spread westward to Britain and eastward to India, *oikoumenē* became a standard word for the civilized world. Though in the New Testament a more comprehensive reference is suggested occasionally (e.g., Heb 2:5), this is to be regarded as an hyperbole. Basically the word means the civilized part of the earth. So, the biblical view of the world shares this much with the common one, ancient and modern—the important part of the world of mankind is that which is integrated into that vast network of persons, ideas, and things which is called civilization. This area, both geographically and demographically, and ideologically as well, has been increasing in size since the Greeks first coined a word for it, until today one must search for a place to get out of it or away from it. A retreat from the world is hard to find these days.

A third word is *aiōn*, appearing forty times in the New Testament. Though the basic notion involved is the temporal concept of age, period of time, this is so closely related to the leading idea in the biblical view of the world, as we shall shortly notice, that in thirty-five of the forty occurrences in the New Testament, it is rendered "world" rather than "age."

The word *kosmos* is the biblical word most important to our study. This is suggested by the fact that the important *Theological Dictionary of the New Testament* devotes twenty-eight pages to it.[6] The primitive idea from which later use developed is structure, order, arrangement. All authorities agree in this.[7] "Insofar as the concept of the beautiful is inseparable from that of the ordered, it is always implied in *kosmos* and finds particular expression in the sense of 'adornment' (usually of women)."[8]

It is clear that when *kosmos* is used to mean "world" in the New Testament, the interpreter will always be on the track of true interpretation when he thinks first of the world of earth and mankind in the sense of the present arrangement, structure, and order.

Word meanings and their uses have now furnished us some aid in understanding the complex biblical thought about the world. The distinctions that may be drawn between the three important ones, *oikoumenē, aiōn* and *kosmos*, though not to be pressed too far, are nevertheless important. It is a fact that *oikoumenē* (literally, inhabited part of the earth), though obviously primarily a geographical term (Greek civilization), became a cultural and then again a geographical one (the Roman empire).[9] Indeed it came to be that when the Hellenic civilization and the Roman empire absorbed one another and they, in the proud opinion of their wise men, summed up all world culture, the *oikoumenē* in their literature is scarcely distinct from the *kosmos* (world) or the *gē* (earth).[10] Although in Mark 16:15 "all the world" of the Great Commission is all the *kosmos*, in Matthew 24:14, the gospel of the kingdom "shall be preached in all the *oikoumenē*.

Although Paul clearly is aware of the difference between the basic meaning of the word *aiōn* and of *kosmos*, he does not always distinctly employ the difference. Viewed in its temporal aspect, the world is an *aiōn;* viewed in its organizational aspect the same world is a *kosmos.* The "world" as such may be either one or both in the mind of the author, and he may employ either word as the one or other idea is dominant in his thought. At Ephesians 2:2, it is quite clear that *aiōn* and *kosmos* are two aspects (temporal and organizational) of the same thing. The believer's former way of living before conversion is spoken of as "according to the *aiōn* of this *kosmos,*" rendered "course of this world."

The New Testament lifts the ideas present in the Old Testament words and expressions, and having gained the terminology of the Greco-Roman *oikoumenē,* it represents them in the Greek language. The distinctions and meanings of both Testaments being represented in the New, we have restricted this summary of the manifoldness of the world idea in the Bible to the New Testament expressions and words.

What assistance does this somewhat extended examination of words yield? At the risk of anticipating later chapters, certain conclusions may be offered.

As "creation," "all things," or "heaven and earth," the entire world, including man in all his social connections, is God's by right of creation. God also maintains the world; He is transcendent above it; He is immanent in it; and He controls it for His own purposes. In addition to benefits mentioned earlier, those who embrace these truths will never voluntarily cooperate in the apotheosis of any human ruler or deify any state by paying exaggerated respect to the totalitarian claims of a state or agency of state, any more than they will acknowledge any supposed absolute sovereignty of individual citizens. On the contrary, God alone has sovereign rights. Hence, doctrinaire democratic theory is no less unscriptural than divine right monarchy. By whatever means men come to positions of rulership—by dynastic descent, aristocratic family connection, plutocratic material resources, or by democratic election, "there is no power but of God" (Ro 13:1). Furthermore, civil government is an instrument, not an end. Men are proximate ends, but only God is ultimate end. The state owns neither its citizens nor their properties, minds, bodies, or children. All of these belong to their Creator-God who has never given to the state rights of eminent domain. Finally, neither society in aggregate, nor any class or group has interest in or claims upon any man which supersede God's claims upon him or contravenes the dignity imparted to him by virtue of the created divine image in him.

In connection with the world as *gē*, earth, men who dwell there are reminded that as "earth dwellers" they are exceedingly limited, for all their natural dignity. Further, they live on a planet appointed to judgment before renovation. Men are advised by grace, not to expect too much here, even under best possible conditions, but rather to seek a "better country, that is, a heavenly" (Heb 11:16). They are instructed that neither church nor civil government is an instrument for inaugurating a golden age, inasmuch as Eden has been irrevocably lost until the kingdom of God shall come. Reformed thinkers of more than one particular school are respectfully reminded hereby that important and commendable as it may be, each program of world renewal—even by evangelism and Christian social action—must come to terms with the Christian doctrine of the world and with biblical eschatology.

The world as *aiōn* (epoch of limited duration) and *kosmos* (system) are treated at length in the next following chapters. Whatever improvement in the times (*aiōn*) or *kosmos* (system) may be effected by government or other social instrument, the basic character of sinful men and of a present evil world will remain just that—a present evil world—until the consummation, when "the kingdom of the world is become the kingdom of our Lord, and of his Christ: and he shall reign for ever and ever" (Rev 11:15).

5

THE NATIONS OF EARTH AND THEIR GOVERNMENTS AS PART OF A SATANIC KINGDOM

THE WORLD viewed as man's habitation is, as we have seen, an *oikoumenē*, a civilization. Viewed from the standpoint of time, *sub specie aeternitatis*, it is only an *aeōn*, an age; it is not a permanent state of affairs. From the standpoint of its inner coherence (system, organization principle) it is a *kosmos*, a world system. In this section, the civilization of the present age of man, as operating under certain invisible but nonetheless real principles and organizations, is seen to be demonic. Later, attention will be directed to what God has done to limit Satanic control in order that life may go on and God's ultimate purposes may be achieved. It is at that point that the place of government and human laws will be discussed.

SATAN'S CLAIMS

The great literary works of Goethe (*Faust*) and Marlowe (*Dr. Faustus*) and the opera of Gounod (*Faust*), employing the motif of the offer by Satan of worldly success in exchange for sale of one's soul to the devil, do exhibit a true biblical notion, even if the superstitious and mythical settings do not. Two of the synoptic gospels report such an offer to Jesus as sober fact. Matthew makes it the climactic enticement. "Again, the devil taketh him unto an exceeding high mountain, and showeth him all the kingdoms of the world, and the glory of them; and he said unto him, All these things will I give thee, if thou wilt fall down and worship me" (Mt 4:8-9). Luke adds: "For it hath been delivered unto me; and to whomsoever I will I give it" (Lk 4:6). It is noteworthy that Jesus did not dispute

49

the claim of dominion over the kingdoms of the world (*kosmos*). His answer was an implicit acknowledgment of the legitimacy of Satan's claim. Under the providence of God it is his to give, or else there was no temptation. In such a case Jesus might have laughed at Satan rather than to have answered with sober quotations of relevant Scripture.*

THE SCRIPTURE STATEMENTS

The scriptural declarations are extensive, clear and overwhelming. Their mere recital is enough to establish that the present world system is, indeed, in some important respects a demonic structure.

Our Lord was certainly not a superstitious man, yet frequently he referred to Satan as ruler of this world. For example, as He contemplated His impending death by crucifixion, He exclaimed cryptically, "Now is the judgment of this world [*kosmos*]: now shall the prince [*archon*, ruler, lord] of this world [*kosmos*] be cast out" (Jn 12:31). As He walked toward the garden of Gethsemane, Jesus remarked to His disciples, "the prince of the world cometh" (Jn 14:30). Later in that last evening, and speaking from an assumed post-crucifixion point of view, he added, "the prince of this world hath been judged" (Jn 16:11). Satan, who at Jesus' temptation offered Him the kingdoms of the world, was thus acknowledged by Jesus to be the ruler of this world.

Several writers of the New Testament refer to him in a similar fashion. To Paul he is "the prince [*archon*] of the powers [*authority*] of the air, . . . the spirit that now worketh in the sons of disobedience" (Eph 2:2). The powers thus noticed, of which he is ruler, are held to be an organized structure of evil beings against whom believers must fight if they are to be victors, "For our wrestling is not against flesh and blood [i.e., visible human opponents], but against the principalities, against the powers, against the world-

---

*John Howard Yoder in *The Politics of Jesus* (Grand Rapids: Eerdmans, 1972) supports this interpretation, saying: "There is a very strong strand of Gospel teaching which sees secular government as the province of the sovereignty of Satan. This position is perhaps most typically expressed by the temptation story, in which Jesus did not challenge the claim of Satan" (p. 195). He cites Archie Penner (*The New Testament, the Christian and the State* [Scottdale, Pa.: Herald, 1959]) in further support.

rulers [kosmocrats!] of this darkness, against the spiritual hosts of wickedness in the heavenly places" (Eph 6:12). In his letter to the Corinthians, people all too familiar with vain heathen gods and the silly claims made for them (see 1 Co 8:4-5), Paul yet acknowledged sacrifice to idols to be, in sober reality, sacrifice to demons: "But I say, that the things which the Gentiles sacrifice, they sacrifice to demons, and not to God. . . . Ye cannot drink the cup of the Lord, and the cup of demons: ye cannot partake of the table of the Lord, and of the table of demons" (1 Co 10:20-21). He affirmed further the persistence of unbelieving rejection of the claims of Christ to be due to the darkening influence of the devil and his agents—human and demonic—upon the minds of men. Says he, "even if our gospel is veiled, it is veiled in them that perish: in whom the god of this world [*aiōn*] hath blinded the minds of the unbelieving, that the light of the gospel of the glory of Christ . . . should not dawn upon them" (2 Co 4:3-4). And later, of the purveyors of false religion, he declares, "Such men are false apostles, deceitful workers, fashioning themselves into apostles of Christ. And no marvel; for even Satan fashioneth himself into an angel of light. It is no great thing if his ministers fashion themselves as ministers of righteousness" (2 Co 11:13-15). Satan and his spiritual armies are behind "the rulers of this world"; indeed, they are the real rulers of this world, together with the heathen magistrates of the day, the ones who "crucified the Lord of glory" (1 Co 2:8). Very highly-regarded interpreters even take the view that "the powers that be" of Romans 13:1 are these same demon powers.

John's first epistle warns the readers by observing that this evil being is "he that is in the world" (4:4) and that "the whole world lieth in the evil one" (5:19). John's point of view is that Satan's power in the world at the present time is pervasive. (See also Rev 20:3, 8, 10, where Satan is said to deceive the nations.)

These considerations regarding the nature of evil, its origin, and the connection of evil with the present providence which leaves Satan relatively free to rule the world, are productive now of significant conclusions regarding the pervasive and permanent (as far as the present age is concerned) possibilities for elimination of evil and evils by mere social action or civil power.

THE NATIONS AS PART OF SATAN'S KINGDOM ON EARTH

In the next chapter the rightful place of government in God's wise providence will be treated. Here, however, the unhappy fact must be noted that national governments (a modern term intended here to cover all those systems by which the various geographical and civil units of mankind have ruled themselves throughout history) are part of Satan's sphere of prevailing influence on earth. They are a sphere of special Satanic activity.

Government always has had a religious foundation.* This is because government must always operate with some authority. To exercise authority there must be some theory of authority. Another name for authority is sovereignty, or right of rulership. If the rulers of the populace hold that man himself is the source of authority (as in all political thought stemming from the so-called Enlightenment), then a religious commitment has been made regarding man. He is master of his fate, captain of his soul, and it is held to be right that he should so be. In this case, the voice of the people is the voice of God because man is his own God. This was the theory of sovereignty underlying the French Revolution. It is the explicit rationale of modern secular socialism. It is no accident that the more thoroughly secular socialistic the political theory controlling a nation becomes, the more sub- or post-Christian it becomes. Even in parliamentary and constitutional republics such as the United States of America, the actual working philosophy is to regard the voice of the majority as ultimate. Constitutions, eternal laws of God (the Christian God), and innate rights mean nothing ultimately. The public opinion poll becomes the ultimate instrument of determining policy. An elite party may become the trustee of the nation as in most socialistic states, but in any case, man is ultimate.

Kuyper has shown that "popular choice gains the day, as a matter of course, where no other rule exists, or where the existing rule falls away."[1] Yet there are many other ways by which government has been and continues to be bestowed on rulers or magistrates—none of which imply any innate right of men to choose their own

---

*"No political scheme has ever become dominant which was not founded in a specific religious or anti-religious conception." (Abraham Kuyper, *Lectures on Calvinism* [Grand Rapids: Eerdmans, 1961], p. 78.)

rulers, desirable as that may be where men are both righteous and free. "This bestowal may flow from the right of inheritance, as in a hereditary monarchy. It may result from a hard-fought war, even as Pilate had power over Jesus, given him from above. It may proceed from electors, as it did in the old German empire. It may rest with the States of the country, as was the case of the old Dutch republic. In a word it may assume a variety of forms, because there is an endless difference in the development of nations."[2] Thus the democratic theory of sovereignty has proven unexportable to Viet Nam, granted that it might be desirable in abstract. The people do not understand it, do not want it, and could not make it work if they had it. Most of the peoples of the so-called third world who, in forming nations, expected to be truly free now that they were rid of the old colonialism find themselves instead being ruled by native military or party dictatorships. There is no general agreement even on what democracy is. According to the Bible, this is because God has divided the nations according to His own will, assigned them their territories, and determined their histories according to His own inscrutible but nevertheless powerful governance.

This, however, is not theocracy; it is divine providence. There has been but one true theocracy, Old Testament Israel governed by God's supernaturally selected men, ruled by His revealed law, informed by Urim and Thummim and by divinely chosen prophets.

There is no biblical theory of human political sovereignty—monarchial, aristocratic, plutocratic, democratic, republican, or otherwise. God's is the only sovereignty recognized in the Bible. In biblical doctrine, all political sovereignty is bestowed by God. Biblically speaking, there is no such thing as either popular sovereignty as in Western democracies, or state sovereignty as in the various totalitarian states. The various human methods by which political power is conveyed to magistrates are just that—methods of conveyance only.

Kuyper summarizes biblical faith in the area of political sovereignty, saying:

It . . . may be summarily expressed in these three theses: 1. God only—and never any creature—is possessed of sovereign rights, in the destiny of nations, because God alone created them, maintains them by his almighty power, and rules them by his ordinances. 2. Sin has, in the realm of politics, broken down the direct government of God, and therefore the exercise of authority, for the purpose of government, has subsequently been invested in men as a mechanical remedy. And 3. In whatever form this authority may reveal itself, man never possesses power over his fellow-man in any other way than by an authority which descends upon him from the majesty of God.[3]

Historically, however, most governments of earth have had a more self-consciously specific religious basis than does secular socialism. In the ancient classical world the prevailing theory of government, except for nomadic cultures, was some form of monarchy. Practically every ancient classical dialect from Persia to Scandinavia had a word properly translated in English as "king."[4] The rulers were properly called kings. Strictly speaking, none of these rulers claimed independent power. Rather, the prevailing theory was that the king reigned by the authority of whatever god the people of the locality accepted. In those cases where several gods competed for supremacy in different parts of a given country, the king ruled by right of the gods of the various sections. Not infrequently the king was held to be the incarnation or the actual offspring of the god, and the most horrendous myths were created to explain this.† With due allowance for oversimplification, we may endorse the views of S. H. Hooke:

> The cult of all ancient near eastern religions was dominated by a coherent complex of ritual and myth which served as a "pattern" for all these religions, and which had its home in Babylonia. Babylonian cultic practice in historical times, and also Canaanite, Israelite [Christianity does not endorse this inclusion of faithful Israelite], and other cultic systems are variations of this original "pattern." At its centre stands the king, himself divine, the offspring or the incarnation of

---

†Old Testament scholars, especially those interested in Psalm interpretation, have sifted the literature of the ancient Near and Middle East and of Egypt in this connection. Two symposiums edited by S. H. Hooke, *The Labyrinth; Further Studies in the Revelation Between Myth and Ritual in the Ancient World* (New York: Macmillan Co., 1935) and *Myth, Ritual and Kingship; Essays on the Theory and Practice of Kingship in the Ancient Near East and in Israel* (Oxford: Clarendon, 1958) provide a key to much of this literature. Another important source is "The Psalms," by A. R. Johnson in the symposium *The Old Testament in Modern Study*, H. H. Rowley, ed. (Oxford: U. Press, 1952). But for a summary in relation to the present subject, refer to Chapter III, 1. of *He That Cometh* by Sigmund Mowinckel, trans. G. W. Anderson (Oxford: Blackwell, 1956), the section entitled "The Royal Ideology of the Ancient Near East," pp. 23-56.

the god, who in the cult is at the same time the god himself, so that in dramatic form he lives or endures the entire "myth" of the god, his deeds and his experiences.[5]

Among the Greeks and Romans there was the theory of apotheosis whereby the king or emperor was declared god (the senate cooperating), usually at the king's death. "Julius Caesar was deified after his death . . . and the example thus set was followed in the case of the other emperors."[6]

Now many modern people living in a secular society, products of secular schools, usually biblically illiterate and ignorant of the Christian religious foundations upon which their inherited value systems are built, are apt to be totally oblivious to the religious nature of all statements regarding sovereignty. "To whom ye yield yourselves servants to obey, his servants ye are" (Ro 6:16, KJV) is true in the political realm. If one obeys no higher authority than man, whether individual or aggregate, then he has made man his lord.

The Bible frequently recognizes this relationship between sovereignty and religion in connection with its teachings regarding Satan's present powers on earth. Let us note a prominent example. Ezekiel prophesied against the prince of Tyre, "Thus saith the Lord GOD; Because thine heart is lifted up, and thou hast said, I am a God, I sit in the seat of God" (Eze 28:2, KJV, cf. context). A well-recognized commentary notes on this passage: "Throughout the east the majesty and glory of a people were collected in the person of their monarch, who was not feared as a man, but actually worshipped as a god . . . The word prince is here the embodiment of the community. Their glory is his glory, their pride is his pride."[7] The same Ezekiel reports the divine claims of the pharaoh of Egypt: "Thus saith the Lord GOD; Behold I am against thee, Pharaoh king of Egypt, the great dragon that lieth in the midst of his rivers, which hath said, My river is mine own, and I have made it for myself" (Eze 29:3, KJV).

The Pharaoh claims divine powers for himself—claiming to be creator of the Nile, and therefore creator also of Egypt and sole author of all life and liberty there. The religious hymns and rituals of ancient Egypt acknowledged their Paraoh so to be.‡ These examples could be multiplied at great length.

The apostle taught the Corinthians not to fear these pagan gods and their idols. The Old Testament prophets called them all vanity—nonentities. Paul's words agree: "We know that an idol is nothing in the world, and that there is none other God but one. For though there be that are called gods, whether in heaven or in earth, (as there be gods many, and lords many,) But unto us there is but one God" (1 Co 8:4-6).

The same apostle goes on to equate idol worship with demon worship: "What say I then? that the idol is anything, or that which is offered in sacrifice to idols is any thing? But I say, that the things which the Gentiles sacrifice, they sacrifice to devils, and not to God" (1 Co 10:19-20, KJV). So idol worship is devil worship. Further, Satan, in biblical doctrine, among many other things, is prince of demons. The Jews of Jesus' time believed this, and Jesus did not correct them (Mt 9:34; 12:24, 27). Idolatrous kingdoms are therefore in Satan's power.

It is a source of amazement to modern men—that is, to those few who take the trouble to discover it—how seriously the Bible takes this doctrine of satanic and demonic dominion over the nations. The book of Daniel represents God's holy angels (archangels) Michael and Gabriel as in conflict with evil spiritual beings known as the prince of Persia and the prince of Grecia, and as holding up arrival of the holy angel at Daniel's side for three weeks (see Dan 8:16; 9:21; 10:13, 21). St. Paul speaks of satanic spirits in such a way as to suggest a hierarchy of evil angels and spirits organized to do Satan's work for him (Eph 6:12; Ro 8:38). The victory of Christ wrought at Calvary over these spirits manifested at His ascension, session at God's right hand, and second coming is referred to in the New Testament at Philippians 2:6-10, Colossians 1:20, 2:15, 1 Peter 3:22, and several other passages. Perhaps, as many competent exegetes have thought, the "elements of the world" (Gal 4:3, 9) should be understood as "elemental spirits."[8] Several of

---

‡That Ezekiel did not exaggerate the pharaoh's claims to the Creator's power and prerogative is made plain by J. H. Breasted, who gives very impressive documentation of the divinity attributed to the pharaoh in the priestly literature of ancient Egypt in his *Development of Religion and Thought in Ancient Egypt*, Harper Torchbook ed. (New York: Harper, 1959), pp. 122-26.

Europe's leading theologians of the last three generations, beginning with Martin Dibelius (*Die Geisterwelt im Glauben des Paulus* [The Spirit-world in the Faith of Paul], 1909) have supported the proposition that the "powers that be" of Romans 13:1 and perhaps also "the princes of this world" of 1 Corinthians 2:6, 8 are the evil spirits of Satan's forces on earth. Some of these authors would not agree that the New Testament authors are correct, being quite ready to label the New Testament teachings superstition and to "demythologize" them. Yet they hold that such is what the New Testament documents teach.[9]

As I shall have occasion to argue at length in a later chapter, Dibelius, Barth, Cullmann, and company are mistaken in their treatment of "the powers that be" of Romans 13:1-7. They carry the satanic connection too far. But they do provide valuable support for the affirmation that national governments, under the limitations imposed by divine providence, are a part of Satan's sphere of uncommonly successful activity. The claim, then, of the devil, when pressing his trials hard upon the Saviour, to be master of all the kingdoms of the world with authority to give it to whomever he wished (Mt 4:8-9; cf Lk 4:6) was no idle claim. As far as the Bible is concerned, it is certified fact. Even the elaborately organized regiments and officiaries of fallen spirits and angels set forth in Milton's *Paradise Lost* and *Paradise Regained* are not wrong in conception—if imaginary in detail.

The Bible in plain fact breathes the atmosphere of such a conception. One may reject it, re-interpret it, or believe it. One may hardly deny that the Bible presents it as true. If one takes the Bible seriously, he must take this fact into consideration in deciding what are the church's place and mission in relation to civil government and society in general in such a world.

PART

II

Interpretation of the Essential Biblical Data

6

CIVIL GOVERNMENT IN BIBLICAL HISTORY

To TRACE OUT SUCH INFORMATION as Scripture provides, bearing directly upon the subject of rule of men by men and the place of such rulership in God's own government of mankind, is a large task, but not an impossible one. The Bible is a large book, and the subject of civil government pervades it; yet it is possible to generalize without commenting on every reference to kings and queens, government agents and agencies, and the people they govern. Happily, there are also several comprehensive texts which treat the subject in systematic fashion.

No attempt will be made to trace the careers of particular governments, biblical or otherwise. To do so would be to write a history of the nations. Though comments on certain political theories will be presented, no attempt will be made to provide a history of that subject. Nor will this study be strictly a biblical theology as scholars nowadays conceive it, though attention to organic development through the Bible is an important aspect of the treatment. Neither will the method be strictly that of a systematic theology with the structure of logical categories and classifications characteristic of the method. The plan of treatment has been suggested simply by the fact that civil government appears on several levels in the Scriptures. On the basic level it is *a fact of biblical history,* a recorded occurrence, quite as much as it is a phenomenon of history observed by all men in all times. Civil government also comes before the Bible student as a *topic of preaching and writing* by the prophets of Judah and Israel.

On another level it is *the subject of divine legislation* in several important sections of the Pentateuch, and a matter for *reflection* by the authors of the books of biblical wisdom. On still another level,

61

it is a matter of *special instruction,* wherein not only our Lord but the prophets and apostles also provide the essential ingredients of a doctrine of civil government. Finally, there are the *New Testament exhortations and warnings* to Christians with regard to their response to and duties toward governments, their laws, agencies, and representatives.

DIVINE PROVIDENCE IN BIBLICAL HISTORY

As we proceed with analysis and exposition of these aspects of the biblical theology of civil government, we must at all times acknowledge God's rule as well as His reign in and over every aspect of reality. This biblical teaching is known as the doctrine of providence. An Aramaic or Hebrew word or phrase to be precisely translated "providence" in this sense does not appear in the Old Testament, though the idea is frequent. It is expressed as thoughts of God (Ps 33:11; Is 55:8-9) counsels of God (Ps 33:11; Is 5:19), and so forth. Perhaps the closest word to providence in essential meaning is *pēqudâh* (visitation, or care, Job 10:12). The English word appears only once in the King James Version (Ac 24:2), but not in the precise theological sense. Pagan conceptions of the world have no consistent view of the power shaping of events either in nature or in the society of men. It is sometimes asserted that the ancient Greeks believed the world to be "tychistic"; that is, events in the world all come to pass by chance. It is true that Democritus and his fellow materialists supposed that the "atoms" combining in the great "void" to form things and events are controlled by chance. The Latin word is *fortuna,* hence the designation of the concept in English by *fortune* and *fortuitous.* But other concepts of the power in control of nature coexisted with the tychistic view. There was widespread belief in *fatum* (Latin) or *moira* (Greek), perhaps best translated by our word "destiny." Sometimes fate, or impersonally determined destiny, was thought of as controlling even the gods. But chance and destiny were but inconsistent aspects of a pervasive pantheism which cannot now, any more than then, decide between fortune (chance) and destiny. Obviously, chance is complete rejection of the principle of purposes and goals, while destiny is the complete affirmation of them. A later development was the determinism of Islam. None of these, any more than the doctrine of karma in several Eastern religions, is truly comparable to the Christian doctrine of providence.

Although providence has been mentioned several times in previous discussion, it is now necessary to discuss the doctrine somewhat more fully, relating it more precisely to the subject of civil government of man by men.

Providence is a work of the triune God. He who planned the world, created it, and preserves it, also governs it. His plan for the world is from eternity. His work of creating is finished, but His work of preservation goes on, as does His government of it.

That God's providence extends to the setting up of governments as well as their continuation and dissolution is scarcely a matter of debate among Christians, for it is direct biblical teaching. Men may call the forces which shape success or failure at cards by the name of chance, but Scripture does not—"The lot is cast into the lap; but the whole disposing thereof is of Jehovah" (Pr 16:33). What men call chance, the Hebrew Bible calls a meeting or encounter (*miq-reh*, from the word to meet, Ru 2:3; 1 Sa 6:9), though the English translations are usually "chance" and "hap." In the outlook of biblical faith, God brings all such encounters to pass (see Ru 2:3, 20). Men may trace the human and natural forces causing the rise of kings, parties, dictators, governors, and presidents to power in politics—and the Bible does also—but beyond and behind stands God directing. "By me kings reign, And princes decree justice, By me princes rule, And nobles, even all the judges of the earth" (Pr 8:15-16). "That the living may know that the Most High ruleth in the kingdom of men, and giveth it to whomsoever he will, and setteth up over it the lowest of men" (Dan 4:17 cf. Pr 21:1).

Some writers claim it was the Old Testament writers (especially of apocalypses, as Dan 2 and 7) who originated the idea of linear progressive movement in history, deriving it from their faith in God's providence. It is commonly asserted by scholars that the Hebrew authors, both Christian and Jewish, of apocalypse adopted the idea of ages of the world from the Greeks. If so, they also rejected the essentially hopeless cyclical view of history inherent in the Greek thought, favoring the hopeful view of the Bible that the world is God's kingdom wherein He rules and ultimately will bring His counsels to pass.

To deny this teaching is to deny Christian theism in general and
the efficacy of prayer in particular, for there is obviously no value
in asking God to intervene in history if he is not in charge of it.[1]
Objections to the doctrine of providence turn out invariably to be
objections to Christianity itself.

According to this scriptural doctrine, in God's rule over mankind—
Protestant, Catholic, Jew; Hindu, Buddhist, Muslim; atheist, in-
fidel, secularist: among all creeds, races, and cultures—civil government has a divinely ordained place. With regard to many aspects of
the Christian's relation to civil government, there is no detailed
biblical information; in essentials there is clear information. Where
there is not, there are guiding principles. It is our purpose to discover and report what can be known, and to obtain some suggestions as to procedures to follow where the Word of God is silent
or not clearly understood.

Our point of view and goals are quite well summed up in a Lutheran publication:

> Despite the fact that there is a great distance between us and the way
> of life prevailing in the centuries during which the documents of the
> Scriptures were written, the essence of the question as to how church
> and state must live and work together is very clearly set forth in the
> Word of God. In point of fact the whole matter of church-and-state
> relations lies near the center of our theology. At the moment when
> Jesus was sentenced to be crucified, the relationship between Christ
> and Caesar was moved to the very heart of the Christian faith. More-
> over, the problem of church and state, with its many ramifications, is
> posed for the church of all times by the circumstance that we stand in
> the succession of those disciples to whom Jesus once said: "You will
> be dragged before governors and kings for My sake, to bear testimony
> before them and the Gentiles [Mt 10:18]."[2]

First Appearance

The first appearance in the Bible of something fairly equivalent
to that which we now call the state, or civil government, poses a
minor problem. It has been found in the creation of man with his
duty to take dominion over creation; in the presumed pre-fall prescribed relation of the sexes in the family and in the position of the

father in the home. Some today see all human civil government as primarily an extension of the family authority of fathers. Civil government has been discovered in the sword of Lamech and the city-building of Cain. It appears that the first mention of an officer of government in the Bible is in Genesis 14, where in connection with Abraham, nine kings are mentioned. The names of several city-states of both earlier and later times are given in Genesis 10, along with the first use of the word "nation" (v. 5) and of the word "kingdom" (v. 10). None of these is irrelevant, for it is likely that each is connected with some aspect of the beginning of civil government.

But civil government, like the presence of evil in the world, is mainly presupposed in the Bible. We are not told much about how it got here, even though we are sufficiently informed as to what it is, what we must do about it, and of God's relation to it.

Some remarks of John Calvin in connection with the creation of and nature of angels are appropriate at this juncture. In his usual deft way of coming directly to the point, he says: "Not to take too long, let us remember here, as in all religious doctrine, that we ought to hold to one rule of modesty and sobriety: not to speak, or guess, or even to seek to know, concerning obscure matters anything except what has been imparted to us by God's Word."[3] Then after mentioning the then famous *Celestial Hierarchy* (a work of Pseudo Dionysius on angels) he comments: "But if anyone examine it more closely, he will find it for the most part nothing but talk. The theologian's task is not to divert the ears with chatter, but to strengthen the consciences by teaching things true, sure, and profitable."[4]

BASIS IN MAN'S CONSTITUTION

The basis for civil government was laid by God in the original constitution of man. We do not mean that civil government of any kind is a necessary or inevitable expression of human nature (either before or after the fall) or of natural law. Philosophers as far apart in their views as Thomas Aquinas and Georg Hegel have asserted that civil government of the sort each approved was rooted in the very nature of reality. Hegel exalted the state as an ideal. Although he is not widely read today, his ideas have greatly influenced European history since his death in 1831. An absolute idealist, his doctrine was that man becomes fully man only in the state. Man is not only naturally a family member, but naturally a citizen. The state is the whole which synthesizes all human activities and institutions. The state expresses the absolute idea in the social realm in the same way that the order of nature expresses it—or Him, for Hegel was essentially pantheistic—in the physical realm. The three main functions of the state—legislative, executive, and judicial—are best carried on in a monarchy, wherein the cohesion and reciprocal support of all the individuals are best attained.[5]

Human excellence, according to Hegel, is attained in obedience to the community, in conformity with its mores. The state is the "highest and most perfect embodiment of social morality; it both sustains my personality as a being with freedom of will and transcends my personality by compelling me to contemplate a good beyond my own personal interests.[6] For the Christian, freedom consists in obedience to the personal God, Creator of man; for Kant, in obedience to one's own moral will; for Hegel in obedience to the demands of the community, to the dictates of social morality. There is no higher norm, no more authoritative source of instruction; for in the community or state, the god of Hegelian pantheism speaks more distinctly, superior to all personal conviction.

Thomas Aquinas (1227-1274) arrived on the scene of European history at a period when the Roman church, through its popes, ruled over the whole of ecclesiastical and political life. The reasons for this lie in medieval European history, but the times of Aquinas called not for historical explanations—these came later in the generations of the Reformation—but for intellectual justification. Aquinas' mission was not to explain the medieval feudal system of civil rulership, but to defend it. As Thomas worked it out, man's nature at the fall did not receive corruption so much as injury by the loss of the superadded graces of holiness, righteousness, and so on. Thus with his reasoning power fully intact, man is supposed to be able under proper divine guidance to form a society that is good and just.*

---

‡The reader will find useful and dependable information on views of government in the Medieval period, especially Aquinas, has been (in addition to standard reference works) in the long chapter (including 43 pages of very fine print notes) of Ernst Troeltsch's classic, *The Social Teaching of the Churches.* I also found E. L. H. Taylor (*The Philosophy of Law, Politics and the State*) very helpful, especially for additional bibliography. Troeltsch is objective and descriptive. Taylor is laying ground-

A recent British writer has summarized St. Thomas' effort in this regard:

> Accordingly, Thomas had to show that the existing feudal ordering of political and social relationships, so far from being the product of sin and lust for power, were natural and therefore just. Just as Aristotle had tried to answer his Sophist critics by trying to prove that the existing institutions of the Greek city-state, such as slavery and the exploitation of women and the working classes, were natural and reflected the very order of the universe, so now Aquinas tried to show that such feudal institutions as serfdom, the monarchy and papal theocracy were also natural, and arose out of the very nature of things. Aquinas in fact borrowed much of his argument from Aristotle because he discovered in the *Politics* a conception of man in society that could easily be adapted to implement the papal program to build up a Christian society and to provide a rational justification for it. With Aristotle's help he tried to prove that the feudal state was grounded in nature rather than in sin as Paul and Augustine had supposed.[7]

Dooyeweerd criticizes the Thomist view as falsely representing the state as the whole of society of which other aspects are only parts. He asserts that this appears to make man "by nature a state-oriented being, for already in the forming of marriage, family, and blood-relations the natural compulsion to form the state is germinating."[8]

But Scripture does not support either Hegel or Thomas. A refinement of meaning is in order. A distinction must be made between social organization and coercive civil government per se. For example, the Bible rather clearly indicates that the holy angels, who are rational creatures, are organized into ranks with gradations of authority at various levels. But no mention is made of coercive obedience or threats of punishment. No mention is made of any self-ordering of angels by police. What human social organization might have been without sin, we have no way of knowing, but as we

---

work for the Dooyeweerdian position, though this does not seem to prevent a comprehensive and incisive treatment. Troeltsch is immensely informative and indispensable but impossible to summarize. Much of the current second-time-over study of Christian response to the challenge of civil government in particular and society in general would be greatly simplified by attention to Troeltsch. He is practically exhaustive down to 1911. A respectable treatment with guide to the literature since 1911 on to 1941 is *Democracy and the Churches*, by J. H. Nichols (Philadelphia: Westminster, 1941).

have earlier shown, some ordering of society inevitably would have developed.

When we say the basis for civil government lies in man's constitution by creation, we mean to say that since man is rational being, possessing the power of choice, not determined by necessity or any inner or external law toward particular decisions, he is capable of exercising delegated power over his fellows and likewise of obeying or disobeying that power. His nature does not demand for its expression or perfection or fulfillment that he be coercively governed, nor does human society only come to flower in the state. The Bible simply cannot be made to teach such a statist doctrine.

Certain Christian writers who stand far away from either the Thomist or the Hegelians do, however, find an impulse, if not a necessity, for civil government in the nature of man. For example, Abraham Kuyper has said, "We admit that the impulse to form states arises from man's social nature, which was expressed already by Aristotle, when he called man a *'zōon polilikon.'* God might have created men as disconnected individuals, standing side by side . . . but this was not the case."[9]

Whether or not this impulse to form states is in man by virtue of the organic connection of all, as Kuyper states, seems uncertain.† It can hardly be doubted that part of his *capacity* for social organization as opposed to pure anarchy roots in the organic connection of all men. Mankind is divided into various organized units of civil government because given also the changes later introduced by sin, God wrote it into their nature so to be. It has been contended since early in the Christian era that the necessity for civil government grows out of sin.‡ It appears to me that, if by government one means social

---

† "Organic" is not used here in the sense which identifies man with nature or spirit as in some Greek or Hegelian thought, but in the biblical sense wherein the human race is seen to be *ex henos*, "out of one" (Ac 17:26, cf. Gen 2:21-22; 3:20).

*There is a work by Karl Werner of Vienna, *Der heilige Thomas von Aquino* [St. Thomas Aquinas] in three volumes (1858-59) wherein the question of development of civil government apart from the fall in St. Thomas's doctrine is fully canvassed. Ernst Troeltsch, who relies heavily on Werner, says Thomas contended that "Whether the Fall had taken place or not, human beings would still have created social institutions, only the process would have been carried out in the spirit of love and voluntary submission and control" (*The Social Teaching of the Churches*, 1:283; see Troeltsch's discussion, pp. 280ff. and references to the literature of the subject). Werner holds that it was Thomas's teaching that a natural evolution of society, even among men in a prelapsarian primitive state, would have led not only to dominion and holding of property but also to slavery as a proper social institution (ibid., p. 411).

organization with coercive power, then, indeed, sin was and is the occasion for civil government—though apparently the race existed for many generations, according to the Genesis record, under the condition of sin, without coercive civil government.

The existence of what is called natural law is not to be denied, but the contention is held that man has no liberty to construct doctrine on that basis alone. Inductions based upon theories of natural law may have some validity, and both induction and deduction are parts of doctrinal Bible study. But we must start with Scripture, not with reason or nature.

It is written: "There be four things which are little upon the earth, but they are exceeding wise: The ants are a people not strong, yet they prepare their meat in the summer; The conies are but a feeble folk, yet make they their houses in the rocks; The locusts have no king, yet go they forth all of them by bands; The spider taketh hold with her hands, and is in kings' palaces" (Pr 30:24-28, KJV). This is to say, ants, conies, locusts, and spiders are so made by God that their activities throughout life are directed by instinct. They do not need kings. They do as their natural impulses direct them. In the moral sense, they are neither obedient nor disobedient; they can have no king, for a king could neither oppose nor assist them. In contrast, man is made with a moral nature, powers of reflective thought, the faculty of volition, and the precious gift of freedom. This is summarized in Genesis 1:27, "So God created man in his own image, in the image of God created he him."

Because he is like God, man has a natural love of order. "God is not a God of confusion, but of peace" (1 Co 14:33). Thus we have reason to assert that something of voluntary social organization, or government, was inherent in man from the start. There is precedent for it in the Godhead. The three Persons of the Trinity are equal in dignity and power and possess all the divine attributes in perfect degree, yet the Father *sent* the Son; the Spirit *proceeds* from the Father and the Son. The Scriptures display an eternal economy of relationship between the three Persons and distinguish important differences in their relationships to creation and redemption. These are aspects of that love of order in the Godhead which depraved men can not fully root out of their own nature. In his own way, each man on earth has a different place to fill. He does not find it automatically as does an ant or a locust or a coney or a spider. He may have to be assigned it by authority. Present exaltation of a democratic individualistic process in choosing one's place in life has its drawbacks. The lack of a sense of meaning and the aimlessness of many young adults in modern democratic society bears sad testimony to this fact. In a sinless enlightened society, assignment of individual social function—baker, carpenter, teacher, etc.—would always have been done well. In any case, organization of society would have been necessary. Even the first pair, before sin's entrance, had relations to each other involving wielding of authority and submission to it in mutual relations.[10]

The command to "be fruitful, and multiply" (Gen 1:28), coupled with the institution of the monogamous family (Gen 2:24), seems to imply, as a number of Bible commentators notice, the development of the race into families, tribes, and so on. We cannot press this too far, but granted the known facts and the natural precedence of parents—especially of the male parent—and the survival of many contemporaneous generations (if death had not entered), the necessity of extensive social organization can hardly be doubted.

Further, there is the command, "replenish the earth, and subdue it; and have dominion over the fish of the sea, and over the birds of the heavens, and over every living thing that moveth upon the earth" (Gen 1:28). Think what exploitation of natural resources that involved, what feats of exploration, what organization of human resources! No romantic's dream of man in paradisaical anarchy, undisciplined by social organization and external channeling of his mind and muscle, has a ghost of a chance for acceptance in the light of that verse, sin or no. Man was so made that to do all his Creator wanted him to do, human social organization had to come—it was incipiently present from the first day.

ACUTE NEED

Acute need for social organization with the features now associated with coercive civil government came about through the fall of man. Some, as noted previously, would say that sin is the only reason for human government, and they are partly right.§ Sin made

---

§This view has been the traditional Lutheran doctrine.

it urgent that man govern himself, not to be fully man, but to carry out divine commissions and to stay in existence.

The third and fourth chapters of Genesis are instructive. At that sad confrontation following man's initial disobedience, the Lord God said to Eve: "Thy desire shall be to thy husband, and he, himself [emphatic in the Hebrew], shall rule over thee" (Gen 3:16). "Rule" (Heb. *mashal*) is the common word for the function of kings or governors in exercising civil dominion and is the root of several Hebrew words for realm, ruler, rule. Coercive power can hardly be eliminated from the word. So woman, constrained by bonds of natural attraction, emotional dependence, lesser physical strength, and the will of God, accepts the rule of her husband. Happy the woman who finds her husband personally worthy of her obedience, and happy the man who finds his wife's obedience willingly given.

The story of Cain and Abel shows how early appeared the acute need for coercive restraint on violent impulses by some police action (Gen 4:1-16). There follows the incident of Lamech and his sword-brandishing bravado before his family in a polygamous household (Gen 4:19-24). His boastful song manifests all the madness of armed violent wickedness throughout man's long history. The perversity of "reeking tube and iron shard, all valiant dust that builds on dust, and guarding calls not thee to guard" (Kipling; *Recessional*) is suggested in those couplet lines, "Adah and Zillah, hear my voice; Ye wives of Lamech, hearken unto my speech: For I have slain a man for wounding me, And a young man for bruising me: If Cain shall be avenged sevenfold, truly Lamech seventy and sevenfold" (Gen 4:23-24). As a matter of fact, the Genesis narrative relates that it was precisely this tendency to violence, unrestrained by any formal organized social control, that in part brought on the judgment of the deluge, for, "God said unto Noah, The end of all flesh is come before me; for the eatrh is filled with violence through them; and, behold, I will destroy them with the earth" (Gen 6:13).

So in the antediluvian age, though certain elements of social organization may have existed, particularly in the family—perhaps extending to the larger family units such as clans and tribes—it was not enough. God brought that epoch to an end by the flood and started out again with further aspects of social control explicitly imbedded in the new order of things.

FORMAL ESTABLISHMENT

The formal establishment of human government under divine auspices took place in the form of a covenant of God with the survivors of the flood.

The conditions of violence and corruption that occasioned the flood manifested that a new world order was necessary if the human race was to continue and not perish in moral decay. But with the flood, that first sad epoch ended. By inaugurating a new one, God recognized the incorrigible sinfulness of the heart of man, and by covenant with the sinful race, He established a stronger basis for social control. If sin's violence to man cannot be kept in check by voluntary controls, then God in His grace would control it by coercive means. The world would never again be destroyed as it had been (see Gen 8:21-22), because disorder would now be brought under control in a better way. The violent tendencies of men would now be put under such restraint that they would never again get so far out of hand.

This is the significance of the following quotation. After reaffirming man's viceregency over earth and all its nonhuman inhabitants and extending to man the right to eat animal flesh, God said: "But flesh with the life thereof, which is the blood thereof, shall ye not eat. And surely your blood, the blood of your lives will I require; . . . at the hand of every man's brother will I require the life of man. Whoso sheddeth man's blood, by man shall his blood be shed: for in the image of God made he man" (Gen 9:4-6). Protestant identification of this text with the original formal establishment of coercive human government begins with Martin Luther. From the pages he devotes to Genesis 9:6, the following is pertinent. Having pointed out that Cain was punished only by excommunication, Luther adds: "Here, however, God shares his power with man and grants him power over life and death among men, provided that the person is guilty of shedding blood . . . him God makes liable not only to his own judgment but also to the human sword."[11] Luther finds the establishment of all coercive government forces here: "Therefore we must take careful note of this passage, in which God establishes government, to render judgment not only about matters involving life but also about matters less important than life. Thus a government should punish the disobedience of children, theft, adultery and perjury . . . This text is outstanding . . . for here God establishes government and gives it the sword, to hold wantonness in check, lest violence and other sins proceed without limit."[12]

Calvin took a similar but broader view, asserting:

> On the whole, they are deceived (in my judgment) who think that a political law, for the punishment of homicides, is here simply intended. Truly I do not deny that the punishment which the laws ordain, and which the judges execute, are founded on this divine sentence; but I say the words are more comprehensive. It is written, 'Men of blood shall not live out half their days,' (Ps. lv. 25). And we see some die in highways, some in stews, and many in wars. Therefore, however magistrates may connive at the crime, God sends executioners from other quarters, who shall render unto sanguinary men their reward. God so threatens and denounces vengeance against the murderer, that he even arms the magistrate with the sword for the avenging of slaughter, in order that the blood of men may not be shed with impunity.[13]

Except for the commentators who, rejecting the presence of authentic history in the passage make it a sort of anachronous flashback from Israel's monarchial times,[14] almost every grammatical commentary and theological treatment of it gives this obvious and undoubted interpretation—C. F. Keil, F. Delitzsch, and J. G. Murphy, are examples among older exegetical writers; H. C. Leupold among more recent. Erich Sauer, a contemporary European writer; and A. J. McClain and John Murray, recent American writers on biblical theology, have expressed similar views.[15] In a class by himself is C. S. Lewis, whose powerful pen has struck some mighty blows on this subject.

The provisions of God's covenant with Noah are not temporary elements of revelation to be superseded or done away, for the covenant is specifically for perpetual generations (9:12). It is important to note that the temporary nature of the provisions of the Mosaic law does not prevail in the case of the Noahic covenant.

It is a covenant with the entire human race for perpetual generations, no more done away by the coming of a better testament than is the narrative of the call of Abraham. There will be occasion to call attention to this fact later.

Since critical significance as a foundational text for a biblical doctrine of civil government belongs to Genesis 9:4-6 and context, more extensive exposition must now follow. Four provisions regarding human civil government are set forth in this passage, commonly called the Noahic or Noachian covenant.

First, civil government is for "the protection, conservation, fostering, and improvement of human life."[16] God made man for Himself and longs to see human life blossom, even under the curse of sin. Government has a general welfare design here at inception.

Second, government does not have its origin in some primeval social contract among our ancestors, as Hobbes, Locke, Rousseau, and their secular democratic followers would have it; neither does it arise out of some immanent force in the world culminating in the state, as supposed Hegel and certain other later nineteenth century German philosophers. It has its origin in God's sovereignty. He alone is sovereign, but has delegated the power of civil government to magistrates—the manner of their placement not being specified.

Third, "the humane civil organization of men must have a moral basis,"[17] that is, it is acknowledged that in an important sense every man is brother to every other man. "At the hand of every man's brother will I require the life of man" (9:5) The Hebrew idiom may be rendered, "from the hand of mankind [the man], that is to say, from the hand of each man's brother I will require life from man." This has its negative requirement in forbidding the killing of man by any individual. It has its positive side in making each man owe a debt of love to his neighbor (Ro 13:8-9).

This is closely connected, in the fourth place, with the religious foundation of civil government, "for in the image of God made he man" (Gen 9:6). This is a fact of divine revelation and is not only a matter of religious faith but of veritable reality. It is precisely this fact which gives the individual man his value. He is more than "valiant dust that builds on dust."He is better than the beasts which perish. Take away this religious relation of man, and all the evils of totalitarian exploitation and oppression of men come in—man has no value, no inalienable rights except the ones the state says he has. Obviously the only adequate religious foundation is true biblical religion. Liberty has never flourished long in any other setting.

The religious basis of civil government is a general concern of Scripture. A short examination of Psalms 92 through 99 will serve to make clear the connection of all sovereignty by which kings reign and lesser magistrates administer government as well as the justice which they maintain with God the Creator. This is to say that the very brief information in Genesis 9 is the first surfacing of a truth which pervades the whole of biblical doctrine. Due to the length of these passages, our treatment of them will be condensed.

Actually only the eighth verse of Psalm 92 connects that member of the psalter in thought with the following seven psalms. In the manner of the ancient Hebrew editors of Psalms and the prophetic books, this was sufficient to give it the position it has. The verse reads: "But thou, O Lord, art on high for evermore" (Ps 92:8). This is an epitome of what all the following psalms of the section have to say: God is King over all the world; He always has been, now is, ever shall be; hence all nations of men should acknowledge His reign. They must also submit to it and praise God for it, because ultimately that reign will become visible. "Whatever allusions to Israel's history or assaults of world powers against Israel may be discovered in this remarkable group of theocratic Psalms, they witness to God's present reign and anticipate the period of his personal visible manifestation as king of the whole earth."[18] A selection of phrases and sentences will serve to clarify and support these assertions: "The Lord reigneth, . . . The world also is established, that it cannot be moved. Thy throne is established of old: Thou art from everlasting" (93:1-2). "O LORD God, to whom vengeance belongeth; . . . shew thyself. Lift up thyself, thou judge of the earth" (94:1-2, cf. Gen 18:25). "He that chastiseth the nations . . . that teacheth man knowledge" (94:10). "The Lord is a great God, And a great King above all gods. In his hand are the deep places of the earth; the heights . . . the sea . . . the dry land . . . Let us kneel before the Lord our Maker" (95:3-6). "Declare his glory among the nations . . . among all the peoples . . . great is the Lord" (96:3-4). "All the gods of the peoples are idols; But the Lord made the heavens . . . Ascribe unto the Lord, ye kindreds of the peoples, Ascribe unto the Lord glory and strength . . . The glory due unto his name: . . . Tremble before him, all the earth. Say among the nations, the Lord reigneth: the world also is established that it cannot be moved: he will judge the people with equity. . . . Exult . . . before the Lord; for he cometh . . . to judge the the earth: He will judge the world with righteousness, and the peoples with his truth" (96:5, 7-10, 12-13). "The Lord reigneth; let the earth rejoice . . . the Lord of the whole earth . . . all the peoples have seen his glory" (97:1, 5-6). "His righteousness hath he openly showed in the sight of the nations . . . Make a joyful noise before the King, the Lord. . . . The world, and they that dwell therein . . . for he cometh to judge the earth: He will judge the world with righteousness, And the people with equity" (98:2, 6-7, 9).

Finally, the ninety-ninth Psalm draws the conclusion: "The king's strength also loveth justice; Thou dost establish equity" (99:4). Not only Israel's rulers, but all human civil rulers, derive their strength for justice and equity from God, Lord of all creation, "For there is no power but of God; and the powers that be are ordained of God" (Ro 13:1).

Whether or not this means that all government is theocracy depends upon what one conceives theocracy to be. Josephus coined the word to indicate contrast between the government of the Jews as established by Moses and the governments of non-Jewish nations such as monarchy, oligarchy, and democracy, particularly to distinguish the Mosaic form of government, wherein there was not only an acknowledged divine ordering of government structures, but also a revealed divine law for the community. It would seem best to retain this narrow sense of the word. Franz Delitzsch, prince of commentators on the Psalms, says in this connection, after giving Josephus credit for inventing the term "theocracy:"

> The coining of the expression is thankworthy; only one has to free one's self from the false conception that the theocracy is a particular constitution. The alternating forms of government were only various modes of its adjustment. The theocracy itself is a reciprocal relationship between God and men, exalted above these intermediary forms, which had its first manifest beginning when Jahve became Israel's

king (Deut. 23:5, cf. Ex. 15:18), and which will be finally perfected by its breaking through this national self-limitation when the King of Israel becomes King of the whole world, that is overcome both outwardly and spiritually. Hence the theocracy is an object of prediction and of hope. And the word *ma-lakh* [reign as king] is used of Jahve not merely of the first beginning of his imperial dominion, and of the manifestation of the same in facts in the most prominent points of the redemptive history, but also of the commencement of the imperial dominion in its perfected glory.[19]

So, theocracy in the original sense of the word, and as Delitzsch explains it, is not the correct name for the biblical doctrine of civil government, even though all governments derive their power from God. Worldwide theocracy, to employ Delitzsch's pattern of thought, until the kingdom of God shall come, is only "an object of prediction and hope."

The likeness of man to God by creation is, as just noted, a wholly religious notion. In this text, that likeness, and thereby relation to God, is made the basis for the prescription of the death penalty for murder, quite aside from later provisions of Mosaic law. No informed person can doubt that capital punishment in certain epochs has been extended far beyond proper bounds, and Christians, as in eighteenth-century England, were vocal in seeking to reduce the number of crimes so punished. But on the contrary, it has been precisely where biblical religion has been set aside and the secular enlightenment view of man as his own god has prevailed that capital punishment for murder has been abolished. It is precisely man's likeness to God that makes him both a sinner, and in the case of killing for personal reasons, a murderer. God has honored Himself and man's likeness to Himself in giving government the power of the sword (cf. Ro 12:19—13:5). This has been presented with great clarity by John Murray, who writes:

> The accent falls upon the divine image in man as the rationale of the execution of the death penalty. Whether the fact of God's image in man is the reason why man is charged to take the life of another, or whether it is the reason why life is taken, we must perceive that the institution of capital punishment is grounded in the fact that the divine image constitutes man's uniqueness. . . . when we ask about the per-

petuity of this institution, no consideration is more pertinent than
this: the reason given for the exacting of such a penalty . . . is one
that has permanent relevance and validity. There is no suspension
of the fact that man was made in the image of God; it is as true
today as it was in the days of Noah.[20]

All of Murray's discussion in his chapter, "The Sanctity of Life," is
of great value in this connection.[21]

The concept of justice, rooted in God's person, to which all men
are responsible and by which they are judged, is a religious one.||[22]
Where theistic religion grows weak, this concept will weaken. Crimes
then are defined as antisocial activity, which in turn is then merely
what the majority says it is. Then punishments seem to be the result of the majority's ganging up on the minority. This in turn
seems inconsistent with democratic feelings. The result is a decline
in uniform application of penalties for crime, resultant miscarriage
of justice, trampling on the rights of law-abiding people, together

---

||These pages shall not assay more than a provisional excursion along the thorny road
to a theology of "justice," though it will be obvious that I consider it to be primarily
a religious-theological issue. What is fair, right, equitable—that is, just—is necessarily
determined by the nature of reality as a whole. This is a matter of ultimates—ultimate
concerns, as Tillich has taught the present generation to say. Authorities assert that,
when what is just is known, men ought to serve it; and universal conscience, I suppose, concurs. But what is justice? There appear to be three main theories:
1. The Positive Law Theory. Justice is posterior to law; law being prior to justice
   cannot be judged by justice. Hence, justice is primarily conformity to law.
2. The Social Good Theory. The source of justice is society, arising out of the agree-
   ments men make to promote their own welfare. Justice is therefore utilitarian and
   conventional.
3. The Natural Right Theory. Justice for man is rooted in what man is by nature.
   It is obligatory in itself apart from positive law or social good.
Though there have been Christian ethical philosophers among each of these schools
of thought, it does not seem to me that any one of the three is wholly correct or
wholly wrong. A fourth element must surely be added—the givenness of the divine
order for the world, including natural light and revelation (or, in the ambiguous
terms of the present time, general and special revelation). If I understand Dooyeweerd and his disciples, this is what they also are saying. For a survey of views, see
Otto A. Bird, *The Idea of Justice* (New York: Frederick A. Praeger, 1967), 192 pp.
For a guide to Christian literature on the subject, especially on the thought of the
Dooyeweerdian schools, see E. L. H. Taylor's chapter, "The Christian Philosophy of
Law" in *The Philosophy of Law, Politics and the State*, (pp. 278-358). A contemporary Christian discussion from quite a different point of view will be met in *The
Theological Foundation of Law* by Jacques Ellul, translated from French by Marguerite Wieser (New York: Seabury, 1960). A careful reading did not yield for me
a distinct impression of the author's views. He seems closest to the natural law
theory. Though there is presently quite a vogue of citing and praising Ellul's many
works in the areas of society, law, government (and I was reading him long before
he became popular among evangelicals) and he does have wholesome things to say, I
find his works somewhat lacking in clear-cut definitions and conclusions. I have not
yet had opportunity thoroughly to digest *Institutes of Biblical Law* by R. J. Rushdoony (Nutley, N.J.: Craig, 1973). It is a massive study.

with an increase in what ought to be called crime. Thus when the Psalms represent the reign of the messianic king, they represent God's people as praying: "Give the king thy justice, O God, and thy righteousness to the royal son! May he judge thy people with righteousness, and thy poor with justice!" (Ps 72:1-2, RSV).[23] The terms which alternate for civil authority in Psalm 72, and usually throughout the Old Testament, are *mishpat* (judgment, justice) and *tsedhaqah* (righteousness). As used in the Old Testament in this connection, these words refer to that which is God's and His alone. In the biblical view, all civil right, justice, and authority are God's; hence, all government is conceived as religious in foundation. Mankind invariably start speaking in religious language of ultimate concerns, for example, when they speak seriously about their views of right government, bearing witness thereby to this biblical insight. Thus one's religious convictions are of formative force in shaping political views. Politics and religion, at the level of personal opinion, cannote be separated. Thus when a country has no common religious faith, and a pluralistic approach is tried, disorder at various levels is likely to result, despite formal commitment to equal rights for everyone.

R. J. Rushdoony has well stated his view of these matters, and in doing so has issued a needed warning: "Every social order rests on a creed, on a concept of life and law, and represents a religion in action. Culture is religion externalized. . . . Wherever there is an attack on the organization of society, there is an attack on its religion. The basic faith of a society means growth in terms of that faith, but any tampering with its basic structure is revolutionary activity. The Marxists are in this respect more astute than their adversaries: they recognize hostility to their structure as counter-revolutionary activity."[24]

In the fifth place, the institution of government with coercive power ("by man shall his blood be shed") shows that fallen humanity, even among a pious remnant such as the eight who survived the deluge, has "unmeasured potentialities for evil which must be curbed."[25] That the biblical sentence quoted describes formal collective action by man is indicated by the Hebrew idiom, which employs the generic term for mankind rather than the individual person, and by the fact that it is followed immediately by "for in the image of

God made he him." This would be meaningless if the sentence in question were a simple prediction that murderers will be killed somehow by other people. It is quite usual in the Hebrew Bible for commands of God or of kings, governors, or parents, to be expressed by the simple future indicative form while conveying the imperative mood.# Several of the Ten Commandments fall into this category. So Jeremiah was right: "It is good for a man that he bear the yoke" (Lam 3:27). The policeman at the corner with the law, the judge, and the hangman standing behind him are necessary for society among sinful man.

In the sixth place, it must be emphasized that the death penalty for murder, the ultimate crime against one's neighbor, is not personal revenge by the dead man's family against his murderer, but divine vengeance, the just retribution upon the offender for wrong done against the God in whose image every man has been made.

This leads to the seventh point, that we have here the basis of all penalty or punishment—not reformation primarily (in the case of murderers certainly out of the question if they are executed), not protection of society (though society is protected), but the purpose of God to vindicate Himself as Governor of the universe. For this reason, Christian writers commonly speak of divine punishments—in this case delegated in execution to magistrates—as vindicative (but not vindictive).

Eighth and finally, the moral justification for the institution of human government and for the capital punishment of murder is the sacredness of human life—man's dignity as a responsible being. "In the image of God made he man." Another way of saying this is that it is man's relatedness to God, as created in the image of God, that demands that he receive treatment as a morally responsible being rather than a thing or commodity, the unresponsible creature of heredity and environment. Take a murderer promptly to court, convict and punish him just as promptly, and you treat him as a responsible man. Treat him as a mere victim of his environment and history, attempt merely to rehabilitate him from his murdering tendencies, and you treat him as a thing or commodity to be manipulated.

#The Hebrew language employs imperative forms only for positive commands; imperfect forms (either regular or modified) with certain negative particles for negative commands. Context only can determine when the sense of many imperfect verbs, usually translated future indicative, is declarative in sense or imperative.

LATER BIBLICAL HISTORY OF CIVIL GOVERNMENT

The biblical history of human government is given a large place in later portions of the Old Testament. The special form which government took among the chosen people will call for treatment later. The Old Testament treatment of the nations other than Israel is quite extensive, though almost always in relation to Israel.

The tenth chapter of Genesis speaks of the division of Noah's family and of their geographical spread, being summarized in the last verse: "These are the families of the sons of Noah, after their generations, in their nations: and of these were the nations divided in the earth after the flood" (Gen 10:32). The story of how men originally resisted the forces leading to dispersion and were compelled by God to spread abroad is told in Genesis 11:1-9.

It is apparently not God's will, however, under the present condition of sin, that the world should be governed as a unified world state. Furthermore, it is probably impossible. One of the truly great statesmen of the past century, member of the Netherlands Parliament, founder of the Free University of Amsterdam, and Prime Minister of the Netherlands 1901-1905, was Abraham Kuyper. In 1898 he lectured at Princeton Theological Seminary, and on that occasion said:

> Man is created from man, and by virtue of his birth he is organically united with the whole race. Together we form one humanity, not only with those who are living now, but also with all the generations behind us and with those who shall come after us—pulverized into millions though we may be. All the human race is from one blood. The conception of States, however, which subdivide the earth into continents, and each continent into morsels does not harmonize with this idea. Then only would the organic unity of our race be realized politically if one State could embrace all the world, and if the whole of humanity were associated in one world empire. Had not sin intervened, no doubt this would actually have been so. If sin, as a disintegrating force, had not divided humanity into different sections, nothing would have marred or broken the unity of our race. And the mistake of the Alexanders, and of the Augusti, and of the Napoleons, was not that they were charmed with the thought of One World-Empire, but it was this—that they endeavored to realize this idea notwithstanding that the force of sin had dissolved our unity. . . . I say, all this is nothing but a looking backward after a lost paradise.[26]

At any rate, the nations of men—governed already no doubt by a great variety of forms of social organization and employing as many varieties of magistrates—are on the scene when the story of the Hebrews is introduced at chapter 12 of Genesis. Some form of monarchy prevailed already in the more advanced centers, but we know that patriarchal clans, as in Israel, also often joined with monarchy.

Many great nations appear in the Old Testament narrative. Before the recent recovery and deciphering of considerable literature of antiquity, our knowledge of them came mainly from the Old Testament. Assyria, Babylon, Elam, Media, Persia, the Hittite empire, Egypt, Ethiopia, and others come readily to the mind of the Bible reader. There is mention of numerous small nations also, mainly neighboring to Israel in the land of Canaan. Among these are Philistia, Edom, Moab, Ammon, and Syria, although sometimes these terms refer to geological areas rather than the people who lived there.

The appearance of national governments of various sorts is no less pervasive in the New Testament than in the Old. The Jewish kingdom, as such, had disappeared, and a complicated system of overlapping jurisdictions had replaced it, the variety and number of which are confusing to all readers of the New Testament, whether lay or learned.

After 27 B.C. the Roman Empire, of which all of Palestine was a part, was placed under three regular kinds of jurisdictions and more than one irregular kind. In the former lands of Israel, there were sections representing several of these types of jurisdiction. In addition, many aspects of public law relating to domestic matters were in the hands of religious authorities, giving them a quasicivil status. So, in the New Testament there are many types of government, many grades of magistrates and executive officers represented: local kings ("Herod the king," Mt 2:1; "Agrippa the king," Ac 25:13); provincial *hegemoni* (Gr.; "Quirinius . . . governor of Syria," Lk 2:2); *ethnarks* (Gr.; 2 Co 11:32); *politarks* (Gr.; Ac 17:6, 8); besides judges, centurions, jailors, temple police, prison guards, and so on.

The New Testament narrative begins with reference to the births of John the Baptist and Jesus "in the days of Herod the king" (Mt 2:1; Lk 1:5). It is related that Jesus' parents were subjects of Caesar

Augustus, whose decrees vitally affected their lives and even the place of Jesus' birth (Lk 2:1-7). The four gospels report several incidents, good and bad, in connection with local governments. The slaughter of certain Galileans by Pilate and the beheading of John the Baptist by Herod are examples. Each gospel devotes several chapters to the connection of the provincial Roman governor (Pilate) and the Jewish king (Herod Antipas) with the death of Jesus. The book of Acts is laced with references first to civil and quasi-civil officers at Jerusalem, and then to the various local and provincial officials into whose territories the churches first sent their missionaries. The Acts include tales of police actions, arraignments, deportations, extraditions, imprisonments, floggings, trials, and executions. The New Testament ends with a book whose author, John, notes that he is in exile on a government prison island.

Treatment in detail of these data, in the main, must be the same as that given similar Old Testament data. We simply note that government is a pervasive and enduring fact. It takes many forms and is administered with varying degrees of righteousness and of success.

7

CIVIL GOVERNMENT IN OLD TESTAMENT
BIBLICAL PROPHECY

EVALUATION AND CRITICISM of the nations of earth, their peoples, capitals, organization, armies, and rulers of Old Testament times is found mainly in the books of the major and minor prophets. These are Isaiah, Jeremiah and Lamentations, Ezekiel, Daniel, Hosea, Joel, Amos, Obadiah, Jonah, Micah, Nahum, Habakkuk, Zephaniah, Haggai, Zechariah, and Malachi—sixteen books varying in size from one page in the English Bible (Obadiah) to three books each about the same size as the collection of all the Pauline epistles (Isaiah, Jeremiah, and Ezekiel). Each of these three largest books has a large section containing oracles directed to or against the various national neighbors of Israel, large and small. These sections are Isaiah 13-24, Jeremiah 46-51, and Ezekiel 25-32, 35, 38, 39. Daniel, the fourth major prophet, is concerned almost entirely with Israel's career as a nation in relation to other nations, recounting fascinating details of incidents in the lives of famous kings of antiquity—Nebuchadnezzar (chaps. 3-4), Belshazzar (chap. 5), Darius (chap. 6), Cyrus (6:28), as well as prophecies of Xerxes (11:2), Alexander (8:5-8, 20-22), and others. Many of the minor prophets contain oracles relating directly to the nations—Joel (2:20; 3:1-21), Amos (1:3-2:3), Zephaniah (2:4-15), Haggai (2:7), and Zechariah (2:6-13; 6:1-15; 8:23; 9:1-8; 12:1-14; 14:9-21); Obadiah (1-21) is entirely related to the little nation of Edom; Jonah is the story of a preaching mission to Nineveh, capital of Assyria; Nahum is the burden of Nineveh throughout, while Habakkuk is a vision concerning the Chaldeans. So we are embarrassed by the abundance of materials to be assessed.

Some of these passages are among the least known and read in the Bible. The geographical and historical setting is obscure to any-

84

one who has not made biblical history and geography a matter of special study. Though there are excellent published treatments of biblical history and geography, they are the sort of works which even ministers do not often read except in seminary courses or in preparation for travel to Bible lands. Further, the prophetic method, employing poetic style, elaborate figures of speech, archaisms, local color, and references to myths, renders them obscure to the casual reader.

The present effort cannot include a survey of exposition of these Scripture passages. Their bearing on our subject, however, is not difficult to extract and summarize. Our procedure will be to summarize each of the main teachings in a sentence, then to expand it and support it by quotations and explanations.

It is an error to assume that the prophets addressed themselves only to Israel.* The prophets were commissioned to address the nations. In the call of Jeremiah, the Lord explicitly states that the prophet's commission was a mission to many nations: "Then the LORD put forth his hand, and touched my mouth. And the LORD said unto me, Behold, I have put my words in thy mouth. See, I have this day set thee over the nations and over the kingdoms, to root out, and to pull down, and to destroy, and to throw down, to build, and to plant" (Jer 1:9-10, KJV). There are not many statements as strong as this one, in the prophetic corpus, though there are instances in the historical books wherein a Hebrew prophet sent his message to foreign authorities. The fact that so much is addressed to and about foreign nations speaks for itself: the principles announced apply to all men and nations, not merely to Israel.

The doctrines set forth in the Old Testament prophetical books are not rooted in inferences drawn from history by the prophets, or in any insights into "natural law." Rather, the leading function of the prophets was to explain and enforce the pentateuchal revelation, the Mosaic foundation of all later biblical revelation. Some forms of modern critical scholarship have turned this relationship between the Pentateuch and the prophetical books upside down. But many

---

*"The philosophy of history contained in the Bible is that of the universal providence of God and not merely of Jewish particularism. . . . It is fair to say that the prophets of the Old Testament as well as the apostles of the New Testament were no less conscious of God's universal providence than the most actively missionary-minded pastor in a Bible-believing church in our day" (J. O. Buswell, *A Systematic Theology of the Christian Religion* [Grand Rapids: Zondervan, 1962], 1:350-51).

scholars and multitudes of informed Bible-reading Christians remain unconvinced by the arguments of this sort of criticism, regretting more the erroneous assumptions on which it rests than the specific changes in interpretation to which it leads. In the area of present interest, the prophets speak plainly to all who read them, irrespective of critical position.

The nations addressed by the prophets had varying legal foundations, only Judah and Israel had special divinely-revealed law—as distinct from customary law and "natural law." Thus, when addressing Judah and Israel, the prophets bring them to the bar of Mosaic law and prophetic revelation. Though not holding pagans responsible to Mosaic law, when addressing the neighboring nations and their rulers, the prophets assume that all these peoples know and accept certain valid concepts of right and wrong. These ethical notions they hold to be no mere customary righteousness, nor deposit of inherited experience of mankind, nor social exigency, but rather moral laws known by man because he is man. This is an assumption, not a theory, presumably based on the created order of the world. Paul's well-known words summarize the prophetic assumptions at this point: "For when Gentiles [Gr. *ethnoi, nations*], which have not the law [i.e., biblical law], do by nature the things contained in the law, these, not having the law, are a law unto themselves: which shew the work of the law written in their hearts, their conscience also bearing witness, and their thoughts the mean while accusing or else excusing one another" (Ro 2:14-15, KJV). Like these prophets, then, Paul could appeal directly to the conscience of kings and potentates in demanding justice for himself, as well as to specific Roman laws (see Ac 22-28). It has frequently been asserted quite correctly that there is very little in the Ten Commandments that is unique to revealed religion. Men of all times, climes, and cultures, except for the perversely sophisticated, have acknowledged most of the same ten laws, and even the sophisticated who deny them are often in schizophrenic inward rebellion against the persisting testimony of their own consciences.

It is beyond the scope of this book to discuss fully how men of all ages and of all nations seem to possess common knowledge of elemental righteousness. Some have traced it to the light of reason, others to natural law, general revelation, or common grace. It even has been reasoned that in the period of man's probation man was given this knowledge in order to do the law of God, and that in corrupt form it has survived the fall. This is sometimes called primeval or primitive revelation. All men do have some knowledge of elemental righteous requirements of God from man, inasmuch as Scripture plainly says so and many teachings of the Scriptures presuppose it. The Bible appeals to reason, to natural light, to general revelation (though this is a defective name for what man knows without revelation in the best sense of the word). The Scriptures demonstrate the existence of such general knowledge and assign the cause to divine grace imparted in common to all men. If there is sufficient validity in the reasoning powers of fallen men to arrive at such truth, it is by God's grace. The same is true of the other proposed means. If such knowledge did not exist in men, theoretically they might exist as men, but hardly as a *society* of men. As good Bible students, we are not required to choose among these controverted channels of information. Theologians not especially interested in association with any particular school of thought will be found unselfconsciously employing such arguments—not the least of them John Calvin, as anyone who has read the first book of the *Institutes* should know.[1]

Without commitment to any formal theory to account for this general knowledge, turn directly to the books themselves to learn what the prophets have to tell us about civil government.

First, God, the Architect, Creator, and Sustainer of the universe, directs the rise of nations and their course in history. The histories and prophecies of Daniel speak most directly to this point. When, for example, Nebuchadnezzar's army conquered Jerusalem it was because "the Lord gave Jehoiakim king of Judah into his hand (Dan 1:2). Certain experiences taught Nebuchadnezzar that God could confound his executioners for the benefit of his servants (2:1-30). Still later Nebuchadnezzar testified that "the most High . . . liveth for ever, whose dominion is an everlasting dominion, and his kingdom is from generation to generation: And all the inhabitants of the earth are reputed as nothing; and he doeth according to his will in the army of heaven, and among the inhabitants of the earth; and none can stay his hand, or say unto him, What doest thou?" (Dan 4:35). The same chapter delivers a decree of watchers, or "to the intent that the living may know that the most High ruleth in the kingdom of men, and giveth it to whomsoever he will, and setteth up over it the basest of men" (4:17). The story of Belshazzar's feast is prophetically connected with the same truth of divine control over the affairs of nations (esp. 5:21). Later in the book, king Darius is forced to confess the same: "For he is the living God, and stedfast for ever, and his kingdom that which shall not be destroyed; and his dominion shall be even unto the end" (6:26). The prophecy of chapter seven, a survey of the future of nations to the consummation, discloses God in evident control at last: "And the kingdom and the dominion, and the greatness of the kingdoms under the whole heaven, shall be given to the people of the saints of the Most High: his kingdom is an everlasting kingdom, and all dominions shall serve and obey him" (7:27).

Isaiah declares that when King Cyrus of Medo-Persia shall overwhelm the kingdom of Babylon and restore the Jews to their land, it shall be because God raised him up to do so (Is 44:28; 45:13). When God used Babylon to destroy Assyria, and again later used the Medes and Persians to humble Babylon, it was because God by His secret counsel directed and enabled them so to do (Jer 50:15-18).

All the prophets emphasize that God is sovereign Lord of the nations and that all human civil authority is only delegated divine authority. Many other Scripture writers make the same point: "God is the judge: he putteth down one, and lifteth up another" (Ps 75:7, cf. Job 12:18-25; Ps. 107:40; Ec 8:9; Lk 1:52; Ro 13:1).

Speaking more of his own time than of ours, Calvin ruefully notes: "All indeed confess this but scarcely one in a hundred feels in his mind the dominion of God over the earth, and that no man can raise himself, or remain in any post of honour, since this is the peculiar gift of God."[2]

In the second place, Magistrates are responsible to God; hence they must be humble, serious-minded, hard-working men, faithful to their tasks, loyal to truth and justice.

This is the message of Isaiah to the king of Babylon. Though Babylon was not yet a leading world power in the latter part of the eighth century B.C. when Isaiah wrote, he foresaw its advance. Hence the largest of his oracles against the nations concerns

Babylonians and their king. He reminds them that God's government extends to the whole world. Therefore, he will in "the day of Jehovah . . . punish the world for their evil" (Is 13:9, 11). Then in a remarkable display of word power, the prophet denounces the king of Babylon for his oppression of peoples (14:4-6), his vain pomp (14:11), his pride and self-will (14:12-14).

The denunciation of the Pharaoh and of Egypt by Jeremiah, though in different language, is of similar import (chap. 46), as is also Ezekiel's message of judgment on Tyre and its king (chaps. 26-28). Though possessing great wisdom (28:12) and vast resources (28:4-7), the king of Tyre had used both only to exalt himself, his city, and his gods. His special sin had been pride, going so far as even to claim divine honors (28:2). Therefore his reign and his realm will be destroyed.

Daniel rebuked Nebuchadnezzar also for his pride (Dan 4:25-26) and oppression of the poor (v. 27) and, by implication, for his suppression of the truth (v. 37). He pronounced judgment on Belshazzar for indolence and willful stupidity, for his sacrilege in using the Jewish temple vessels for a drunken feast, for dereliction of duty, for his pride, and especially for his failure to acknowledge and glorify God (5:1-30). Darius also smarted from the rebukes of Daniel for his pride and cupidity (chap. 6). As these messages show, it is part of the peculiarity of Old Testament prophecy that many prophetic deliverances are in negatives. The prophets were to serve as critics; to this function they were faithful.

Third, governments are expected to maintain order, and in the process thereof, their magistrates are to enforce laws justly. There is of course no disjunction between law and order on the one hand and justice on the other.

In preserving internal order, the Hebrew magistrates sometimes honored justice and sometimes did not. The prophets often commented on it. A striking example in connection with the Jews is an incident reported in Jeremiah 34:8-22. A law of Moses (Ex 21-2; Deu 15:1-12) forbade making permanent slaves of fellow Hebrews. That indentured servitude (a more accurate name than slavery for the Hebrew institution) always be humane was a concern of the Mosaic law. After six years a man was legally required to release his servant. But this had been disobeyed by the rapacious slaveholders of Jerusalem in the last period of that expiring kingdom (Jer 34:12-14). In a moment of foxhole faith, however, they had tardily obeyed, for when it looked as if the beseiging Babylonian armies were about to breach the walls and destroy the inhabitants, the slaveholders released their unlawfully and unrighteously retained slaves. Then, strangely, the armies of Nebuchadnezzar retired from Jerusalem to pursue Pharoah's army (Jer 37:6-12). To the embattled citizens of Jerusalem who did not know the practical reason why the Babylonians raised the seige, it looked for a while as if the city had been delivered. So the well-to-do former slaveholders simply compelled their former Jewish servants to resume their servitude. For this lawless injustice Jeremiah scolded the king and the people.

Never in the history of the world has the importance of elemental justice honestly upheld and fairly administered by civil magistrates been more forcefully declared than by the prophet Jeremiah, though there are strong sections on the subject in several of the prophets. Shallum (or Jehoahaz, 2 Ki 23:30, cf. 1 Ch 3:15), son of good king Josiah, had a very brief reign of only three months (2 Ki 23:31-33). The reason he was to die in captivity as Jeremiah had foretold, was that "Jehoahaz . . . did that which is evil in the sight of the Lord" (2 Ki 23:31-32). And what might the evil have been? Jeremiah's own bill of particulars is very pertinent to our inquiry:

> Woe unto him that buildeth his house by unrighteousness, and his chambers by injustice; that useth his neighbor's service without wages, and giveth him not his hire; that saith, I will build me a wide house and spacious chambers, and cutteth him out windows; and it is ceiled with cedar and it is painted with vermilion. Shalt thou reign, because thou strivest to excell in cedar? Did not thy father [good king Josiah] eat and drink, and do justice and righteousness [*mishpat* and *tsedhaqah*]? then it was well with him. He judged the cause of the poor and needy; then it was well. Was not this to know me? saith the Lord. But thine eyes and thy heart are not but for thy covetousness, and for shedding innocent blood, and for oppression, and for violence, to do it (Jer 22:13-17).

Then immediately turning his wrath toward the equally venal but more long-reigned Jehoiakim, an older son of Josiah, the present incumbent of the throne, Jeremiah adds: "Therefore thus saith Jehovah concerning Jehoiakim the son of Josiah, king of Judah: They shall not lament for him, saying, Ah my brother! or, Ah my sister! They shall not lament for him, saying, Ah lord! or, Ah his glory! He shall be buried with the burial of an ass, drawn and cast forth beyond the gates of Jerusalem" (22:18-19). When shortly his dead body was cast out to be exposed, unburied, to the carnivores and the elements (see 36:30), the prophet had made his point: magistrates are responsible to God to maintain civil order over themselves as well as among their people, and to do so with justice. This includes elements of what has come to be called social justice. None can say that the prophetic object lesson is not graphic or impressive!

In our day of common reaction against extremes in secularized assistance to the poor, it is proper to emphasize that neglect of the Mosaic provisions for assistance to the poor, as well as disobedience to Moses' prohibitions against exploiting the misfortunes of the poor, were strongly condemned by the prophets. Let us cite only one particularly vivid passage: "Woe unto them that decree unrighteous decrees, and to the writers who prepare trouble; to force away the needy from demanding justice, and to rob the suffering of my people of their rightful claims, that widows may become their prey, and they plunder orphans" (Is 10:1-2 F. Delitzsch's translation, cf. Is 26:4-6; Mt 5:5). Delitzsch explains the passage: "Poor persons who wanted to commence legal proceedings were not even allowed to do so, and possessions to which widows and orphans had a well-founded claim were welcome booty to them."[3]

Large sections of many of the prophets are devoted to this sort of moral judgment of Hebrew rulers. (See Hosea, Amos, Micah, Habakkuk, Zephaniah, Malachi).

For Gentiles, the prophets had a similar burden and expressed it more extensively than is generally realized. Cyrus is praised for his justice in handling conquered peoples (Is 44:24—45:7), but in the book of Obadiah, Edom is condemned for unjustified malice toward Judah. Amos in particular brings Judah's neighbors under the righteous judgment of God. Damascus, capital of Syria, is judged guilty of wrong for unnecessary violence toward the civilian population of a neighbor land with whom they happened to be at war (Amos 1:3-5). Gaza and three other Philistine cities are judged guilty of unlawful deportation of a civilian population, and condemned to perish (vv. 6-8). Tyre is castigated for a similar crime against common justice, also for dishonesty in breaking an international treaty (vv. 9-10). Edom is to be punished by God for lack of humane compassion (vv. 11-12); Ammon for brutal treatment of women of enemy populations in time of war (vv. 13-15); Moab for sacrilege and disregard of ordinary civilized decency. The sacrilege in this case was flagrant violation of the cemeteries of enemy dead (2:1-3). Respect for the customary decencies of mankind is thus recognized as a just requirement of all men. It is significant that no Mosaic law speaks of respect for cemeteries. Even if there were such a law, the Moabites were not subject to Mosaic laws and did not know them. There is evidently some general knowledge of righteousness, call it natural law or common sense, to which God holds all men accountable. The divine controversy with man is not that he has no information about righteousness, but that he refuses to abide by what he knows: "They hold down the truth in unrighteousness . . . they refused to retain God in their knowledge" (Ro 1:18, 28, KJV).

Significantly, though Amos accuses neither Judah nor Israel of such barbaric crimes, he nevertheless judges them worthy to perish. Their magistrates had taken unfair advantage of poor people (Amos 2:6-7); they had permitted the general populace to become involved in many irregular sexual habits, including incest, specifically forbidden in the Mosaic law (Amos 2:7, cf. Lev 18:7, 15; 20:11). They had also misused property not their own (Amos 2:8). Amos condemns Judah severely for the rather tame sins (compared to others in this context) of rejecting truth and telling lies (Amos 2:4-5). These sins he declares to be especially offensive because they knew better—their sins were against light.

It should be noticed that many of the prophets specifically mention the complicity of religious and cultural leaders with civil officers in these self-destroying violations of the divine majesty. Jeremiah laments: "A wonderful and horrible thing is come to pass in the land: the prophets prophesy falsely, and the priests bear rule by their means; and my people love to have it so: and what will ye do in the end thereof?" (Jer 5:30-31). There are several prophetic sections wherein kings, priests, prophets, princes, and other leaders are jointly charged with joining an abandoned people in hearty pursuit of unrighteousness.

Fourth, though not responsible directly for the secret, private conduct of subjects, God expects governments to enforce public morality. The essentials of civic morality, as noted earlier, are presumed to be known, even among pagans. Jewish people, who had special revelation and a higher standard, were held responsible for more light. The prophet does not say what the specific sins of the people of Nineveh were, but the Lord sent Jonah to "go to Nineveh, that great city, and cry against it; for their wickedness is come up before me" (Jon 1:2). The God of the Bible is King over pagan Nineveh quite as much as over Jerusalem, the divinely-chosen capital city of the chosen people. Furthermore, the whole story of Jonah and his preaching mission to Nineveh presupposes that the Ninevites were responsible men, accountable to God for the divine righteousness they knew and flouted long before Jonah arrived. As consideration is given to this sort of evidence, it is readily understood why the Mosaic law omits many things necessary in basic law for a civil commonwealth. The Mosaic system incorporated the customary civil and moral observances of the time—except as corrected where they were inconsistent with the divine righteousness and God's special purpose for Israel.† Natural light, therefore, is light, indeed, even though it is not clear light and it is not unmixed with darkness; or perhaps we should say, common grace *is* grace, even though it is much less than special or saving grace. When Jonah finally obeyed, not only the common people, but the king also engaged in public display of repentance. When magistrates permit murder, theft, forni-

---

†Trustworthy authorities agree on this: Keil, for example, asserts: "For civil right the Mosaic legislation lays down precepts only in regard to the relations of social and political life, which either stood in immediate connection with morality and religion, or required to be modified by the principles of the theocracy. On the law of succession [referring to inheritance of family name and properties], e.g., it only contains three particular specifications, two of which (on the succession of daughters) were given on special occasions; the third, Deut. xxi.15 ff., is intended to banish an iniquity. All the rest is *presupposed as already exising right* [italics added]. Further, it contains no laws regarding buying and selling, but only regarding redeeming and such like. What has no connection with religious life in general, or with the special form given to it by the covenant with God, *is not changed by the theocratic legislation* [italics added]" (*Manual of Biblical Archaeology* [Edinburgh: T. & T. Clark, 1888], 2:323).
  Partly on this account, no effort to construct a civil constitution on the basis of Mosaic law alone can ever be effectual. The Mosaic legislation per se is not a complete record of the civil system of ancient Israel.

cation and the like to go unchecked and unpunished, God calls the whole nation to accounting. The unpunished crimes pollute the land, becoming a growing mortgage against all, upon which God may finally foreclose, driving some inhabitants away, destroying others and permitting different peoples to dwell in the land. This is a recurring theme in the Old Testament, especially in the prophetic books. (e.g., Gen 15:12-18; Lev 18:24-28; Is 1:4-7; Jer 5:7-17).

But do men everywhere really have a knowledge of God and of elemental morality, such as is embodied in the second table of the decalogue: "Honor thy father and thy mother. . . . Thou shalt not kill. Thou shalt not commit adultery. Thou shalt not steal. Thou shalt not bear false witness. Thou shalt not covet." (Ex 20:12-17)? I have argued above that, since God judges the nations for sins against these and other divine laws, they do know them; and I have still earlier introduced the statement of Paul about the conscience of pagans, to the same effect. Let us now take a close look at Isaiah 24, which, in the opinion of the highest exegetical authority, teaches the doctrine we are defending.

The chapter has many features indicating that its author is thinking of the whole earth rather than the land of Israel. Let us consider some of the evidence. In the first place, it serves as grand finale to that section of Isaiah (chaps. 13-23) wherein Isaiah pronounces various judgments on the Gentile neighbor nations, including all the major world powers. The theme of the prophecies herein does not relate at all to Israel and Judah, but to the sins of Babylon (13:1—14:23), Assyria (14:24-27), Philistia (vv. 28-32), Moab (chaps. 15-16), Syria (chap. 17), Ethiopia (chap. 18), Egypt (chap. 19), Babylon again (chap. 21), the foreign-interest element in Jerusalem (chap. 22), and Tyre (chap. 23). Then comes chapter 24 in apparent summation and pronouncement of final judgment on them all.

Eretz, with the limited meaning of "land," or with the worldwide meaning of "earth" is rendered "earth" throughout the chapter in three leading English translations (KJV, RV, RSV), showing what the many scholars involved in those translations deemed to be the case. At verse 4, "earth" is in parallel structure with "world" (Heb. *tēbhēl)* which is certainly the globe and its inhabitants (cf. Ps 90:2). In verse 13, "For thus it shall be in the midst of the earth among the peoples" shows that it is not a single people in a single land, but all peoples in the whole earth that the author has in mind. At verse 21, there is a very strong indication of a universal reference, for "the kings of the earth upon the earth" therein is properly "the kings of the ground [Heb. *ha' adhāmāh*] upon the ground [Heb. *ăl ha' adhāmāh*]." "The ground" is the word used, for example, of the earth's substance ("dust of the ground," Gen. 2:7) and has no special connection with the land of Israel. The kings of the whole world are in mind. So it seems quite certain that Isaiah is speaking of all mankind.

The chapter closes with a microcosmic view of final judgment, and not with some providential event such as the capture of Samaria or of Jerusalem. The theology of Daniel 7 and of Revelation 4-20 is there in germ.[4] Even the supernatural spirits, associated elsewhere in Scripture with governments, are to be finally judged. Isaiah 24:21-23 is connected with the judgment of the last day, not with the providential occurrences of history.

Come the questions, Why? On what basis? Chapter 24, verse 5 answers: "The earth also is polluted under the inhabitants thereof; because they have transgressed the laws, violated the statutes, broken the everlasting covenant." Laws, statutes, and covenant are known by men and are broken by them. It may possibly be that Scripture here refers to the various national laws (Heb. *tôrōth*), and statutes (Heb. *hoq*, statute, in singular). It would more accurately be rendered, "they have transgressed laws, violated statute." If these are human laws and statute, what a resounding affirmation of the validity of human civil law, the disobedience thereof being punished in the final great assize! How this enlarges Paul's "for conscience sake" (Ro 13:5). "Broken the everlasting covenant," however, can refer only to God's law. If laws and statute are human, they are not eternal except only that willful disobedience has eternal consequences, as do all sins. But God's everlasting covenant, in the context of God's rules and judgments, is the divine will in expression— divine law. C. Von Orelli of Basel had said, in comment on this verse: "The whole human world knows God's ordinances and laws transmitted to it and testified to by conscience (cf. Gen. ix.4ff.), and is in covenant with God so far as God's revelations are known to it (Rom. ii.14ff.)."[5] Delitzsch's remarks are very strong in support of the interpretation advocated here, bringing not only his own valued opinion to bear, but also the weight of Jewish interpretation which his special Jewish training and background equipped him to explore: "Understanding 'the earth' as we do in a general sense, 'the law' cannot signify merely the positive law of Israel. The Gentile world had also a *tōrâh* or divine teaching within, which contained an abundance of divine directions (*tōrôth*). They also had a law written in their hearts; and it was with the whole human race that God concluded a covenant in the person of Noah, at a time when the nations had none of them come into existence at all. This is the explanation given even by Jewish commentators."[6]

The same doctrine, responsibility of rulers and citizens of all countries to obey the moral laws of God, with judgment threatened both here and hereafter, is the theme of several other biblical portions, notably Jeremiah 25, wherein "all the kings . . . and all the kingdoms of the world" are clearly designated (25:26).

The last four kings of Judah were knaves, hypocrites, fools, and weaklings: Jehoahaz, Jehoiakim, Jeconiah, and Zedekiah. Jeremiah was contemporary with them all. He said that Jehoahaz (or Shallum) would die in a foreign land (Egypt, cf. Jer 22:10-17); Jehoiakim was to be killed and to receive the burial of an ass (vv. 18-19). Of Coniah (or Jeconiah or Jehoiachin), the same prophet, speaking for God, said, "I will cast thee out, and thy mother that bare thee, into another country, where ye were not born; and there shall ye die" (v. 26, see vv. 24-29). Zedekiah, the last of the unhappy four, honored Jeremiah by asking for his prayers and advice, but received word only of certain defeat and death by the armies of Nebuchadnezzar (21:1-7). To the ruling family Jeremiah said: "O house of David, thus saith the Jehovah, Execute justice in the morning, and deliver him that is robbed out of the hand of the oppressor, lest my wrath go forth like fire, and burn so none can quench it, because of the evil of your doings" (Jer 21:12). The impressively stated explanation given in 2 Chronicles 36:11-21 as to why Zedekiah and his nation were to come to such an unhappy end contains these sad words concerning the people and their king, "they mocked the messengers of God, and despised his words, and scoffed at his prophets, until the wrath of Jehovah arose against his people, till there was no remedy" (v. 16). Then they were killed or taken away "until the land had enjoyed its sabbaths."

It should be emphasized again that according to the standards of the Old Testament prophets, when citizens of any country blaspheme God without civil restraint, break laws against chastity, against persons, against property, against civic peace and order, and the crimes go unpunished, there is accumulating a debt of offense against the majesty of God, the judge of all the earth, which cannot indefinitely go unpaid. Thus the God-fearing citizens have more than an incidental interest in the maintenance not only of good church order, but also of public order and decency. This theme is important to many sections of the Bible, and in light of contemporary life it deserves more attention than it receives.

Fifth, governments are required by God not only to rule justly, but also to ensure justice in the relationship between individual citizens and between what have come to be called socio-economic classes. It has already been observed that provision of what the United States Constitution calls "the general welfare" of nations was in the original mandate (Gen 9:1-7) for rule of man by man.

Those who by reason of industry and prudence or inheritance have the power that wealth and possessions bring are to be prevented from taking unfair advantage of the less powerful. A passage in Jeremiah is noteworthy in this connection.

> And touching the house of the king of Judah, hear ye the word of Jehovah: O house of David, thus saith Jehovah, Execute justice in the morning [i.e., get to his case early!], and deliver him that is robbed out of the hand of the oppressor, lest my wrath go forth like fire, and burn so that none can quench it. . . . O king of Judah, that sittest upon the throne of David, thou, and thy servants, and thy people that enter in by these gates [the courts were held in rooms at the gates or in the open near them]. Thus saith Jehovah: Execute ye justice and righteousness, and deliver him that is robbed out of the hand of the oppressor: and do no wrong, do no violence, to the sojourner, the fatherless, nor the widow; neither shed innocent blood in this place (Jer 21:11-12; 22:2-3; cf. Pr 14:28; Is 11:4; Amos 2:6-7; 4:1; 5:11-12; 8:6).

Promises and threats follow. Rulers then, as now, needed prodding to do their duty for the obscure, who have "no clout," as conscientiously and promptly as for the prominent citizen with influence. It is instructive that the shepherd (or pastor) is used as a figure for rulers in the civil-political sphere more frequently than in the religious-spiritual sphere (as in Psalm 23 and often in the New Testament). This figure appears quite frequently even among pagans, in whose literature the ruler is often designated a shepherd‡ The Shepherd's care for the needs of the sheep and his protection of them is the source of the pleasing comparison. Thus Cyrus, the Persian conqueror who, as a matter of state policy, returned many deported populations, including the Jews, to their native lands, is described by God as "Cyrus ... my shepherd, ... [who] shall perform all my pleasure, even saying of Jerusalem, She shall be built" (Is 44:28). § It is interesting that although the King James Version renders Jeremiah 2:8, "they that handle the law knew me not: the pastors [shepherds] also transgressed against me," the American Standard Version ren-

‡Evidence for use of the shepherd figure (Heb., *ro'eh;* Gr. *poimēn*) for a political person or ruler rather than an ecclesiastical person or pastor outside the Scriptures is neatly summarized in the *Theological Dictionary of the New Testament* article on *poimēn.* Under the rubric "In the Ancient Orient," it is said, "Already on Sumerian royal inscriptions the king ... is described as the shepherd appointed by deity. In Babylonian and Assyrian *re'u* ('shepherd') is a common epithet for rulers and the verb *re'u* ('to pasture') is a common figure of speech for the rule. ... Gathering the dispersed, righteous government and care for the weak are marks of the shepherd function of the ruler. Gods, too, hear the title of shepherd." The author finds the same usage in Egypt.

Even cognate modern Arabic carries over this political sense of "shepherd" in various uses of and derivatives of the verb *ra'a. Ri'aya,* for example, means patron, protectorate, guardianship; and *ra'awiya* means citizenship, nationality.

§An important contemporary cuneiform inscription, evidently authorized by Cyrus himself, points out that his permission for the Jews to return to their homeland was part of a general policy and, showing how little he understood the divine providence that made him God's servant, likewise announces his essentially pagan reasons for doing so: he expected all the priests of various religions to pray to their gods for his health. The most significant portion of the inscription follows.

"I returned to [these] sacred cities on the other side of the Tigris, the sanctuaries of which have been ruins for a long time, the images which [used] to live therein and established for them permanent sanctuaries. I [also] gathered all their [former] inhabitants and returned [to them] their habitations. Furthermore, I resettled upon the command of Marduk, the great lord, all the gods of Sumer and Akkad whom Nabonidus had brought into Babylon to the anger of the lord of the gods, unharmed, in their [former] chapels, the places which make them happy.

"May all the gods whom I have resettled in their sacred cities ask daily Bel and Nebo for a long life for me and may they recommend me."

This text was inscribed on a clay barrel usually referred to as the Cyrus Cylinder, published by H. C. Rawlinson, *The Cuneiform Inscriptions of Western Asia* (London, 1861-84). The above translation is from *Ancient Near Eastern Texts Relating to the Old Testament,* ed. J. B. Pritchard (Princeton, N.J.: U. Press, 1955), p. 316.

See discussions in Martin Noth, *The History of Israel,* 2ᵈ ed. (London: A. & C. Black, 1958), pp. 303-5; John Bright, *A History of Israel* (Philadelphia: Westminster, 1959), pp. 343-44; and G. A. Barton, *Archaeology and the Bible,* 7th ed. (Philadelphia: Amer. Sun. Sch. Union, 1937), pp. 484-85.

ders "pastors" according to the meaning of the figure as "rulers" [Heb. *harō'im*, the shepherds]. Jeremiah speaks of good rulers as "shepherds according to [God's] heart, who shall feed you with knowledge and understanding" (Jer 3:15); and of evil rulers as shepherds who have "become brutish, and have not inquired of Jehovah: therefore they have not prospered, and all their flocks are scattered" (10:21; see also 12:10; 22:22; 23:1, 2, 4; 25:34-36; 50:6, 44; Eze 34:2, 5, 7-10, 12, 23; 34:23; 37:24; Mic 5:5; Nah 3:18; Zec 10:2-3; 11:3, 5, 8, 15-16).

Contrariwise, those whose inheritance includes neither power nor riches as individuals are not to be permitted to unite their forces unjustly to despoil the rich. The prophets were not advocates of social and economic leveling; "liberty, equality, fraternity," as in French Jacobin social political propaganda and recent secular socialist thought, had no place in their vocabulary. They cannot be made to teach either political democracy or economic socialism. It is written in the law, "Thou shalt not follow a multitude to do evil; neither shalt thou speak in a cause to turn aside after a multitude to wrest justice: neither shalt thou favor a poor man in his cause" (Ex 23:2-3). This falls in a section on reciprocal civic duties. Likewise, it is written, "Ye shall do no unrighteousness in judgment: thou shalt not respect the person of the poor, nor honor the person of the mighty: but in righteousness shalt thou judge thy neighbor: I am Jehovah" (Lev 19:15-16).

The prophets as exponents and expositors of the law did not fail to announce these principles. For example, early in his ministry, Jeremiah made a search for righteous persons among his fellow citizens in Jerusalem (5:1). He found that among the poor there were none. They were not only poor in goods, but "foolish; for they know not the way of Jehovah, nor the law of their God" (5:4). The rich and mighty were not less unrighteous, foolish, and ignorant (vv. 5-6). In fact all, small and great, rich and poor, were given over to covetousness (6:13) and sins of sexual impurity (vv. 7-8). When Nebuzaradan, the Babylonian general, left "the poor of the people, that had nothing, in the land of Judah, and gave them vineyards and fields" (39:10), they showed themselves to be morally worse, if anything, than their more well-born and prosperous countrymen who had been taken captive away (Jer 40-44).

The prophets reprove the wealthy for dishonesty in gaining riches and for lack of mercy in using it; the poor for violence or deceit or laziness; both rich and poor for covetousness; but neither rich nor poor for their economic condition. For each, his economic and social station is traced to the divine providence, and he is to use his position for service and spiritual growth. Riches may be a blessing, but the poor may be rich in faith, holiness, piety.

There is no passage more illuminating of the special place of the poor in God's program for Messiah than Psalm 72, one of several psalms declaring a prophetic message. It is rendered into hymn lines by Isaac Watts in "Jesus Shall Reign." Therein the beneficiaries of the reign of the coming righteous king are "thy people . . . thy poor" (v. 2), "the poor of the people . . . the children of the needy" (v. 4), "the needy . . . the poor, that hath no helper" (v. 12), "He will have pity on the poor and needy, And the souls of the needy he will save. He will redeem their soul from oppression and violence: And precious will their blood be in his sight" (vv. 13-14). True, "the poor" is transmuted into a spiritual rather than material quality, but this tends to emphasize some of the possible spiritual values of genuine material poverty. Jesus interprets the psalm for today in the Beatitudes of Matthew 5.

Likewise in the Psalms, a certain type of rich man is occasionally presented as an example of materialistic venality (e.g., Ps 17:14).

Since, however, the rich and great have much power while the poor have little of it, the laws are so to be enforced that the rich are not allowed to take unfair advantage of the poor. There is no doubt that biblical religion acknowledges that great riches, though a blessing, are also a temptation.

These principles, important as they are for good government, will never be put into practice simply by passing laws. Rather, men everywhere, especially in this epoch of prevalent democratic social and political theory, must know them and promote them in personal practice. Perhaps then government will acknowledge and employ them. Robert Lawrence Ottley in his Bampton Lectures of 1898 not only summarized well the significance of Old Testament prophecy for general national life but emphasized this way of actuating the truths of prophecy:

The Old Testament may be studied . . . as an instructor in social

Righteousness. It exhibits the moral government of God as attested in his dealings with nations rather than with individuals; and it was their consciousness of the action and presence of God in history that made the prophets preachers, not merely to their countrymen, but to the world at large. The study of prophecy cannot but deepen our sense of the continuity of national life, of the reality of national vocation and responsibility, of the principle of judgment visibly at work in national history. . . . It was their hold upon law, their inspired sense of the claims of an objective moral order embracing all nations that enabled them to predict. . . . There is indeed significance in the fact that in spite of their ardent zeal for social reform they did not as a rule take part in political life or demand political reforms. They desired, it has been justly said, not better institutions but better men.[7]

8

CIVIL GOVERNMENT IN OLD TESTAMENT MESSIANIC EXPECTATION

EXPECTATION regarding Messiah is an aspect of prophetic teaching regarding government that should not be neglected. The prophets refer to the coming Saviour of men as the anointed (i.e., Messiah, or Christ, Dan 9:26) Son of man (Dan 7:13), son of David (Is 9:6-7; 11:1-2; Jer 33:15), or servant of the Lord (Is 42:1-4). In each case the prophet was thinking of a great human figure through whom the ills and sins of mankind would be cured, issuing in mediation of a just and holy reign of God through man. It is in prophecy of this coming figure that the ideals of the prophets for human government are made most fully known in positive language.

The hopes of the prophets were not utopian. They had no faith in a merely human leader to bring about an ideal state of human affairs. Coupled with expectation of a great human figure who would be the ideal king was the recurring theme: "Behold your God will come." As Franz Delitzsch skillfully presents the explanation for this duality, the human aspect of the hope is a star that marches from the horizon upward; the divine hope is a star that looses itself from the zenith downward in the same meridian of the sky. At last the two stars meet to form one constellation—the God-man, our Lord Jesus Christ.[1]

Delitzsch was right. Many Bible students through the centuries have expected the promises of an ideal earthly government yet to be fulfilled at the second advent of Christ. Evaluation of these claims does not suit the present purpose. Rather, without assuming either literal or figurative fulfillment to have been intended, but taking the predictions of the prophets in relation to good civil government as expressions of legitimate expectations from government, we seek some suggestions regarding good government in every age of mankind. Granting that the sin factor prohibits the ideals from being fully realized, these ideals still constitute values to work for as legitimate goals of human government.

Some of the prophetic ideals must wait. One, for example, is world government under one political structure. The prophecies of that coming day present the sinless Son of man who, as the God-man, can fulfill the prediction that "the Lord shall be King over all the earth" (Zec 14:9) as the head of world government (Dan 7:13). That kingdom will be possessed by the saints (Dan 7:18, 22, 27).

In the meantime, we must make do with the best that we can get, for until that day, the most men can even hope for is an unsteady balance somewhere between the ideal and the possible. The founding fathers of the United States understood this, and acknowledging the depravity of man, they formulated a constitution with a set of checks and balances to restrain unrighteous ambition and oppressive designs. The *Federalist Papers* by James Madison and Alexander Hamilton elaborated this view of affairs, saying in one important passage: "It may be a reflection on human nature that such [constitutional] devices should be necessary to control the abuses of government. But what is government itself but the greatest of all reflections on human nature? If men were angels, no government would be necessary. If angels were to govern men, neither external nor internal controls on government would be necessary. In framing of a government which is to be administered by men over men, the greatest difficulty lies in this: you must first enable the government to control the governed, and in the next place oblige it to control itself."[2]

Will Herberg, in comment on the Christian doctrine of man embodied by the founding fathers in the United States Constitution, has well observed that the basic argument was drawn from Romans 13 by way of Augustine and the Protestant reformers. He notes:

> This argument for the just state is also an argument for constitutional democracy as the best type of regime. The argument for the state as an order of preservation [rather than an order of creation as in Thomist thought] in effect, maintains that government is made necessary by human sinfulness and serves to protect society from the destructive consequences of sinful self-aggrandizement. But rulers are surely themselves human beings, and subject to the same temptations that beset other human beings; hence institutional curbs on

the power entrusted to them are necessary, and for the same reason—
to prevent the inevitable abuse of power that is not in some manner
systematically checked and restrained. Calvin in his own way understood this, and so did the Puritans; so also did the framers of the
United States Constitution, for however far the Founding Fathers may
have strayed from the Christian faith, they 'believed in original sin'
and exhibited a 'hearty Puritanism in [their] view of human nature.'[3]

The policy of George Washington extended these cautions to international relationships, for he warned against permanent alliances
with Old World powers. This he did for practical reasons rather
than for overtly theological reasons. The same may be said of Jefferson's cautions against enlarging alliances.

Without attempting to be exhaustive in examination of the Messianic prophecies of the Old Testament, let us note several principles of sound government in the prophetic expectation of the coming times of Messiah.

1. A balance of powers within each state is desirable. In Isaiah
33:17-22, the now-conventional balanced division of powers is suggested as that of "judge" (judicial), "lawgiver" (legislative), and
"king" (executive). Note especially verse 22, "the Lord is our judge,
the Lord is our lawgiver, the Lord is our king." The passage does not
directly teach balance of powers. Nor do the words judge, lawgiver,
and king invariably designate distinct functions. Coming to the passage with knowledge of the customary analysis, the division of powers necessary in government under the condition of sin appears. Under messianic conditions of the coming kingdom of God, they are
united. Government always has difficulty in maintaining unity and
harmony among these powers. The tensions between judicial and
legislative departments in connection with the House discipline of
Adam Clayton Powell demonstrate this. Tensions between the executive and judicial branches are indicated in the frequent collisions
between the edicts of federal agencies and the courts; between legislative and executive as the Presidents' frequent spats with successive
national congresses show. Yet somehow unity must be preserved.
"Human government . . . always swings between the two opposite
poles of regimentation and fragmentation: the former leading to
sacrifice of liberty in the interest of strength; the latter to sacrifice

of strength in the interest of liberty. And the head of state tends to become either a dictator or a mere symbol."[4]

A related fact is the prophetic appreciation for the legitimate place of various special functions in the social structure. The utmost variety of areas of professional competency, of vocational preference, of artistic and industrial expression is recognized and encouraged; however, all must be conducted within the unifying limits of the service and worship of the one true and living God. The doctrine of sovereignty according to which certain spheres of human activity are each autonomous within their realm is an extension of this teaching. It is too much to load this freight on the prophets, though doubtless it is there. The seed of the teaching is to be found in both Calvin and Luther.* In recent times it has been elaborated into a complete system of thought relating itself to all reality in the writings of Herman Dooyeweerd,[5] interpreted now to English speaking people by E. L. Hebden Taylor.[6] In this philosophy, the state, or civil government, co-exists with church, industry, education, agriculture, art, individual genius, and so forth. All are aspects of God's works of creation, preservation, and providence. Each is autonomous, that is, each operates according to laws of its nature as a creature. The state is only one among the several. Its task is to police them all so that they stay within their autonomies and do not infringe upon one another even though they must impinge on one another. When the state steps in to take charge of any one of the others, a wrong is committed, and disorder is introduced, just as would be the case if civil government were made a department of the church or of the university. God alone has claims of sovereignty over them all.

2. A balance between mercy and justice in executing the demands of law is held up as ideal. A typical expression of this prophetic hope for the Messiah is found in the following scriptural passages:

> Behold, the days come, saith the Lord, that I will raise unto David a righteous Branch, and he shall reign as king and deal wisely, and shall execute justice and righteousness in the land. In his days Judah shall be saved, and Israel shall dwell safely (Jer 23:5-6).

---

*This analysis, now being widely advocated in orthodox reformed circles in America, is not peculiar in concept to the Netherlands Calvinists. In slightly variant language, it is advocated by Emil Brunner, another reformed thinker of a different country; and by Helmut Thielicke and Werner Elert, both German Lutherans, and others.

Say unto the cities of Judah, Behold, your God! Behold the Lord
God will come as a mighty one, and his arm will rule for him:
Behold, his reward is with him, and his recompence before him. He
will feed his flock like a shepherd, he will gather the lambs in his
arm, and carry them in his bosom, and will gently lead those that have
their young (Is 40:9-11).

This balance might be summarized simply as wisdom. Recent
political and social controversy has made men acutely aware of the
need for a balance between "law and order" on the one hand, and
"justice" on the other. The dispossessed are commonly supposed to cry
for justice; the owners of goods and property for law and order.
But rightminded people know that there is need for exact enforcement of the laws against violence and wanton destruction of property. Such enforcement is an aspect of justice. Everyone loses from the
destruction brought by civil disorder, the poor most of all. Criminals
must be apprehended and punished appropriately. Yet it seems right
that the very young, the ignorant, the culturally deprived be punished for lawbreaking in such a way that they profit from the experience
and are given such aid as they need to help them to more constructive
and peaceful ways. Further, it is widely acknowledged that when
the rich and powerful citizen demands justice, he often means nothing more than protection of his possessions, while when the poor
man demands justice he may sometimes be thinking only of what he
supposes is a rightful share in the fruits of the nation's bounty and
industry. These interests, so difficult to meet to the satisfaction of all,
since they often seem to contradict one another, can be merged. The
Old Testament prophetic picture of Messiah's reign speaks of how
"he shall reign as king and deal wisely, and shall execute righteousness in the land" (Jer 23:5); "His arm will rule for him: behold
his reward is with him, and his recompense before him. He will
feed his flock like a shepherd, he will gather the lambs in his arm,
and carry them in his bosom, and will gently lead those that have
their young" (Is 40:10-11). The Psalms speak of the reign of God
as one of such balance: "Righteousness and justice are the foundation of thy throne: Lovingkindness and truth go before thy face"
(Ps 89:14). Yet they also reflect the perplexity of godly men about
lack of clarity with regard to this balance between justice and mercy.
To many saints it has seemed that the wicked always prosper, the

arrogant always triumph, while the righteous suffer (Ps 10:9-10; 73:1-16). "Truth forever on the scaffold; wrong forever on the throne" (James Russell Lowell). The prophets also contain passages which raise questions about this balance (Hab 1:1-17, cf. Ps. 2:7-9). Yet in each case, the answer follows in the later context wherein the questions and complaints are voiced. Thus Lincoln could truthfully say, quoting Scripture, "The judgments of the Lord are true and righteous altogether."

Some of the most enlightened modern states have failed to bring about this balance. Crimes against persons, their property, their rights, and their basic human freedoms now as then go unchecked: "Justice is turned away backward, and righteousness standeth afar off; for truth is fallen in the street, and uprightness cannot enter" (Is 59:14). Until "the inhabitants of the world learn righteousness" (Is 26:9), this balance will be impossible to achieve fully. "To maintain a perfect balance between mercy and justice is never an easy achievement. Historically, governments have been prone to swing between the two opposite poles of legal harshness on the one hand or sentimental laxness on the other. And the end is disaster in either case."[7]

The biblical ideal of balance between mercy and justice in enforcement of law is prominent, especially in the predictions of Messiah's reign. It is a legitimate expectation of a people from their government at all times, yet a very delicate matter in actual occurrence.

We must not fail to notice, however, that there is a merciful quality in strict law enforcement, which punishes all lawbreakers whether old or young, rich or poor, reformable or incorrigible, that must not be overlooked. Penalties assessed, which for the last several decades have been mainly prison terms, thus making severe punishment merely a long sentence, obscure this fact. Corporal punishment, in many situations, would be much more merciful, and much more likely to produce reformation of offenders. Prison terms, as is generally recognized, actually tend to encourage criminality. Severe punishment in former times was corporal more often than not, as is also the case in scriptural prescription.

The mercy in strict judgment was plainly observed by Dietrich

Bonhoeffer. Seeing secular government as part of the dominion of Christ,† he wrote:

> The primary implication for secular institutions of the dominion of Christ and of the decalogue [Bonhoeffer believed that it applies to everyone] is not, therefore, the conversion of the statesman or the economist, nor yet the elimination of the harshness and unmercifulness of the state for the sake of a falsely interpreted christianization of the state and its transformation into a part of the church. It is precisely in the dispensation of strict justice and in the administration of the office of the sword, in maintaining the unmerciful character of the institutions of the state, that is to say, their genuine worldliness, that the dominion of Christ, i.e., the rule of mercy, is given its due. The incarnation of God, that is to say, the incarnation of love, would be misinterpreted if one were to fail to perceive that the worldly institutions of strict justice, of punishment and of the wrath of God are also a fulfillment of this incarnate love and that the commandment of the sermon on the mount is also observed in genuine action by the state. The purpose and aim of the dominion of Christ is not to make the worldly order godly or to subordinate it to the church but to set it free for true worldliness.[8]

3. Closely connected with the foregoing and scarcely distinguishable from it is the balance between freedom and order in the prophetic hope of Messiah's reign. In the course of human affairs, even in that most balanced of governmental traditions, the Anglo-Saxon, on at least two occasions large numbers of citizens felt that government regulation stymied the natural and proper demand for efficiency in government and popular impulses toward freedom of movement, expression, and investment. That government was overthrown and new governments were established. These were the "Glorious Revolution" of Great Britain in 1688 and the American Revolution of 1776. Both were conservative revolutions, not radical ones. Both were undertaken with great reluctance by leaders who were at heart socially self-appointed or popularly-designated representatives of the people. Such was not the case with the French revolution of 1789 nor of

---

†It is the firm position of this book that this is a wrong approach to a Christian doctrine of civil government. Civil government is an extension of the doctrines of man and sin. Christ as king is where the story *ends,* not where it begins. This does not mean that many of Bonhoeffer's conclusions, though approached differently, are not essentially correct.

the Bolshevik revolution of 1917. Each of these was a coup d'etat. The state was overthrown, not conserved.‡ The French and American Revolutions have been put in contrast by many writers, but by none more graphically than Abraham Kuyper, who in a striking passage quotes Alexander Hamilton as saying that he considered "the French Revolution to be no more akin to the American Revolution than the faithless wife in a French novel is like the Puritan matron in New England."[9]

Luigi Sturzo reflects the opinion of several generations of historians about the American expereince. Within the last generation, however, there has been a revision of the opinion that the assertion of independence which led to the American War of Independence was motivated chiefly by secular ideals of liberty emanating from the same sources as the later French Revolution. Present-day researchers in the period beginning with the Great Awakening of the 1740s and continuing to 1775 have demonstrated that rather the motives derived mainly from American Orthodox Calvinism were more important than those derived from the "enlightenment" philosophers of Europe. The present project does not allow a survey of the evidence. I am, however, quite convinced that Alan Heimert has expertly shown by exhaustive research into the sermons and other writings of the pre-Revolution Protestant ministry, both conservative-Calvinist and Liberal or Unitarian, that religious motives were paramount.[10] William G. McLoughlin in an essay review of Heimert's book suggestively entitles it: "The American Revolution as a Religious Revival."[11] McLoughlin thinks that religious motives for reform have dominated American history ever since: "The great contribution of Heimert's monumental work is that it so clearly demonstrates how this existential human characteristic was given a uniquely American formulation in the formative years of the republic so that it became permanently imbedded in our national character."[12]

---

‡This thesis has been maintained by many writers. Those interested in the comparison of the two revolutions should start with chapter four of Vernon Grounds, *Revolution and the Christian Faith* (Philadelphia: Lippincott, 1971), entitled "A Revolutionary Tradition," and move from there. Gregg Singer, *A Theological Interpretation of American History* (Nutley, N.J.: Craig, 1964), shows clearly that the sentiment of American leadership was much more radical in 1776, when Jefferson formulated the Declaration of Independence, than it was thirteen years later when, with Madison supplying greater leadership, the Constitution was shaped up. Viewed from the perspective of our time, the United States Constitution is one of the most conservative government documents in the history of such things.

In many parts of the world, less orderly and law-honoring revolutions have come with wearying regularity. In most cases, however, the new regime immediately becomes self-protective. This requires safeguards that take away the very freedoms for which the revolution was fought.

The prophets knew about this too. They rooted their hope of the future in a King who would possess in His person that balance of goodness and wisdom on the one hand with power and severity on the other so that His government would preserve freedom for the people together with civil discipline and order. He is most fully described by Isaiah.

> And there shall come forth a shoot out of the stock of Jesse, and a branch out of his roots shall bear fruit. And the Spirit of the Lord shall rest upon him, the spirit of wisdom and understanding, the spirit of counsel and might [note particularly the balance of wisdom, understanding, and counsel on the one hand with might on the other.], the spirit of knowledge and of the fear of the Lord [i.e., of human knowledge balanced with godly piety]; and his delight shall be in the fear of the Lord; and he shall not judge after the sight of his eyes, neither decide after the hearing of his ears; but with righteousness shall he judge the poor, and decide with equity for the meek of the earth; and he shall smite the earth with the rod of his mouth, and with the breath of his lips shall he slay the wicked [cf. Jer 23:5-8; 33:15-18]. And righteousness shall be the girdle of his waist, and faithfulness the girdle of his loins (Is 11:1-5).

The ideas in this passage are richly expanded in the later parts of Isaiah, and the later prophets mention them too. This passage appears to be in the background of several New Testament prophecies of the consummation of human affairs on earth in the future reign of Christ. Thus this section becomes very important to biblical prophecy. The present purpose, however, has already been achieved: to show the built-in balance between strength and wisdom, regulation and freedom, justice and mercy, necessary in the central government if there is to be a proper balance between order and freedom in civil life. Free people cannot tolerate a situation that threatens a man with imprisonment or execution for trivial offenses or mere failure to comply with unnecessary governmental regulation any more than they can tolerate a situation wherein known murderers, robbers, and rapists prowl without restraint, or wherein barons of finance and industry strip the countryside, destroying both natural and human resources. The current vexing problem of pollution of natural environment is coming to focus as a proper balance between individual freedom and government control. How can I have freedom to drive my car, for example, and yet avoid polluting the air unless there is government control over all cars? Where men have anything to say about who their rulers shall be, here are some ideals to aim for at election time.

4. Again, though definitely an aspect of the foregoing, it is certain also that the prophets contemplate a rule by the best people available. Their ideal is aristocracy—an aristocracy of wisdom, character, ability, intelligence, and morality. True, in the person of the King, the Son of man, it is a monarchy. Associated with Him, however, and represented in governing capacity, are other persons. Daniel envisions the government in the hand of "saints" or "holy people," and sees nothing illusory or impractical about it. It is a conceit of many shallow irreligious people that the Bible-reading, church-going, morally upright Christian is either a hypocrite or a fool, in any case incompetent in the affairs of day-to-day commerce, industry, or government. On the other hand, there is quite a bit of literature, not entirely friendly to evangelical faith, which seeks to prove that the prosperity of northern and western Europe, together with the rise of capitalism, is derived from these very people, the evangelical Protestants.§

---

§I have reference to the theory given initial articulation by Max Weber in a lengthy two-part essay (1905-6) in *Archiv fuer Socialwissenschaft*, published in English as *The Rise of Protestantism and the Spirit of Capitalism*. Weber, a sociologist and jurist, developed an idea first presented in germ in *Der Moderne Kapiatlismus* (1902) of economic historian Werner Sombart. The most influential book in the field of Christian theology as related to social history, *De Sociallehren der Christlichen Kirchen und Gruppen* by Ernst Troeltsch, appearing in 1911, adopted Weber's thesis, giving it wider disseminaiton and considerable strengthening. An English socialist and economic historian, R. H. Tawney, gave the theory further articulation when in 1926 he published *Religion and the Rise of Capitalism*. Though modified somewhat by its successive exponents, the thesis remains today essentially the same. It is contended that certain doctrines found seminally in Luther but more thoroughly developed and articulated by Calvin produced psychological effects among the Reformed Christians, which encouraged economic and commercial expansion, resulting in the development of capitalism as we know it—deemed by its detractors to be a form of mammon worship. The Weber theory has not wanted for critics. In fact, cutting across sociology, history, philosophy, law, economics, and theology, it has attracted attention from learned writers of several fields up to the present. It has been attacked almost from

In Daniel's prophecies, the course of the nations to the consummation is a frightful succession of unreasoning, bloodthirsty, violent beasts—a lion, a bear, a leopard, and an unnatural monster. They are succeeded by the reign of God through the Son of man. At this juncture, Daniel's prophecy asserts: "These great beasts, which are four, are four kings [i.e., governments and their realms], that shall arise out of the earth. But the saints of the Most High shall receive the kingdom, and possess the kingdom. . . . And the same horn [final form of world rule before the consummation] made war with the saints . . . until . . . judgment was given to the saints of the Most High" (Dan 7:17-18, 21-22, cf. 23-27). A similar passage in the Psalms asserts that "in his days shall the righteous flourish" (72:7). Elsewhere, Isaiah notes that when this "king shall reign in righteousness," then also "princes shall rule in justice . . . the fool shall be no more called noble, nor the churl said to be bountiful . . .

---

the beginning (*Protestantism and Capitalism: The Weber Thesis and Its Critics*, ed. Robert W. Green [Boston: D. C. Heath, 1959]). F. Rachfall (1909) argued that other factors in the rise of capitalism render Protestantism unimportant to its rise and that the rise started long before the Reformation (Ibid., p. viii). Werner Sombart (*Der Bourgeois*, 1913, English trans., *The Quintessence of Capitalism*) argued persuasively that, as a matter of fact, Protestant economic theory was the medieval theory, not only Luther's, as most readily agree, but Calvin's also—that Weber and company had misread or not read the Reformers; further, that the Roman Catholic popes and especially the Jews were far more responsible for capitalism's rise. More recent critics are H. M. Robertson, who argued, among other things, that capitalism, far from arising out of Calvinistic Puritanism, actually was related to Calvinism only by corrupting it after its spirit had grown flabby (*Aspects of the Rise of Economic Individualism*, 1933); Albert Hyma, who endorsed Robertson's arguments, saying that, if professed Puritans became infected with mammon worship, all the evidence is to the effect that they had "ignored the injunctions of their spiritual fathers" in doing so (*Renaissance to Reformation*, 1951); and Winthrop Hudson, who said of the capitalist economic opportunists of Great Britain, who in the seventeenth century went whoring after unearned riches, that they "represent the infiltration of a spirit which the convinced Puritan did not hesitate to label pagan and antichristian. . . . The victory of the spirit of capitalism in a very real sense meant the defeat of Puritanism" ("Puritanism and the Spirit of Capitalism," *Church History* 18 [March 1949]:15).

The industrious reader will find the literature referred to in the works even of Weber and Troeltsch more than can be mastered in any sensible amount of time. Scholars working in the field suggest that one begin with Green.

Weber's theory, though gaining in fascination for the "popular mind" and currently enjoying quite a vogue, seems to be steadily losing ground among the scholars. "What Germany thought yesterday, Britain thinks today, and America will think tomorrow." Perhaps the day after tomorrow no one will think it!

Alan Hemiert has recently shown that an important aspect of the preaching of Jonathan Edwards in the religious revival known today as the Great Awakening (in large part a Puritan-Calvinist affair) was to rebuke the covetous money-grabbing capitalism and crass materialism of the colonial peoples. He also shows that Edward's name was most prestigious long after his death right on through the times of the Revolution and its aftermath (*Religion and the American Mind; From the Great Awakening to the Revolution* [Cambridge, Mass.: Harvard U., 1966]).

But the noble deviseth noble things; and in noble things shall he continue" (32:1, 5, 8).

These ideals share much with Aristotle's *Politics*, Plato's *Republic* and *The Statesman*, and Augustine's *City of God*, as well as the last pages of Book 2 of Calvin's *Institutes*. It is instructive that practical experience at close quarters with the rulers of Syracuse and of Athens over a long life caused Plato to give up the notion he held early in his career that any particular constitutional basis was either an essential to good government or a guarantee against bad. He came to believe that statesmanship, or benevolent wisdom in rulers under constitutional restraints, is the true key to good government. Aristotle also held that constitutional law administered in accordance with strict principles of justice is essential. Calvin and Augustine both were influenced decisively by the same biblical materials which are the subject of this study. All agree that the men of greatest wisdom and good character should rule. By whatever means chosen, they must be found, and the venal, avaricious, lazy, and stupid must be rooted out of government. True, in recent times we pray for a government of laws rather than of men, but bad laws can be changed when good men rule. Contrariwise, no matter how good the laws, oppression and violence ride to war against the public weal when lawless men rule.

5. The prophets envision an ideal government within great variety of social and political structure. The New Testament emphasizes that the gospel is for all men because God is the God of all (Ro 3:29). But the prophets and psalmists said so first. Many nations shall be among those who beat their swords into plowshares and their spears to pruninghooks (see Is 2:1-5; Mic 4:1-13). Many nations shall be owned by the Lord as "nations that are called by my name" (Amos 9:12). Certain even of the nations, famous of old as enemies of God, will be restored and blessed. Nothing is said to the effect that these various nations must change their form of government or reconstruct their social structure and observances before admission to God's favor. The exclusion of certain nations and inclusion of others demonstrates that the authors did not have in mind the extension of gospel preaching and establishment of churches in these nations as the theme of their prophecies. They are to be received as national establishments. They shall, of course, be converted as well. Their unbelief and paganism will be left behind if they come

to God as nations. Any individual could always convert to the true faith and be accepted quite as much as Israel (see 2 Ch 6:32-33).

The principle upon which divine restoration and blessing shall take place is stated in Jeremiah 12:14-17: to "learn the ways of my people, to swear by my [the Lord's] name." Moab and Ammon, relentless foes of Israel, are to be restored (Jer 48:47; 49:6, cf. Is 16:12) though Edom shall not (Jer 49:7-22). So also Elam shall be restored (Jer 49:39). In a manner surely disconcerting to those who see only narrow selfish national interest in the prophetic deliverances, Isaiah prophesies a warm friendship and holy alliance between a latter day Israel, in times of Messiah, with two of its transformed neighbors: "And Jehovah will smite Egypt, smiting and healing; and they shall return unto Jehovah, and he will be entreated of them, and will heal them. In that day shall there be a highway out of Egypt to Assyria, and the Assyrian shall come into Egypt, and the Egyptian into Assyria; and the Egyptians shall worship with the Assyrians. In that day shall Israel be the third with Egypt and with Assyria, a blessing in the midst of the earth; for that Jehovah of hosts hath blessed them, saying, Blessed be Egypt my people, and Assyria the work of my hands, and Israel my inheritance" (Is 19:22-25, cf. 17:5-8; 18:6-7; 19:21). Is it this on a worldwide scale which the author of the book of Revelation has in mind when he says of the coming city of God to descend to earth that "the nations shall walk amidst the light thereof: and the kings of the earth shall bring their glory into it" (21:24)?

6. Social and cultural aspects of the government of Messiah's kingdom are also prominent in prophetic forecasts. Messiah's government will foster a society in which all aesthetic and artistic impulses, every moral and spiritual value, every constructive industry and science will be fostered to the glory of God. These ideals are so beautifully expressed in the prophecies of Scripture that even the secular utopians have found them useful for their propaganda. Someone has said that until the very recent near total secularization of life in the West, there was hardly a leader of social reform who did not draw some of his ideas and much of his most persuasive language from these prophecies.

There have been some who have seen the social and cultural features of the predicted Messianic kingdom in their full biblical perspective. One whose aptly-composed comments have been quoted by others deserves to be cited here. The lines are among those with which Talbot W. Chambers closes his comments on the book of Zechariah, as follows:

> The consequence of such streams of blessing is a degree of consecration never seen before. The form in which the universal prevalence of holiness is expressed [Zech 14:1-21] is noteworthy. Men are not to become monks or anchorites, the ordinary conditions of life are not to be reversed; but on the contrary the infusion of grace will be so large and general that every rank and class will feel it, and its effects will be seen in all the relations of life, purifying and elevating without upturning or destroying. In business, in recreation, in politics, in art, in literature, in social life, in the domestic circle, there will be a distinct and cordial recognition of the claims of God and of the supremacy of his law. There will be no divorce anywhere between religion and morality, no demand that any department of human activity shall be deemed beyond the domain of conscience. When even the bells on the horses bear the same sacred inscription which once flashed from the diadem of the High Priest [Zech 14:20, cf. Ex 28:36], nothing can be found too small or too familiar to be consecrated to the Lord. The religious spirit will prevail everywhere, securing justice, truth, kindness, and courtesy among men; doing away with wars, contentions, jealousies, and competitions; hallowing trades and handicrafts, softening the inevitable contrasts of ranks, gifts, and conditions; binding men to one another by their common devotion to a common master in heaven; and thus introducing the true city of God on earth for which all saints long with an ever increasing desire. The idea of such a commonwealth originated in the Scriptures, and it can be realized only in the way they point out. All schemes of political, social, or even moral reform, apart from the principles of the Word, are the merest chimeras. They are impossible of accomplishment, and if accomplished, would disappoint their projectors. True religion, restoring the Lord to his rightful place in human thought and action, alone furnishes the sanction, the authority, and the power by which men become what they ought to be to themselves, to each other, and to the community.[13]

9

CIVIL GOVERNMENT IN OLD TESTAMENT LEGISLATION

THIS STUDY now shifts to a consideration of the legal portions of the Old Testament. Prime attention is directed first to the question of the relevance of Scripture to the subject of civil government and guiding principles for that government; then the discussion will move to the connection between the religion of a people and their state.

The New Testament furnishes no legislation in the strict sense of specific enactments with specific penalties attached for violation. Although Christians are not without law, the gospel is not a new law, nor is Jesus a new Moses. Jesus inaugurated a new epoch of *heilsgeschichte* and a new stage of revelation; He brought the Mosaic legal dispensation to an end.* But the New Testament in general and the gospel in particular are not legislation. Those commentators and theological writers who refer to the gospel as a new *torah* do not contribute to an understanding of the true unity of the Bible.

On the other hand, though grace is prevalent even within the law,[1] the very heart of the Old Testament is its legislative portion—Exodus, Leviticus, Numbers, and Deuteronomy. Herein lie the prescriptions which, until the legal epoch was brought to an end through the redemption wrought by Christ, were regarded as normative for the whole of Jewish life. The massive Jewish Talmud is the literary deposit of the effort of those Jews who rejected Jesus to find ways to make those prescriptions work in diaspora, when they were ex-

---

*John Calvin devoted chapters VII to XI of Book Two of his *Institutes of the Christian Religion* to this area. Of this, the most important chapters to amplify and explain this statement are Chapter X, "The Similarity of the Old and New Testaments," and Chapter XI, "The Difference Between the Two Testaments." Calvin's is still as good a treatment, faithful to the Scriptures, as has been written. Later Calvinists have refined his doctrine, perhaps improving it. See especially *Calvinism and the Amyraut Heresy: Protestant Scholasticism and Humanism in Seventeenth Century France* (Milwaukee: U. of Wisconsin, 1969), pp. 140-221, which explain the doctrine of Calvinism.

pelled from the land of Israel. Residence in Canaan provided the only historical situation wherein the Mosaic law was designed ever truly to operate fully.

The last four books of the Pentateuch relate how God Himself formed a nation from a mass of miserable slaves, entering with them into a covenant which became the constitution of the Israelite nation. This constitution related not only to religious and political matters, but to all aspects of human life, so that Mosaism was not only a religion, but also a civil constitution and a complete way of living. This is not to say that Moses' words were the only considerations in ordering national life and administering justice. "The processes by which justice was administered among the Hebrews were largely dependent on ancient usage. The Mosaic Law, of course, where it spoke was the highest rule; but in many cases it was silent. Even as it respected the principles upon which decisions were to be reached, it was far from being a complete guide in civil affairs. The judge, accordingly, was often left to that spirit of fairness and wisdom with which, from the nature of his office, it was expected he would be endowed. It was because so much depended on the impartiality of the magistrate that this quality was so strongly insisted on in the law."[2]

As a code or specific constitution, the Mosaic law was temporary, some provisions being designed only for the brief period of forty years of wandering, preliminary to settlement in Canaan, all of it rendered null as a code by the fullfillment that came through Christ's revelational and redemptive work. Our interest in the Mosaic legislation is not therefore to find laws directly applicable to men today.

Our present interest is threefold. First, many items of the so-called legislation were factual and revelational—matters of fact are reported by revelation. For example, Deuteronomy 18:9-22 states that prophets would succeed Moses as divine messengers and also provides for signs by which these prophets were to be recognized and their messages verified. Some of these factual revelations relate to civil government. Second, many principles of divine law (quite apart from the Mosaic dispensation) are set forth in connection with the legislation. For example, in the same eighteenth chapter of Deuteronomy, Moses lists several practices of occult religion—child sacrifice, divination, augury, enchanting, sorcery, charmers, spiritism,

wizardry, consulting the dead (vv. 10-11)—then affirms, "whosoever doeth these things is an abomination unto Jehovah" (v. 12). That
is a statement of fact concerning the eternal changeless God. God
abominated such religious quackery at that time, and unquestion-
ably He still does. Many matters of this sort are unmentioned in the
New Testament for the reason that the Old Testament, part of God's
eternal Word, treats them fully. Not only Jesus, but the many New
Testament authors find it sufficient on many occasions simply to refer
to the teaching of the Old Testament as commonly known, accepted
and sufficient. Paul, for example, without quoting a word, once cited
all the Old Testament teaching about the place of women in support of his own command (1 Co 14:34, "as also saith the law").
Elsewhere he states that "All scripture [i.e., the Old Testament] . . .
is profitable for doctrine" (2 Ti 3:16). Third, many items of legislation regarding the life of a people provide ground for generaliza-
tions and inferences. For example, the dozens of references to provision for the poor, the widows and orphans, and so on, are grounds
for inference that these honestly poor have some claim on the
generosity of their neighbors as a matter of justice, not merely as
a matter of charity. Conclusions drawn from this third class of data
are on a less firm foundation than those resting on the first two
classes.

Something needs to be said preliminarily about the concepts conveyed by the words *nation, state,* and *people,* as used in this section.
According to one authority, in the English-speaking part of the world,
state is "that department of political science which concerns itself . . . with the political composition of society."[3] It expresses the
abstract idea of government in general. In countries where conflict
has existed between civil and ecclesiastical authorities, *state* is a
word for civil authority,[4] yet these statements require qualification.
They are oriented wholly to the modern world.

Using the word *state* of the civil organization of ancient Israel
in any epoch involves us necessarily in a certain amount of distor-
tion of fact. For *state* is essentially a modern notion. The ancients
thought in terms of family and local community rather than of that
governmental creation of modern times. On this point, Pierre de
Vaux has fairly asserted:

Clearly we cannot speak of one Israelite idea of the State. The federation of the Twelve tribes, the kingship of Saul, that of David and Solomon, the kingdoms of Israel and Judah, the post-exilic community, all these are so many independent regimes. We may go even further and say that there never was any Israelite idea of the State. Neither the federation of the tribes nor the post-exilic community were states. Between the two, the monarchy, in its varying forms, held its ground for three centuries over the tribes of the north, for four and a half over Judah, but it is hard to say how far it penetrated or modified the people's mentality. The post-exilic community returned to the pre-monarchial type of life with remarkable ease; this suggests some continuity of institutions at the level of clan and town. This municipal life is also the only aspect of public life considered by the legislative texts. There is indeed the 'law of the king' (Deut. 17:14-20), and the 'rights of the king' in I Samuel 8:11-18 (cf. 10:25), but these in no way resemble political charters. These texts accept the fact of kingship as something tolerated by Yahweh (I Sam. 8:7-9) or as subordinate to his choice (Deut. 17:15); they warn against imitating aliens (I Sam. 8:5; Deut. 17:14), and the evil which kingship entails (I Sam. 8:11-18; Deut. 17:16-17). And that is all. To study royal institutions we must glean what information we can from the historical books.[5]

De Vaux goes on to say that there was only one conception of power which is fundamental to Israelite thought: the conception of theocracy. Israel is Yahweh's people and has no master but Him. That is why from the beginning of its history, Israel remained a religious community.[6]

Nation has less of a connotation of civil government than does *state*, but, as derivation from *natus* (born) suggests, relates to a "historically developed community of people with a territory, economic life, distinctive culture, and language in common."[7] Thus several nations may exist under one government. One thinks of the land of India, a multiplicity of nations under one government. In the case of a migratory people or a scattered people, part of the people may reside in the territory of one state, part in another. In this regard, one thinks of the Armenian nation, scattered through several Levantine territorial states and in Russia near the Black Sea, yet existing as a separate nation with common language, history, religion, and culture.

The idea of national identity connected with a specific territory, form of government, or common political history has varied through the ages and in various places. Arabs living in the West Bank area of Palestine before 1967, for example, had small loyalty to King Hussein and the kingdom of Jordan. They were loyal to their land, and they felt a certain unity with Arabs everywhere, but they were not self-conscious Jordanians. They now claim to be Palestinians. Israel's Knesset and Golda Meir do not charm them, but to lose Amman and King Hussein does not break their hearts either. The Montagnards of Viet Nam live in South Viet Nam, but they are a nation to themselves. The same has been true since time out of mind with the Kurds of Persia and Iraq.

A personal anecdote will strengthen this point. I served as a professor teaching biblical history and archaeology at the Mount of Olives for several months in 1962. In October, while exploring archaeological excavations with one of my students in the Zion area of the southwest corner of the Old City of Jerusalem, I stepped up from an eight-foot excavation, only to hear the Jordanian sentry shouting at me. I sensed immediately that I was in trouble and decided to try bluffing it out. I called back, waved in a friendly manner, and moved a step away. But the sentry shouted again, and I heard him throw a shell into the chamber of his rifle—at about forty yards. So I turned back facing him and put my hands high over my head. After what seemed like all day, a small, typically stocky townsman who ran the nearby bakery across from the Armenian compound, stood beside me and started shouting in Arabic to the sentry. The baker saw my camera with telescopic lens, and he noted the student with me. Then he knew I was a harmless foreigner and not a Jewish spy. But the sentry had seen me draw a map on the ground with a stick for the benefit of my student companion. The significant part of this dangerous but harmless incident was this: Between Arabic sallies toward the sentry by the baker, the baker bitterly reproached King Hussein's army as animals, barbarians, and so on. To him, they were illiterate bedouins from the wilderness east of the River Jordan. As far as the baker was concerned, the bedouin sentry was more the foreigner than I, though both of them were citizens of the Hashemite kingdom of the Jordan. The baker was a townsman of Jerusalem, and if one were to explore further he would find the baker to feel himself a Palestinian—by no means a Jordanian. National feeling was practically nonexistent as far as the Hashemite kingdom of the Jordan was concerned. So it was in ancient times in the land of Syria (which includes Palestine) and so apparently it ever shall be.

No fully satisfactory definition can be provided for the terms *state* and *nation*. For the present purpose, it will suffice to make clear that civil government on whatever level, of whatever form, whether territorially limited as in modern states, or among migratory tribes or clans is our interest. Let us forget for the moment our particular government and consider the question of information on the proper sphere and function of any civil government as seen in the Old Testament Mosaic legislation.

The Mosaic system of government was built upon and absorbed a previously existing system. The children of Israel had existed for generations as a foreign enclave in Egypt, exposed to a foreign language, and foreign customs (cf. Ps 114:1-2). During this epoch, they had been segregated in a section of Lower Egypt known as Goshen. There, over a period of many generations, they had been growing into a "great nation" (cf. Gen 12:2; 15:12-15). They had already accepted patriarchial laws and customs derived from their ancestors and had become accustomed to new ones derived from the Egyptians when Moses assumed their leadership. These could not be, nor need they be, canceled out. Keil asserts rightly: "So we find among the Israelites a consuetudinary [customary] law, which is partly completed by the Mosaic legislation, partly modified and, so far as it was incompatible with the mission of Israel to be God's people, abolished and replaced by new institutions and ordinances corresponding to the new life relations."[8]

They were already carrying on under a form of patriarchial self-government, or as it is called when it grows large, tribal government. In such a government, the elders are the magistrates of the tribes. In the case of the Israelites, development of a system of tribal government "came about naturally with the progressive increase of the children of Israel in Egypt in successive generations. The tribes were founded by the twelve sons of Jacob as the tribal fathers of the people, the clans by Jacob's grandchildren, and the families or fathers' houses by his great-grandchildren, the latter further branching."[9] The division into twelve tribes early became thirteen because each of Joseph's two sons, Ephraim and Manasseh, became a tribal head. From Moses' time onward, however, it was customary to speak of them as twelve (see e.g., Ex 24:4; Josh 4:2) since Levi, the priestly tribe received no tribal territory (Josh 13:14, 33, cf. Num 17:21; Josh 13:7 ff. Compare Num 26:28, cf. v. 57; Josh 16:1, 14, 17).

There is some evidence in the Old Testament records of a manner of looking at family relationships different from ours, so what seem to us to be somewhat artificial genealogical connections appear. For example Genesis 47:8, 21 lists Benjamin and his ten sons, more offspring than for any other of the twelve sons of Jacob, as among the seventy souls that came with Jacob into Egypt. Yet later it turns out that two of these ten are grandsons, and a comparison of texts shows that Benjamin was not more than twenty-three or twenty-four years old at the time of the descent to Egypt.[10] "From all this it necessarily follows, that in the lists . . . grandsons and great-grandsons of Jacob are named who were born afterwards in Egypt, and who, therefore according to a view which we frequently meet with in the Old Testament, though strange to our modes of thought, came into Egypt *in lumbis patrum* [in the loins of the father]."[11]

Certain writers, rejecting the factuality of the reports, have different explanations for the origin of the twelve tribes of Israel.

John Bright writes: "The normative twelve-tribe system emerged only in Palestine. . . . It is probable that each of the tribes included originally heterogeneous elements, some of them participants in the conquest, some long sedentary, others of miscellaneous origin."[12]

In this view, Bright is indebted to his teacher, W. F. Albright.[13] Several epochs of Greek history furnish examples of leagues of several tribes united in worship about a central sanctuary (or sanctuaries). These leagues also had political significance. The name in Greek for such a league is *amphictyony*. Scholars now frequently call the twelve-tribe organization an amphictyony. Interestingly, the most famous of these Greek leagues, called by way of eminence the Amphictyonic League, originally was composed, like Israel's amphictyony, of exactly twelve tribes.[14]

This tribal organization, wherein government was by elders, persisted through all stages of Old Testament history and was a part of the Mosaic system. Even the division of the country into new

administrative districts in Solomon's time did not destroy it. The
Mosaic system presupposes a tribal structure. Moses foresaw the rise
of monarchy without prescribing it (Deu 17:14-20).

The system established at Sinai was primarily religious; that is,
it was a covenant between Israel and God. Underlying all relationships of every sort in Israel was a commitment to the supremacy of
the God of Abraham, of Isaac, and of Jacob. There was a self-conscious recognition that God's was the only sovereignty (Deut 33:1-5).
Family relationships arose out of God's gracious provision of life
through conception and birth (Ps 113:9; 126; 127; Gen 15:2-5; 1
Sa 1:27; Ru 4:11), occupations flourished by divine power (Ex
31:1ff., cf. 1 Co 7:17), wealth was accumulated through divine grace
(Deu 8:17-18) and of great importance for the present consideration, the authority of magistrates and of government in general was
God's authority (e.g., Deu 1:17-18), the only true sovereignty in
heaven or on earth. For, even though they did not know it, the
heathen magistrates received their power from God (Jer 27:5; Ps
83:18; Ex 9:16).

It is to the civil-political-governmental aspect that we now direct
attention. Moses and Aaron were acknowledged by the elders of the
people in Egypt as heaven-sent civil-religious leaders (Ex 4:29-31).
Their accreditation was miraculous, and their initial acceptance by
Israel was thereby irresistible. Ultimately even the heathen Pharaoh
was compelled to accept their miraculous credentials, as indicated
by his response to the plagues, culminating in the death of the firstborn of all Egypt (Ex 12:29-32). The Mosaic system was held to be
supernaturally verified as valid.† Something new was taking place.
This is spelled out specifically many times in the Pentateuch, but
never more impressively than in the case of the rebellion of Korah
(Num 16). The critical section of the story follows: "And Moses
said, Hereby ye shall know that the Lord hath sent me to do all
these works; for I have not done them of mine own mind. If these
men die the common death of all men, or if they be visited after

---

†Unfortunately, many writers of the presently reigning school of biblical theology, in
proposing a theology based on the acts of God, seem to deny the factuality of these
reports—upon which alone an understanding of Israel's religion and the Christian
faith in God, resurrection, and eternal life can be based. This misspent effort is another of the perennial efforts somehow to make unbelief and faith compatible, somehow to make spiritual apostasy and loyal faith commensurable, to make the life-
less idol of rationalism acceptable to worship of the living God.

the visitation of all men; then the Lord hath not sent me. But if the Lord make a new thing [Heb. *we'im berîāh yibhrā'*, if he create a creation], and the ground open its mouth, and swallow them up, with all that appertain unto them, and they go down alive into Sheol; then ye shall understand that these men have despised the Lord" (Num 16:28-30). Thus God magnified the leadership of Moses and Aaron in the establishment of a divinely constituted civil-religious commonwealth of Israel. God stepped out of His role (so to speak) as hidden providential Ruler of all nations and became a more immediate Sovereign through a mediatorial ruler specially called and certified. On to the end of Old Testament history, God required that their ruler, be he judge or king, should be a man "whom the Lord thy God shall choose" (Deu 17:15).

There can be no doubt that Moses was a civil magistrate. The chief distinction between his administration and the reign of a king was that he established no dynasty, employed no royal trappings of office, and was not called *mĕlĕkh*, Hebrew for king or monarch. The Pentateuch presents in some detail the features of his magistracy, even reporting how he associated subordinate associate judges with him (Ex 18:13-25; 24:1-11; Num 11:16-30). As chief magistrate, Moses directed the administration of civil laws; he was director of ordinance and supply, transport, international diplomacy, finance— he was the man in charge of all public life. On his administration of the national law hung life and death (Lev 24:10-23; Num 15:32-36). Another has well said: "As the administrator of a law on the observance of which life and death depended, Moses exercised the office of a king. He represented the invisible King (Deut. 33:5); and he passed on to Joshua, to the judges, and to the kings, the duty of enforcing this law" [Deu 17:18][15] Stephen's words indicate the correctness of this view: "This Moses whom they refused, saying, Who made thee a ruler and a judge? him hath God sent to be both a ruler and a deliverer" (Ac 7:35). A. J. McClain has wisely observed: "This divinely bestowed authority of Moses was generally recognized among the people of Israel, although upon various occasions they were prone to murmur against their great leader; but only once in his long ruling career did the murmuring break out in open insurrection, and then the authority of Moses was underscored in terrible fashion [Num 16:1-50]."[16]

It is equally certain that the twelve tribes constituted a nation, or "state." Israel had existed as a nation within the "state" of Egypt before the Exodus. Under Moses she truly had become an independent civil unit, exercising national sovereignty, in events culminating at Mt. Sinai.‡ Israel was not as yet a territorial state, but she was a civil commonwealth nonetheless. For this civil commonwealth, Moses, under God, framed a constitution. This is well put by M. G. Kyle: "The statesman-prophet framed a civil government which illustrated the kingdom of God upon earth. The theocracy did not simulate any government of earth, monarchy, republic or socialistic state. It combined the best elements in all of these and set up the most effective checks which have ever been devised against the evils of each."[17]

---

‡Moses' office as ruler indicates the independence of the state of Israel; she is called a nation in parallel with other nation-states. In Genesis 12:2, for example, Israel is called "a great nation," and in 15:14 Egypt is called a nation. Similar language is used of Edom (17:20), and so on through the Pentateuch.

10

RELIGIOUS FOUNDATIONS OF THE MOSAIC COMMONWEALTH OF ISRAEL

THE TERM "Mosaic commonwealth of Israel" requires some clarification. This study indicates a view of biblical history and a definite entity within it. Questions of literary criticism aside, the position is taken that the picture of Israel at the exodus and settlement given in the last four books of the Pentateuch and in Joshua is factual according to the standards of reporting of the time, and that the story of the establishment of the national institutions—social, religious, ethical, civil—therein is what actually occurred. If so, then the central books of the Pentateuch describe a Mosaic commonwealth of Israel, and Moses was indeed a monotheist; we need not look for the first true monotheism in an Amos or "second Isaiah." The Mosaic religion of the Pentateuch underlies the history of Israel from the beginning of the settlement in Canaan. Granting modifications, Hebrew religion, as the plain man who reads the Bible finds it, is not something which took that shape only as it developed in the millenium between the thirteenth and fourth or third centuries B.C.

The Israelite nation was located precisely between two great ancient cultures, each with distinct features. These were Egypt on the southwest and Mesopotamia on the northeast. A scholarly literature has arisen treating the history, culture, languages, and religion of these lands in the past 150 years. Some compare the two areas with each other; and a few compare the two with the Hebrew nation. Some have even focused on the political developments in the three cultures. Most of these authors have sought along cultural-anthropological lines to trace developments to some material-physical root— weather, degree of isolation, geography, foods available, technology, etc.—and, it must be granted, with considerable appearance of success. Others have looked deeper, and with greater success. This significant minority of scholars has more wisely traced the most important

126

aspects of culture in these countries back to a cosmological outlook. A. N. Whitehead, mathematician, logician, and philosopher, is a leading exponent of this approach to historical research. In one of his latest books he wrote:

> In each age of the world distinguished by high activity, there will be found at its culmination, and among the agencies leading to that culmination, some profound cosmological outlook, implicitly accepted, impressing its own type upon the current springs of action. This ultimate cosmology is only partly expressed, and the details of such expression issue into derivative specialized questions . . . which conceal a general agreement upon first principles almost too obvious to need expression, and almost too general to be capable of expression. In each period there is a general form of the forms of thought; and, like the air we breathe, such a form is so translucent that only by extreme effort can we become aware of it.[1]

Authors who write from such perspective will not be committed to some scheme of development or retrogression (evolutionary or otherwise) which characterizes so much recent writing, such as that of Spengler and Toynbee. They will rather be seeking for some pervasive idea or ideas which persist in a people, giving shape to their on-going culture. Whitehead's felicitous term is "cosmological outlook." This will be an always-present pervasive force in shaping a culture and in relation to which it will flourish or fade. I follow this approach, though I have not the space and perhaps not the competence to develop and defend it.

Such is the working basis of an important minority of scholars. Among the notable scholars adopting this approach were H. Frankfort, H. A. Frankfort, John A. Wilson, Thorkild Jacobsen, and William A. Irwin, who cooperated in the important work, *The Intellectual Adventure of Ancient Man, An Essay on Speculative Thought in the Ancient Near East.*[2] Better known than these is A. N. Whitehead. In his volume, he explains Egyptian civilization as an expression of a cosmic outlook in which religion and ethics were never significantly united. Though the cosmic outlook was different, the same lack of connection between religion and ethics characterized Mesopotamian civilization.[3] In this the two were alike, but they were a world of thought away from the Hebrew outlook. In the section on Hebrew life and culture—the largest section, unfortunately omitted from the current Penguin edition—Irwin points out that among the Hebrews, religion and ethics were interwined, both being aspects of the profound cosmological outlook of monotheism—the Mosaic monotheism of the Bible (though Irwin is ambivalent on the precise time of first appearance of the idea). This, he holds, has given Israel the greatness which caused the biblical outlook in such matters to be pervasive in the West throughout the present era.

Let us proceed to refine the "cosmological outlook" idea and to focus on the question of religious foundations of government.

Many foundational factors go into the structure of a society. Another way of saying this is to assert that every society has many concerns, most of which are the same in all societies, for all the concerns spring forth from the nature of man himself. Something can be said for the place of varieties of environment in producing varieties of culture, especially on their material side. But it can also be said truthfully that in its ethical and judicial aspects at least, and to high degree in all aspects, a society is the expression of the ultimate concern of its people, especially of its ruling elite. Another name for ultimate concern is religion.[4] This is why importance is assigned to the religious foundations of the Mosaic commonwealth of Israel.

Though it be an aspect of culture, the crucial importance of a people's religion to the development of culture, including civil government, is not limited to ancient civilizations, even though modern secularist attitudes and assumptions obscure the fact. The difference, for example, between the culture today in Latin America and in North America above Mexico stems greatly from the religious beliefs of the pioneers who shaped the separate cultures. The other factors—gifts and abilities of the colonists, their level of education, natural resources of the lands settled, etc.—cannot account for the immense differences in the two kinds of culture that have developed in the last four centuries. The most decisive differences lie in the two religious faiths: the Tridentine Roman Catholic faith of the one and the dominant Calvinistic Protestant faith of the other. This has been amply explained and documented by competent scholarship.[5] A social order (as opposed to anarchy) has at least three distinguishable foundations. Of these the most basic is ultimate concern, that is, religion or creed; the second is the state structure itself which expresses the beliefs of its people about ultimate things; and third is the seat of ultimate authority or sovereignty.[6]

A great deal depends on the order of precedence of these three. If the state structure, for example, were to be first, then it shapes the religion so as to make the state itself of ultimate concern—as in ancient Rome and pre-World War II Japan. In such a case, state and religion have been merged, with state being determinative.

It is also important to observe that if the basic convictions of a populace, their ultimate concern, their views on ultimate value—that is to say, their religion—change through the generations, the structure of government and the ideas about authority or sovereignty will also change. This accounts in smaller part for the prophets' concern to preserve Mosaic religion as long as the Mosaic state lasted (e.g., Deu 32:17; Judg 5:8; Jer 2:1-37). It also accounts in part for the breakdown in America of law, order, and justice. The mass of alienated Americans today neither know nor understand the religious presuppositions underlying their form of government, and they would not be in sympathy with them if they did understand them.

Will Herberg has correctly written in his introduction to the English edition of Barth's treatment of this question: "In Western thinking, there have been two ways in which the political order embodied in the state has been understood and related to the God of faith. The first is the doctrine of natural law . . . the other philosophy of the state that has been very influential in Western thought is drawn . . . from the Church Fathers, who themselves derived it from the Scriptures."[7]

Herberg goes on to say that this second view is one taken over by the Protestant Reformation. According to this view (which we agree with Herberg in asserting seems to stem from Romans 13 though that chapter only brings the teachings of the whole Bible on government to focus) there are three orders in God's relation to the world. The first is the order of creation, of which man is a part and which sets the limits within which man as a creature of God has been intended to live. The second is the order of preservation. This consists of those forms and institutions made necessary by the fall. The third, the order of redemption, is that brought into existence by Christ's redemption. The Word of God and the church are within this order. Human civil government is a part of neither the order of redemption nor of creation, but of the order of preservation. This view, Herberg goes on to say, accepts original sin and the natural depravity of man; it acknowledges that though the state exists within society for the preservation of society, no one, either the ruler or ruled, is completely to be trusted, hence a balance of powers is necessary. Then he writes:

> It will be noted that this argument for the just state is also an argument for constitutional democracy as the best type of regime. The argument for the state as an order of preservation, in effect, maintains that government is made necessary by human sinfulness and serves to protect society from the destructive consequences of sinful self-aggrandizement. But rulers are surely themselves human beings, and subject to the same temptations that beset other human beings; hence institutional curbs on the power entrusted to them is necessary, and for the same reason—to prevent the inevitable abuse of power that is not in some manner checked and restrained. Calvin in his way understood this, and so did the Puritans. So also did the framers of the United States Constitution, for however far the founding fathers may have strayed from the Christian faith, they 'believed in original sin' and exhibited a 'hearty Puritanism in their [view] of human nature!' In the Augustinian-Reformation argument, we may therefore find a significant justification of constitutional democracy; yet we should not forget there are other types of regime compatible with the legitimate state, and that *constitutional Democracy as we understand it is actually possible only under certain historical conditions, which are by no means always present* [Italics added].[8]

This extensive quotation is introduced here to witness further to the inevitable connection between a peoples' religious beliefs and their views of the sources of government and their expectations from it, as well as responsibilities toward it, whatever the form of it may be—democracy, oligarchy, republic, monarchy, or as in Israel's case, a formal theocracy. In the case of the Mosaic state, the one explains the other; the state is built on its faith commitment. So also as Christianity wanes in the West, giving way to humanistic secularism everywhere, a socialistic-humanistic-welfare state is gradually taking the place of genuine constitutional democracy of the sort enshrined in the American constitution.*

---

*A growing number of writers charge the system of compulsory education with great-

As Moses, after forty years of unparalleled national leadership, was giving his parting words to the nation, he reviewed the circumstances and events of the covenant at Sinai together with subsequent events up to the apostasy in connection with the worship of the golden calf. Then by way of summary he said, "And now, Israel, what doth the Lord thy God require of thee, but to fear the Lord thy God, to walk in all his ways, and to love him, and to serve the Lord thy God with all thy heart and with all thy soul, to keep the commandments of the Lord, and his statutes, which I commanded thee this day for thy good?" (Deu 10:12-13).

After that, Moses reaffirmed that they were privileged people only by divine grace, and in that connection he reminded them of that civic righteousness which necessarily flows from faithful operation of government under such a covenant-constitution: "For the Lord your God, he is God of gods, and Lord of lords, the great God, the mighty, and the terrible, who regardeth not persons, nor taketh reward [bribe]. He doth execute justice for the fatherless and widow, and loveth the sojourner, in giving him food and raiment. Love ye therefore the sojourner; for ye were sojourners in the land of Egypt" (Deu 10:17-19).

This same Mosaic law which announced the religious foundation of the nation's government, also outlined careful procedures to preserve the people at every level—home, community, nation—perpetually aware of that foundation. At the very beginning of the famed lawgiver's career, the religious foundation in the ancient covenant established with Abraham and confirmed to Isaac and Jacob is intro-

---

est guilt for loss of the religious-spiritual underpinning of our American system of government. A famous Jewish liberal observer as long ago as 1940, in an address to the American Association for the Advancement of Science, charged, "That during the past forty or fifty years those who are responsible for education have progressively removed from the curriculum of studies the Western [Christian?] culture which produced the modern democratic state; That the schools and colleges have therefore been sending out into the world men who no longer understand the creative principle of the society in which they must live; That deprived of their cultural tradition, the newly educated Western men no longer possess in the form and substance of their own minds and spirits the ideas, the premises, the rationale, the logic, the method, the values of the deposited wisdom which are the genius of the development of Western civilization; That the prevailing education is destined, if it continues, to destroy Western civilization and is in fact destroying it" (as quoted by Walter Lippmann, *Education versus Western Civilization*, as cited by T. Robert Ingram, *The Christian News*, Feb. 2, 1970, p. 5). A thorough historical study of this matter, tracing the subject from the work of Horace Mann to the latest educational theorists and practitioners in America will be found in R. J. Rushdoony, *The Messianic Character of American Education* (Nutley, N. J.: Craig, 1958).

duced (Ex 3:6-7). The connection of the nation with the God of Abraham, Isaac, and Jacob was even to be called to Pharaoh's attention—Israel is God's firstborn son (Ex 4:22-23). Shortly after that, Moses significantly carried out the rite of circumcision, sign of the covenant, in the presence of his Gentile wife (Ex 4:25). The rite of circumcision was to remind the Israelites of their personal and national pledge to love and serve Jehovah-God. Their God was holy, therefore they were so to be (e.g., Lev 19:2, 10-11, 14, 16), as the decalogue spelled out in detail (Ex 20; Deu 5, cf Lev 19). Their family life, the sabbath law, their abstention from idolatry, their sacrificial system, and their civil laws were likewise to remind them of the religious foundation of their national life and welfare (Lev 19:2-22; Deu 6:5-6).

The specific religious foundation of the Old Testament Mosaic commonwealth of Israel is neatly summed up by S. D. Press:

> From the beginning of its existence as a nation it bore the character of a religious and moral community, a theocratic commonwealth, having Jehovah himself as Head and Ruler. The theocracy is not to be mistaken as a hierarchy, nor can it be strictly identified with any existent form of political organization. It was rather something over and above, and therefore independent of the political organization. It did not supersede the tribal organization of Israel, but it supplied the centralizing power, constituting Israel as a nation. In lieu of a strong political center, the unifying bond of a common allegiance to Jehovah, i.e., the common faith in him, the God of Israel, kept the tribes together. The consciousness that Jehovah was Israel's king was deeply rooted as a national feeling, and the inspiration of a true patriotism.[9]

The prophets as expositors of the Mosaic law sought to keep the Israelite "state," its officers, its courts, and its people inwardly loyal to the law and consistent with it in outward practice. The sentiments, even the phraseology, of the tenth chapter of Deuteronomy recur again and again in the prophets. The prophets call attention to disorder, poverty, injustice in the land, point back to the pentateuchal moral and religious laws, and bring back the divine blessing on the nation. They threaten national destruction if repentance and improvement do not take place (e.g., Is 1:2-31; Jer 6:16-21; Dan 9; Eze 20). Likewise many of the poetical worship sections treat the subject of national health (e.g., Ps 50, 74), while the historical books ring the changes of them. The entire book of Judges is specifically a development of this theme as indicated in its prologue (2:6-23). In fact the entire section of Joshua through Esther—nearly a third of the entire Old Testament—has an overarching purpose to trace the fortunes of the nation, success and failure, in relation to faithfulness or unfaithfulness to the Mosaic religious foundation of the nation.

This is never more strikingly evident than at the very end of the narrative of Israel and Judah, the two kingdoms which developed, where it stands written, "Moreover all the chiefs of the priests, and the people, trespassed very greatly after all the abominations of the nations; and they polluted the house of Jehovah which he had hallowed in Jerusalem. And Jehovah, the God of their fathers sent to them by his messengers, rising up early and sending; because he had compassion on his people, and on his dwelling place: but they mocked the messengers of God, and despised his words, and scoffed at his prophets, until the wrath of Jehovah arose against his people, till there was no remedy" (2 Ch 36:14-16).

One cannot expect to win the minds of many nonbelievers of the present day to this conviction as to the decisive place of religious commitment—in our culture, Christian commitment—for the form and quality of every aspect of the cultural life of a people. No one has seen this more clearly than Emil Brunner, whose striking words appear in his "Christianity and Civilization": "It is precisely the man whose first concern is not culture but the kingdom of God that has the necessary distance from cultural aims and the necessary perspective to serve them in freedom, and to grasp that order which prevents the various sections of civilisation from monopolising the totality of life. Only from beyond civilisation can its order and harmony come. It is a humanistic superstition to believe that the man to whom culture is everything is the true bearer of culture. The opposite is true . . . Culture-idolatry is the sure road to cultural decay."[10]

11

POLITICAL STRUCTURE AND CHARACTERISTICS OF THE MOSAIC COMMONWEALTH OF ISRAEL

IT IS BASIC to understanding the Mosaic commonwealth to know it was a theocracy.* This does not mean that it was ruled by religious professionals (priests or ministers), but that God Himself was the ruler of the nation through His own chosen representatives; the laws were of His own ordination and the whole nation—leader and gentry, magistrate and citizen, priest and layman, elder and youth— was directly responsible to him.

In his volume of Old Testament theology, J. Barton Payne has pointed out that in the Hebrew theocracy God Himself was the true leader in the group's battles (Ex 14:14; 15:1; 23:22; Num 10:35)—even the collection of poems celebrating the victories being denominated, "The Book of the Wars of the Lord" (Num 21:14)— while the nation was His army (Ex 7:4; 12:41) and God Himself the King (Deu 33:5). Payne notes also that Moses did not originate government, but only mediated it (Ex 18:16, 22). He also contends that: "For this reason, Israel's judges were called *Elōhīm*, divine representatives . . . and later David's sons as rulers were styled *kōhēn*, 'priest,' authorized ministers for God (II Sam. 8:18). . . . As Isaiah summed it up, 'Yahweh is our judge, Yahweh is our lawgiver, Yahweh is our king; He will save us!' (Isa. 33:22). . . . And in truth this union of civil and religious life *is* the ideal social relationship. As a form of government, it will some day be fully carried out in God's yet future theocratic kingdom (Zech. 14:20)."[1]

---

*Evidently Josephus invented this word. After mentioning monarchies, oligarchies, and republics, he asserted, "But our legislator . . . ordained . . . our government to be what, by a strained expression, may be termed a theocracy, by ascribing the authority and power to God" (*Against Apion*, 2:17).

134

Josephus, even though he somewhat misrepresents the pentateuchal narrative in making Moses, himself, the author of the theocracy, nevertheless got the point of the records. Moses was directly chosen of God in a theophany which launched his career as deliverer, legislator, and ruler (Ex 3:1—5:18). The choice was confirmed to Moses himself, to the elders of Israel (Ex 4:1-9), and to the Egyptians by a series of miraculous divine manifestations. Responsible people in all epochs of Israel's history not only acknowledged God as king, but the literature frequently points to Moses as the first example of theocratic ruler. Psalm 99, beginning, "the Lord reigneth," mentions Moses in that connection at verse 6. In Psalm 103:7, Moses is mentioned as the one to whom he "made known his ways." Moses' part, under God, in the deliverance from Egypt which led to establishment of the commonwealth is celebrated in Psalm 105:26-43. Moses' theocratic authority is praised in Psalm 106 (see vv. 16, 23, 32). Moses himself represents all his laws as proceeding immediately from either "the finger of God" (Ex 31:18; Deu 9:10, cf. Ex 8:19) or "the mouth of God" (Num 12:8; Deu 8:3).

At all times the voice of God, heard in the law, later also in the prophets (Deu 18:9-22), and by Urim and Thummim (Ex 28:30, Lev 8:8, Num 27:21, Deu 33:8, 1 Sa 28:6, Ezra 2:63, Neh 7:65), was final. Though honored often only in breach, the scriptural annals trace the causes of the nation's disasters precisely to breaches of the covenant, or theocratic law.

Many features of civil law and justice, present in the milieu of the ancient world in general and in Israel in particular, were accepted by Moses and incorporated into the Mosaic system. On the other hand, certain elements intended only for the wilderness wanderings were null after the settlement. The former has been compared to the incorporation of a useful but inadequate older building into the plan and execution of a larger structure. The latter has been compared to the scaffolding employed while a building is in process of construction but removed once the building is complete.

FOREIGN AFFAIRS

The law was concerned not only with internal regulation of the Mosaic commonwealth, but also with the treatment of foreign nations, and of foreigners within the nation of Israel. The Mosaic law taught Israel to treat strangers of their own nation and foreigners within their borders with love and respect. A man of one tribe of Israel was regarded as a sojourner if he resided in the territory of a different tribe. "A sojourner shalt thou not wrong, neither shalt thou oppress him: for ye were sojourners in the land of Egypt" (Ex 22:21). This text, setting forth this idea for the first time in Scripture, sets the pace for the matter. Moses enlarged and amplified this idea of kindness to strangers as an aspect of justice in one of his final addresses: "For the Lord . . . regardeth not persons. . . . He doth execute justice for the fatherless and widow, and loveth the sojourner, in giving him food and raiment. Love ye therefore the sojourner." (Deu 10:17-19; see Ex 23:9; Lev 19:33).

Love of strangers and foreigners was not unconditional, however. Two of Israel's neighbor nations, nearby Edom (see Gen 35:29—36:8) and the distant Babylon are treated semi-symbolically in certain Old Testament passages—as representing, in the case of Edom, the ultimate in secularity, vulgar unbelief, utter spiritual insensitivity (compare Is 34; 63:1-6; Amos 1:11; Ob with the stories about Edom and Jacob in Gen). Esau (Edom or Idumea) is the antithesis of Israel (Jacob) who, for all his faults, treasured the gifts of God and true spirituality. Babylon (Is 13:1—14:23) is described with such extravagant language that some important symbolical meaning naturally is sought. Again Genesis furnishes the key. Babylon is the place where systematic false religion began, where efforts by the united human race to outdo the most High by man-built towers (Gen 11) were first attempted. It stands in contrast to Zion and "the Holy One of Israel" (contrast Is 12:6; 13:1-11). Likewise Esau stands, even in the New Testament, for the profane person (Heb 12:16-17, cf. Ro 9:13) as Babylon for the ultimate of corrupt religion (Rev 14:8; 16:19; 17:5; 18:2, 10, 21). Even so, the Edomites were not to be mistreated unnecessarily, nor were they to be excluded forever from the commonwealth of Israel (Deu 23:7-8). Herod the great was an Edomite, and truly lived up to the profane secularism which his nation represented in the Old Testament Scriptures.[2]

There were certain nations against whom the Israelites were commanded to carry out total destruction. In every case where the reason for this is treated by the Scriptures, it is said to be on account of their consummate degree of corruption or some particularly vile offense against the divine holiness and majesty (see Ex 23:27-32; 34:10-17; Lev 20:28; Num 34:12-29; Deu 7:1-5). Leviticus 18 suggests specifically why such drastic measures were necessary (see Ex 23:32-33; 34:12-29; Deu 6). The specific sins of the Canaanites were particularly vile and destructive of all that is good in social intercourse. Yet at the same time, they were very enticing—all in the area of impure relations between the sexes. They deserved destruction, as do all sinners, but they were granted no further grace (cf. Gen 15:16) lest they be a snare to Israel (Ex 34:12). Some of these sins are set forth with startling detail in Leviticus 18. The section is concluded with the solemn warning: "Defile not ye yourselves in any of these things: for in all these the nations are defiled which I cast out from before you; and the land is defiled: therefore I do visit the iniquity thereof upon it, and the land vomiteth out her inhabitants" (vv. 24-25). The specific procedure for submission or annihilation of the nations of Canaan, together with the divine rationale for it is stated succinctly at Deuteronomy 20:10-18. The Amalekites, who were to be destroyed, "had attacked Israel with treacherous malice after his glorious deliverance from Egypt, and thus laid their hand on the throne of God"[3] (see Ex 17:14, 16; Num 24:20; Deu 25:17-19). Similarly, the war of annihilation waged against the Midianites was on account of their particularly offensive effort to corrupt the faith and morals of Israel, which, if successful, would have entirely prevented Israel's messianic mission (Num 25; 31:16).

There was another class of nations with whom peaceful relations were to be maintained as far as possible. These nations were not to be attacked or invaded. God had given them their lands the same as He had given Israel hers. Among these were Edom (Esau or Seir), Ammon, and Moab (Deu 2:4-19). These three were immediate neighbors. Their treatment is prescribed in detail at Deuteronomy 20:10-15.

With a third class, the Israelites were apparently simply to respond as necessary for the preservation and protection of their commonwealth. Some of these (e.g., Philistia) ultimately had to be vanquished; with others (e.g., the Tyrians) useful treaties were formed; with others sporadic conflict and cooperation persisted through the centuries (e.g., the Syrians of Damascus); and, sadly, still others were, under God, to be the instruments of divine judgment on Israel's apostasy (Assyria and Babylon).

Israel was aware of being a chosen nation with a distinct divine mission. However much the true spiritual dimension of that fact may have been obscured or denied in practice, the Scriptures are most plain. When God says through Amos, "You only have I known of all the families of the earth" (3:2), he is only echoing what the whole Pentateuch from Genesis 12 on through Deuteronomy renders plain as day. Their privilege was also their responsibility, and resulted, as God had fearfully promised (Deu 4:25-40) in their severe chastening by repeated national calamities. The book of Jonah is a witness to Israel's own failure to understand their privilege as one of mission. Yet in the providence of God, their failures were overruled, and the Abrahamic promise, "In thee shall all the families of the earth be blessed" (Gen 12:3) came to pass "when the fulness of time came" when "God sent forth his Son . . . born under the law" (Gal 4:4).

INTERNAL GOVERNMENT

Most modern secular national states have three departments—legislative, executive, and judicial. In the Mosaic theocratic structure, there were elements corresponding to these but no departments strictly defined as such. Moses himself was the legislative department. Nothing like a congress or parliament of representatives for making more laws was contemplated in the Mosaic state structure, though the various councils of elders and officers (Heb. *shoterim*) continued to function and may be presumed to have enacted legislative changes from time to time without altering the Mosaic constitution. On the other hand, executive and judicial functions are present in abundance. It is not possible, however, in this situation, wherein all of the national life was connected with the reign of God, to follow the lines of analysis that might be applied to a modern secular state. But various aspects of internal government as they furnish information regarding guiding principles underlying all of the government of Israel should be noted.

One of the first impressions drawn from the reading of the books of Exodus through Deuteronomy is the complete absence of any strong centralized political authority. The structure based on twelve (or thirteen) tribes was taken into the Mosaic scheme. This was the norm. Neither Moses nor Joshua founded a dynasty, nor did they have successors. For hundreds of years there was no continuing central authority except the high priest, and his authority was limited mostly to matters of ritual law. Administration of civil law was essentially on a local level, in the hands of tribal elders. The judges were charismatic leaders of sectional authority only. A single passage leads us to suppose that Moses contemplated that a central national judiciary, parallel to the national high priesthood would develop, presumably through the regular tribal channels (Deu 17:8-11).

Another impression is the great concern for justice impartially and effectively administered. Every tribal group and locality had its judge or magistrate. This is presented very explicitly: "Judges and officers shalt thou make thee in all thy gates, which the Lord thy God giveth thee, according to thy tribes; and they shall judge the people with righteous judgment. Thou shalt not wrest justice: thou shalt not respect persons; neither shalt thou take a bribe; for a bribe doth blind the eyes of the wise, and pervert the words of the righteous. That which is altogether just shalt thou follow, that thou mayest live, and inherit the land which the Lord thy God giveth thee" (Deu 16:18-20). The various patriarchal heads of different levels (Josh 7:16-18) each were judges. For a brief time at the beginning, Moses was the only judge. On the advice of his father-in-law, however, he chose seventy elders to assist him. Significantly, by comparing the several accounts in the Pentateuch (Ex 18:13-27; Num 11:16-17; Deu 1:13), we discover that these seventy elders were all previously officials within the tribal structure, and that Moses was only returning to them, in the freedom of the new independent Israelite civil commonwealth, the magistracy which they had previously exercised in their subservient situation in Egypt.

In all this, God Himself was the supreme judge; hence to go before a judge was the same as going before God (Ex 18:15-16; 21:6; 22:8). This, in the theocratic situation, sometimes involved also the magisterial assistance of a priest (Deu 19:16, 19) as interpreter of the law.

There was no system of appeal to higher courts by plaintiffs. A judge's decision on any level was final. Yet the judge on any level could refer cases, even to the highest magistrate or priest at the central sanctuary. There were to be judges over tens, judges over fifties, and so on, but as Keil asserts, "The relation of these judges to one another is not exactly defined in the Biblical text; but from what has been said, we are not at liberty to conceive of it as a succession of courts rising in order above one another so that litigants could appeal from the judge over ten to the judge over fifty, and so on."[4] The highest court, to which cases too complicated or beyond the competence of the lesser magistrates were to be sent, was a national court. This court is somewhat obscure, but the basic text is Deuteronomy 17:8-13. It must be realized that many articles of the Mosaic law are designed to regulate or employ the usages of unwritten customary law. Since the customs have been lost to us, it would be impossible even if it were desirable to reconstitute a national system strictly according to the usages of Mosaic laws.

The actual operation of these courts has been the subject of considerable research by ancient scholars[5] and by modern scholars as well. With the judge in each court, there were officers (Heb. *shoterîm*) who constituted a jury. These juries were of various sizes, as Keil has shown.[6] The great council, called the Sanhedrin, originated during the two centuries immediately before Christ, after the Mosaic kingdom had been broken up.[7]

Most cases, even those involving death penalties, such as adultery (Lev 20:10), persistent rebellion of sons (Ex 21:15), apostasy (Deu 13:1-11), blasphemy (Num 24:11), were to be adjudicated locally by the magistrate. Furthermore, the citizens of the locality were responsible to inflict the punishment of death, where called for, by stoning (Deu 17:5).

In addition to the judges, there were certain other officers involved in at least some of the court proceedings. The word "officer" is about as indefinite in the Old Testament as in our present usage. Although these officers performed a number of duties in earliest times (see Ex 5:6, 14-16) and had certain military connections (see Deu 20:5, 8-9; Josh 1:10; 3:2), there were *shoterîm* associated with the judges also. "Judges and officers shalt thou make thee in all thy gates . . . and they shall judge the people" (Deu 16:18). Derivation of the word suggests that the officers were court recorders or registrars.[8] The priests also had a court function, for always, where such was necessary, they were the authentic official interpreters of the law. Sometimes priests even served as judges (cf. Lev 10:10-11; Deu 21:5).

The main elements in court procedures are excellent. Courts were public, the location being at the city gates or the central sanctuary (Deu 16:18-20). Moses heard cases at the door of the tent of meeting (Num 16:18-19). Deborah heard them under a palm tree (Judg 4:15). We must assume that the litigants argued their own cases before the judges, since there is no evidence either of public prosecutors or of public or private defense attorneys. Oaths were not used except in certain exceptional cases, and witnesses could be summoned.

There is little evidence of significant variation from the Mosaic court system in Old Testament times. During the time of Jehoshaphat, who reigned after a long period of civil and religious decay, the king did set up a supreme tribunal in Jerusalem. This was in connection with strenuous efforts to turn his people back to their covenant faith by instructing the whole nation in the law (2 Ch 17:7-9). The tribunal, while not prescribed by the law, was lawfully constituted (2 Ch 19:8-11). Jehoshaphat did not neglect administration of law courts in the districts (2 Ch 19:4-7).

That which interests us most is the principles upon which Mosaic justice was administered. What constituted justice? First of principles to be noted is recognition of the equality of all men before the law. It was regarded as the height of impiety for the judges to respect persons. This was spelled out. The magistrate was to decide for minorities against majorities if truth called for it; he must not decide for the poor and weak man merely because he is small, nor for the rich and powerful because he is great. Bribes and gifts to magistrates were a great offense, and the law abounds with exhortations to magistrates on this count.

Second, there was an enlightened view of what constitutes guilt. For example, the law recognized several degrees of guilt for murder. Premeditated deliberate homicide only was punishable by the death penalty; a homicide inflicted in a spontaneous fight or out of sudden passion had a lesser penalty; out of negligence still less; and a pure inadvertence, or act of God, received no punishment at all. Children could not be punished for their parents' crimes. God could visit the evil consequences of sinful actions upon offspring to the third and fourth generations, presumably through heredity or social consequences, but not so with men.

> There is prohibited one of the most common of ancient practices, the visitation by human authority upon an offender's family of the penalty which belonged only to him. "The fathers shall not be put to death for the children," says Moses in Deuteronomy, "neither shall the children be put to death for the fathers: every man shall be put to death for his own sin" [24:16]. The mysterious influence of heredity is not hereby denied. The inexorable law of cause and effect, by which sins of the fathers are actually visited upon the children to the third and fourth generation, is not disputed or repealed. But to fallible men there is properly denied the right to trench upon the prerogative of the Almighty. The divine ways, as the prophet Ezekiel shows in speaking of this very matter, are equal; man's ways are unequal [Eze 18:20].[9]

Third, there was a concern that penalty should be adjusted to fit the crime. "The quality and form of punishments were, as far as possible, fixed in harmony with the principle that satisfaction was to be rendered for harm done. Guilt and its requital were in some sense to correspond. What the evil man had done, or purposed to do, to another, was to be visited in punishment on his own head."[10]

The so-called *lex talionis*, which required "eye for eye, tooth for tooth" (Ex 21:23; Lev 24:17-18; Deu 19:21), was a vivid expression of this law of proportion. Laws of neighbor nations, frequently designed to discourage theft and assault rather than strictly to vindicate divine righteousness, more often extracted several times more than the strict assessment of guilt required. So, far from teaching cruelty and hate, this formula was part of Israel's unique message of mercy, although it did not always prevent miscarriage of justice.

Penalties under Mosaic law were severe by current standards, but they were neither degrading nor cruel. The ruling principle was that the punishment must fit the offense. Hence crimes against life were punished mainly by comparable forfeit of the life of the convicted offender. It was "life for life," usually by stoning. In cases of other offenses against the body, it was to be "stripe for stripe." Jesus made reference to "few stripes" and "many stripes," reflecting the usual method of corporal punishment. The method, though admittedly severe, was limited to forty stripes (Deu 25:1-3). In the case of offenses against property, punishment was compensation for loss plus a fine paid to the plaintiff. In minor cases, the fine might be a fifth of the value of the restored property (Num 5:6-7); or in more serious cases, it might be double the value of the theft (Ex 22:4).

The element of moral discipline of the population is prominent in all of these arrangements, together with proper regard for the majesty of a holy God.

The severity of penalties prescribed by the law of Moses indicates that some of the worst offenses were deemed to be those against the structure of society itself. Thus the penalty for murder, the violation of the sanctity of life, was death; likewise for adultery, the violation of the sanctity of the home, the basic social unit; and for incorrigible rebellion of children, the violation of the integrity of the home. The same is true of violation of the holiness of God—blasphemy—and for violation of the integrity of His worship—sacrilege (cf. Lev 10).

Fourth, rules of evidence were strict. The accused nor witnesses could be tortured when evidence was not forthcoming. Where crime was charged and no competent witnesses could be produced, a solemn oath on the part of the accused was sufficient to release him (Ex 22:11).† An accusation had to be supported by facts. Though in a minor case, a king-judge might be guided by circumstantial evidence (1 Ki 3:26), conviction for a serious crime required witnesses. A Roman Catholic authority writes, "For a death sentence the law required at least two witnesses for the prosecution (Num. 35:30; Deut. 17:6; cf. I Ki. 21:10; Matt. 26:59-60; Heb. 10:28) and possibly for every case, according to Deuteronomy 19:15; cf. Isaiah 8:2. These witnesses accepted responsibility for the sentence, which is why they had to throw the first stones if the condemned party were stoned (Deut. 17:7; cf. 13:10; Jn. 8:7). But their evidence had to be verified by the judges, and false witnesses were condemned to the punishment which would have befallen the accused (Deut. 19:18, 19; cf. Dan. 13:62 [i.e., Susanna])."[11] Mankind being what it is, this did not entirely prevent miscarriages of justice, as the stories

---

†Compare No. 131 of the Laws of Hammurabi: "If the wife of a man is accused by her husband, and she has not been caught lying with another man, she shall swear her innocence and return to her house."

of Naboth (1 Ki 21:10-16), Jesus (Mt 26:59-68), and Stephen (Ac 6:8—7:60) amply demonstrate.

Fifth, the purposes of punishment of offenders were primarily vindicative and restitutional and only secondarily to correct offenders or to prevent further crimes. This is very important.

"Punishments were inflicted in order specially to express the sacred indignation of the divine Lawgiver against wilful transgression of his commandments, and not for any purposes of human vengeance, or for the sake of frightening other criminals."[12]

By "vindicative" is meant the acknowledgment of and honoring of the righteousness of God. In all biblical teaching regarding man and his societies, righteousness grows out of the divine character of the government of the world. This is only rendered more prominent in a formal theocracy wherein all laws are more obviously given God's direct sanction. To break a law is to reject the government of God. God intends that civil magistrates should not let lawbreakers get away with their lawlessness. "Be ye holy, for I am holy," is the fundamental concept. Hence in the Mosaic code, punishment is retribution, strict return upon the offender of appropriate suffering for his offense. Coupled with this is the "intention . . . to extirpate evil and produce reverence in the heart of the people."[13]

The high pedagogical value of the law, not merely in the punishments prescribed in case of its fracture but throughout the entire system, has been noticed by many writers and experienced by multitudes of its readers. I, for one, was spared the grosser sins by quite undesignedly, but providentially, at the age of ten, choosing to read all the Pentateuch at the Christmas season in connection with a Bible reading contest. A girl who read the shortest Psalms over and over won the contest, but I won a precious treasure of "sin-prevention" which I needed badly a short time later.

An instructive article on this subject states:

> But perhaps the most important consequence of the theocratic nature of the Law was the peculiar character of goodness which it sought to impress upon the people. Goodness in its relation to man takes the form of righteousness and love; in its independence of all relation, the form of purity; and in its relation to God, that of piety. Laws which contemplate men chiefly in their mutual relations endeavor to enforce or protect in them the first two qualities [righteousness and love];

the Mosaic Law [on the contrary], beginning with piety as its first object, enforces most emphatically the purity essential to those who by their union with God, have recovered the hope of intrinsic goodness, while it views righteousness [i.e., justice] and love rather as deductions from these than as independent objects. Not that it neglects these qualities; on the contrary, it is full of precepts which show a high conception and tender care of our relative duties to man (see, for example, Ex 21:7-11, 28-36; 23:1-9; Deu 22:1-4; 24:10-22, etc.); but these can hardly be called its distinguishing features. It is most instructive to refer to the religious preface of the Law in Deuteronomy 6–9 (esp. to 6:4-13), where all is based on the first great commandment, and to observe the subordinate and dependent character of 'the second that is like unto it'—'Thou shalt love thy neighbor as thyself; I am the Lord' (Lev. 19:18). On the contrary, the care for the purity of the people stands out remarkably, not only in the enforcement of ceremonial 'cleanness,' and the multitude of precautions or remedies against any breach of it, but in the several laws against self-pollution, a severity which distinguishes the Mosaic code before all others ancient or modern. In punishing these sins, as committed against a man's own self, without reference to their effect on others, and in recognizing purity as having a substantive value and glory, it sets up a standard of individual morality such as even in Greece and Rome, philosophy reserved for its most esoteric teaching.[14]

In a society where all wrongdoing is regarded as primarily against God, this principle of just retribution will extend even to offenses against property, for "he that killeth a beast shall make it good and he that killeth a man shall be put to death" (Lev 24:21). This approach to penology produced what our age might regard as severe punishments. Yet, on the other hand, the system was surprisingly mild, and for many offenses no punishment at all was prescribed.

Furthermore, the Mosaic law really was much milder than many systems in modern times in so-called enlightened countries. It is instructive, for example, that a burglar might be killed by the proprietor only if it was night, when the intruder's purpose would be uncertain. In the daylight a proprietor was not permitted to slay a housebreaker bent on thievery only. What might have been prescribed if daylight burglars carried instant death to opponents in the form of firearms is uncertain, for such, as we know today, heightens the tension and danger involved. Mutilation was allowed in the single case of a very repulsive act for which such punishment might seem appropriate even today. The case is just such a one as might occur among a disorderly and violent people, wherein even the women are caught up in the spirit of violence. See Deuteronomy 25:11-12: "When men strive together one with another, and the wife of the one draweth near to deliver her husband out of the hand of him that smiteth him, and putteth forth her hand, and taketh him by the secrets [i.e., the genitals]; then shalt thou cut off her hand, thine eye shall have no pity."

By "restitutional" is meant that penalties were designed to restore the proper state of affairs. So apprehended thieves were to restore to the proper owner what they had stolen. Thus the intruding evil was to be rooted out of the land. Hence imprisonment, as a punishment, had no place at all in the Mosaic system, while flogging was prescribed. "Simply to deprive a person of his liberty and support him at the expense of the state was punishment neither in the form of retaliation nor compensation."[15]

The Pentateuch says less of the corrective effect of certain types of punishment than do certain other sections of the Old Testament. Significantly, this is principally in regard to parental punishment of the misdeeds of the children. (Deu 21:18; 2 Sa 7:14; Pr 13:24; 19:18; 23:13). There is little doubt that many of the penalties assessed by the Mosaic laws tended to correct the behavior, if not the thinking, of the offenders who suffered from it.

Any preventive effect to be derived from civil punishments is seldom mentioned; but where it is mentioned it is put forcefully. Moreover, the preventive secondary effect is traced specifically to the exact retributive character of just punishment. This is to say that punishment tends to prevent lawlessness only when it is deserved, or retributive, and just—in equal proportion to guilt or desert. If punishment is less or more than equal, the preventive effect may be largely lost. The principle is set forth specifically in relation to punishment of a false witness in Deuteronomy 19:19-21. "Then shall ye do unto him, as he had thought to do unto his brother: so shalt thou put away the evil from the midst of thee. And those that remain shall hear, and fear, and shall henceforth commit no more any such evil in the midst of thee. And thine eye shall not pity; life shall go for life, eye for eye, tooth for tooth, hand for hand, foot for foot." Eye, hand, and foot are to be understood symbolically, of course, for with a single exception, as noted above, mutilation or corporal punishment of any kind other than flogging was not allowed under the Mosaic laws.

Any punishment out of proportion to the magnitude of offense would not have the effect to put away the evil—that is, it would not correct the situation or prevent future occurrences. If the punishment were too severe, a second offense would have been perpetrated by the very worst possible party, the agent of the law of the land. Law and police are made to seem unjust; organized society appears to be an oppressive establishment interested not at all in fairness to all, but interested only in defending the privileges of the present social, political, and economic elite. If the punishment were too lenient, the offense is not seen as a serious matter, the law itself is brought to seem trivial, the persons harmed by the offender are further insulted while the offender himself remains essentially unrebuked, uncorrected, and unimproved, and he is educated by the judicial agencies to go further toward inevitable self-destruction.‡

---

‡Carl Friederich Keil has put the issues squarely in his section entitled "Character of Theocratic Penal Law" in his *Commentary on the Pentateuch*. He opens the section by observing, "The Mosaic penal code shows itself to be a manifestation of the divine righteousness by its combination of two elements. At the root of its enactment lies the principle of strict but righteous retribution, and its intention is to extirpate evil and produce reverence for the righteousness of the holy God in the hearts of the people." Then after showing how the *jus talionis* was a general principle in Israel's law, not merely one relating to bodily injuries, he writes more at length:

"The Mosaic law carries out the principle that punishment should correspond to the heinousness of the offence, that there shall fall on the head of the culprit what he has done to his neighbor. Hence it limits the punishment to the guilty person without extending it to his children (Deut. 24:6); and in any case of property, it requires it only in order to restoration and by way of penal restitution, if the guilty man had invaded his neighbor's property or violated the integrity of his house. By punishment it is intended only that evil be rooted out and right be preserved or restored. What is said (Deut. 19:19 f.) in regard to the false witness holds good of all the penal enactments of the Mosaic Law: 'Do unto him as he thought to do unto his brother, and put away the evil from the midst of thee.' When, however, it is added: 'Those which remain shall hear and fear, and shall henceforth commit no more any such evil in the midst of thee' (vs. 20, cf. 17:13), this general object of punishment must not be in the least identified with the deterrent theory, i.e., with the tendency to deter from crime by the way and manner of punishing it. By removing the evil by means of punishment, it is intended to bring into view the earnestness of divine retributive justice, that the wicked may not merely be afraid of the penalty, but much more the righteous judgment which overtakes transgressors, without respect of persons. How far removed the theocratic penal code is from the theory referred to, appears from the strict limits set to the number of stripes and the amount of fines, and still more clearly from the absence of every kind of torture or infamy from the penalties.

"If, however, partly owing to this cause, partly to the careful distinguishing between presumptuous crimes and trespasses arising from weakness, thoughtlessness, or negligence, milder penalties are fixed corresponding to the degree of guilt, yet

Sixth, the Law of Moses gave special attention to the sacredness and value of human life. For this reason the extreme penalty was required for murder. The dreadful consequences of failure to properly punish all murderers according to the law's requirements are constantly reiterated. Several chapters of the Pentateuch are devoted to careful instruction in the handling of murder cases (see esp. Ex 21:12-25; Lev 24:17-21; Num 35:9-34; Deu 21:1-9). In this connection it is important to understand that murder is held to pollute the very land whereon the nation dwells, as does fornication; further that the only way to rid the land of the pollution of first degree murder was by the death of the murderer, officially inflicted by civil action after due process of law. "So ye shall not defile the land wherein ye are: for blood it defileth the land: and the land cannot be cleansed of the blood that is shed therein, but by the blood of him that shed it. Defile not therefore the land which ye shall inhabit" (Num 35:33-34, cf. Deu 9:1-5; 19:10-13; 21:1-9). Unlawful violence was one of the reasons why God brought the flood; the prophets of both the kingdom of Israel and the kingdom of Judah pronounced coming judgment because of murder unpunished by the responsible magistrates of both kingdoms (cf., e.g., Jer 2:34-37; Ho 1:4; 4:1-5).

Closely connected are the sins of uncleanness in sexual matters, for both sexual immorality and murder are direct offenses against the God in whose image man is made. Therefore, after a list of the sexual practices of the Canaanites (Lev 18:1-23), this solemn warning follows. "Defile not ye yourselves in any of these things: for in all these the nations are defiled which I cast out from before you; and the land is defiled: therefore I do visit the iniquity thereof upon it, and the land vomiteth out her inhabitants. Ye therefore

there is no weakening thereby of the earnestness of retributive justice. On the contrary, greatly as the Mosaic Law takes account of human weaknesses, and even forbids many a thing without attaching to the transgression of it any civil penalty (comp. e.g., Lev. 19), yet it insists unreservedly on the hallowing of Israel in the fear of the holiness of Jehovah, the covenant God. Hence it designates even the trespasses arising from weakness as sin, and appoints forms of expiation for them, the omission of which is threatened with cutting off. It commands with unsparing severity the punishment of all presumptuous disobedience to God, the Holy One of Israel, and to his holy ordinances. Finally, it threatens a curse and severe punishments from God, the avenger of all evil, for offences which either escape the eye of civil justice, or which, like apostasy from the Lord to idolatry, may at times prevail to such a degree, that the arm of the earthly magistrate is overpowered and paralyzed by the spirit of the time [Zeitgeist]" (pp. 354-56).

shall keep my statutes and mine ordinances, and shall not do any of these abominations . . . that the land vomit not you out also, when ye defile it, as it vomited out the nation that was before you" (vv. 24-26, 28, cf. 20:22-27).

As has already been observed, it is not possible to transfer Mosaic laws into the civil structure of any state today, owing to their special theocratic character. Yet this does not mean that they have no relevance. In the case just cited, note how God holds the Canaanite people quite responsible to keep their land free from unrestrained vice. In many respects, Mosaic laws are special enactments for Israel of general divine law applicable everywhere.

Before passing on, we note that the doctrine of collective national responsibility for enforcement of basic public morality, as well as justice, through legal magistrates, is integral to many parts of Scripture. This has been noted earlier in these pages. Israel's land was held in responsible trust. God was proprietor; they the tenants; eviction the result of misuse or immoral use of the premises. This is clearly set forth in the twenty-fifth and twenty-sixth chapters of Leviticus. But the principle does not stop there, for as we have seen, the prophets explicitly declare the heathen nations likewise responsible to see that justice and public morality are maintained. They are not held to the standards of special revelation—biblical truth—but they are responsible for natural light, the knowledge of His existence that God has given to all men. To draw from one further source, Psalm 94 refers to Jehovah as the "God, to whom vengeance belongeth" (v. 1) and "judge of the earth" (v. 2). God is "He that chastiseth the nations" and "he that teacheth man [Heb. *'ādhām*, mankind, the whole human race] knowledge" (v. 10). The international extent of the psalmist's prayer for a divine intervention to correct national evils, especially those perpetrated by public officials, is thus put in sharp profile. All twenty-three verses should be read, but we cite only a brief selection:

> Lift up thyself, thou judge of the earth:
> Render to the proud their desert.
>
> .   .   .   .
>
> They slay the widow and the sojourner,
> And murder the fatherless.

. . . .

He that chastiseth the nations, shall not he correct,
Even he that teacheth man knowledge?

. . . .

Shall the throne of wickedness have fellowship with thee,
Which frameth mischief by statute?

. . . .

And condemn the innocent blood.

(vv. 2, 6, 10, 20, 21)

The author is Jewish and his standpoint is Jewish, but he argues from general principles, not special laws; and he has faith that what God does in moral government of Israel, He does everywhere. The sins and crimes of public officers named, even using statutes of public law (v. 20) to oppress the people, need no special revelation to be known as evil.

It is of great importance to observe that the basic divine laws of sexual purity are presumed by authors of Scripture to be known by all men (cf. Ro 1:18—2:16). Thus, for example, the pagan Canaanites were held accountable to God with regard to these standards of sexual purity. Though Israel might be (and was) evicted from her homeland for breaking laws of both general and special revelation, other nations under no special theocratic constitution and custodians of no special revelation are accountable in matters of common morality. There can be no doubt that, biblically considered, matters of public morality are proper subjects for civil legislation and civil penalties. The state has both a right and a duty to enforce minimum standards of public morality. If abortion is a crime against life, then laws and penalties for it are necessary. Furthermore, considering the stake Christians have in rearing children in an atmosphere where morality in the thought life, as well as in external acts, is supported, they have a stake in legislation against pornography in the mails and against gross uncleanness in all public media for dissemination of information. Their land may spew out the chaste and law-abiding along with the immoral if they are not successful in securing and enforcing legislation against crimes and public immorality. They may utterly fail, as did Hosea in Israel and Jeremiah and his helpers in Judah, but they should not cease to try.

12

PROPERTY AND SLAVERY IN THE MOSAIC COMMONWEALTH OF ISRAEL

THIS STUDY of the Mosaic legislation closes with consideration of aspects of the Mosaic laws in regard to property or economics, and in that context, slavery. "It is certain that no laws better represent the characteristic principles of the Mosaic legislation or serve more to separate the Hebrews from all other nations of antiquity than those relating to property."[1]

The commands of the law regarding wealth and its use are all addressed to the heart, aimed at quenching the desire for earthly riches and mammon-worship.[2] Yet on the other hand, they were not intended to dull enthusiasm for honest industry and proper gain thereby, and certainly not to encourage sloth, waste, or indolence. If work and thrift are part of the Puritan ethic, we know where the Puritans, famous for their interest in the Scriptures, got such ideas. The balance between greed and generosity, thrift and parsimony, freedom to eat and care also for one's neighbor's welfare is brought out in a number of ways. A hungry man might lawfully eat grapes in another's vineyard, yet he could not lawfully carry away any in a container; in similar circumstances he might pluck corn from his neighbor's field, as did Jesus and His disciples (Mt 12:1), but he might not lawfully take more than enough to care for his present hunger (Deu 23:24-25). Creditors were insured by laws quite severe, by our present standards, against loss from insolvent debtors (Lev 25:24-46; cf. 2 Ki 4:1; Neh 5:5; Job 24:9), even to the extent of claiming debtors as slaves—though slavery in this case amounts only to working off a debt. Yet there were many cushions against rapacity of creditors. Owners were protected against damage (Ex 21:23-36; 22:4-5; Lev 24:18), fraud (Ex 22:6-14), and theft (Ex 22:1-3). In some cases penalties were

151

severe. Yet all was designed as moral discipline as well as to insure civil equity. This is demonstrated by the fact that in both theft and fraud, a penitent could rectify the situation before the law simply by making good the loss to the victim and adding a fifth part. The lesson was pointed up in the conscience of the offender by a necessary trespass offering to God (Lev 6:1-7).

The sources of the wealth of the children of Israel were several. There was chiefly the land of Canaan itself, a section of the Near East considered by the people of that part of the world, then and now, as a very favored area. Perhaps the most detailed biblical description of its natural wealth is in the words of the great lawgiver, "For the LORD thy God bringeth thee into a good land, a land of brooks of water, of fountains and depths that spring out of valleys and hills; A land of wheat, and barley, and vines, and fig trees, and pomegranates; a land of oil olive, and honey; A land wherein thou shalt eat bread without scarceness, thou shalt not lack any thing in it; a land whose stones are iron, and out of whose hills thou mayest dig brass" (Deu 8:7-10, KJV). These natural endowments include all important agricultural resources, both soil and water—elsewhere said to include sufficient rain—plus minerals for a metal industry. Not mentioned are the forests that then covered most of the highlands. "The rich forests of Gilead were almost as famous as those of Lebanon, the two often being mentioned together (Jer. 22:6; Zech. 10:10). The people of Gilead lived from the forest. The balm, of course, was proverbial (Jer. 8:22; 46:11), and was exported to the Phenicians at Tyre (Ez. 27:17) and also to the Egyptians; for Joseph was sold to a travelling company of Ishmaelites who were 'coming down from Gilead, with their camels bearing gum, balm, and myrrh, on their way to carry it down to Egypt' (Gen. 37:25)."³ As late as the reign of David, the forest of Ephraim was extensive (2 Sa 18:6-8). The visitor to the Holy Land today should know that in spite of appearances to the contrary, the annual rainfall of Jerusalem—about twenty-five inches—is about the same as that of London and slightly more than that of Berlin;⁴ that the present prevalent barrenness is the fruit of man's· folly. At various periods of its history, the country has supported millions of people, as it is even now beginning to do again.

Other sources of wealth were the livestock of the children of

Israel, which had multiplied in Goshen (Gen 47:1, 6, 27), and the moveable properties such as silver, gold, and jewelry, with which the exasperated Egyptians had endowed them at the time of their exodus (Ex 11:1-3; 12:35-36), together with the properties which they had taken from their enemies just previous to entering upon the wars of conquest (Num 31:32-54).

Notices in the Pentateuch report that the portable wealth gained during the exodus and the travels to Canaan's border were divided among all the families (Num 31:25-54). Explicit instructions were left by Moses that every Israelite family was to receive an allotment of real estate in the land of promise. This was to be done proportionately—larger or more valuable properties to larger groups, smaller properties to smaller groups (Num 26:52-56; 33:54). The Levites were excepted from this benefit, being provided for by other means. The book of Joshua witnesses how carefully this division was carried out. There were differences in personal wealth of course, for they had not left Egypt with equal possessions, and half a century had passed before the settlement took place.

There are three principles which the Mosaic laws held to underlie all land proprietorship in Canaan. First, ownership lay in families rather than in persons. Since the family is an on-going entity, surviving the decease of its members, a second principle prevailed: the land originally allotted to a family could not be alienated by any means whatsoever from that family. Third, all land ownership was a trust or stewardship from the Lord Himself, the true proprietor of all the land of Canaan. All three of these principles appear in the following passage:

> And the land shall not be sold in perpetuity; for the land is mine: for ye are strangers and sojourners with me. And in all the land of your possession ye shall grant a redemption for the land. If thy brother be waxed poor, and sell some of his possession, then shall his kinsman that is next unto him come, and shall redeem that which his brother hath sold. And if a man have no one to redeem it, and he be waxed rich and find sufficient to redeem it; then let him reckon the years of the sale thereof, and restore the overplus unto the man to whom he sold it; and he shall return unto his possession. But if he be not able to get it back for himself, then that which he hath sold shall remain in the hand of him that bought it until the year of jubilee:

and in the jubilee it shall go out, and he shall return unto his possession (Lev 25:23-28).

As a parenthetical, but important matter, many scholars have noted that Mosaic law paid due respect to older customs in many enactments regarding inheritance. Polygamy, for example, complicated the laws of inheritance, for there might be more than one firstborn son among the wives. How this was handled is set forth in Deuteronomy 21:15-17.[5] Levirate marriage whereby the brother of a deceased man was obliged to marry the widow of the deceased, incorporated into Mosaic law, was a pre-Mosaic custom. There is no evidence for wills in the Old Testament. Paul's discussion of certain aspects of the work of Christ wherein he uses the idea of a will or testament and the death of a testator is apparently based on Roman usage. Also, before Moses, the firstborn designate could be changed by a father, but evidently not afterward (see Gen 25:31-34; 49:3-4; 48:20-22; 1 Ch 5:1).

A number of interesting and instructive episodes and laws relate to the actual implementation of the provisions of Leviticus 25:23-28 quoted above. The jubilee was a recurring fiftieth year when all land that had been sold in the interval was returned to its original owner or to his heirs. Further, a kinsman of one who sold a property could buy it back at any time in order to return it to the original owner or his heirs. There is much doubt expressed among certain authorities as to whether some of the features of the jubilee really were observed. Skepticism is expressed regarding letting the land lie fallow all year in addition to the fallow sabbath year preceeding (cf. 2 Ch 36:21). In any case, it seems likely that the land reversion feature was adhered to, for frequent reference to it occurs outside the Pentateuch, being coupled as it was with the right of redemption (Num 27:4, 36; cf. Josh 17:3ff; Ruth 4:3; 1 Ki 21; cf. 2 Ki 8:3; Jer 32:7; Eze 7:12-13; 46:16). Whether or not the provisions were kept is not important for our study. For, granting the authenticity and truthfulness of the penteteuchal accounts, God was the author of the laws. Such being the case, those authors who label the plan impractical or utopian or deny the authenticity of the accounts by following the reigning theories of higher criticism appear to manifest more religious doubt than literary insight.[6]

Under the rules for property-holding in Israel, property is seen to be an important human right. There is no basis for distinction between property rights and human rights. There is a valid distinction to be discovered and a range of value among the several human rights, however. Thus a proprietor's right to his property is lower in scale than that of another man to his own life, even though he be a thief caught in the act of breaking and entering during daylight hours. For though at night, when the burglar's purposes would be obscure—perhaps murder of a man's sleeping family—he might be slain with impunity, neither the proprietor nor his friends obstructing a simple daylight burglary were allowed to take the life of the thief.

It has already been seen that land ownership had some very special features not prevalent in any Western country today. And ideas about ownership vary from place to place and from culture to culture. The Mosaic law, while it clearly endorses private ownership and private initiative (as does all Scripture), does not legislate against other forms of ownership. The law's rules for land-holding are certainly as much like family ownership as strictly private personal ownership. A suggestion by a distinguished legal philosopher, Jacques Ellul, of Reformed faith, professor of law at Bordeaux University, is helpful:

> It is divinely ordained, for instance, that ownership is the mode of relationship between man and things, that this ownership has a Christocentric significance, and that this is a sign of grace, a part of man's inheritance. But absolutely nothing is said about the form of this ownership as exercised by a person, a family, or a collectivity, nor about the modalities it should assume in a given society for its representation or transmission. Nonetheless the fact of ownership as a divine institution presupposes practical limitations for the extent, the permanency, and the exclusive character of ownership. In other words, if there is to be order, the form of this ownership will be conditioned by two considerations: the fact of being created by God, and the fact of a specific political, social, and economic environment.[7]

Although Professor Ellul is not referring specifically to the Pentateuch, his words apply. If the laws of Moses cannot be made directly to teach socialism, neither can they, without bending, be made to support all the doctrines of any other economic theory claiming universal and exclusive validity.

A. J. McClain introduces a remarkably perceptive analysis of this economic system.

> Now the approach of the Mosaic law to the matter of wealth and its distribution is both novel and realistic. It envisioned no perfect utopia in which all men would be equal in ability and possessions. On the contrary, there was a frank recognition of the perennial nature of the economic problem in a sinful race, even under the beneficient rule of a kingdom of God on earth: 'For the poor shall never cease out of the land' (Deut. 15:11). This is not a *laissez faire* form of economic fatalism, but simply one price which a society must pay for human freedom. For, if men are to enjoy any satisfactory measure of personal liberty in economic affairs—men being what they are, widely different in disposition and ability—some will gain and others will lose. Historically, no perfect way has ever been found to reconcile personal liberty with complete economic equality; the reason being that the root of the problem is in the nature of man himself, and consequently individual action is never wholly predictable. The law of the historical kingdom [i.e., the Mosaic law] accepted these facts and laid down its rules accordingly. Since men could not be left wholly free and at the same time be fully protected from their own economic follies, certain provisions were established to safeguard them in the exercise of their economic rights and also to ameliorate some of the inequalities arising therefrom.[8]

Both the wisdom and the benevolence of the Mosaic laws respecting property, especially as regards the needs of the poor, are evident. Great wisdom may be seen in the way the laws pay due respect to the emotional, psychological, moral, and spiritual needs of men, as well as to their sheer physical necessities. In the land of Israel, any man had the right to try, and thereby also the right to fail, but he had no right to starve! In Old Testament legislation, the poor are neither things nor statistics; they are persons and families. There were no paternalistic rules or procedures to limit the owner of a plot of ground from using it as he saw fit. He could farm it well, or he could deplete its soils for nought. He could rent it, sell it, or abandon it. The only restriction was that he could not surrender title to the land in perpetuity. He could redeem it any time he was able and willing; or a more wealthy kinsman could do it for him or his heirs after him. In any case, in the year of jubilee, recurring every fifty years, the land returned, free of any encumbrance, to the original owner or his heirs.* No law gave king or government rights of eminent domain, and it is doubtful if even exchanges of properties within tribal boundaries were allowed (see 2 Ki 21). All of this was given a religious-theological foundation, as the frequently reiterated "I am the Lord" in connection with these laws ominously emphasizes.

Nothing speaks more distinctly of the benevolent spirit of the civil regulations than the provisions therein for the honest poor. Professional vagrancy or mendicancy and many of the evils attendant upon some of the aids to the poor in the welfare provision of the modern secular states are not contemplated; nor were they possible. It is hard to say what specific laws Moses might have laid down for the protection of the rights both of poor and rich under God if the children of Israel had been a nation of corporations and stockholders, employers and employees, capitalists and laborers, merchants and consumers as in a modern industrialized state. In any case, it is certain that the spirit of the legislation he did provide would have been carried over. Some of those provisions are here summarized. The list is impressive and certainly ought to give pause to those on the one hand who think government owes everyone an

---

*The work of Robert North, *Sociology of the Biblical Jubilee* (Rome: Pontifical Biblical Institute, 1954) is at almost every point in agreement with the affirmations of this chapter. The author concludes:

"In claiming for himself the ownership of the land, God did not intend to exclude the right of private property, but rather emphasized it to the point of making it inalienable. This inalienability was *relative*. It applied only in the particular and theocratic domain of Israel. . . . Its more permanent enunciation would be "No contingent circumstances can force a man to alienate his share of the world's goods in such wise that he and his family will be left destitute while others immoderately abound" (pp. 213-14).

"But even in the more narrow and proper sense, the unity of the family is inculcated by the jubilee law. Like the doctrine of the living wage, the property-restitution aims to guarantee to the family the means of worthy independence, the basis of contented cohabitation. If the claims of commutative justice made it necessary to restrict this independence temporarily, the family even during this period had the stimulus of guaranteed hope. . . . This guarantee was equivalent to old-age security, a powerful factor in the economic struggles of the family.

"Pride in one's modest property and resolve to preserve and improve it through generations is a strong incentive to hold the family together through the temporary agitations which may threaten any marriage. There is also a basic morality in the concept that a son should plan to carry on the establishment of his father. It cannot be doubted that the precipitate flight to "rise above one's father's station' is responsible for much of the instability in the modern family (p. 215)."

equal income, and to those on the other hand who think all the poor are both stupid and lazy, possessing no rights except to starve to death.[9]

First, all acts of willful cheating or of oppression were outlawed. We cite only a few references, for it would require several pages merely to quote the passages in the Old Testament in this regard. "Thou shalt neither vex a stranger nor oppress him: for ye were strangers in the land of Egypt" (Ex 22:21 KJV, cf. 23:9; Deu 27:19). This concern was to extend to foreigners as well as to widows and orphans (Ex 22:22-24). Money was to be lent to poor countrymen in a kindly way and without interest (Ex 22:25, cf. Deu 23:19-20), and no pledge should be kept that would deprive a poor man of things necessary for health, comfort, and decency. Even escaped slaves, presumably from neighboring lands, were to be granted asylum (Deu 23:15.) A "hired servant that is poor and needy," whether native or alien, was to be given fair treatment, just wages, and prompt payment for his services (Deu 24:14-15). The book of Proverbs, which greatly praises the law, reenforces the law at this point with striking warnings: "Rob not the poor, because he is poor; Neither oppress the afflicted in the gate: For Jehovah will plead their cause, And despoil of life those that despoil them" (Pr 22:22-23, cf. 28:3).

Second, the affluent person, or even one of moderate means, was enjoined to give generously to the needy, as a matter of the needy man's right, as well as out of charity. The Mosaic system really lifts the care of honest poor far above any mere legal obligation to the realm of brotherly kindness. The Jewish people were in very truth a family wherein the fraternal spirit was to prevail, regardless of wealth or the lack of it. This is brilliantly set forth in the following striking passage.

> If there be with thee a poor man, one of thy brethren, within any of thy gates in thy land which Jehovah thy God giveth thee, thou shalt not harden thy heart, nor shut thy hand from thy poor brother; but thou shalt surely lend him sufficient for his need in that which he wanteth. Beware lest there be a base thought in thy heart, saying, The seventh year, the year of release is at hand; and thine eye be evil against thy poor brother, and thou give him nought; and he cry unto Jehovah against thee, and it be sin unto thee. Thou shalt surely

give him, and thy heart shall not be grieved when thou givest unto him; because that for this thing the Lord thy God will bless thee in all thy work, and in all that thou puttest thy hand unto. For the poor will never cease out of the land: therefore I command thee, saying, Thou shalt surely open thy hand unto thy brother, to thy needy, and to thy poor, in thy land (Deu 15:7-11).

The prophets also uphold the Mosaic standards for treatment of the poor (Eze 18:12-17; 22:29; Jer 5:28; 22:13, 16; Is 10:2; Amos 2:6, 7; Zec 7:9, 10), as do also Job (20:19; 24:3, 4, 9-14; 29:12-16; 31:17) and the psalmists. Postbiblical Jewish books continue the same (e.g., Tobit 12:8-9; Ec'us 4:1, 4; 7:32).

Third, there were two benefits for the poor derived from the recurring sabbatical year. Just as every seventh day was a rest day for man and beast, so every seventh year was a rest for the land. All fields were to remain unplanted and all vineyards and orchards untended. During this year there was to be no harvest of grain, no systematic vintage of grapes or gathering of fruits. Rather they were to "let it rest and lie fallow, that the poor of thy people may eat" (Ex 23:11, cf. Lev 25:6). This was the first benefit—extra food. The owner of land, himself, could gather from what grew "volunteer," as farmers used to say, but he could not exclude slaves, hired servants, and sojourners. The sabbatical year was also twelve months of relief for debtors wherein there was a moratorium on all debts. (Deuteronomy 15:7-11 makes it plain that the year of release from debts was a regularly recurring seventh year, the same calendar year throughout the land, rather than the seventh year of any particular indebtedness.) This is the second benefit. Though the language of Deuteronomy 15:1-6 is not free of ambiguity on the subject, it is close to certain that the year did not signal a general cancellation of all debts; rather a general twelve months' postponement of responsibility for payment.[10] Foreigners were not extended this particular exemption. This was logical, for the sabbatical rest of the land did not apply to them, and presumably they were as active in earning during the sabbatical year as any other, while the Israelite had no opportunity to earn from the usual agricultural pursuits.

Fourth, there was also a triennial tithe of all the produce of the land to be brought to the various city gates for the support of landless persons (Deu 14:28-29; 26:12-13). The sin of failing to care for this matter was rebuked by certain of the prophets (Amos 4:4; Mal 3:9-11).

Fifth, a truly enlightened aspect of the provisions of the Mosaic law for those whom modern people call unfortunate lies in the regulations on slavery. The parochial mind is almost sure to respond to this statement by asserting that any enlightened government would simply abolish slavery by laws, for it is a curious conceit of secularized modernity that slavery has been abolished in the modern world. This conceit arises out of a very narrow understanding of what constitutes slavery.

Consider the following. All persons forcibly detained in jails and prisons fall into categories ancient people called slavery. Indentured service, that is, a contractual relation whereby one man agrees to work wholly for another for a given period of time in return for payment of a certain amount of money or in consideration of some other value—say transportation from Europe to America as in the colonial era—would, in ancient times, have been called slavery. If we were to count all the people in Western society falling into these two categories, we would find that a very large proportion of our population turns out to be slaves in the ancient sense. Add to these the millions of persons virtually chained to their benches in factories or to the fields on plantations in many modern countries. In fact, a case can be made for the existence of less involuntary servitude (which is what we tend to mean by the word *slavery* in modern usage) in the ancient world, during many periods, than among us today. A penal system such as we have, wherein an adult man may be put in prison for a year for deliberate destruction of property or ten years for embezzlement, did not exist anywhere in ancient times. Beatings were given for many offenses, but restitution in money or by work was the way to pay for crimes against property. Thieves especially were put to work—usually for the benefit of those they robbed—until full restitution had been made. So while we do not sell into involuntary servitude populations of cities conquered in war as the ancients did, slavery in the ancient sense of the word is still with us.

The Mosaic law was keyed to the times in which it was given. The law therefore overtly acknowledged the existence of slavery—

something Western governments of today do not do—and regulated it in such a way as to protect the rights of all concerned. According to the customs of the time, even hired service was regarded as incompatible with freedom, though it was not regarded as degrading, for both hired persons and slaves enjoyed high regard. There are numerous stories favorable to stewards recorded in Scripture. The existence of a highly paid wage-and-salary-earning section of the population, enjoying political franchise and complete social freedom, is a recent development. According to the customary usage of the times, slavery is not treated as a moral evil at all in the Bible. Rather, even in the very Hebrew word for slave, the value of work is emphasized, especially willing labor for another. "A servant in the Hebrew mind (and the Bible is a Hebrew book) was primarily one who did work. The root of the word means that. But because most of the hardest work was often done by slaves, the word came to mean slave, and this word *'ebhedh* is the one so often rendered 'bondservant.' By extension it came to mean one who, like a slave, had no will of his own, no liberty of his own, save to do the will of his master."[11] The laws of Moses made any such permanent arrangement wholly voluntary. Hence the prophecies of Isaiah (esp. 52:13—53:12) innocently and approvingly use this word for slave of the coming Saviour of men who knew no law save the will of His Father, and calls Him "the slave of the Lord." Hence kings are called slaves (English Bible, servants) of God, persons in the public service are honored to call themselves slaves of the king, and even prophets and priests are known as slaves of God. Paul does not feel degraded to be known as the slave (Gr. *doulos,* Ro 1:1) of Jesus Christ, and he did not hesitate to return to his Christian master a slave, Onesimus, converted through his ministry. He encouraged slaves to give obedient service (Eph 6:5; Col 3:22), not even recommending manumission (1 Co 7:21-23).

But men being evil, innumerable evils existed in connection with slavery, especially in the exploitation of the services of women and girls, their charms and graces. We shall restrict our remarks here to certain features illustrating the law's care for the rights and needs of both slaves and their masters.

There were three circumstances under which an Israelite could become the slave of another Israelite: (*a*) a man in poverty could voluntarily sell himself (Lev 25:39), that is, his services, to another, in order to maintain himself and his family or to gain anything else he might wish. He could do so in order to redeem mortgaged family property (Lev 25:25), to buy a desired article, pay a debt, and so on. He could not be seized by a creditor and sold as a slave nor could his children be seized and sold as slaves to pay their father's debt;* (*b*) the law of restitution basic to all Mosaic legislation provided that a thief was bound to work out the value of his theft in bondservice, presuming him to be without other resources, to the one robbed, plus indemnities (Ex 22:1-4). The law does not elaborate, but Jewish sources show that this was interpreted to mean that when the thief had worked out his debt and indemnities, he was to be freed.[12] Like all Hebrew slaves, he would be free in any case after the maximum of six years of servitude. An Israelite thief could not be sold to a foreigner, for that in effect would put him outside the sphere of Israel's religion;[13] (*c*) a father could sell a daughter of tender years to another with a view to his taking her to wife for himself or for his son (Ex 21:7-11). All her usual rights were protected, and the "sale" price was hardly different from the usual dowry. While the female slave was in the service of her master, though subject to his discipline as would have been the case if she were his daughter, her chastity was to be protected, her physical welfare provided for and, in case of marriage, she was to receive the same treatment as any other Jewish woman: "If he espouse her unto his son, he shall deal with her after the manner of daughters" (Ex 21:9).

These various indications render it close to certain that personal poverty was the only reason for one Israelite's bondslavery to another Israelite. The kidnapping of persons for sale later as slaves, familiar to us in the case of all the African slaves imported to the new world, was a capital crime in Mosaic law (Ex 21:16; Deu 24:7). It is therefore improper to draw exact parallels between the humane and merciful institution of slavery in the Bible and the

---

*Second Kings 4:1 and Nehemiah 5:5 report cases of seizure of children of debtors. These appear to be cases of flagrant breaking of Mosaic law and accommodation to heathen practices in degenerate times. The case of selling a debtor and his family by a creditor in the parable of Jesus (Mt 18:23-35) is drawn from Roman usage, not biblical.

cruel exploitation of kidnapped African primitives and their off-spring. The latter was both immoral and criminal from the start. The law prescribed treatment for slaves that was in every way humane and just. The bondman could always look forward to a termination of servitude not indefinitely removed, for the law limited his term to no more than six years (Ex 21:2). If his debt was paid, he was released; and if the year of jubilee occurred before the six years were up, his servitude became automatically terminated (Lev 25:40-41).

While he was a bondservant, he could expect, as one of the children of Israel, to have all his personal, civil, and religious rights carefully respected, being in no manner disenfranchised by his temporary bondservitude (Lev 25:39-46). During his six-year term, he was not to be oppressed. When his time of servitude came to an end, he was not to be sent out naked and without provision (Deu 15:14-15, 18). There would be cases when, for fear of promptly falling into debt again and then to resume slavery under a less generous master, the slave would go through the process of becoming a perpetual slave of his master (Ex 21:5-6; Deu 15:16-17).

He was protected by law against personal injury from his master (Ex 21:20, 27-28). Jewish interpreters have taken these regulations seriously. Authorities assert: "The Rabbinists [medieval Jewish scholars] specified a variety of duties as coming under these general precepts [Lev 25:39-43]; for instance, compensation for personal injury, exemption from menial duties, such as unbinding the master's sandals† or carrying him in a litter, the use of gentle language on the part of the master, and the maintenance of the servant's wife and children, though the master was not allowed to exact work of them."[14]

Though the lot of an Israelite bondman might be hard, ordinarily it was not so:

> In a community which attached such importance to the family, in which work was scarcely conceivable outside the framework of the family, a man or woman on his own was without protection or means of support. The slave was at least assured of the necessities of life.

---

†This gives depth to John the Baptist's statement, "Whose shoes I am not worthy to bear" (Mt. 3:11), and explains why Peter recoiled so when Jesus came to wash his feet (Jn 13:8).

More than that, he really formed part of the family, he was a "domestic" in the original sense of the word. . . . He joined in family worship, rested on the sabbath (Ex. 20:10; 23:12), shared in the sacrificial meals (Deut. 12:12, 18) and in the celebration of religious feasts (Deut. 16:11, 14 . . . Ex. 12:44), from which the visitor and the wage-earner were excluded. A priest's slave could eat the holy offerings (Lev. 22:11), which visitors and wage-earners could not (Lev 22:10).[15]

One slave is reported to have married his master's daughter (1 Ch 2:34-35). Good men cared for the religious life of their domestics, who, as Job declares, are God's creatures as well as their masters (Job 31:13-15). There was therefore little social stigma attached to the slavery of citizens of Israel and it was not regarded as degrading to be a slave or to have slaves.

13

CIVIL GOVERNMENT IN BIBLICAL WISDOM

THE COMMENT of an eminent Old Testament authority will make immediately apparent the necessity for a chapter on the contributions of Proverbs to a book on the subject of civil government in the Bible.* "So far as concerns the sayings and wisdom poems which make up the book [Proverbs] consisting as they do of general truths about life and specific commands and prohibitions, warnings against evil and exhortations to right action, they cover the whole realm of life in all its vicissitudes—government and civil life, trade and justice, crafts and agriculture, family and slaves, work and holiday, joy and sorrow."[1]

There is a bulk of material on the subject of civil government. There are thirty-one chapters in Proverbs, averaging about twenty-seven verses each. Of these, at least sixty-five verses, equivalent of well over two chapters, relate to civil government. In addition, Proverbs treats many features of civil life indirectly related to government, such as real property; buying and selling; marriage and family; wealth and debts; the rich and the poor; suretyship and wages; weights and measures; loans, creditors and debtors; courts, plaintiffs, defendants, and witnesses; industry and thrift; laziness and ambition; wife and husband; harlotry; children and parents. All of these features have connection with civil government, especially in the Mosaic theocracy wherein all of life was of one piece with both government and religion. The present discussion restricts treatment mainly to texts of Proverbs which have direct bearing on civil government. Finally, there is the striking use of and dependence upon Proverbs by Paul in connection with the most outstanding text in

---

*Although other Old Testament books are categorized as wisdom literature, this chapter will restrict attention to the book of Proverbs.

the whole Bible on the subject of civil government, Romans 12:17—13:14.

The often noticed prevalence of secular concerns in the Proverbs should not obscure the fact the Mosaic religion underlay it all. Furthermore, the ideal harmonious community of human life wherein each lives happily and well is presupposed to be a believing community.[2] Even where no such community exists, the wisdom to guide the believer is from the Lord.

Whatever the ultimate human source of individual sayings (striking similarity between sections of Proverbs and portions of the Egyptian wisdom Teaching of Amen-em-ope and Teaching of Ahikar suggests verbal borrowing, though the borrowing may have been from the Hebrew Scriptures rather than the other way around),[3] the aphoristic sayings of Proverbs are fully commensurable with Israel's Mosaic monotheism and essentially spiritual faith. The sayings of Proverbs are indeed practical, but this scarcely renders them non-religious! They explain not merely how one may conduct practically successful social relationships in harmony with true morality, but also how such a life may be lived in harmony with spiritual faith engendered by a proper understanding of spiritual Mosaism and full commitment to it. It is no accident that even though there are few references to the Pentateuch in Proverbs, all of the Ten Commandments are supported by sayings in Proverbs. "The Jew was to be taught to recognize, in spite of all that kept him aloof from other races, a common ground on which he and they alike stood, in the law written in the hearts of all men, and was prepared to receive the teaching that the love of God and man was more than all whole burnt-offerings and sacrifices."[4]

Yet the wisdom of Proverbs can stand by itself. It is wisdom because it is truth. Though not understood fully in pagan circles, there is a commonality of sense, within limits, between the wisdom of Proverbs and the light of nature.

ESSENTIAL FEATURES OF CIVIL GOVERNMENT

The remark has already been made in connection with Mosaic legislation that a great deal of what in Anglo-Saxon countries would be called unwritten common (customary) law underlies the ancient Hebrew civil commonwealth. A state could not operate on the basis of Mosaic laws alone, then or now. Furthermore, government was by the rule of magistrates. They were *rulers* in a greater sense than are rulers in the West today. For though they were responsible to Mosaic laws in areas covered by those laws, and to a degree to customary law, part of that custom was to rely simply on the decisions of the ruler for whatever the people expected from their government. Government was therefore in much larger degree than in Western lands today a rule by just men rather than just laws.†

The essential elements in the Old Testament concept of civil magistrate are found in focus in a short text of Proverbs (8:15-16). The Hebrew text followed exactly in the margin of the American Standard Version reads:

> By me kings reign,
> And princes decree justice.
> By me rulers rule,
> And nobles, even all the judges of the earth.

"Kings . . . princes . . . rulers . . . nobles . . . judges," five words for the magistrates of the nations are heaped one upon another to exhaust the list.‡ These five names for the executive civil office divulge a good bit of what the Old Testament concept of such civil office was.

"Kings," from which is derived the Hebrew word "to reign," is the least definite of the words. The visible head of any civil government, whether strictly monarchial in constitution or otherwise, was called a *melekh*, king.

"Princes," is a word (*rōzēn*) occurring only six times, always in poetry. Authorities explain it by reference to a cognate Arabic word meaning to be "weighty, grave, firm of judgment"—incapable of be-

---

†This is true today, in spite of carefully worded constitutions and mountainous volumes of legislation. In spite of hopeful division of powers between legislative, judicial, and executive departments, men feel that hope for justice lies quite as much in the character and wisdom of the men exercising office as in the laws. Witness the almost frantic interest of the US electorate in the choice of the President, who though nowadays proposes much legislation, technically makes no laws at all, but only executes them.

‡C. H. Toy in *International Critical Commentary* (New York: Scribner, 1903) rearranges verse 16b to eliminate one of the four terms on (*a*) the basis of the Septuagint; (*b*) symmetry of the clause obtained thereby; and (*c*) supposed assimilation of the Proverbs text to Psalm 148:11 in transmission. Other recent translations follow ICC. Involved is changing *kal-shopetey* to *yish-phetû* and *'eretz* to *teritz*. There is not sufficient objective evidence to warrant those drastic changes.

ing shaken, figuratively of majestic repose, dignity in speech and action such as befits one invested with power.

"Rulers" (*sārîm*) is common, meaning about the same as "head man" in colloquial English, a person of recognized authority in the realm where he operates, hence "authority." There is apparently no metaphor when leading merchants are called princes (*sārîm*, Is 23:8). Similarly, in the time of David, a tribal elder said to be ruler (*nāgʰidʰ*) is called prince (*sar*). Certain angels are called princes (Dan 10:13), a leading prince being Michael (10:21).

"Nobles," singular *nadhibh*, primarily one who is inwardly inclined toward liberality, one of noble character; by extension, one of noble position.

The fifth word, *shōphēt*, "judge," is a comprehensive term for one who exercises civil authority, whether executive, judicial, or otherwise.

A sixth, and favorite word for Hebrew rulers used throughout the Old Testament, twice in Proverbs (8:6, 28:16) is *nāgʰidʰ*.§ The literal and obvious meaning is one who stands in front.

Note that absent from all these terms is the sense of "people's representative." The idea that authority moves from people to ruler is difficult to find anywhere in the Bible, and least of all in Proverbs. A striking example of the reverse of modern Western thinking is the story of the demand for a change from charismatic judges to dynastic kings in Samuel's time. The Israelites demand of Samuel: "Now make us a king to judge us like all the nations" (1 Sa 8:5) — no suggestion of a representative president to be designated by plebicite. They further project, "Nay; but we will have a king over us, that we also may be like all the nations, and that our king may judge us, and go out before us, and fight our battles" (vv. 19-20).

We next examine the terms in Proverbs 8:15-16 for the functions of civil officers. There are three. The first, "reign," is cognate with the word "king" in the passage, for in the frequent Semitic fashion of classes of denominative verbs, the verb "reign"—to play the part of a king—is derived from the noun. In such cases the noun and verb are often in subject-predicate relation. The first clause—noun

---

§Apparently the only place in the Bible among the forty-three occurrences where it is used of things instead of persons is Proverbs 8:6, though even there one is tempted to render it "rulers."

and verb—is literally "kings king" (noun, verb). But "reign" is the idea. What the queen of Britain does when she sits or stands in royal regalia, with symbols of her "power" on her person or in her hand or in view nearby is the idea. Nor is absent the sense of what Elizabeth's remote royal ancestors did when they overruled judges and parliaments to secure their own programs for the realm.

The second term is a phrase, "decree justice." Our modern democratic mind will automatically think of a legislative process, "but the usage of the language determines . . . only the significations of commanding, decreeing, or judging.[5] The word "justice" speaks plainly enough. So the sense is of a ruler promoting the welfare of his people, especially making decisions and giving orders in harmony with divine righteousness.

The third, "rule," is like "reign" and "king" above, cognate with "princes," so whatever the noun means, the verb derived from it also essentially means. Hence, "play the part of a ruler" or "do the job of a ruler" gets at the basic meaning. The civil power, originating in higher sources, rather than democratic ones, is sardonically put by the rebels against Moses, where they charge that he has, without warrant, kept on "playing the prince over us [see Num 16:3]."[6]

There is a fourth term implicitly employed here, *shōphēt*, the word for "judge." It comprehends all the functions of the magistrate as ruler. Once only elsewhere in Proverbs (31:9) the word appears in this customary sense.||

Now let us return to examine the nature of the power or sovereignty by which magistrates exercise their office: "By me kings reign," and so on (see Pr 8:15). This is spoken by "Wisdom," which is personified and associated with God the Creator and sovereign Lord of providence in a remarkable way in this portion of Proverbs.#

Without pressing the hypostatizing of Wisdom to the point of making her (the Hebrew word is feminine in gender) identical with God, and

---

||*Māshăl*, a broader terms for "rule," appears three times in Proverbs (12:24; 17:2; 22:7), but not in the sense of civil ruler. Three others which have overtones of oppressive rule do not appear in Proverbs (*shālăt, rādhāh, and rûdh*). Finllay, *shālît*, used several times in the Bible, occurs only once in Proverbs, but not in the sense of ruler (22:20).

#Certain authors, notably Dietrich Bonhoeffer (*Ethics*, trans. N. H. Smith [New York: Macmillan, 1965], pp. 332-39), have a theory that all government is Christological, that in some special way rulers are all Christ's representatives, ruling by His power. This passage on wisdom (cf. 1 Co 1:24) might be employed to strengthen that case.

certainly not equating her with wisdom, the attribute of God, the wisdom of rulers certainly is a divinely imparted wisdom. In verses 12 to 15, Wisdom is said to comprehend prudence, knowledge, discretion, fear of God, counsel, effectual working, and understanding. She is dissociated from evil, pride, arrogancy, and perversity. She claims, "I have might. By me kings reign." The "might" (*gebhurah*) —greatness—of wisdom is nothing different from the authority (*mishpāt, tsedhāqāh*, Ps 72:1-2) by which the Messianic kings reign. It is none other than Paul's, "there is no power but of God" (Ro 13:1) and Jesus' "no power . . . except it were given thee from above" (Jn 9:11). As in the case of a Saul or a Pilate, the gifts associated with the divine wisdom may be perverted and lost. Nevertheless, the gifts and qualities associated with civil rule are divinely conferred.

This seems to present a contrast with the low level of average accomplishment of rulers envisioned in many passages of Scripture (e.g., 1 Sa 8:10-20; Ps 2:1-5; 149:8). If so, it is man's failure, not God's. The divinely given powers of rulers are no basis for hope of utopia just yet!

OBSERVATIONS ABOUT RULERS AND THEIR FUNCTIONS

There is no clear way of arranging the seeming random aphorisms of the book of Proverbs. It is simplest to present the sayings in the order in which they come, with comment. "In the multitude of people is the king's glory; But in the want of people is the destruction of the prince" (Pr 14:28). This political precept appears striking among personal morality maxims. It is a protest against the prevalent Oriental kings' false ideal of national greatness. In neither conquest nor pompous display is the true greatness of a king, but in numerous people dwelling happily together.[7]

Next is a substantial section on the functions of kings, Proverbs 16:10-15:

> A divine sentence is in the lips of the king;
> His mouth should not transgress in judgment.
>
> A just balance and scales are the Lord's;
> All the weights of the bag are his work.

It is an abomination to kings to commit wickedness;
For the throne is established by righteousness.

Righteous lips are the delight of kings;
And they love him that speaketh right.

The wrath of a king is as messengers of death;
But a wise man will pacify it.

In the light of the king's countenance is life;
And his favor is as a cloud of the latter rain.

Toy points out that "the reference is to all sovereigns, not merely to those of Israel" and that though it is "the ideal king whose character is . . . sketched" in verses 10-13, the actual kings are in view in verses 14-15.[8] The reader gains knowledge of what a king ought to be and do as well as some insight into what most kings actually are and do. Delitzsch points out, "For as little as the New Testament teaches that the Pope . . . is infallible so little does the Old Testament [teach] that the theocratic king . . . was infallible.[9]

Some interpreters regard verse 10 as saying that when the king makes judicial decisions, the decision has divine force. If infallibility be not affirmed, this is sound biblical teaching. Yet others, who surely are correct, agree with Stuart that "what is here meant is, that what a king utters is of high import and authority. . . . Since this is the case, he should look well to it, that he utters nothing perfidious or prevaricating."[10]

The teaching of verse 11 about honest weights and measures in commercial dealings is a poetical reframing of the laws of Leviticus 19:36 and Deuteronomy 25:13-16, and an extension of the eighth commandment, "Thou shalt not steal." Micah 6:11 shows that the God of justice will judge the man who misuses the national system of weights and measures, even though the king rather than God has fixed the standards and ordered their use. There is no sphere wherein one must be subject to civil law "for conscience sake" (Ro 13:5) to a greater degree than in weighing and measuring items for sale (cf. Lev 19:35-36).

The teaching of verse 12 may be taken in two ways: It is abomination to God for the king to do wrong, or, It is abomination to the king for the people to do so. In either case, especially the second, as many passages already cited in these pages from Pentateuch and prophetic books amply prove, "the throne," (i.e., the orderly peaceful conduct of civil life) cannot continue. Verse 13 amplifies this thought.

Verses 14 and 15 are practical advice to citizens, considering the weaknesses and faults of rulers, for success in dealing with them. There will be no infallible perfect king until Messiah comes (Is 16:5).

Several scattered maxims offer guidance to magistrates in wise and fair treatment of their subjects. It is wrong to punish righteous high-minded folk (17:26). The magistrate must not render decisions hastily without hearing both sides of a matter (18.13). False witnesses must be punished severely and invariably (19:5, 9; 21:28). As in the Pentateuch and prophetic books, there are frequent admonitions to magistrates concerning fair merciful treatment of God's poor. They are not to be further deprived because seemingly defenseless, for God is their defender and will ultimately avenge them of mistreatment (22:22-23).

Among these maxims is a striking set of observations on stable government: "For the transgression of a land many are the princes thereof: but by a man of understanding and knowledge the state thereof shall be prolonged. A poor man that oppresseth the poor is like a sweeping rain which leaveth no food" (Pr 28:2-3, KJV). There is a question whether the word for transgression (*pësha*^{c}), meaning "rebellion," should be thought of as against God, by various sins of the people, or against the king, as in a revolution. Many commentators prefer the latter. In the former case, the familiar teaching is "that a land which apostatises from revealed religion becomes at once the victim of party spirit, and a subject of contention to many would-be rulers,"[11] In the latter case, "A revolt against a ruler leads to rapid changes of dynasty,"[12] as the history of the kingdom of Israel illustrates. If, however, a wise magistrate is at the helm of state, stable government continues, to the benefit of all concerned. The best interpretation of Proverbs 28:3 is that in times of civil turmoil, men frequently elevate a poor man of the people, like themselves, to be head of government. Such a ruler usually turns out to be the most avaricious oppressor of all, plundering the people and countryside of the little they have, like a torrential rain which washes away the seed grain instead of moistening, nourishing, and bringing it to harvest.

Still other proverbs warn against wicked or stupid men in public office (e.g. 28:15-16) and note how the people sigh in unhappiness as result of rule by such men (e.g. 29:2). The benefit of securing rights by just administration is contrasted against the destruction brought by securing favors through bribes given to corrupt officials (29:4).

Near the close of Proverbs there is a greater density of material to and about civil rulers—about twenty verses in chapters 29-31. Two of these have been just treated. One we reserve for later. The remaining seventeen consist chiefly of advice to or information about certain features of administration. First is 29:12-14:

> If a ruler hearkeneth to falsehood, all his servants are wicked.
> The poor man and the oppressor meet together;
> The Lord lighteneth the eyes of them both.
> The king that faithfully judgeth the poor,
> His throne shall be established forever.

The teaching is that subordinate civil administrators tend to conform to the weaknesses of their head. If the chief has an ear for falsehood, self-serving advice, and so on, that is what his subordinate civil administrators will provide for him in return. The twelfth verse might also be taken to mean that after the king's appetite for gossipy falsehood has been whetted a bit, he ceases to trust any of his subordinates, for they all seem like liars. Verse 13 teaches the familiar doctrine of providence met throughout the Bible, with its presently much-resented implication: God is the benign Creator of all social classes; whatever evil may result therefrom can be overruled for good. Earlier in the Proverbs it is said in this connection, "A good name is rather to be chosen than great riches, and loving favor rather than silver and gold. The rich and the poor meet together: The Lord is the maker of them all" (22:1-2). The author of these sentences was hardly either a capitalist or a socialist! Yet there is positively no support here for any national policy which neglects justice for the poor classes, for the fourth verse makes clear that so to do is to endanger the permanence of any government at all. As we have noted in connection with the Mosaic law, the poor have certain claims for relief rooted in justice, not merely in mercy. Disapproval is expressed concerning those sudden elevations of persons of inferior rank to head of state by coup d'etat. A similar statement appears at 19:10. Biblical history furnishes several such disasters (e.g., Zimri, 1 Kings 16:9), while the Egyptian and various Asiatic monarchies furnish many examples. Sometimes even slave eunuchs were so elevated or assisted others' violent elevation. Verses 29-31 of chapter 30 are in praise of stable government, discouraging any form of violent internal resistance to central authority.

The materials end with a queen mother's hopeful warmhearted advice to her son, consisting chiefly (and from a mother's viewpoint) of cautions against overindulgence in the pleasures of the harem and against the use of intoxicating liquor by kings (31:1-7). According to the Syriac reading of verse 3 ("the food of kings" instead of "that which destroyeth kings"), overindulgence in luxurious food is advised against also.

OBSERVATIONS ABOUT CITIZENSHIP

There are at least twenty-one maxims of this category in Proverbs. The first two (11:10-11) clearly identify true community prosperity of every sort with the fruit of righteousness. This should not be pressed to the point of making *rich* equal to *righteous* and *poor* equal to *wicked,* for the Proverbs clearly are not on the side of that perversion. Rather the doctrine is that if the wicked prosper, the community will reap disaster: "When it goes well with the righteous, the city rejoices; and when the wicked perish there are shouts of gladness. By the blessing of the upright a city is exalted, but it is overthrown by the mouth of the wicked." Further, the greatness of a country lies in its righteous people and their righteous actions not in its wealth, military prowess or prestige, for "Righteousness exalteth a nation: but sin is a reproach to any people" (14:34). Therefore, the king should favor the righteous elements of the commonwealth and suppress the influence of those who bring shame on the land by immoral living (14:35, KJV), "The king's favor is toward a wise servant: but his wrath is against him that causeth shame." A valid aristocratic principle is introduced at 19:10, "Delicate living is not seemly for a fool; Much less for a servant to have rule over princes." That is, not only are the material benefits of high position inappropriate for certain types of persons, but in every case, those properly equipped should rule. The teaching is, as noted elsewhere, that the best government is ruled by the best (morally, intellectually, spiritually) people. The problem on any constitutional theory is how to find such people and install them in office and keep them there. The righteous nevertheless are cautioned to trust in God more than in national armies, though military preparedness is not discouraged (21:31).

Special warning is given to heed the ancient property rights of the families of Israel—as would be natural considering the large importance of permanent family land. tenure in the Pentateuch and the detailed descriptions of the tribal-family lands in Joshua and other Old Testament books: "Remove not the ancient landmark, Which thy fathers have set. . . . Remove not the old landmark; And enter not into the fields of the fatherless: For their Redeemer is strong; He will plead their cause against thee" (Pr 22:28; 23:10-11). These aphorisms appear to have a relation to the land tenure system of Israel. As I have elaborated at length in connection with the Mosaic laws in this regard, there was, strictly speaking, no landless class in ancient Israel. Proprietorship was vested in the various families or clans, all of whom received lands in the original settlement. Some place was everyone's home. *Use* of land, only, could be alienated, and that only for forty-nine years at most. Encumbered real estate was always subject to redemption by a member of the clan. This system apparently was observed up to the very latest periods of Hebrew history. But there was no scientific system of survey. Therefore ancient landmarks—mainly stonepiles—were of great importance. Hence, though a powerful person could not steal property or alienate it permanently except by gross violence scarcely possible even for a king (as the story of Ahab and Naboth's vineyard illustrates) he might by stealth or bold terror reduce a poor man's territory by unlawfully moving a landmark. It is precisely this crime which the passages condemn. The sanctions open to the poor are surprising. The magistrate, police, and courts are not mentioned. Rather, God Himself, as next of kin, is introduced as the poor man's resource. Among the duties of able kinsmen toward their brethren were to buy back alienated family property as *redeemer* (*go'ĕl*); to perform unspecified favors, or do the part of a *kinsman* (*gā'ăl*); in the days before systematic civil procedures were available to punish his kinsman's murderer as *avenger* (*go'ĕl*); to present favorable testimony for a kinsman in court as *vindicator* (*go'ĕl*). It is in this last sense that *go'ĕl* is used in Proverbs 23:11. We are to understand that when human justice fails to right wrongs perpetrated on the godly, the case ultimately will be carried to the highest court, at which God will vindicate the rights of His own people. This seems to discourage use of any private physical force to restore the loss. Modern situations wherein certain governments expropriate the private property of great industrial corporations or wherein socialist regimes confiscate the landholdings of great hereditary estates to distribute them to landless poor or to make collective state farms scarcely is the sort of situation contemplated by these proverbs—whatever the morality of such actions.

Hints about success in private dealing with government function-aries are offered. In a general way, diligence in business will bring advancement (22:29). One is advised to display modesty and re-straint in the presence of high officials (23:1-2). A quiet manner and great forbearance will favorably impress the good ruler (25:15).

Proverbs 25:2-7 makes a point about the behavior of kings which is coupled with some remarks on wise behavior of citizens before kings. Perhaps the best interpretation of verses 2 and 3 is that just as the greatness of God in creation and providence are great mysteries, challenging even kings to discover God's ways insofar as they relate to the state, so the mysterious workings of the king's mind are ground for serious reflection for those under them. Furthermore, verses 4 and 5 seem to say that "the true ideal of government is that of a watchful rule separating the evil from the good. The king himself, like the Lord Whom he represents, is to sit as 'a refiner of silver.' "[13] In view of this, pushing and lobbying for favors is said to be not merely unsuccessful, but self-destructive in the long run: "Put not thyself forward in the presence of the king, And stand not in the place of great men: For better is it that it be said unto thee, Come up hither, Than that thou shouldest be put lower in the presence of the prince" vv. 6-7). Jesus employed these very words to discourage boastful aggressive social manners for selfish purposes (Lk 14:8-10).

This section closes with some remarks on two passages which specifically condemn both deliberate social agitation aimed at com-munity disruption and violent political revolution. Toy translates Proverbs 24:21-22, "Fear Yahweh, my son, and the king, And with those who change have naught to do; For suddenly arises their ruin, and the destruction of them both." "Those who change," according to Toy, "can mean only political agitators."[14] Most interpreters understand verse 22 to say that both God and the king, who represents God, join in bringing sudden destruction to agitators against civil peace, together with those who join with them. The second text reads, "Scoffers set a city in a flame, But wise men turn away wrath" (29:8). The scoffers are the irreverent activists who mock standards, laws, authorities, and those who support them. They are the strident voices, sometimes claiming to be prophetic, but really quite the contrary. They "laugh at moral obligations and stir up the passions of their fellow citizens."[15] "They . . . excite the city . . . by the dissolution of the bonds of mutual respect and of piety, by the letting loose of passion, they disturb the peace and excite the classes of the community and individuals against each other."[16] Contrariwise, wise men—those in touch with the divine Spirit, being true servants of God (cf. Is 52:13) will turn away wrath, that is to say, they will use their strength to reduce the animosities and to calm the excesses of excitement and to support the constituted authority in the community as far as possible.

Any reader of Proverbs of politically radical sentiments who is offended by this line of doctrine, or on the other hand, anyone too hopefully dedicated to the social-political status quo, might well ponder the rebuke to both kinds of thinking in the last aphorism to be introduced in this connection: "Many seek the ruler's favor [whether of the present establishment or the new regime]; but a man's judgment [justice] cometh from Jehovah" (29:26, cf. v. 25). Government is of divine institution and a necessary instrument for the ordering of society. But it does not solve many problems. It cannot even guarantee physical safety. Man's only sure hope for this world or the one to come is in God.

Before passing on to other matters, we pause to note the link between these biblical teachings and ourselves. They are, indeed, in part addressed to persons living under the theocratic government of the Mosaic constitution. Yet no direct appeal is made to Mosaic formulae. The authors of Proverbs speak in general terms throughout; they enunciate universal truths. As noted earlier, many of the sayings have near exact verbal equivalence to portions of the wisdom writings of Gentiles. Two portions may even be addressed to Gentile heads of state (see 30:1-10; 31:1-9).** In a world which has a basic moral order, such as the Bible says it has, wherein God is the king, the Lord of providence, as the Bible claims, no civil community can operate apart from those principles of human action and of human association, which God has ordained. They have been woven into the structure of the whole economy of society. Therefore there should be no hesitation about applying the principles of divine wisdom in Proverbs to civil relationships in all ages.

The primary interest of this book is in biblical teachings on only one aspect of society, civil government. Other aspects of society, however, impinge on this subject. Furthermore, throughout history, various peoples have made civil government a sort of comprehensive category for all aspects and functions of society, tending toward the idea that society equals civil community. This is a growing trend at present. Inasmuch as Proverbs has much to say on many aspects of society, brief attention is directed at several of these.

FEATURES OF SOCIETY ASSOCIATED WITH CIVIL GOVERNMENT

MARRIAGE AND FAMILY

One normally should provide some degree of material security before marriage (24:27). A good marriage partner and a sound marriage are among the greatest divine benefits (Pr 18:22; 19:14). Wives are cautioned against several familiar faults—nagging (21:9, 19), boisterous manners (9:13), quarrelsomeness (19:13; 27:15). Husbands are encouraged to love their own wives, the physical aspects being mentioned (5:15-19), and to eschew adultery (5:20). Wives are to be faithful, too, remembering that marriage is a covenant with God (2:17), and while not restricted to the home as an outlet for her energy (31:16), the wife is to make her home a career (12:4). If she neglects her home, she is foolish (14:1). The good wife described in 31:10-31 is not only industrious and loyal to her home, but she is also generous and kind to others outside her home, with a wide range of interests and activities. Children are to be taught true faith

---

**Commentators in the main do not favor the idea that either "Agur, son of Jakeh" or "Lemuel, king of Massa" are Gentiles, but they have not eliminated it as a possibility.

(14:26). They are to be disciplined (22:15; 23:13) and trained for useful adult responsibility (22:6). Children are already building character and reputation (20:11), being thereby either a joy or a pain to parents, depending on their character and behavior (10:1; 15:20). They are to respect parents as long as life lasts (6:20; 19:26; 23:22). They fail to do so with peril of eternal destruction (20:20).

PROPERTY AND ECONOMICS

While the right of acquisition of private property is assumed, and in a measure is approved, in many sayings the form of ownership is not prescribed. Family proprietorship of real estate has already been noted. Other types of property were personally owned. Such are properly passed down by inheritance—specifically houses and riches (19:14). It is proper to work for profit (13:4; 14:23), and wisdom may be employed to gain wealth (3:16; 24:3). Industrious people shall make legitimate material gain while indolent shall not (10:4; 13:4). Idle chatter is the road to poverty (14:23). Theft and fraud are condemned (13:11; 20:10; 21:6); they lead to ultimate loss (28:20, 22). Borrowing is discouraged (22:7). A puzzling statement on taking of interest on money lent to others, seems to be only against excessive interest (28:8).[17] Taking interest from Israelites is forbidden in the Pentateuch (Ex 22:25), since money was usually lent to poor people to sustain life, rather than to the well-to-do to promote commerce.

Acquisition of wealth, though entailing certain spiritual perils, is approved (13:8; 14:20; 21:20). This does not quite constitute a blessing on the modern capitalistic system, many features of which Solomon, no less than the financially uninitiated of today, would have found hard even to understand, much less approve. Yet some basic features of simple, non-doctrinaire capitalism are accepted as right. Material blessings must not be squandered away (29:3). We have already noticed rights of inheritance, private ownership and private enterprise. There is no hint that privately held wealth is a sin against those who are not wealthy. Wealth has a necessary place and many uses. Practically, it is hard to get along without, for it provides at least some self-respect and social esteem (12:9), is helpful in adding to the number of one's friends (19:4), and in providing peace (21:14) and protection (10:15).

Yet the dangers of wealth are noted, for "he that trusteth in his riches shall fall" (11:28), and stewardship of wealth in the service of God and man is recommended (3:27-28; 14:31; 21:3). Moral and spiritual riches are of greater value than material riches (15-16; 17:1), for "a good name is rather to be chosen than great riches" (22:1). Wealth must not take God's place in one's life (11:28), on pain of divine judgment (11:4).

Some concluding observations are in order. First, complete absence of any theoretical, doctrinaire approach to civil life is a pervasive feature of the biblical wisdom. One gains the impression that the magistrates mentioned in the book might receive pretty much the same counsel in whatever land they lived and under whatever sort of social-political-economic systems. Some systems are more amicable to biblical religion than others, yet except where biblical faith is proscribed and persecuted as a matter of state policy, it seems likely that the wisdom of this book is generally applicable. Of course, when ungodly theories of man and society are made a matter of state policy, there will be special difficulties, in which case the man of faith can only pray for a change of regime. Second, the general force of biblical wisdom in the social sphere is conservative in the best sense of that word. The best things are to be preserved, never rightly destroyed by mere human initiative for any reason whatsoever. Stable institutions, stable social relationships, strengthening of civil order and authority are supported. Disruptive agitation, revolution, and active civil disobedience all are condemned. It is perhaps significant in this connection that the first important modern political party, put together by biblically committed Christians—party of Abraham Kuyper in the Netherlands almost a century ago—was called the Anti-revolutionary Party.[18]†† Third, the biblical wisdom is also "liberal" in the best sense of that word. It aims at relief of poverty by public justice and private generosity (though assistance of the poor by public funds

††In this connection, it is noteworthy that theologians of the Reformation found the principle of civil disobedience following hard on the principle of civil obedience. The latter is the normal and almost invariable procedure. The former applies only in the extraordinary situation when the sovereign claims of God take precedence over the claims of civil government. This type of thinking is found in both Calvin and Luther and among their followers to the present day.

is not condemned thereby). Extension of the benefits of nature's bounty and the gifts of God are encouraged, but never at the cost of robbery of the rich, nor to the encouragement of indolence or avarice on the part of anyone. The tone of the book is calm. It offers no encouragement to the people and parties who are determined to push the public into some preconceived economic or social pattern; it tends to hush the strident voices.

14

THE PRACTICE AND EXAMPLE OF JESUS WITH REGARD TO CIVIL GOVERNMENT

AT THIS STAGE of discussion, we are interested in what Jesus and the apostles did in their personal relationships with government and what they manifest in their attitudes toward it, rather than specific instructions which they may have given. One is justified in saying that if their example be taken as normative—and properly interpreted, in historical context, it is—there is very helpful guidance for finding one's way through the intricate problems of Christian relation to government on the personal level.

Let it be observed that Jesus was an ancient Jew, not a modern Englishman or American. He lived out His life in a particular historical situation as regards social, political, and governmental matters. He began His life in a pious Jewish home wherein the Mosaic biblical religion was fervently believed and carefully practiced. Modifications of that system of religion imparted by exile, restoration, submission to Persian and Greek overlords, and brief national independence, followed by resubmission, this time to Roman conquerors, were familiar to him, as were the special problems created by the Roman political suzerainty. It is from that historical setting that Jesus' example speaks to us today.

Jesus lived out childhood and youth in obedient submission to His parents. Home life in Israel had a civil aspect more explicit than in American life. The fifth commandment, "Honor thy father and thy mother" was connected with the land (Ex 20:12), and the law of the land stood behind it. There was no distinction between religious laws and civil laws in ancient Israel. Church and state were one. Death by public stoning was the punishment prescribed for incorrigible disobedience to parents (Deu 21:18-21). It is thus certain that Jesus was fulfilling a civil, as well as religious duty, when at the beginning of his teenage years it is written of him that "he went down with them [i.e., from Jerusalem with Joseph and Mary], and came to Nazareth; and he was subject unto them" (Lk 2:51).

It is true that "the law was given through Moses; but grace and truth came through Jesus Christ" (Jn 1:17). There are, however, firm principles even in the teachings of grace relating to one's civil relationships, for the grace of God that appeared in Jesus came "teaching us that . . . we should live soberly, righteously, and godly, in this present world" (Titus 2:12, KJV). "Soberly" has primary reference to one's personal demeanor, mainly an attitude rather than action; "godly" has specific reference to formal duties toward God; while "righteously" refers to an external manner of living before God and man that conforms in act (hopefully, also in intention) to the laws of God. Thus conformity to divine revelations about conduct is part of the grace of God that appeared in Jesus. This grace of God began with a life of civil obedience to His parents, for Jesus "came to Nazareth; and he was subject unto them."

As an adult, Jesus likewise conformed to the laws of man on every level. He made no distinctions as far as obedience is concerned, between good laws and bad ones, between pertinent ones and outdated ones. This was true of the religious laws of that segment of society in which he was brought up—Mosaic rituals, festival observances, personal, family, and community obligations—the whole complicated, burdensome business of it. And, though the record is plain to the effect that He thought the administration both of religious and of civil laws to be unjust, He obeyed those laws nevertheless.

This comes very much as a contrast and rebuke to Western peoples and their so-called democratic ideas. It is quite contrary to the particular temper of our time. Yet it is doubtful if His high standard of civil obedience was quite approved of generally in the hearts of young men ever, for "foolishness is bound up in the heart of a child" (Pr 22:15), and the hearts of adults are more prone to wander than to serve God.

Peter's words relating the example of Jesus to our subject cannot be overlooked. He has admonished Christians, as sojourners and pilgrims—citizens of the kingdom of heaven whose affections are set on things above—to live in a manner that would point their pagan neighbors toward God (1 Pe 2:11-12). Then more specifically: "Submit yourselves to every ordinance of man for the Lord's sake . . . to the king . . . governors . . . . Fear God. Honour the king" (1 Pe 2:13-14, 17). Then admonishing even slaves to bear their subjugation respectfully, whether their masters be gentle or contrary, he presents the example of God's great servant prophesied in Isaiah 53, fulfilled in Jesus, as follows: "Because Christ also suffered for us, leaving us an example, that ye should follow his steps: Who did no sin, neither was guile found in his mouth: Who, when he was reviled, reviled not again" (1 Pe 2:21-23). So Christian duty toward human laws, whether of kings, governors, magistrates, parents, masters, slaves, schoolteachers, or shop foremen is that of obedience, not of rebellion. The example of Jesus teaches it, and the words of Peter concerning Jesus' example enforce it. It is not counsel of perfection for a few Christians who excel; rather it is a formula for all Christians in society.* It is not the complete formula, but it may not be omitted.

In light of these things, the frequent references to Jesus as a great nonconformist or revolutionary are not only brash, but patently untrue and grossly misleading, wholly misrepresenting the attitude and behavior both of Jesus and of the first generations of His disciples.

This is not to say that Jesus approved of everything in the religious and civil laws of his day, nor that he was silent regarding ineffective or unjust administration of laws, nor that he was obsequious or excessively deferential to official personages. His verbal tirades against Pharisees, Sadducees, scribes, priests, and prelates are well known. There is scarcely any passage in our language so fiercely denunciatory as Matthew 23, which reports His harsh public condemnation of the deeds of the scribes and Pharisees (vv. 13-29). Yet, even these hot words are in a context of respect for laws and for the officers who execute them. No one who ever heard an address by Jesus left with an angry impulse to storm the bastille, barricade the dormitory, invade the offices of the draft board, or occupy the president's office.

*Among the teachings of the Roman Catholic church is one that certain of the more rigorous ethical demands of the Bible were never intended for all Christians, but only for certain spiritual athletes to obey. This spiritual elite is composed mainly of the religious orders. See Vernon J. Bourke, *Ethics, a Textbook in Moral Philosophy* (New York: Macmillan, 1966); and *A New Catechism* (New York: Herder & Herder, 1967), pp. 122-24, 231-33, 410-16.

Those impulses arise from quite another source. Jesus' words were: "The scribes and the Pharisees sit on Moses' seat: all things therefore whatsoever they bid you these do and observe: But do not ye after their works: For they say, and do not. Yea, they bind heavy burdens and grievous to be borne, and lay them on men's shoulders; but they themselves will not move them with their finger" (vv. 2-4).

It was not different with civil laws and rulers. The two most important civil rulers of Palestine in Jesus' adult life were Pilate and Herod Antipas. When at home in Nazareth, Jesus was in Herod's dominions, as also when, as a Jerusalem-bound pilgrim south of the Sea of Galilee, He crossed the Jordan to walk its east bank southward, through a region then called Perea, toward a recrossing of Jordan near Jericho. In and around Jerusalem He was in territory controlled by the Roman governor, Pilate. Both of these civil authorities appear in the discourses of Jesus reported in the thirteenth chapter of Luke. Pilate is held up as something of a bloodthirsty tyrant (vv. 1-3), and Herod as "that fox," suggesting that the Pharisees who had just warned Him of Herod should go tell on him (vv. 31-32). Then Jesus showed Himself to be aware that His death would not take place in Galilee anyway. It would take place at Jerusalem, which was under Pilate's jurisdiction. So, though He was not disobedient toward civil officers, He gave them only their due, and no more. One suspects that He would not have enjoyed any time-serving job under any of them. He had none of the usual politicians' proclivity to sacrifice principle for the expedient. Yet near the end of His life, when Jesus stood before both Herod and Pilate, His conduct, while not obsequious, was correct.

In His public ministry, however, Jesus manifested no prejudice against official functionaries of religious or civil government, though He showed that He was familiar with their failings. Gentile rulers lorded it over their subjects, and cynically, in spite of such pompous effrontery, called themselves benefactors (Mt 20:25); publicans— the hated Jewish collectors of Roman taxes—were to be classified with harlots, heathen, and sinners (Mt 18:17; 21:31); His disciples would be ill-treated by Jewish councils and synagogue officials as well as by pagan governors and kings (Mt 10:16-18). Furthermore, Jesus was aware that His own unjust execution would occur when jealous chief priests and scribes delivered Him over to pagan magistrates for crucifixion (Mt 20:17-19, cf. Mk 10:32-34; Lk 18:31-33). Yet He was very friendly with a centurion, healing his servant and praising his faith extravagantly (Mt 8:5-13, cf. Lk 7:1-10); He was house-guest of publicans, even converting one into an apostle (Lk 5:27-32). Jesus was kind to the questions of several rulers, of one of whom it is said that Jesus looking upon him loved him (Mk 10:21; cf. vv. 17-22, cf. Lk 18:18). He seemed to have accepted the protection given citizens by the legal procedures of His country and religion (Jn 7:45-51, cf. Ex 23:1; Deu 17:6; 19:15; Pr 18:13), as did Paul later (Ac 23:1-3).

Though Jesus was poor, He had no poor man's prejudices against the well-to-do and the privileges accompanying wealth and property ownership. There is small comfort for economic egalitarianism or socialism in Jesus. He spoke approvingly of owners of vineyards who expected a reasonable return from investment (Lk 20:9-18); He accepted the generosity of rich people with cheerfulness (Lk 19:1-10) while pointing out the perils to the soul of great riches (Mk 10:17-25; Lk 16:19-31). Landowners, stewards, hired servants, merchants, bankers, generals, soldiers, kings, all the various personnel of the secular aspects of society wherein farming and business, government and military activity go on a profit-and-loss, earn-what-you-eat, get-what-you-can basis—were treated without pejorative overtones in the life and words of Jesus.

He apparently had no idea that society is corrupting, defiling, per se, to persons who get involved in it. He undoubtedly approved of John the Baptist's instructions to converted tax gatherers: Be fair in your assessments and collections! (Lk 3:12-13), rather than: Get out of the dirty work! and of his words to conscience-smitten soldiers: Don't use your professional position to extort money nor to gain vengeance on people you do not like, and quit bellyaching about army life! (Lk 3:14). If this is the secular Christianity that Bonhoeffer means, it must be approved by all right-minded Christians.

There remain two important questions: To what extent, if at all, did Jesus conceive of His mission as a political program? and Precisely how was political power involved in His condemnation and execution? The two questions are related.

In answer to the first question, two classes of texts emerge. First, a large number do definitely and in unmistakable language announce what sounds much like a public, political program. The angel Gabriel's words to our Lord's virgin mother, considered in the light of Old Testament prophecies lying directly behind them, must be placed in this category: "The Lord God shall give unto him the throne of his father David: and shall reign over the house of Jacob for ever" (Lk 1:32-33). This announcement unmistakably points to Jesus as the person designated by all the Old Testament prophecies of Messiah, the Son of David (narrowly considered apart from prophecies of the Son of man, Servant of the Lord, "that Prophet," etc.). The Messiah was to have a political program, exercising direct regal civil authority over all Israel, making Zion His capital, and extending His sway over all the earth. There was to be a program of spiritual renewal too, for prophets saw nothing inconsistent between a worldwide political commonwealth of Messiah and His work of worldwide spiritual judgment and spiritual renewal.

So also must His words be interpreted about seeing the kingdom of God come with power (e.g., Mk 9:1) and His bold acceptance of and even insistence upon the hosannas of the festival crowds on the occasion of His triumphal entry. They cried, "Blessed is the King that cometh in the name of the Lord" (Lk 19:38). Certain Pharisees demanded that He rebuke such words, whereupon He replied with this strong assertion: "I tell you that, if these shall hold their peace, the stones will cry out" (Lk 19:40). Before that day had passed, He assumed Messianic authority within the capital, for "he entered into the temple, and began to cast out them that sold and them that bought in the temple, and overthrew the tables of the money-changers, and the seats of them that sold doves; and he would not suffer that any man should carry a vessel through the temple" (Mk 11:15-16). The infuriated ecclesiastical authorities immediately set in motion definite steps to destroy Him, demanding the next day that He show cause for the "outrage" (Mk 11:27-33). At about the same time, during the last week, Jesus spoke several parables related to the future of the kingdom, in at least two of which, both directed against the Jewish ecclesiastical rulers, He spoke of violent overthrow of the Jewish capital and disruption of all national Jewish life. In the first of these two (Mt 21:33-41), a great deal of physical violence is spoken of, both by the partisans of the Jews and by the partisans of Jesus. A metaphorical interpretation may be given, and often is, but the bare narrative is still freighted with violence. Immediately follows the second parable (Mt 22:1-14), in which Jesus speaks of a king (God) making a marriage feast for his son (the Lord Jesus) and inviting guests (the Jews) through servants (the first gospel messengers). Those messengers are rejected, whereupon another set is sent out (usually now viewed as the gospel messengers to the Jews as reported in the early chapters of Acts). These messengers also the Jews rebuffed, abusing them and even killing some. In punishment, the father-king sends forth his armies (Vespasian and Titus, A.D. 68-70), destroys their city (Jerusalem), and furnishes his wedding feast with guests from everywhere.

Now, every verse in these sections gives the learned commentators an exegetical field day. They invite comment and discussion. But the point made earlier, a program of military-political action, is strongly suggested. Even at the Last Supper, Jesus encouraged His apostles to expect someday to "sit on thrones judging the twelve tribes of Israel" (Lk 22:30).

Second, there is another class of texts which plainly declare that Jesus' mission was thoroughly nonpolitical, that He had no intention to assume any civil functions at all, even among His own followers, much less over the Jews at large or over the nations in general. Here fall the several references to Jesus' refusal to cooperate with efforts to make Him king, His steadfast rejection of Zealot-supernationalist associations, and His mysterious discouragement of publicity to the effect that He was the promised Messiah, obviously preferring the title of "Son of man" to the title "Christ" (Messiah) and to be associated in the minds of his auditors with the suffering servant prophecies of Isaiah rather than with the "Son of David" prophecies. He did not, however, deny that He was the Christ nor reject the Son of David connection of His mission. Although the meaning of His responses to Pilate's inquiries is to this day obscure, it is plain that He did not think of Himself as a contender with Herod Antipas or Pilate for political leadership of the Jewish nation. Just how complete His dissociation was appears in a text not often noticed: "And one out of the multitude said unto him, Teacher, bid my brother divide the inheritance with me. But he [Jesus] said unto him, Man, who made me a judge or a divider over you?" (Lk

12:13-14). This is a clear disavowal of any civil jurisdiction over His followers.

Only by doctoring the biblical evidence through some form of source-criticism is it possible to get rid either of the political-visible kingdom element or of the spiritual, kingdom-of-love-and-grace element. Nor is such effort necessary.

There is a better way to bring these two elements into harmony. It became clear before long that the death of Christ, His subsequent resurrection, and His ascension were stages in a redemption which would ultimately win for Christ the bended knee of all His enemies. Our Lord's reign as King was inaugurated at His ascension to the Father and session at the Father's right hand (see Mk 16:19; Ac 2:34; 5:31; 7:55; Ro 8:34; 1 Co 15:25; Eph 1:20; Phil 2:6-11; Col 3:1; Heb 1:3; 8:1; 10:12-13; 1 Pe 3:22; Rev 3:21).[1] But His reign, though real, is not everywhere acknowledged. It will be acknowledged after the second advent. Thus unfolds the twofold-ness of Christ's advent. That which from the Old Testament perspective presented an enigma—suffering servant versus reigning king—unfolds as cross first, then crown; cross at first advent, crown at second; inauguration of reign at first advent, consummation of it at second. During the interval, the program of spiritual conquest by evangelism and Christian nurture proceeds quietly. To what extent some of the military-like language of conquest and rule may stand figuratively for that extension of a spiritual kingdom is difficult to say; perhaps none of it, and certainly not all of it, for there are features of many of the statements related specifically in other passages to our Lord's second advent. Psalm 110:1-2's sturdy language: "Until I make thine enemies thy footstool . . . Rule thou in the midst of thine enemies" is the formula applied in many places in the New Testament to explain the present epoch. The enemies of our Lord do not know it, but they were placed on a leash at Calvary. They now seem to have liberty. Insofar as they are constrained, it is by an invisible and unrecognized providence. Some day they will be snubbed to the post and brought to servile obedience. Our Lord set the example for nonpolitical, nonmilitary, spiritual extension of His kingdom throughout the present age. The arts of His servants are persuasion, prayer, preaching, and testimony; through the Word of God and through His Spirit.

Two quotations from later portions of the New Testament show how those closest to our Lord understood this—first Paul, the mighty missionary and intrepid churchman: "For though we walk in the flesh, we do not war according to the flesh (for the weapons of our warfare are not of the flesh, but mighty before God to the casting down of strongholds); casting down imaginations, and every high thing that exalted against the knowledge of God, and bringing every thought into captivity to the obedience of Christ" (2 Co 10:3-5).

The final testimony of inspiration is that of the author of the Apocalypse, a man who was in exile "for the word of God and the testimony of Jesus" (Rev 1:9), and who had seen martyr Christian souls in heaven "slain for the word of God, and for the testimony which they held" (Rev 6:9), who hears a great voice in heaven reporting how the brethren win their victories over the great dragon, the devil, as follows: "And they overcame him because of the blood of the Lamb, and because of the word of their testimony; and they loved not their life even unto death" (12:11).

The second question, How was political power involved in Jesus' trial and execution? (though of secondary importance, for Jesus' attitude is only secondarily involved) has bearing on our search, since the understanding Jesus' enemies had of His mission is involved. Modern critical study, much of it unfriendly to Christian orthodoxy and taking a low view of the Scriptures, has played fast and loose with this issue. There is little to be gained by reviewing all the critical discussion here.

Some of the facts are plain. At least a dozen times in the New Testament, the part of unbelieving Jews in the condemnation of Jesus is mentioned—by way of prediction, historical narrative, and retrospect. It is clear from these that the primary responsibility for Jesus' execution must be attributed to the Jewish nation, represented truly by the national religious leaders (the high priest and the Sanhedrin; see Mt 16:21; 20:17-19; 26:63-66; 27:20-26; Mk 8:31; 10:33-34; 14:61-65; Lk 9:22, 51; 13:22-35; 18:32). Theirs was the primary responsibility for His killing, and it was for an alleged crime against their law that they condemned Him and remanded Him to the Romans. This crime was blasphemy. Jesus acknowledged before the high priest that He was the promised Messiah and the divine Son of man of Daniel's prophecy (see Mt 26:63-64; Mk 14:61-62; Lk

22:66-71). To make such a claim falsely, of course, was blasphemy (i.e., to attribute to any mere creature the attributes and works of God). Jesus predicted that He would be condemned by the Sanhedrin and delivered to the Gentiles for execution. On that last sad trip "up" to Jerusalem, Jesus forewarned His twelve of Jewish plans to condemn Him: "And as Jesus was going up to Jerusalem, he took the twelve disciples apart, and on the way he said unto them, Behold, we go up to Jerusalem; and the Son of man shall be delivered unto the chief priests and scribes; and they shall condemn him to death, and shall deliver him unto the Gentiles to mock, and to scourge, and to crucify" (Mt 20:17-19). Another report of the same incident is even more explicit, if possible, that the Jewish court was the one that condemned Him, while the part of the Gentiles (Pilate and his soldiers) was not to conduct a trial of Jesus in the formal sense, but to execute (albeit reluctantly) the sentence of condemnation passed by the Sanhedrin: "Behold we go up to Jerusalem; and the Son of man shall be delivered unto the chief priests and the scribes; and they shall condemn him to death, and shall deliver him unto the Gentiles: and they shall mock him, and shall spit upon him, and shall scourge him, and shall kill him" (Mk 10:33-34).

One contemporary scholar, Oscar Cullmann, among others, has contended that the words of the supposed Aramic *Vorlage* lying behind the synoptic records were misunderstood by Matthew and Mark, the authors of the above quotations.[2] Neither, he claims, did they understand their sources on the exchange between Caiaphas and Jesus on whether or not Jesus claimed under oath ("I adjure thee") to be "the Christ, the Son of God" (Mt 26:63-65). Interpreters have quite uniformly taught that Jesus' words, "Thou hast said" mean "Yes, I am." This author says he meant, "No, I am not." Maybe, this author asserts, the Jews had the authority to execute those condemned by the Sanhedrin.[3]†

But evidence of Scripture is missing, and the logic is lame. This view cannot be sustained on the basis of the text of the gospels without subjectively grounded higher critical doctoring. The plain sense makes common sense. Certain conclusions of this author to

---

†T. W. Manson sees in the adulterous woman incident (Jn 7:53–8:11) a reference to the question of competence of Jewish courts in capital cases (*Only to the House of Israel: Jesus and Non-Jews* [Philadelphia: Fortress, 1964], pp. 11-12).

whom we refer we will cite later with approval. He does not need to wrest the Scripture to reach them. Rather,

> [Caiaphas], assembling the Sanhedrin at daylight . . . at length . . . with great difficulty, procured two witnesses who testified to Jesus' threat of destroying the temple . . . but with such discrepancy between themselves that Caiaphas broke the silence of Jesus by adjuring him respecting his Messianic claims, and on his avowal of his [Messianic] character made use of this admission to charge him with a sentence of death . . . after a formal vote of the full Sanhedrin early in the forenoon. Jesus was next led to the procurator Pilate's mansion for his legal sanctions upon the determination of the religious court. . . . The procurator . . . compelled to exercise jurisdiction . . . at length yielded to their demands, and . . . pronounced sentence for his execution on the cross.[4]

Long before this point in our discussion, certain interpreters will want to know why we have not introduced two passages which are frequently supposed to be Jesus' most important statements regarding our subject—one thought to disclaim any worldly political aspects of Jesus' program. The earlier statement falls at the point of Jesus' arrest in the garden, the later at the point of His second interrogation by Pilate. The earlier is: "Then they came and laid hands on Jesus and took him. And behold, one of them that were with Jesus . . . smote the servant of the high priest, and struck off his ear. Then saith Jesus unto him, Put up again thy sword into its place: for all they that take the sword shall perish with the sword. Or thinkest thou that I cannot beseech the Father, and he shall even now send me more than twelve legions of angels? How then should the scriptures be fulfilled that thus it must be?" (Mt 26:50-54, cf. Mk 14:47-50; Jn 18:10-11).

It will be helpful here to note that Jesus did not pronounce the use of military force ("the sword") immoral or improper in the hands of state authorities. In fact, Jesus even said Pilate's power, including evidently both that of sword (to wage war against enemy nations and seditious elements within the country) and of cross (to execute those judged guilty of capital crimes), had been given to Pilate by God (Jn 19:10-11). Nowhere did Jesus denounce the legitimate use of these powers of state. What is clear is that that stage of Jesus' course in the plan of God for His career, was not amenable to the use of physical force in its accomplishment. The New Testament in all parts rings the changes on the teaching that "thus it must be," that is, that Jesus must be delivered up to wicked men to die for the sins of mankind. God's "determinate counsel and foreknowledge" (Ac 2:23) appointed Him as the Lamb slain from the foundation of the world (1 Pe 1:19-20). Jesus was fully aware of this, and thus (the word is needed) on this occasion exclaimed, "The cup which the Father hath given me, shall I not drink it?" (Jn 18:11). In such a case, neither Peter's puny sword, nor God the Lord of armies' legions of angels were to be used to deliver God's Son from death. The fact that shortly before, Jesus had told His disciples that they might carry a sword is inconsistent with the notion that Jesus was hereby outlawing swords for everybody. These words are fully consistent with His doctrine that His present program for the disciples did not allow the use of the sword by them, as disciples, to advance their program. "All they that take the sword shall perish with the sword" is "an ordinary axiom in law adduced for the purpose of enforcing his disapproval of the unwarrantable conduct of Peter."[5] Pilate's soldiers (whose assistance the Jewish authorities had legally solicited hours earlier) and the high priest's officers were performing a legal arrest. The actions were certainly ill-conceived, but the government was not yet doing anything unlawful. One private citizen may not legally prevent the lawful arrest of another citizen. Peter was putting himself in the category of lawbreaker, and Jesus told him so. "All they that take the sword [unlawfully] shall perish with the sword [lawfully]" (Mt 26:52). "We know that the law is good if a man use it lawfully, as knowing this, that law is not made for a righteous man, but for the lawless and unruly . . . for murderers of fathers and murderers of mothers, for manslayers" (1 Ti 1:8-9).

The second passage thought by many to express in clear and unmistakable language Jesus' absolute rejection of any visible, political, nationalistic program within His "kingdom of heaven," relates to an exchange between Pilate and Jesus which transpired during his second interrogation by the procurator: "Pilate . . . said unto him, Art thou the King of the Jews? Jesus answered, Sayest thou this of thyself, or did others tell it thee concerning me? Pilate answered, Am I a Jew? Thine own nation and the chief priests have delivered thee unto me: what hast thou done? Jesus answered, My kingdom is not of this world: if my kingdom were of this world, then would my servants fight, that I should not be delivered to the Jews: but now is my kingdom not from hence. Pilate therefore said unto him, Art thou a king then? Jesus answered, Thou sayest that I am a king. To this end am I come into the world, that I should bear witness unto the truth" (Jn 18:33-37).

An interpretation common among many commentators and discussions of the kingdom message of Jesus is that when Jesus declared, "My kingdom is not of this world," He was clearly and unmistakably insisting that He had no plan, then or ever, to establish on earth a visible realm (call it state, nation, kingdom, government) comparable in any sense to the states of history. Those who take Old Testament prophecies of Messiah and His Jewish kingdom seriously and who yet follow this interpretation of the above text frequently then discover a "spiritual" or strictly symbolic interpretation of the Old Testament prophecies of Messiah's visible earthly kingdom. Others simply refer all those prophecies vaguely to the future. Still others find a place for literal fulfillment of Old Testament prophecies of a visible kingdom of Messiah in a future millennium, according to the system of interpretation called premillennialism.

It will not be necessary to treat all of this interesting passage as yet. A better explanation than the ones described above will be furnished by a closer examination of "My kingdom is not of this world" and "now my kingdom is not from hence" (v. 36). The chief features of this line of thinking now ensue. There is a presently inaugurated aspect of the kingdom of God, which, though as real as sunshine, is presently invisible to faithless men. It was inaugurated at the ascension of Christ and His session at the Father's right hand. The disciples (and certainly Pilate) evidence no understanding of this until Peter first expressed it (Ac 2:29-36). But there is an aspect of the kingdom that will be visible in the world when "the kingdom of the world is become the kingdom of our Lord, and of his Christ: and he shall reign for ever and ever" (Rev 11:15). This aspect of His kingdom, as our Lord carefully and painfully explained to his followers shortly before His passion, would transpire only "after a long time" (Mt 25:19, cf. the whole context of the parable of the talents). The disciples were in error, Luke distinctly indicates, "because they supposed that the kingdom of God was immediately to appear" (Lk 19:11, cf. context to follow in the parable of the pounds). Now certain interpreters would like us to believe that the two parables teach that the visible kingdom of God on earth was *never* to appear. But the Scripture, including Jesus' pregnant words, cannot be made to say it without wresting the Scriptures. Quite to the contrary, the apostles still were looking forward to a visible earthly kingdom of Christ after the resurrection of the Lord. Jesus, on His part, during His postresurrection ministry, while informing them that the visible kingdom was, indeed, as He had previously taught, to be delayed, gave no hint of a suggestion that it would never appear (see Ac 1:6-8). It is to be, as both of these parables amply demonstrate, at His second advent (see Rev 19:11—20:4). So, whether the present invisible inaugurated kingdom or the future visible consummated kingdom, the kingdom of Christ is not "of this world." The words, "of this world," translate *ek tou kosmou toutou,* that is, out of this world. Source rather than realm is the sense. Christ's kingdom comes from heaven and needs no human soldiers to fight for it. The "zeal of Jehovah of hosts will perform this" (Is 9:7). The present reign of Christ in heaven was to be secured by redemption, not by military conquest; it is fully visible only in heaven where Christ sits at the right hand of God, not in Rome or Jerusalem. Pilate need feel no challenge to his authority from such a king as this. The future consummation of the kingdom of Christ cannot rightly be said to be beyond history. No indeed! It will occur in history and is history's goal.

Pontius Pilate, however, had nothing to fear from any man or men, in this case Jesus and His disciples, from this quarter. As John later wrote, the visible kingdom of Christ is to be established when "the Word of God" comes with "the armies of heaven" at the end of this age (Rev. 19:11-16). It will not be secured by revolt from beneath, but by power from above, acting directly and visibly. So Jesus said, "My kingdom is not of this world . . . not from hence" (Jn 18:36). "From hence" is *enteuthen,* meaning, in relation to place, "from here" and "to indicate the reason or source."[6] So Jesus very clearly is making no comment on either the nature of His kingdom or its realm, rather on the power source of its establishment. The power source might well have been Pilate's concern if he had been impressed at all by the Jewish charges. But he was not so impressed for he knew that envy was the real basis of their charges (see Mk 15:10). This agrees with the very highest expressions of Old Testament Messianic prophecy, for it is there written of Him that: "The government shall be upon his shoulder . . . of the increase of his government . . . there shall be no end, upon the throne of David . . . *The zeal of Jehovah of hosts will perform this*" (Is 9:6-7 italics added).

15

THE TEACHINGS OF JESUS WITH REGARD
TO CIVIL GOVERNMENT

MOST DISCUSSION of Jesus' teaching on the reciprocal duties pertaining to the Christian and civil government begins and ends with the incident about rendering Caesar's things to Caesar and God's things to God (Mt 22:15-22; Mk 12:13-17; Lk 20:20-26). It is indeed Jesus' most extensive discussion of the subject. But a careful sifting of the gospels will yield a bit more than that.

The materials at hand are not extensive, nor do they insistently demand any particular logical or chronological order of treatment. I shall restrict my discussion in the main to two pivotal texts. Attention to some of Jesus' more random remarks and to the inferences which some propose on the basis of certain parables would be interesting but not decisive and would unduly prolong this chapter.

ON PAYING THE TEMPLE TAX

Our attention is first directed to an incident and attendant teaching reported only by Matthew. Since Matthew, as the only professional tax collector in the apostolic company, would have had an interest in the subject of the conversation between Jesus and His bumptious disciple, Peter, it is readily understandable why this seemed important enough to report quite fully.

> And when they were come to Capernaum, they that received the half-shekel came to Peter, and said, Doth not your teacher pay the half-shekel? He saith, Yea. And when he came into the house, Jesus spake first to him, saying, What thinkest thou, Simon? the kings of the earth, from whom do they receive toll or tribute? from their sons, or from strangers? And when he said, From strangers, Jesus said unto him, Therefore the sons are free. But lest we cause them

> to stumble, go thou to the sea, and cast a hook, and take up the fish that first cometh up; and when thou hast opened his mouth, thou shalt find a shekel: that take, and give unto them for me and thee (Mt 17:24-27).

As is frequently true in real life, there is a strong mixture of humor with pathos here. Jesus had recently announced His coming passion and violent death at the instigation of priestly authorities at Jerusalem (Mt 16:21). Peter had tried to talk his Lord out of pressing a course leading to such undesired results and had been given a scolding for his efforts (Mt 16:22-27). Now, here were temple authorities asking for money from this Teacher of his—money to support the public religious rituals conducted by these very priestly authorities (cf. Ex 30:13; 38:26). Peter had also heard Jesus speak of a coming end to Jerusalem-centered worship and by various other indications had shown less than wholehearted approval of what was going on at the Jewish temple. So when these somewhat tarnished characters wanted to know about Jesus' payment of the legally required temple tax, Peter was fearful that perhaps Jesus did not pay the half-shekel. Yet characteristically impulsive, he blurted out the defensive assertion, "Yes, sure he does." Then Jesus, knowing what Peter had done, (we must leave that to the mystery of the incarnation, for there are quite dissimilar incidents, eg., Mk 5:30-31) somewhat slyly let Peter know that He was aware of what had happened and proceeded to answer the question Peter really never had a chance to ask.

We must not lose sight of the fact that though the tax involved in the question was originally a Mosaic law, it was now also a Roman law. By accepting the status of an established regional religion, the Jewish religious authorities had extensive civil powers, behind which stood the sword of Rome. The crucifixion story is clear enough on that point. When later, after the further subjugation of Jewry and the destruction of Jerusalem and its temple, the Mosaic sacrifices ceased to be offered, the Roman government directed that this particular tax be continued and the proceeds thereof be used to pay for the support of pagan worship, specifically the building of the temple of Jupiter Capitolinus.[1] So the issue was partially one of support of the apostate, but divinely and legally established, public services of religion and partially that of paying taxes demanded by a hated, oppressive, foreign, civil power.

Although the design of the inquiring tax collectors may just possibly have been to bring Jesus into collision with civil or religious authorities, He does not treat the problem they raised as one of duty to authorities, but rather with reference to overly curious neighbors—the sleazy temple tax gatherers. Does one have responsibilities and duties to such mistakenly religious persons? Yes. It is worth a half-shekel not to offend them. Jesus does not raise the non-offense-to-neighbor principle to the level of an absolute (one can hardly think of these tax men as "little ones," Mt 18:6, or fellow believers "weak in faith," Ro 14:1). But He makes plain that one ought to live in the civil commonwealth in such a manner as to support peace and public order. Your tax may go to pay for religious functions (one may think of the local Roman Catholic mass in Italy where the church is supported out of public funds, or of nominal Protestantism in certain countries where it is the state church) of which you specifically disapprove. Nevertheless, as a matter of peace and good public order, you will not want to encourage other people who do not share your own religious scruples, to give up obedience to public authority. So pay your taxes, all kinds of them. You are not forbidden to try to modify or eliminate them. But while they are legal and enforceable, pay them.

ON THE QUESTION OF PAYING TRIBUTE TO CAESAR

During the last week of our Lord's natural life, the incident and instruction occurred which is best known and most frequently cited:

> Then went the Pharisees, and took counsel how they might ensnare him in his talk. And they send to him their disciples, with the Herodians, saying, Teacher, we know that thou art true, and teachest the way of God in truth, and carest not for any one: for thou regardest not the person of men. Tell us therefore, what thinkest thou? Is it lawful to give tribute unto Caesar, or not? But Jesus perceived their wickedness, and said, Why make ye trial of me, ye hypocrites? Show me the tribute money. And they brought him a denarius. And he saith unto them, Whose is this image and superscription? They say unto him, Caesar's. Then saith he unto them, Render therefore unto Caesar the things that are Caesar's; and unto God the things that are God's. And when they heard it, they marvelled, and left him, and went away (Mt 22:15-22).

Over a generation later, Josephus called this party Zealots. If they went by this name in Jesus' time (doubtful), one of them, Simon by name, may have become one of Jesus' apostolate of twelve. Two Jewish parties, Pharisees and Herodians, are mentioned. The Pharisees were loyal to what they deemed to be Mosaic-biblical religion and were generally unfavorable to unnecessary collaboration with the Roman conquerors. Presumably, many of the twelve had been drawn from this party. To their political right were the ultra-nationalists (Lk 6:15; Ac 1:13). Oscar Cullmann has sought to prove that several more, including Peter, were also Zealots.

Cullman's thesis that Simon certainly belonged to the Zealots and that others (such as Judas Iscariot and Peter) probably did, is doubtful in extreme. If several were Zealots, then there is no reason why one of them should have been called "The Zealot" ("Zelotes," Ac 1:13, KJV). This seems to throw out Cullman's theory immediately. It was quite gratuitous to theorize that he stood out preeminently among the several apostle-Zealots, hence "the Zealot." It is much more reasonable to suppose that he was called the Zealot for the obvious reason that he was the only former Zealot in the company, or simply that he was a zealous person in some other way. Cullman holds, to point out one of several other weak spots in his arguments, that Iscariot means "man from Kerioth" (he refers to Codex Sinaiticus on John 6:71). Then he strangely adds, "But we know of no place by this name." In truth, this is a simple error of fact. There are two cities of that name Kerioth (qᵉrî yôth) mentioned in the Bible. One is a city of Moab mentioned with Beth-meon and Bozrah (Jer 48:24, 40). In that city was a temple of Chemosh, whose altar is mentioned in the Mesha Inscription. Amos 2:2 also places a Kerioth in Moab. The other Kerioth is located in the extreme south of Judah (Josh 15:24). For this reason it has frequently been observed by New Testament students that Judas, man of Kerioth, likely came from the opposite end of the country from that of most of the twelve, who were mainly Galileans. Cullman has lost his way badly here.*

*S. G. F. Brandon (*Jesus and the Zealots* [New York: Scribner, 1968]) has an elaborate theory which in effect makes Jesus Himself a Zealot and each of the gospel writers a perpetrator of pious fraud. Brandon's curious books make interesting reading (and I have read several of them in whole or in part), but unless one is prepared to believe that the gospel writers—especially Mark—actually mean to convey the very opposite of what they knew to be true, his books are not very persuasive. The spate of books on a supposed radical revolutionary Jesus brought forth by this sort of scholar-

To the liberal collaborationist left were the Sadducees, who likely furnished no apostles. How the Herodians fit into this scheme is hard to say. The New Testament authorities by no means agree; and it is by no means certain that the Herodians, contrary to the Pharisees, favored the Romans. It has been cogently argued that they favored Herod, who though an Idumean (Edomite) by descent, was at least some kind of a practicing Jew, and gave the Jewish national feeling at least small encouragement thereby. This much only is certain: all the various segments of Jewish society were gradually uniting in feeling against Jesus, so much so that a few hours later the people and leaders, even those who really hated Rome and its Caesar, would cry, "Crucify Jesus; we have no king but Caesar." It likewise certain that the two parties mentioned hoped to ensnare Jesus into opening up His inner sentiments by incautious speech. If He spoke out in favor of paying tribute to Caesar, He was apt to alienate the populace on the one hand, and if He should say, "It is not lawful to pay tribute to Caesar," He then would bring upon Himself swift arrest and possible execution as an ultranationalist Zealot. And, although Jesus marvelously demolished their sinister effort, there was enough impression of guilt of Zealotism left in deposit on the public mind that when Jesus shortly was put on trial before Pilate, a crowd of Jews could accuse Him, saying "We found this man . . . forbidding to give tribute to Caesar" (Lk 23:2).

Long ago, Alfred Edersheim pointed out that "the Nationalist [Zealot] movement may have had an important preparatory bearing on some of the earlier followers of Jesus,"[2] while recently, Cullmann has made this theory a leading idea in his important small work, *The State in the New Testament.* At any rate, there were Zealots in the community, and for Jesus to have identified Himself with them would have brought about His end very quickly. Cullmann's remarks

ship in English and in German speaking lands cannot detain us here. I have the distinct impression that to attempt refutation of Brandon and the unnamed writers in the last previous sentence might be remarkably like conducting a fistic debate with a revolving door. An excellent work by an evangelical writer on the topic is Vernon C. Grounds, *Revolution and the Christian Faith* (New York: Lippincott, 1971), especially chapters 5 and 8. A more recent work, similar in approach to Brandon's and valuable for its discussion of German language studies of the trials and execution of Jesus is William R. Wilson, *The Execution of Jesus* (New York: Charles Scribner's Sons, 1970). See the negative evaluation of this work in a review by H. W. Hohner, *Bibliotheca Sacra,* April 1972, p. 159. Several studies of various particular aspects of the gospel narrative of Jesus' trials and execution have been collected in *The Trial of Jesus,* ed. Ernest Bammel (Naperville, Ill.: Allenson, 1970).

put this in correct perspective. After noting that the disciples of Jesus had to fight on two fronts, the one front being the collaborationist Sadducees, he notes:

> Much more important for emergent Christianity was the contrasting Jewish solution, the theocratic; the confusion between the State and the Jewish congregation, as it was pursued by the Pharisees. On the basis of this idea the Pharisees could oppose the Roman state only on purely negative terms. In view of their theocratic idea, they had to renounce the State unreservedly. . . . The extreme wing of the anti-Roman resistance party is of special interest . . . the so-called Zealots. . . . Here the theocratic ideal finds its sharpest expression. For its realization the Zealots preached a holy war; and they not only preached it: they secretly prepared for it, menacing the Roman garrison by individual resistance-actions and uprisings.[3]

Add another factor. Many scholarly writers point out that later Judaism, and very likely Judaism from early Maccabeean times in the second century B.C., held as a principle that "the right of coinage implies the authority of levying taxes, and indeed constitutes such evidence of *de facto* government as to make it duty absolutely to submit to it."[4]

In this tense situation wherein there was no real agreement even among the Lord's fierce enemies, Jesus brought out in the clearest possible fashion an important guiding principle for all church-state relations among those who desire both peace and justice. He did not evade the question or merely confuse His questioners. Edersheim explains, "It was a very real answer, when, pointing to the image and superscription on the coin, for which He had called, He said, 'What is Caesar's render to Caesar, and what is God's to God.' It did far more than rebuke their hypocrisy and presumption; it answered not only that question of theirs to all earnest men of that time, as it would present itself to their minds, but it settles to all time and for all circumstances the principle underlying it."[5]

Now if this be true (and how can it be gainsaid), it is hardly possible to exaggerate the importance of this text for the basic theme of this book. Edersheim's exposition of Jesus' statements about rendering to Caesar and to God is superbly well-put:

Christ's kingdom is not of this world; a true Theocracy is not in-consistent with submission to the secular power in things that are really its own; politics and religion neither include, nor yet exclude, each other: they are, side by side, in different domains. The State is Divinely sanctioned, and religion is Divinely sanctioned—and both are equally the ordinance of God. On this principle did Apostolic authority regulate the relations between Church and State, even when the latter was heathen. The question about the limits of either province has been hotly discussed by sectarians on either side, who have claimed the saying of Christ in support of one or the opposite extreme which they have advocated. And yet, to the simple searcher after duty, it seems not so difficult to see the distinction, if only we succeed in purging ourselves of logical refinements and strained inferences.[6]

In this assessment, Edersheim has set forth in simple language what others of greater interest in theology, as such, rather than historical-biblical study, have called sphere sovereignty.[7]

It has been a true Christian insight, supported by divine illumina-tion, that has always sent Christians to these very words of Jesus for guidance on the subject of biblical church-state relations.

There is a spirit of love and fairness about these words. Jesus did not plead the cause of Rome; neither did He harshly judge the sincere national aspirations of the Pharisees and the more intensely patriotic Zealots. He lifted the whole controversy above the sphere of partisanship—God has His claims on man in the realm of obedient faith (i.e., of "religion" in the best sense). Pay God's just claims! The civil magistrate (the state) has its claims in the realm of money and many other things. Pay those claims also.

Some suggest that there is a latent warning in Jesus' words to the effect that one pay Caesar no more than what is Caesar's right—mainly taxes. Cullmann warns that if Jesus had really assigned the same value to Caesar's sphere as to God's, He would have placed Himself on the side of the collaborationists. Instead, Jesus simply recognized that, within its sphere, the state can demand what belongs to it: money, taxes. But it is not placed on the same level as God. Give God what is His! That means, give Him your life.[8] On another occasion, Jesus put God in contrast with mammon (money, Mt 6:24; Lk 16:9-13). As the Greek word (*apodote,* "give back") suggests, give the mammon—money—back to Caesar; it belongs to him; it even has his picture on it. But you, yourself, have God's image impressed in your nature. Give God's own back to Him. Thus Tertullian (A.D. 160-220) in a celebrated passage on the righteousness of religious freedom within the Roman Empire, asserted in a comment on Jesus' words about rendering unto Caesar: "We have, for Caesar, the image of Caesar which is impressed upon the coin, for God the image of God which is impressed on human beings. Give Caesar his money; give yourself to God . . . . Accordingly we follow the apostle's injunction to submit to magistracies, principalities and powers, but only within the limits of discipline; that is, so long as we keep ourselves clear of idolatry."[9]

Thus, while Jesus placed no limits on God's claims, Caesar's claims, while valid, are strictly circumscribed. To quote Cullmann with endorsement once more:

> Thus Jesus' whole position toward the State is clearly circumscribed, precisely in the duality it entails throughout. On the one hand, the State is nothing final. On the other hand, it has the right to demand what is necessary to its existence—but no more. Every totalitarian claim of the State is thereby disallowed. And the double imperative logically follows: on the one hand, do not let the Zealots draw you into a purely political martial action against the existence of the Roman State; on the other, do not give the State what belongs to God! In the background we hear the challenge: if ever the State demands what belongs to God, if ever it hinders you in the proclamation of the kingdom of God, then resist it. The whole leitmotiv of the complex New Testament attitude toward the State is formulated by Jesus here in this saying [i.e., Mk 12:13; Mt 22:21].[10]

An Explanatory Digression

Our treatment of the teachings of Jesus regarding civil government is now complete. No doubt someone will want to know why Jesus' Sermon on the Mount, with His remarks therein about feeding one's enemies and doing good to those who despitefully use them, are not given exposition and related to a biblical Christian view of civil government. Someone else will inquire why Jesus' doctrine of His lordship over all, the universality of His kingdom, is not introduced. There are decisive reasons for passing by both the sermon and the kingdom as essentially irrelevant to the subject of this investigation.

First, what is the relevance of the Sermon on the Mount and other ethical teachings of Jesus to a Christian view of civil government? Let us now consider some evidences and a conclusion, employing chiefly one of the adages of Jesus from the famous sermon: "Ye have heard that it was said, An eye for an eye, and a tooth for a tooth: But I say unto you, Resist not him that is evil: but whosoever smiteth thee on thy right cheek, turn to him the other also" (Mt 5:38-39). The then current saying cited by Jesus in this excerpt is part of a larger pentateuchal precept which appears several times in the legal section of the Old Testament. The first occurrence (Ex 21:24-25) is in a clear context of guidance to civil magistrates in execution of public law. The specific case is one of guidance to civil judges in assessing penalties when a fight has occurred between two men with resultant harm of some sort to themselves or to others. The larger context with the text assures the reluctant assessor of these remarks that the case is being represented truly. This is important to the argument, especially since the famous formula, "an eye for an eye," is almost universally misrepresented. "And if men strive together, and hurt a woman with child, so that her fruit depart, and yet no harm follow; he shall be surely fined, according as the woman's husband shall lay upon him; and he shall pay *as the judges determine.* But if any harm follow, then thou shalt give life for life, eye for eye, tooth for tooth, hand for hand, foot for foot, burning for burning, wound for wound, stripe for stripe" (Ex 21:22-25, italics added). The law in question was given for guidance to civil judges in execution of public law, not to individuals for adjustments of private grievances. The principle is that in public law, penalties exacted should be in proportion to offenses committed. In Leviticus 24:20, where the same law appears in condensed form, again the subject is of penalties for breaking public laws. Several examples are furnished, with added provision that the penalties should be the same for both natives and foreigners (Lev 24:22). The passage closes with a report of divinely authorized execution by stoning of a man convicted of deliberate blasphemy—all in all a rather rough narrative (Lev 24:10-23). The third occurrence of this law (Deu 19:21) is even more specific than the former two: the context of it includes witnesses; litigants; judges, with priests present; official inquiries;

false and true testimonies; as well as penalties (19:15-20). Undoubtedly, therefore, the saying cited by Jesus was to impart and emphasize a basic principle of justice in exacting penalties for offenses against public law in ancient Israel.

To go a step further, the Old Testament is replete with condemnations of any move by individuals to carry out private punishment or revenge on one's adversaries. Let the reader balance off Leviticus 19:17-18 against the earlier citations from Exodus and Leviticus. "Thou shalt not hate thy brother in thy heart: thou shalt surely rebuke thy neighbor, and not bear sin because of him. *Thou shalt not take vengeance,* nor bear any grudge against the children of thy people; but thou shalt love thy neighbor as thyself: I am the Lord (italics added). There is private duty to rebuke the offending neighbor, but no duty to get even with him. Civil magistrates will care for that. The same teaching is on display in the Song of Moses, wherein appears the original of a saying which reappears several times in the Bible: "vengeance is mine [God's], and recompense" (Deu 32:35).

This Mosaic teaching is praised in the Proverbs: "Say not thou, I will recompense evil: Wait on the Lord, and he will save thee" (20:22), and "If thine enemy be hungry, give him bread to eat; And if he be thirsty, give him water to drink: For thou wilt heap coals of fire upon his head, And the Lord will reward thee" (25:21-22).

Furthermore, there is sufficient evidence to know that God-fearing Israelites were aware of the distinction between personal behavior toward enemies and the duty of public officials to punish. Two striking examples are present in Israel's history. Who, having read the story of Nabal's insults to David and his men, does not feel sympathy with his move to destroy Nabal (1 Sa 25:9-38)? There is a bit of the heroic in his vow, "He hath requited me evil for good. So and more also do God unto the enemies of David, if I leave of all that pertain to him by the morning light any that pisseth against the wall" (1 Sa 25:21-22, KJV). Yet Nabal was saved from David's private vengeance, being reserved for divine punishment, by the wise counsel of Nabal's comely wife, Abigail (vv. 28-31), though she acknowledged that in civil capacity, Nabal sometimes fought the Lord's battles. David responded, "Blessed be thy discretion . . . that hast kept me this day from bloodguilness" (v. 33). Shortly afterward, "The Lord smote Nabal, so that he died" (v. 38).

There is a connection between these matters and Jesus' sermon. He spoke to people who were fully aware, from the Scripture and from their own history, of the valid biblical distinction between response to evil in the area of private conduct and in the area of public duty of civil magistrates. Jesus is clearly speaking of the former. His remarks in question are therefore irrelevant, in any direct sense, to His teachings on the subject of responsibilities of public persons toward public law.†

There is another approach to the question of this chapter which seeks to find the answer in the present reign of the ascended Christ from the Father's right hand. Peter announced that at Jesus' session at the Father's right hand, He was proclaimed "Lord and Christ" (Ac 2:33, 36). It is argued that it is right, therefore, to expect His Lordship to be effected in the present age by the work of evangelism and instruction. It is a form of postmillenialism, though not of the usual type. Most of the advocates of this approach are of strong Reformed background, especially the admirers of Kuyper, Dooyeweerd, and Rushdoony. Elements of this approach will also be found in the writings of Dietrich Bonhoeffer (especially in *Ethics*), and of Oscar Cullmann. The Christian doctrine of civil government belongs, as we have placed it herein, in the doctrines of sin and of God, specifically in the work of providence, rather than in Christology, where some would place it.

---

†There is a number of Christian groups, often lumped together as "peace churches," which find important aspects of their distinctive teachings in the Sermon on the Mount. Some of these would agree with all that is written here, while others would seek to attach Jesus' standards to the rules for magistrates and police in their public capacity. Troeltsch gives this movement rather full treatment. (The present writer was reared in one of these denominations stemming out of German pietism of the early eighteenth century.) A representative work of considerable erudition which will introduce the reader to some of the main ideas of the nonresistance doctrine is *War, Peace and Non-resistance*, ed. Guy F. Herschberger (Scottdale, Pa.: Herald, 1959). Herman A. Hoyt, *Then Would My Servants Fight* (Winona Lake, Ind.: Brethren Missionary Herald, n.d.) gives a different peace church view as held by the Brethren, stemming from the German Baptist or Dunker tradition. More recent, reacting to the discussion, is J. H. Yoder, *The Christian Witness to the State* (Newton, Kan.: Faith & Life, 1964). Another is John H. Yoder, *The Politics of Jesus* (Grand Rapids: Eerdmans, 1972). Roland Bainton's works advocating pacifism, though informative as to history of thought, are not particularly geared to biblical doctrine (see his *Christian Attitudes Toward War and Peace* [Nashville: Abingdon, 1960]; neither are the modern works of Quakers. There are several centers of study of this question among Mennonites and Quakers which I have seen. The various writings of Franklin Littel fairly present the views of Mennonites and others with high degree of scholarly competence.

16

THE PRACTICE AND EXAMPLE OF PAUL WITH REGARD TO CIVIL GOVERNMENT—BEFORE JEWISH AUTHORITIES AND ILLEGAL MOBS

A COMPLETE DISCUSSION of the religious and social geography of Palestine in the middle years of the first century would be both relevant to the pursuit of our subject and interesting. A few remarks and summaries are necessary to connect previous observations on the practice and example of Jesus as regards human government with Paul's practice and example in that same regard. Quotation of a recent work by a recognized authority serves to lay these matters before us.

> [The book of] Acts takes us on a conducted tour of the Greco-Roman world. The detail is so interwoven with the narrative of the mission [i.e., of Paul and his associates] as to be inseparable. But when one turns from Acts to the Gospels the impression is totally different. The narrative of the three synoptic gospels is set in a world which reflects hardly a touch of Greek or Roman influence until the arrival of Christ in Jerusalem. What is true of the setting is equally true of the content, and particularly of the pattern of life revealed to a social and economic historian by the parables. . . . Briefly, hardly anything in the parables would suggest at first sight that Alexander and Pompey the Great had brought Hellenistic civilization and Roman organization into the kingdom of the east.[1]

Sherwin-White devotes twenty-four pages of his excellent work to the narrative of the gospels and shows that except for those times when our Lord was in Jerusalem, especially during the final week, the law and authority of Rome do not figure prominently at all in the accounts of Jesus' career. True, there are Roman client kings such as Herod the Great and Herod Antipas, centurions, and publicans, Caesar coinage, and so on, but that is only "background noise." The "broadcast" is in terms of a Jewish society in which the social poles are priest and layman, rich man and poor man, village and country, Judaea and Galilee rather than the much more complicated and wordly structure of the Hellenistic Roman society of the book of Acts from chapter nine onward. Galilee was ruled by the son of a proselyte Edomite apostate who was happy to please Rome's Caesar with as little as possible and to disturb the entrenched orientalism and Judaism of his narrowminded villagers and peasants as little as necessary. Jesus lived in what would have been thought of as a cultural backwater, precisely because outside of a city or two—Tiberias, notably—the Jewish people of Palestine remained outside the world of Greco-Roman civilization.[2]

THE EMPHASIS ON ROMAN LAW AND MAGISTRACY

It is well known that the gospel written upon historical principles and literary standards nearest the standards of the Hellenistic authors of the time is Luke. Luke's gospel does most to connect Jesus' life story chronologically with the history of the Roman Empire. His standards of historical writing have more in common with Herodotus and Thucydides than with the authors of the books of Kings or of Ezra and Nehemiah. This same author, with a predilection for the Western slant in writing, is precisely the one whose narrative of the mission of Paul in the world of Greek letters, Roman law, and Greco-Roman civilization is the major source for the present investigation: the interaction of the most representative and significant New Testament Christian with the custodians of the ordinances of man. It is a story which begins in Jerusalem, and ends in Rome by way of numerous commercial cities of the empire and cultural centers, including Athens, the greatest of them all. Nothing could be better material for our investigation.

Most of the materials for this section have been derived from Acts 13-28, sixteen rather long chapters. A principle which has successfully guided interpreters of the gospels will guide us here—the amount of literary space assigned a given subject is an indication of the emphatic interest of the author. In John, for example, though there are twenty-one chapters in the narrative of Jesus, beginning in eternity past, from chapter 11 onward, the story relates to the last week of Jesus' life, leading up to His death and resurrection. That Jesus' work of redemption, rather than his teachings, per se, is more important to John's message is thus clearly indicated.

In the case of Luke's history of Paul's mission and ministry, the whole epoch of the apostle's earliest missionary activity, wherein he established churches in Syria and that part of Asia Minor near Syria, is largely omitted (cf. Acts 9:30; 11:22-26). Three missionary journeys and a final trip, as a prisoner, to Rome are the subject of all after the opening of chapter 13. Yet herein, though the author does create a general framework of Paul's movements, the bulk of his report relates to selected incidents which are reported in great detail. Many scholars have noted and commented on this.

The first of the journeys of Paul made a subject of Luke's detailed reports is the interest of chapters 13 and 14. The first effort was on the island of Cyprus, described in verses 5 to 12 of chapter 13. Of these eight verses, all except one relate to a Roman proconsul, Sergius Paulus, who is presented in a very favorable light and whose conversion is vividly reported. The missionaries move on by ship to the south coast of Asia Minor (only one and one-half verses devoted to that). Then, according to the rest of the chapter's forty verses, an incident in the Roman city of Antioch resulted in successful evangelism, followed by expulsion from the city at the instigation of Jews aided by leading residents, but no interference one way or another from Roman officials. Chapter 14 is quite similar. It is a period of intensely Jewish ministry wherein Romans or other Gentiles are not prominent. The response of superstitious low-class Gentiles, first favorable and then otherwise, is not a significant result of the mission except as it aroused Jewish opposition.

The story of the missionary journeys resumes with chapter 16. But thirty of the forty verses relate conspicuously to Philippi, a Roman colony wherein an incident occurred that brought Paul mistreatment by minor Roman government personages (praetors, lictors, a jailor) at first, but later brought good treatment when the Roman officials carefully observed the provisions of Roman law with reference to Roman citizenship. Through chapter 17, conflict over decrees of Caesar and a lengthy discourse before the Aereopagus court of Athens continue the emphasis on government and government officials, mainly of Roman aegis. The climax of the story of the Corinth mission, which comes next, is an extensive report of the victory for Christian freedom of worship and related activities under Roman law announced by Gallio (chapter 18), while in chapter 19 a similar victory is the climax of the Ephesian ministry. Chapter 20 reports no such incident, but the rest of the book of Acts, chapters 21-28, is entirely related to an attack upon Paul by Jews, his rescue by a Roman military tribune, and his fortunes in the custody of the Roman military establishment, interrupted by occasional Roman judicial assizes.

It is certain, then, that the relation of the Christian mission to the civil powers in a major theme of the book of Acts. It is greatly to be regretted that the many recent treatments of the state in the New Testament take almost no notice of this material.

Roman Civil Status and Citizenship

There were several grades of civil status among residents of the empire, as well as several grades of political status among the various geographical areas. It may be said of the status of individual residents that it varied from the nonstatus of slaves up through free residents of provincial districts, several grades of citizenship to the solitary imperium of the emperor himself. Accustomed as men of modern democratic countries are to almost automatic citizenship in the country of one's birth and the national sovereignty of each of the countries in which they dwell, it is difficult for them to conceive of the situations in ancient and medieval times.

With a judgment of charity from the reader for a degree of oversimplification, it can be said that in Paul's time the status of an individual resident of the Roman Empire would have been one of four possibilities. He might have been a slave. If so, he would have had almost no rights at all. He would not have been able to contract legal Roman marriage, and would not have been entitled to own property. If he were a non-slave, a free man, he might have been of the lowest grade, *pergerinus*. Ordinarily, the *peregrini* were persons born in lands conquered and annexed to the empire. They would have had such local social and political rights as were appropriate to the particular status of that province in the empire, but they would not have had *connubium* (the right of legal Roman marriage), nor *commercium* (rights of property and trade), accorded citizens of Rome. They could make valid contracts, but they were under the same limitations as nonresidents of Rome. In fact, a citizen of a foreign state having friendly relations with Rome was regarded as a *peregrinus*. This is to say that the *peregrinus* was somewhat like an American in several foreign states of today, wherein he can sell and buy merchandise but cannot own land. An intermediate stage was that of the *Latinus*—halfway to full citizenship—who could own property and engage in trade with full legal rights but could not contract a Roman marriage with all the rights pertaining thereto. Full citizenship (*civitas*), possessed by the *civis,* conferred not only *commercium* and *connubium,* but also the privilege of holding public Roman office and freedom from certain legal penalties such as bonds and beatings, and from certain types of capital punishment such as crucifixion, deemed unworthy of even guilty citizens of the empire. Thus Christian tradition ascribes execution by the sword to citizen (*civis*) Paul but crucifixion to noncitizen (*peregrinus*) Peter.

In Paul's time, most provincials (i.e., nonresidents of Italy) were *peregrini*. Here and there at strategic places were Roman colonies (a city and environs) whose upper classes all enjoyed the same privileges of citizenship (*civitas*) as the inhabitants of Italy. Also scattered throughout the empire were persons, of whom Paul himself was an example, who enjoyed the rights of full citizenship, which, once gained, were passed on to descendents, without diminution or encumbrance. In theory it was the right of the Roman people, transferred to their great generals such as Pompey, Caesar, and the second Triumvirate, and then to Augustus and his successors, to confer citizenship on whom they would.[3] Practically speaking, the way to citizenship was to gain the emperor's favor. How this might be accomplished depended upon the personal character of the emperor, his need for money, and how freely he delegated the citizenship-conferring privilege to his immediately subordinate rulers in the provinces. Incidentally, there is no information as to how Paul's ancestors gained the *civitas* that rendered him "Roman-born."[*]

---

[*]Henry Alford, in his comment on the meaning of Acts 22:28 and the source of Paul's Roman citizenship, sets forth the situation:

There is a streak of a different kind of patriotism connected with a different kind of citizenship in Paul—characteristic of a true Hellenist whose Jewish ancestors had lived prosperously for several generations in a prosperous Greek city whose fame had developed long before Roman suzerainty. It is local city-state patriotism. Love of fatherland throughout history has usually been local. Up until the very recent past, continental Europe has offered few examples of large geographical units for which loyalty might develop among the inhabitants. In America before the Revolution, such American patriotism as existed was for the colonial states. Virginians, for example, thought of themselves as just that, well into the nineteenth century; and they reverted quickly to it in 1861 when the Civil War erupted. Thus after writing at length of the accomplishments of the people of Tarsus, W. M. Ramsay asserts further:

> The Tarsians of the later Greek and Roman times were stimulated and strengthened by the consciousness of their descent from men of earlier times. That is clear from the language of Strabo and Dion; and it is expressed in the words of St. Paul, as may be gathered from Luke's account of the stormiest scene in his chequered and adventurous career, when he replied to the Roman Tribune, "I am a Jew, Tarsian of Cilicia, citizen of no mean city" [see Ac 21:39]. One would have expected him to claim the Roman rights, as indeed he did a few minutes later; but the first words that rose to his lips came direct from his heart and expressed the patriotism and pride in his fatherland, his *patria,* that lay deep in his nature.[4]

On the subject of Paul's citizenship in the Hellenistic city of

---

[I WAS FREE BORN] literally, BUT I (besides having the privilege like thee of being a Roman citizen) WAS ALSO BORN ONE. *How was Paul a Roman citizen by birth?* Certainly not because he was of Tarsus: for (1) that city has no such privilege, but was only a *free city,* not a colony nor a municipal town: and (2) if this had been so, the mention of his being a man of Tarsus (ch. xxi.39) would have of itself prevented his being scourged. It remains, therefore, that his father, or some ancestor, must have obtained the freedom of the city [i.e., citizenship (Culver's interp.)], either as a reward for service or by purchase [*New Testament for English Readers* (Chicago: Moody, n.d.), p. 803].
W. M. Ramsay discusses the question at length in his *Cities of St. Paul: Their Influence on His Life and Thought* (London: Hodder & Stoughton, 1907), pp. 169-91, and suggests that the famous Antiochus, who in the next decade so furiously opposed the religious intransigence of the Jews of Palestine (see 1 Maccabees), granted residence and that Pompey had granted numbers of their descendants, one of whom was Paul's ancestor, the Roman citizenship. In *The Beginnings of Christianity,* edited by F. J. Foakes-Jackson and K. Lake, literature of the subject is cited and views are canvassed, but no commitment is made (4:284-85 [London: Macmillan, 1933]).

Tarsus (we are not here treating his specifically Roman citizenship), both Schuerer and Ramsay have significant contributions to make. Ramsay points out that the franchise in every such city was held by virtue of membership in a *fule* (tribe).

Schuerer asserts that wherever Jews in the empire had citizenship rights, they must have had the legal standing of a separate *fule*, inasmuch the citizens of Greek towns, normally divided into tribes, practiced special religious cultic rites within the tribes. Hence a Jew, as an individual apart from such a legally recognized tribe, could not practice his religion as a loyal Jew and also hold citizenship in a Greek town. The Jews had to form a *fule* of their own if they were to be both Jews and citizens. Hence, if Saul was a citizen of Tarsus as he says (Ac 21:39), all the Jews who had previously settled there must have formed a *fule* and possessed citizenship.

Even so, Jews were in a delicate, self-contradictory position, for citizenship normally involved participation in municipal affairs which, in turn, involved traffic with the native religious cult. The Jews, out of religious scruples, had to abstain. This constituted an apparent ground of complaint by pagan fellow-citizens. This was, in fact, the very complaint of representatives of Ionian cities brought before Agrippa against the Jews.[5] This means that in the Roman Empire, the Jews were most likely to be disliked and even hated and persecuted in the very Greek-style cities where they possessed the privilege of citizenship. Schuerer goes on to say:

> So it was, for instance, at Alexandria (B J [*Wars of the Jews*, Josephus] XII. iii. 7, persecution under Caligula), Antioch (B J VII. iii. 3-4, v. 2), the cities of the Ionian coast (*Ant.* [Antiquities of the Jews, Josephus] XII. iii. 2); and the same was the case at Caesarea in Palestine, where they had obtained through Herod the Great, the *isopoliteia* [equality of citizenship] (*Ant.* XX. viii. 7, 9, B J II. xiii. 1). Everywhere it was only the superior authority of the Roman *imperium* that protected them in the enjoyment of the privileges that were recognized as belonging to them.[6]

The matter of citizenship in the Roman Empire is important to our subject.

William Ramsay, whom many regard even now, several decades after his death as the best informed modern writer on the subject of the church in the Roman Empire, devotes eleven pages of his *Cities of Saint Paul* to these matters, showing by indirect and direct evidence that there was a large community of Jews, such as Schuerer describes above, in the city of Tarsus. He adduces several indirect arguments but clinches the case with an argument of definite and direct proof that there was in Tarsus a body of Jewish citizens. Paul, in Romans 16:7-21, designates six Christian brethren as kinsmen without adding "according to the flesh" as he does in Romans 9:3, where kinsmen by blood and birth is the thought. Since there is reason to believe that the flesh-and-blood family of Paul had not come over to Christianity in large numbers, these kinsmen of Romans 16:7-21 must have been members of the citizens group of Jews at Tarsus—the *fulē* or tribe mentioned above. Nor are they simply members of the Jewish nation, for others mentioned in the passage undoubtedly were Jews, but were not called kinsmen as were Andronicus, Junia, Herodian, Lucius, Jason, and Sosipater. He continues,

> This use of the word "kinsman" was idiomatically Greek, and seems to have risen in other cases to the mouth of the Greek when his feelings of patriotism were moved. Thus, for example, when the Greeks of Ephesus came to Agrippa, to ask him to eject their Jewish fellow-citizens from participation in the rights of citizenship they declared that "if the Jews are kinsmen (i.e., fellow-citizens) to us, they ought to worship our gods," i.e., to practice the religion of the city, participation in which was the natural and (to the Greek mind) necessary expression of patriotism and kinship. This kindred and common citizenship was based on religion. It was in the same sense that Paul calls those six men his "kinsmen" in Romans 16:7, 11, 21.[7]

PAUL AND THE JEWISH AUTHORITIES

When Saul, citizen of Tarsus, citizen of Rome, first appears (Ac 7:57—8:1), it is an approving witness of what appears much like a lynching in the Roman province of Judea,† and next as a kind

---

†Nothing in the story of Stephen's death by stoning indicates that it was other than an unlawful, spontaneous, angry response of furious Jews. There appears to have been nothing deliberate or legal about it. Another view holds: "The execution of Stephen for blasphemy, precipitate though it was, must have rested upon a formal judgment of the court that tried him, and must also have been ratified by the Roman governor, as was required for a capital penalty, though this may have been done in retrospect to cover the invalidity (Acts 7:54-60). But a lynching must be ruled out, partly in view of the terms in which the witnesses are referred to (Acts

of police deputy for the religious authorities of Judea on a mission of the Judean religious authorities in a neighboring Roman province (cf. Ac 8:3-4; 9:1-9; 22:1-19; 26:9-20; 1 Co 15:9; Gal 1:13, 22-24; Phil 3:6; 1 Ti 1:13). It is hard to explain Paul's preconversion activities against the Christians except on the understanding that the high priest at Jerusalem had general control, in matters of religion, over the local synagogues and local Jewish councils of the dispersion at least in the provinces near Judea.[8] It is known for certain that a local ethnarch had such civil authority in Alexandria of Egypt, for, quoting Strabo, Josephus writes of the Jews there that, "There is also an ethnarch allowed them, who governs the nation, and distributes justice to them, and takes care of their contracts, and of laws to them belonging, as if he were the ruler of a free republic."[9]‡ Such an arrangement would not have been thought particularly strange, for: "The mode of dealing with a conquered country was not uniform. When constituted a *Provincia,* it did not become to all purposes an integral part of the Roman State; it retained its national existence, though it lost its sovereignty."[10] The language of the narrative of Acts 9:1-9 and Paul's own shamefaced confessions about it later in Acts and his epistles make clear that he did not act without some civil-religious authority (of the Jerusalem high priest) in undertaking a personal vendetta against the Christians.§ He was therefore all too aware of the terrible misuse of which legitimate

---

8:1; 22:20), and partly because a proper judgment must have been necessary as a basis for the arrests which followed (Acts 8:3; 9:3; 22:5), particularly as the operation extended to Jewish communities in foreign territory" (E. A. Judge, *The Social Pattern of Christian Groups in the First Century* London: [Tyndale, 1960], pp. 65-66).

‡E. M. Blaiklock cites two very interesting documents of Claudius which seem to show the emperor's concern for the protection of the rights of the Jews in various localities to carry on their cult without interference and by the emperor's authority (*The Century of the New Testament* [Chicago: Inter-Varsity, 1962], pp. 40-43).

§Emil Schuerer has written to this point: "A jurisdiction of their own in *criminal cases,* in the complete sense of the expression, was certainly not conceded to the Jews in most places. On the other hand, not only do we meet with undoubted instances of the exercise of a *correctional police authority* (see Mommsen, *Zeitschrift fuer de Neutest. Wissenschaft,* ii. [1901] 88f.), but this would appear to have been permitted by the State authorities. It is from this point of view that we are to understand how Saul of Tarsus applied to the Sanhedrin at Jerusalem for full powers to punish Jewish Christians living outside Palestine (Acts 9:2; 22:19; 26:11). He himself was afterwards as a Christian scourged five times by the Jews (II Cor. 11:24). In these instances we are certainly to think, not of Palestinian but of foreign Jewish communities. At Corinth the proconsul Gallio leaves it to the Jews to proceed against Paul with their own judgment, for he himself will not act as judge when an offense against Jewish religion is concerned (Acts 18:12-16)" (*Hastings Dictionary of the Bible, rev. ed.* [New York: Scribner, 1927], s.v. "Diaspora").

governmental authority is capable. It is significant also that when he wrote as a Christian, Paul never sought to excuse his wrong use of power but severely condemned his actions as wicked use of legitimate authority. He himself was frequently on the receiving end of such monstrous perversions during his missionary career. Though most of Paul's later scrapes with Roman law were at the persistent instigation of envious Jews (beginning at Antioch of Pisidia and then at Iconium and Lystra, Ac 14-15), it does not seem that he was ever in the official custody of Jewish authorities. The Jewish officials frequently pressed charges against him and many times his countrymen unlawfully attacked him, yet never did they lawfully arrest or imprison him—that the Roman authorities did. Yet Paul honored those Jewish authorities and addressed them with more tender appeal and genuine respect than their contumacious behavior merited, though this did not prevent him from rebuking them with his peculiar oriental ferocity on more than one occasion.|| These truly startling demonstrations are reported in several texts: Acts 13:51 where Paul and Barnabas "shook off the dust of their feet against them, and came unto Iconium;" 18:6 where Paul shook out his raiment as he rebuked Jewish unbelief; 22:23 where the opposing Jews "threw off their garments and cast dust into the air" against Paul. Jesus told his disciples to express final exhaustion of effort to evangelize in this way (Mt 10:14). It is clear that the chief significance is asseveration, that is, formal disclaimer of further responsibility. "Rabbinic commentators on the New Testament (Matt. 10:14), from Lightfoot to Strack-Billerbeck, regard the gesture as indicating that the city thus rejected is treated as the heathen."[11] The gestures surely involve testimony and warning, especially warning (see Eze 33:1-9).

As far as conscience would let him, Paul declined, at the cost of great personal inconvenience to himself and not a little embarrassment to his Gentile friends, to offend them in any avoidable fashion. A nice balance of obedience to authority *to a point* against prin-

---

||Henry J. Cadbury in *The Beginnings of Christianity*, Vol. 5, note XXIV on pages 269-77, has written the most extensive treatment I have read of the meaning of these somewhat furious oriental gestures of Paul and his associates, though he draws no firm conclusions. He states, "In spite of prolonged study by scholars, and contexts of the several passages, and the citation of parallels elsewhere, the interpretation of these gestures remains without settled solution" (p. 269).

cipled disobedience *at a point* appears thus very early in the story of Paul.

PAUL AND ILLEGAL LYNCH MOBS

Sometime before the beginning of Paul's second missionary journey, a meeting of leaders from the church at Antioch of Syria and the Jerusalem church took place to settle some differences between them that had grown out of the reception of converted Gentiles under the impact of the Gentile mission of Paul and Barnabas. It was on this occasion that the "whole church" at Jerusalem wrote to Antioch (Acts 15:22), referring to Barnabas and Paul as "men that have hazarded their lives for the name of our Lord Jesus Christ" (v. 26). The hazards involved were several: first, being brusquely ordered out of town and ushered to its edge by leading citizens of Antioch of Pisidia (Ac 13:14, 45-51) acting at the instigation of angry Jews who were jealous of the phenomenal success of the mission of Paul and Barnabas among the Gentile inhabitants (see 13:44-45, 50). To this the two missionaries had responded in their vehement oriental manner of disclaiming further responsibility by shaking off the dust of their feet, as their Lord had said they should. This was hardly a gesture of quietistic pacifism. On the occasion of the second attempt at persecution, in Iconium, the next scene of ministry (14:1-5), the missionaries simply fled the city before a mob bent on stoning them could catch them. At the next stop, Lystra of Lyconia, where their preaching was remarkably successful in winning adherents, their old Jewish enemies from Antioch and Iconium succeeded, where they had failed at Iconium, in stoning Paul. "They stoned Paul, and dragged him out of the city, supposing that he was dead. But as the disciples stood round about him, he rose up, and entered into the city" (14:19-20). It is possible and even probable that Paul feigned death to escape his persecutors. His boldness in reentering the city was obviously a calculated challenge and threat to his recent persecutors, for what the mob had done was illegal under any kind of law, and especially under Roman law. Paul might have pressed charges and won damages.

It is quite clear, as W. M. Ramsay points out, that the ignorant, uneducated, and superstitious native population rather than the

Roman coloni, the ruling class, was involved in the riot.[12] This may account for Paul's reserve in pressing the civil magistrates and courts for justice, because he doubtless had sympathy for them. It seems more likely that he felt that on this occasion the future of the gospel work in the community would be hindered by legal action against the rioters, or even that he simply wished to keep out of sight of Roman civil authorities. There was nothing to be gained by having a reputation among Roman provincial administrators for being everywhere an occasion, if not a cause, of trouble. He was somewhat in the position of the unhappy automobile owner who declines to report minor damage to his insurance company, lest he have his policy canceled or his rate increased.

At this stage of his ministry, Paul was experimenting. Though he was moving in distinctly Roman areas and already had even seen a Roman official converted (Ac. 13:6-12), there does not seem to have developed any pronounced attitude toward Rome except that he simply used its favorable civil climate to move about the world and to work in it. After the first missionary journey, there are reported several incidents very important to our research for light on policy toward civil authority wherein Paul's efforts as a Christian brought him into direct contact with Roman civil magistrates. These furnish a great deal of material by way of precedent for Christians always and everywhere. The next chapter is devoted to these events.

17

THE PRACTICE AND EXAMPLE OF PAUL WITH REGARD TO CIVIL GOVERNMENT—BEFORE LAWFUL CIVIL MAGISTRATES

AT THIS POINT in our study, it will be helpful to make certain observations regarding Paul's missionary diplomacy. These observations are made possible by the advance of archaeological researches over the last hundred years and the careful study of Paul's itineraries by specialists in social, economic, military and administrative history within the provinces of the Roman Empire in the period of our study.

It has already been pointed out that Paul was careful to move not only within the bounds of the empire (long observed), but within certain administrative districts and municipalities. As noted earlier, there were several types of civil administration in the empire. In the eastern regions, many client kings, some of ancient dynasties, were left to rule their kingdoms, paying taxes and rendering certain services to the emperor. In the region of Antioch, Iconium, and Lystra, Paul was nearing such a kingdom—that of Antiochus IV, king of Commagene.* As he proceeded southeasterly from Antioch of Pisidia, via

---

*This Antiochus IV, surnamed Epiphanes (not to be confused with Antiochus IV, also surnamed Epiphanes, of Syria, who shamefully handled the Jews of Palestine in the second century B.C.) and his small realm of Commagene are not well known to biblical scholars.

"Commagene [was] a small country between the Euphrates and Mount Taurus, the capital of which was Samosata. It formerly formed part of the Syrian kingdom of the Seleucidae, but probably became an independent principality during the civil wars of Antiochus Grypus and his brother. . . . Antiochus, the first king of Commagene . . . is first mentioned about B.C. 69, in the campaign of Lucullus and against Tigranes. (Dion Cass. Frag. 2.)." (*Smith's Dictionary of Greek and Roman Biography and Mythology* [New York: AMS, 1880], 1:193-94.

In Paul's time, the country had been in semi-independence from Rome for about a century, though it had no king A.D. 17-38. The Antiochus IV of Paul's time is possibly a descendant of Antiochus I, the first king. Tacitus wrote of Antiochus IV that he was richest of the tributary kings (Tacitus, *Histories*, ii, 81). Josephus mentions him also (*Wars of the Jews*, vii. 7). See W. M. Ramsay's discussion of Paul's missionary diplomacy in regard to Rome (*Cities of St. Paul: Their Influence on His Life and Thought* [London: Hodder & Stoughton, 1907], pp. 407-18, 423-35.

Iconium to Lystra, Paul was moving steadily toward Commagene. If he had continued in that direction, he would have come soon to his native city of Tarsus and shortly afterward—of course barring extended ministries—would have arrived in Antioch of Syria. But in between lay Commagene, which Paul avoided.

Not only did Paul's policy focus on the most fully Roman districts, but he concentrated his ministry on the best educated, and hence most fully Romanized, elements in the population of the various cities. This can hardly have been except by conscious design. The proof of it is hardly necessary for one who has read the book of Acts. Recall the customary beginnings at the synagogues—centers of all Jewish life, not merely of their religion, in the diaspora. Always committed to education and deeply interested in the culture and learning available in the Greek centers, the Jews (of whom Paul with his knowledge of Greek rhetoric and literature, Ac 17:22-31, is an example) took advantage of it all. There were Jewish scholars and literateurs as well as merchants and bankers. They likewise attracted many of the upper social levels (i.e., Romans and Hellenes, rather than native populations, in the provinces), to their religion. Some might go so far as to become proselytes (i.e., fully members of the Jewish religious community), though there were times more who only went so far as to accept the piety and teaching of the synagogue. These were called "God-fearers," of whom Cornelius is a New Testament example (Ac 10:1-22). Many cultivated women (e.g., Lydia, Ac 16:14-15) were in this group.[1] Now it was precisely among these people that the early successes of Paul took place. They were the most fully Roman elements in the community.

It is well known that Antiochus IV, the Seleucid king, persecuted orthodox Judaism in Palestine. What is not so well known is that his fury there was in part rendered more fierce by seeming Jewish ingratitude, inasmuch as he had granted Jews special favors throughout his realm, including his large holdings in Asia Minor. Generally speaking, he had treated Jews of his realm quite benignly. The bearing of this on our subject is that through Antiochus' policy, the Jews had been hellenized through a large part of the East, and hence, when Rome took over, the Jews in diaspora easily adapted to Rome's ways too. Generally speaking, except for the intransigent nationalist fanatics of Palestine, Rome was kind to the Jews.[2]

Recent writings of leading Jewish historical scholars emphasize this point made by Josephus. Salo Wittmayer Baron states, "Early Roman legislation concerning Jews and Judaism in the other provinces of the empire was even more favorable than in Palestine, inasmuch as the imperial masters did not have to contend with ambitious and unreliable princes and often overtly rebellious masses. Rarely in the history of the Diaspora have Jews enjoyed such a high degree of equality of rights and self-government, under the protection of public law, as in the early Roman Empire."[3] Baron provides extensive bibliographical materials on scholarly discussion of Roman treatment of Jews during the early empire. He points out that imperial favor to Jews was a frequent cause of their local persecution and betrayal to civil authorities, their favored treatment producing widespread resentment. The Jews were especially attached to the emperor. There is even a hint in the Sibylline Oracles of the kindness of Rome to the Jews in diaspora, showing that there was a degree of contemporary awareness of the fact among the Jews themselves.[4]

In the lawful order of the empire was their civil peace and safety. It was Jewish religious fanaticism ultimately, not a sustained anti-Jewish policy, that destroyed Judea and Jerusalem.

This explains in part why Paul's ministry had such strong Hellenic and Roman emphases, but it is not the only reason. Think how different and how short his ministry would have been if Paul had gone to the uncivilized parts of the world where governments only partially controlled the areas. There would have been no common language of communication such as existed in the Greco-Roman world. Neither would the lives of the missionaries and their converts have been protected! Paul counted on the protection which Roman civil government gave to him and to the infant church.

There are chiefly five occasions when Paul's activity led him into involvement with lawfully constituted civil authorities: the missions at Philippi (Ac 16:19-40), Thessalonica (Ac 17:1-9), Corinth (Ac 18:1-17), Ephesus (Ac 19:23-41) and the final collision in the Acts narrative, that began at Jerusalem and brought him to Rome in Roman police custody (chaps. 20-28).

PAUL AND THE PRAETORS OF THE ROMAN COLONY OF PHILIPPI

Acts 16:11-40 narrates the story of Paul at Philippi. Luke, author of the story, was likely a citizen of Philippi (according to W. M. Ramsay). Luke writes, therefore, with justifiable local pride that the party proceeded "from thence to Philippi, which is a city of Macedonia, the first of the district, a Roman colony" (v. 12).

Another authority writes: "Why did the author go out of his way to introduce Philippi thus, when he never formally describes the technical status of any other city? [Ramsey thinks it a bit of local pride on the part of Luke.] The reasonable answer could be that it was because Paul had an adventure at Philippi of which the significance depended upon the special status of the place. The notice is a warning. Paul enters a Roman community and encounters special difficulties, such as he had not met earlier at the Roman colonies of Antioch-by-Pisidia and Lystra, where the action taken against him was not formal and official."[5] As noted earlier, a Roman colony was a political extension of Rome into portions of the conquered empire. Here the same laws applied as in Rome itself, and civil administration was wholly in the hands of Roman citizens— the local noncitizens, whether "civilized" Greeks or barbarians, had no franchise and less civil rights. The formal toga, mark of Roman citizenship, was not generally worn, hence there was no clear way to distinguish Roman citizens from others. Since false claim to citizenship was heavily punished, it did not occur; and citizens could carry a certificate of citizenship in the form of a small diphtych— a two-leafed wooden book—to document their civil status should it be questioned.

Upon his arrival in this place, Paul made no display of his citizen status, hence he was treated as any noncitizen when certain persons sought to get rid of his influence in the community by bringing charges to the police. They unceremoniously haled him before the city magistrates. It did not occur to the magistrates that one or both of the strangers (Paul and Silas) might be citizens. In the sixth decade of the first century, citizenship had not yet been widely distributed.

In verse 19, the magistrates are designated "rulers," from the Greek *archon* (singular), the common word for magistrate in any Greek-speaking municipality. But they are called by the Greek word for Roman *praetors* in verse 20, and so on through the chapter (cf. vv. 22, 35, 36, 38). It is affirmed by competent authority that "The title

Praetors was not technically accurate, but was frequently employed as a courtesy title for the supreme magistrates of a Roman colony; and, as usual, Luke moves on the plane of educated conversation in such matters, and not on the plane of rigid technical accuracy."[6]† Later in the narrative, the Greek word *lictors,* about the equivalent of English constable or policeman, is used for the persons who beat Paul and Silas at the command of the *praetors* and who report Paul's protest to them (cf. vv. 22, 38). Their symbol of office, a small bundle of rods with an axe in the midst was called the *fasces.*[7] The *fasces* was the symbol of Roman government authority, much as the American policeman's star or badge. Two *lictors* walked before the *duoviri* or *praetors* of a Roman colonial municipality such as Philippi. When Paul, in announcing his Roman citizenship and protesting the mistreatment, struck these *praetors* numb with fear, it was by appeal to Roman civil law (vv. 37-38).[8] The Romans taught Western civilization the value of rule by law rather than rule by men—at least for Romans—and here it stands on display.

Thus everything about this incident has a setting in Roman civil laws and institutions. Further information about the jailor himself and the architecture of his jail no doubt would enforce this statement.[9]

Some observations are now in order. First, Roman government at the beginning seems to have been a formidable enemy of gospel and church, for the mission was abruptly suspended by Roman arrest of the missionary principals. Second, the authority of the *praetors* was proper authority in the best legal sense. They had been duly appointed by constituted authority. They were the visible executives of the only lawful, orderly, civil power in the area. Third, these civil magistrates were bound by the law they exercised to release their unjustly beaten and imprisoned victims when the facts became

---

†"This title was not quite officially correct, since these men were properly termed *'duoviri,'* but it occurs several times in inscriptions as a popular designation for them" (W. F. Arndt and F. W. Gingrich, *Greek-English Lexicon of the New Testament and Other Early Christian Literature* [Grand Rapids: Zondervan, 1963], p. 778).

The best explanation is that of Sherwin-White that the Latin *duoviri,* official title of the chief rulers of a Roman colony, is untranslatable into any Greek. (It is clumsy likewise in English, "the two men ate".) "The author is simply using the commonest Hellenistic title to render the untranslatable term *duoviri*" (A. N. Sherwin-White, *Roman Law and Society in the New Testament* [London: Oxford, 1965], pp. 92-93).

References to these magistrates in the passage employ a word distinctive of Roman civil officers (cf. *Smith's Dictionary of Greek and Roman Antiquities,* s.v. "Praetor").

known. Presumably Paul and Silas, both Romans (v. 37), had been allowed no opportunity to announce their citizen status before the beating by *lictors*. Fourth, Paul the Christian, the man whose true *civitas* (Gr. *politeuma,* see Phil 3:20) is heaven, nevertheless felt it entirely correct, according to Christian principles, to claim his rights under human civil law to gain his freedom and to demand the protection of the law for his Christian mission as an evangelist and pastor. Thus, fifth, it emerges that while Christians may expect that, occasionally, human government unlawfully exercised will be an instrument of satanic oppression, they must also know that their hope for peaceful existence in the world will come from the same government exercising its powers lawfully. One may further cite Paul's words in 2 Thessalonians 2 about the man of sin with regard to unlawful use of power, or 1 Timothy 1:9 and Romans 13:3 with regard to legal exercise of power.

PAUL BEFORE THE POLITARCHS OF THE FREE CITY OF THESSALONICA

It is in harmony wtih the purpose of this study to call attention to the difference in the political status of Thessalonica from that of the neighboring Philippi. A lengthy quotation from a pair of famous collaborating authorities places that difference before us:

> Thessalonica was not a colony, like Philippi, Troas, or the Pisidian Antioch, but a free city *(Urba libera)*, like the Syrian Antioch, or like Tarsus and Athens. The privilege of what was technically called "freedom" was given to certain cities of the empire for good service in the civil wars, or as a tribute of respect to the old celebrity of the place, or for other reasons of convenient policy. . . . At Thessalonica it was the part which its inhabitants had prudently taken in the great struggle of Augustus and Antony against Brutus and Cassius. When the decisive battle had been fought, Philippi was made a military colony, and Thessalonica became free.
>
> The privilege of such a city consisted in this, that it was entirely self-governed in all its internal affairs, within the territory that might be assigned to it. The governor of the province had no right, under ordinary circumstances to interfere with these affairs. The local magistrates had the power of life and death over the citizens of the place.[10]

Free cities had various forms of government. Some perpetuated ancient local customs. In others, a senate of the Roman pattern, or an assembly along the lines of the Greek cities was installed. Here at Thessalonica there was a popular assembly of the type usually found in a Greek city before the Roman conquest—that is, if "the people" (Gr. *demos*) of verse 5 is a formal gathering of the citizens and supreme magistrates, or politarchs (rulers of the city) as it appears to be (cf. Ac 19:32, 39, 41).

So, though the Roman power was somewhat removed, there was a local civil government recognized by Rome and responsible to Rome.

The narrative begins somewhat like that of the lynching attempts noted earlier. But for some reason the Jews here were unable to find Paul, so directed their efforts at suppressing the successful Christian mission against Jason, Paul's host (17:5). Then, evidently afraid to carry out a lynching, they dragged Jason and some others before the politarchs. The missionaries were charged with seditious activity against Caesar and his laws. Then the politarchs, not wishing to appear in public as insensitive to the alleged speeches against the distant emperor, required monetary guarantees from the new Christian community that Paul and Silas would no longer speak in town. The missionary pair, unwilling to get their friends into further trouble, had no choice but to move on, though Paul did shortly send back Timothy, who was not under the interdict of the magistrates, to help in the work at Thessalonica (1 Th 3:1-3).

Here again, certain observations fruitful for a Christian doctrine of civil government are to be made. First, sometimes lawful government can be used to silence Christian testimony. Paul and Silas had no rights they could claim for recourse against the civil magistrates. Until a later election by the *demos* should replace them with other magistrates hopefully more favorable, the two missionaries had to remain silent in Thessalonica. Christian activity was not under a complete interdict, but the chief Christian spokesmen were. The Christians submitted meekly, evidently having no legal resource and being unwilling to take any action that was unlawful. Paul desired to return, for here had been his most noted success to date. Shortly he wrote from Corinth that he had several times tried to return, "and Satan hindered us" (1 Th 2:18). What was the hindrance? It is nearly certain that it was the civil magistrates of Thessalonica, whose clever way of making the Christians themselves the guarantee of his absence now made it impossible for him to go back.[11] Second, independent local government may be more oppressive toward Christian activity than a more broadly based government. It has advantages, and a high degree of local autonomy is generally thought to be greatly desirable. But local civil government frequently has been more easily directed against an undesired minor group than strong central government, which most of the time needs to keep peace with widely distributed minority groups. Third, the best Christian response to such local suppression seems then to be to subside and wait for a more favorable season. Genuinely seditious groups have practiced this sort of negative diplomacy for ages, and it is certainly open to Christians, who also have used it whenever and wherever circumstances made it useful, and who use it in many parts of the world at the present time. Wisdom is, indeed, sometimes the better part of valor.

Note that we omit Paul's experience with the Areopagus court of Athens, occurring at this point in the narrative of Acts. Though there were civil features of its functions, an assessment has not proved fruitful for our search.

PAUL BEFORE GALLIO, THE ROMAN PROCONSUL OF ACHAIA AT CORINTH

At Corinth, as in every previous encounter with the law reported in Acts, it was Paul's Jewishness (and thereby beginning his work in each locality with at least a brief mission to Jews before turning to Gentiles) that got him in trouble. The nature of the charges leveled against him in Corinth by the Jews makes it important to pursue just a bit more exactly the extent to which Jewish communities were free to enforce their own rules over their own membership and to what extent they could normally call upon Roman civil authority to assist them to enforce their own rules.

We have already noted that the Jewish authorities at Jerusalem apparently had some civil power over their Jewish constituency in the environs of Palestine, though there is little except Saul's mysterious mission to Damascus to prove it. Sherwin-White has written that it was the high priest only who authorized the arrest and binding of Christians at Damascus, and he cites Acts 9:2 and 26:12.[12]

But Paul says in Acts 26:12 that the authority came from chief priests (plural), and in Acts 22:5, Paul mentions that he received his commission to arrest Damascus Christians from "all the estate of the elders"—presumably the great Sanhedrin.

The Jews at Alexandria, for very special reasons, were given special powers of enforcement of their own law in their own community.[13] Beyond that, however, we should accept the well-supported opinion of Sherwin-White: "All that is certain, from the numerous decrees quoted by Josephus, is that the Jewish communities were protected against any interference with their religious and social customs on the part of the local governments of the Hellenistic cities. There is no clear evidence that the local Sanhedrins had any formally recognized right to force obedience on one of their own adherents."[14]

A weighing of the decrees quoted by Josephus, wherein he does the best that could be done to exalt the standing of Jews in the Roman world, supports Sherwin-White's opinion.[15] Josephus reported that during the reign of Claudius, which falls at this time (Ac 18:2), the emperor issued a decree of which a short excerpt seems to prescribe the same limits of Jewish authority over their own constituency elsewhere: "It will therefore be fit to permit the Jews, who are in all the world under us, to keep their ancient customs without being hindered so to do."[16] In other words, they were free to practice their religious customs, but they could not call in civil power to enforce them on Jews who did not choose to cooperate.[17]

Let us now observe the succession of events in Corinth leading up to their consummation in the very significant judgment of Gallio. Paul came alone to Corinth, a Roman colony. There he leagued himself with a Jewish Christian couple, Aquila, (whose Roman name suggests that he may have been a citizen) and his wife, Priscilla. Paul plied his trade of tentmaking with them and quietly "reasoned in the synagogue every sabbath" (18:4). But after Silas and Timothy joined him, Paul went all-out to evangelize the Jewish community. When they responded with concerted resistance, Paul "shook out his raiment and said unto them, Your blood be upon your own heads; I am clean: from henceforth I will go unto the Gentiles" (v. 6). After that, he transferred his lectures to a house next door to the synagogue, owned by a proselyte Jew named Titus Justus. Shortly, even the head of the synagogue, Crispus, and his entire family confessed faith in Christ. After all this, it is no surprise that the members of that synagogue felt outraged. Ramsay has observed, "It must be acknowledged that Paul had not a very conciliatory way with the Jews when he became angry. The shaking out of his garments was undoubtedly a very exasperating gesture; and the occupying of a meeting house next door to the synagogue, with the former *archisynagogos* as a prominent officer, was more than human nature could stand . . . It is not strange that the next stage of proceedings was in a law court."[18]

The civil officer before whom the Jews now brought Paul is called Gallio and is said to be the proconsul of Achaia. Gallio, as extant records of his life show, had only recently become proconsul of Achaia. This may explain why the Jews used this particular occasion to present their case against Paul. The provinces were mainly of two kinds, those administered directly by the emperor, and those administered by the Roman senate. The head of government in a senatorial province, such as Achaia, which included the city of Corinth, was called a proconsul. The proconsul, acting as judge, held court in assize cities, of which Corinth was one.[19] This (because there were several important men of the time named Gallio) Gallio is rather well known to historians. He was brother to Seneca, the famous Stoic teacher and advisor to Nero, emperor following Claudius. Did he share Seneca's fine sentiments regarding mercy, expressed as advice to the unspeakable Nero in *de Clementia?* He did enjoy a fair reputation among his contemporaries, and showed real skill as a judge.[20] Coneybeare and Howson report that Gallio had a reputation "not only as a man of integrity and honesty, but as one who won universal regard by his amiable temper and popular manners."[21]

According to well-known Roman law, private persons could bring an accused person, with charges against him, to the tribunal. Thereafter, the judge, in this case the proconsul, was at liberty to hear, inquire, and investigate, or to refuse to hear. Such was his prerogative.[22] One authority speaks of the "unfettered quality of the provincial governor"—his freedom to hear or not to hear cases as he he chose.[23] There were certain laws covering major offenses against persons, society, and the government, but the many offenses "outside the list" (Lat., *extra ordinem*) were left up to the authority (*imperium*) of the proconsul.[24]

In the light of this information, the ambiguity of the Jews' charge is significant to the course of our study. "This man persuadeth men to worship God contrary to the law" (Ac 18:13).‡ It is true that "officially the Roman citizen may not practice any alien cult that has not received public sanction of the State, but customarily he might do so as long as his cult did not otherwise offend against the laws and usages of Roman life, i.e., so long as it did not involve political or social crimes."[25] So the best way the Jews of Corinth could bring the Roman law down on Paul was to get him convicted of teaching Romans to act contrary to Roman social usages, and that was an interpretation which Gallio might have given to the charge that Paul was teaching unlawful worship of God. But what they really deplored was that Paul was persuading (not compelling) Jews to believe and to do things contrary to their customary interpretation of Mosaic law—then embodied in traditional teachings, later to be collected into Mishna and supplemented by Gemara (the Talmud).

The wording of their charge gave their case away to a person aware in even a slight degree of the Jewish manner of speaking, wherein "the law" means Jewish religious law. Unfortunately for them, Gallio was just such a person. So before Paul was given a chance to speak, "Gallio said unto the Jews, If, indeed, it were a matter of wrong or of wicked villany, O ye Jews, reason would that I should bear with you: but if they are questions about words and names and your law, look to it yourselves; I am not minded to be a judge of these matters. And he drove them from the judgment-seat" (vv. 14-16). This is to say that Gallio threw the case out of court.

Some commentators take a myopic view of this incident. Not so Ramsay, more than any other modern writer, has interpreted the ministry of Paul for English-speaking Christians. He writes:

This action of the Imperial government in protecting him from the

---

‡The Jews were taking advantage of the obscurity of Roman laws regarding the exercise of their religion. "Against their very ntaure, Roman emperors and jurists preferred to leave the legal position of Jews obscure during the first century, as their successors failed to define the status of Christians a century later" (Salo Wittmayer Baron, *A Social and Religious History of the Jews* [New York: Columbia U., 1956], p. 241).

Jews, and (if we are right) declaring freedom in religious matters, seems to have been the crowning fact in determining Paul's line of conduct. According to our view, the residence in Corinth was an epoch in Paul's life. As regards his doctrine he became more clearly conscious of its character as well as more precise and definite in his presentation of it; and as regards practical work he became more clear as to his aim, namely, that Christianity should be spread through the civilized, i.e., the Roman world (not as excluding, but as preparatory to, the entire world Col 3:11), using the freedom of speech which the imperial policy as declared by Gallio seemed to permit. The action of Gallio, as we understand it, seems to pave the way for Paul's appeal a few years later from the petty outlying court of the procurator of Judaea, who was always much under the influence of the ruling party in Jerusalem, to the supreme Tribunal of the empire.[26]

The present author concurs in this judgment.

Paul's experience at Corinth taught him that satanic as orderly human government may be in certain of its manifestations, it is nevertheless the only human promise the Christian has of freedom to speak his mind on the subject that lies closest to his heart, the Lordship of Jesus Christ. F. F. Bruce has written: "Any decision that civic magistrates, such as the politarchs of Thessalonica, might take would be valid only within their civic jurisdiction, but the verdict of a Roman governor would not only be effective within his province but would be followed as a precedent by the governors of other provinces. Had the proconsul of Achaia pronounced a verdict unfavorable to Paul, the story of the progress of Christianity during the next decade or so would have been very different from what it actually was."[27]§

PAUL IN LEGAL DIFFICULTIES IN THE DEMOCRATIC CITY OF EPHESUS

Sherwin-White asserts that "Acts does not show such detailed knowledge of any other city as of Ephesus."[28] Ephesus lay in the

---

§Second Thessalonians 2 is interpreted by some to set forth civil government and the magistrate (on largest scale, the empire and the emperor) as forces restraining evil in the world. Other interpreters find in the blasphemous lawless one of verse 8 a cryptic reference to the emperor (see Robert Culver, *Daniel and the Latter Days* [Chicago: Moody, 1964], pp. 64-69).

territory possessed by the general, Lysymachus, after the death of Alexander. Founded originally by Greek Achaeans in the heroic age, Ephesus had always been a Greek city. After it had passed into the hands of the Romans in 190 B.C., it continued at least in form its ancient internal government under the friendly but firm auspices of Rome. This power was supposed to be vested in the citizens (i.e., the residents) who met in assembly and a smaller executive body known as a council. In Paul's time, however, the city of Ephesus was also the capital of the Roman province of Asia, which included most of western Asia Minor. It was a very important province, Ephesus being the greatest city in the area. Not only so, as center of the cult of Artemis (Diana), it was a great pilgrimage city, and owing to location and port, also a great commercial center. It is most significant that having just established Christianity in Corinth, a city of similar regional importance, Paul's next center of concentrated effort was Ephesus.

The missionaries labored there for many months without hindrance. Paul was compelled to separate from the synagogue after three months, owing to Jewish opposition (Ac 19:8-9). Then, laboring daily from early morning till the end of business hours (presumably as tentmaker, Ac 18:3; 20:34; Ro 16:3; see also 1 Co 16:19 and 4:11-12, written from Ephesus during this period), he pressed the claims of Jesus Christ upon the heathen residents of the city after business hours, which were over at about the fifth hour, or eleven o'clock A.M. (Life starts long before daylight in the Orient, even today.) The lecture hall of Tyrannus would be free for Paul to use, while the people of the city, who employed the afternoon and early evening for home-life and rest, had freedom to hear him.[29] This ministry continued for at least two years and three months (Ac 19:8, 10), though in the manner of speaking of the time, Paul rounded that off to three years, the next superior number (20:31).

The first prominent effect of the mission on the economic life of Ephesus—disposal by burning of valuable paraphernalia of heathen practices by the new Christian converts—caused no immediate trouble Ac 19:18-20). Those who suffered the loss of a value of fifty thousand pieces of silver, being Christians and having counted the cost of becoming believers, joyfully suffered a voluntary loss of goods and livelihood.

:nding very soon to embark on a journey through
.chaia and hoping afterwards to go on to Rome (Ac
me of his plans reenforced (he had to leave town)
:d (he was sent to Rome). After Gallio delivered
licy of freedom to propagate Christianity at Corinth,
ctory among the masses at Ephesus, Paul evidently
:reedom and victory might be expected in the impe-
; city of Rome. Also, as expressed not long after-
o extend his mission to Spain (Ro 15:24, 28). Thus
ins were nothing less than the extension of the faith
:mities of the empire.

i hint in 1 Corinthians 15:32 (where "beasts" seems
reflect Paul's opinion of certain people, for it is ex-
to be literally true that he fought animals in Ephe-
as opposition from the populace. A collision with the
vith the ruling class and Roman officials) was unavoid-
say has written: "The character of the city shows how
vas. The superstition of all Asia was concentrated in
ghout the early centuries the city mob, superstitious,
volous, swayed by the most commonplace motives, was
most dangerous and unfailing enemy of Christianity,
ied the imperial officials farther than they wished in
iecution."[30]

riot and its fortunate conclusion, the disorderly pop-
up in a very bad light, and representatives of govern-
the local city government as represented by the "town
the Roman government of the province as represented
is—are shown in a favorable light.

:e, it was Roman policy to seek the creation of a sense
patriotism in the empire as means to discourage the old
al loyalties. Patriotism needs a common religion among
i order to flourish. In a time when cultivated people
given up belief in the gods of the Greco-Roman pan-
ere not as superstitious as in former times, there was
a new faith. During the reign of Augustus (Octavian),
:ror, who reigned 31 B.C. to A.D. 14, the first rather mild
official worship of the empire in the person of the em-
to develop. It still was not full-grown in Paul's time,

though by that time it was becoming a factor to reckon with. It has been competently stated that:

> Patriotism in ancient times was inseparable from religious feeling, and Roman policy fostered a new imperial religion in which all its subjects should unite, *viz.*, the worship of the divine majesty of Rome incarnate in human form in the series of emperors and especially in the reigning emperor. Each province was united in a formal association for this worship: the association built temples in the great cities of the province, held festivals and games, and had a set of officials, who were in a religious point of view priests and in a political point of view officers of the imperial service. . . . The priests of the imperial religion became by insensible degrees a higher priesthood, exercising a certain influence over the priests of the other religions of the province.[31]

It is quite amazing that these imperial patriotic priests, who in the narrative before us appear by the name of Asiarchs, should turn out to be friends and counselors of Paul, concerned for his person and solicitous about his welfare (19:31). They regarded the new emperor worship in a wholly utilitarian manner, a useful device for creating empire unity, a useful fiction. State-sponsored religions often turn out to be regarded in this way by their priests and sponsors. The Asiarchs evidently saw no threat to their work in Paul's mission, strange as that may appear to us now. The startling fact remains that in this portion of Acts, even the representatives of the official Roman emperor cult appear as friends of the chief exponent of Christianity at Ephesus.

The scholarly authorities amply authenticate the existence of the town clerk in the city of Ephesus.[32] He was the chief executive officer of the city (both of council and of assembly, likely) and the person whom the Roman imperial government would have held first responsible if things had got further out of hand, especially injury to a Roman citizen by an unruly mob. He is, moreover, a quasi-Roman officer, at least recognized by the Roman government, appearing at the proper moment to give an address in defense of the apostolic party which even Paul could not have put better if he had composed it himself. Probably the clerk referred to the disorderly meeting in the theater (the proper place of legal assembly) as an "assembly" only to give it a semblance of being legal, although irregular (i.e., not a scheduled meeting). Like Gallio's speech at Ephesus, it is an announcement of official government policy, upon which Paul was certainly operating in his mission to evangelize the empire. With regard to church and state in the example and experience of Paul, Ramsay declares:

> Luke, having stated the accusation against Paul, does not fail to show up its utter groundlessness in the eyes of responsible officials. The speech of the town clerk, which is given at length, is a very skillful and important document, in its bearing on the whole situation, and on Luke's plan. The clerk was probably the most important official in Ephesus, and therefore in close contact with the court of the proconsul, who generally resided in that city; and his speech is a direct negation of the charges commonly brought against Christianity as flagrantly disrespectful in act and language to the established institutions of the State. He points out that the only permissible method of procedure for those who have complaints against a Christian is action before the courts of the province, or the assembly of the municipality; and he warns the rioters that they are bringing themselves into danger by their disorderly action.[33]

Ramsay goes on to say of the defense of the Christian by the town clerk that "It is included by Luke in his work [Acts], not for its mere Ephesian connection, but as bearing on the universal question of the relations in which the church stood to the Empire."[34]

It may rightfully be said, then, that in the first two centuries of the Christian era, there were at Ephesus three distinct powers which were brought into contact or conflict. These were the government of the city, the Diana temple hierarchy, and the Christian faith of Paul and his disciples. At first there was no municipal opposition to the Christian faith. The municipal secretary, speaking for the city government, asserted that the Christians had committed no acts of disrespect toward the established usages of the municipal system and had not even spoken publicly against it. On the other hand, the rioters had made the whole city liable to reprimand or even punishment from the emperor. The secretary's superior tone was one of near contempt for the superstitious rabble who had rioted in the theater. He asserted Paul's right to free public speech as long as he respected the laws and institutions of the city. If the secretary had been a practicing Christian as well as a man of state affairs, he could not have argued more effectively to show the rioters wrong and Paul right. Ramsay, who writes to this effect, adds:

> We shall probbaly not err in believing that the general tone of the educated officials and the priests of high rank at this time was one of perfect equanimity and general philosophic interest in the preaching of St. Paul, whereas the superstitious and vulgar mob were strongly opposed to him. This state of opinion lasted till near the end of the first century.[35]

PAUL IN THE POWER OF THE ROMAN JUDICIAL SYSTEM

The amount of space in Acts devoted to Paul's arrest, imprisonment and successive examinations by several Roman officials, followed by an appeal to Caesar leading toward an ultimate trial of Paul in Rome and thereby of the legal freedom of Christians to propagate their faith in the Roman empire, indicates that we have now arrived at what in Luke's opinion was the most important part of his book. If Luke wrote according to a controlling purpose (and who can doubt that he did) then his purpose, though never stated, was at least in part to say something about church and state relations in the Roman Empire.

We do not know why Luke closed his narrative with the arrival of Paul in Rome, or why nothing of the trial before Nero (or his surrogate) and its results is related. Perhaps he intended to write a third book and did not; or perhaps he was prevented by illness or other causes from completing this one. It is possible, but doubtful, that he simply quit because he was with Paul at the point of Acts 28, and published his work as a finished product.

At any rate, unless he expected Paul to be vindicated before Caesar, as precedents in chapters 13-20 would have led them to expect, the large section (21-28) seems rather pointless.

It is the opinion of many New Testament scholars that Paul was vindicated and released. At this time, Nero was under the moderating influence of Seneca, his old philosopher-teacher, a man famous even today for generous outlook and high evaluation of human freedom. That such was Seneca's influence is supported by the fact that there are those who think Calvin chose Seneca's work, *Clemency* (*de Clementia,* mercy) for translation and exposition in hopes that it might moderate the persecution of Huguenot Christians by King Francis of France. Later, when Nero did persecute Christians unmercifully, it was a definite change of policy toward Christians in particular and toward opponents in general. Ephesians, Philippians, Colossians, and Philemon, written during Paul's first Roman imprisonment, breathe a spirit of hopefulness. Note especially that though Paul is prepared either to live or to die (Phil 1:20), he thinks "to abide in the flesh is more needful for your sake" (1:24). He is making plans for the future, including a trip back to Macedonia, which was to occur "shortly" (2:19-24). Not only so, but the "brethren" at Rome are "bold to speak the word of God without fear" (1:14). This was written early in the reign of Nero. Shortly afterward, Nero became the monster which history remembers so well, effecting the assassination of many of the people close to him, including his old mentor, Seneca. He also later instituted the first systematic persecution of Christians.

The renewed ministry of Paul after his release—when he was a marked man—was brought to an end by another arrest and another imprisonment. His career during this respite is unknown except for hints mainly in 1 Timothy, Titus (written during the period of freedom after the first imprisonment), and 2 Timothy (written during the final imprisonment, see 4:6-8), and certain statements by very early Fathers. The following quotation puts the matter correctly.

> It is now admitted by nearly all those who are competent to decide on such a question, first, that the historical facts mentioned in the Epistles to Timotheus and Titus cannot be placed in any portion of Paul's life before or during his first imprisonment in Rome; and, secondly, that the style in which those Epistles are written, and the condition of the Church described in them, forbids the supposition of such a date. Consequently we must acknowledge (unless we deny the authenticity of the Pastoral Epistles) that after St. Paul's Roman imprisonment he was travelling at liberty in Ephesus, Crete, Macedonia, Miletus, and Nicopolis, and that he was afterwards a second time in prison at Rome.[36]

Important texts bearing on the above are 1 Timothy 1:3; 2 Timothy 1:16-17; 4:20; Titus 1:5; 3:12. Most convincing are references to a ministry in Crete—for which there is no evidence or place in Acts—and the prison condition of Paul described in 2 Timothy 4 as contrasted with that of the book of Philippians.

It is also of interest to note that Paul's attitude toward the lawful authorities through his lengthy period of detention was one of respect and courtesy, never once questioning the propriety of their actions nor accusing them of wrongdoing in detaining him. He insisted, however, on remaining in Roman custody, the proposal of a return to Jewish custody being the occasion of his appeal to Caesar (Ac 25:9-10). He plainly expected more justice, and certainly more kind treatment, from the secular Roman power than from the bigoted Jewish hierarchy, meanwhile making bold claim to all his rights as a Roman citizen (Ac 22:24-25, 28). His respect for police, for the government's power of the sword—to restrain lawbreakers and to execute those guilty of capital crimes—he boldly declares (Ac 22:25; 25:10-12). Paul had argued convincingly for his innocence of any wrongdoing against Jewish or Roman law; before the tribune at Jerusalem; Felix, the governor at Caesarea; and his successor, Festus. These men had declared him innocent, but for policy's sake (appeasing the Jews) had kept Paul in prison. But Paul stuck with the system, as he had no other course of escape from indefinite detention, and trusted himself to Caesar.

Nero was up to then a moderately good emperor; only later did he become a monstrous one.‖ Paul was aware that "the powers that be" (Ro 13:1) are not always benign. But the travel and life-record of the Acts and the biographical material of the epistles manifest a constant esteem and respect for human government, God's order of preservation.

Before closing this treatment of Paul's personal response to the civil powers of his time, the possible bearing of a controverted passage on the subject requires some notice. This is in reference to the one "that restraineth now" (*ho katechōn*, 2 Th 2:7) and "that which restraineth" (*to katechon*, 2 Th 2:6) in Paul's great discussion of Christian expectation of the second advent in 2 Thessalonians 2. An eschatological interpretation should be given to the entire passage.[37]

‖Expositors of Romans 13 frequently make quite a point of the fact that Nero was a monster of iniquity to lend force to "the powers that be are ordained of God" (v. 1). The force is lessened somewhat when it is seen that Nero was still quite a benevolent-appearing monarch when Paul wrote the epistle to the Romans.

Even so, granting Paul's expectation of an imminent *parousia* and the foreshortening of the future in predictive prophecy of the Bible, it is not impossible that he may have had the Roman Caesar and his empire in mind as the "one that restraineth" and "that which restraineth." In such a view of the passage, civil officials (Nero-Caesar being chief of them) and civil governments (Roman government being most universal) are providential divine agencies for restraining lawlessness (v. 7) and men of sin (v.3). The "catena of passages," cited by Henry Alford, supports the assertion of Sanday and Hedlam that this was "the commonest interpretation of these words among the Fathers."[38] Without fully endorsing their view of 2 Thessalonians 2:6-7, I pass on their words as essentially correct in interpreting Paul's experience with civil authority:

> St. Paul's experience had taught him that there were lying restrained and checked great forces of evil which might at any time burst out, and this he called the "mystery of iniquity," and describes in the language of the Old Testament prophets. But everywhere the power of civil government, as embodied in the Roman Empire (*to katechon*) and visibly personified in the Emperor (*ho katechōn*) restrained these forces. Such an interpretation, either of the eschatological passages of the Epistle or the Apocalypse, does not destroy their deeper spiritual meaning; for the writers of the New Testament, as the prophets of the Old, reveal to us and generalize the spiritual forces of good and evil which underlie the surface of society.[39]

These same authors go on to remind us that the name of Rome greatly influenced Paul. He was determined to go to Rome. "After I have been there, I must also see Rome" (Ac 19:21); he understood that God was sending him there: "so must thou bear witness also at Rome" (Ac 23:11). The imagery of Roman citizenship had impressed itself upon his diction (Ac 23:1; Eph 2:19; Phil 1:27; 3:20). This was the effect not only of birth to Roman citizenship, but also of experience as Christian traveler and missioner. As Sanday and Hedlam claim and our studies have concluded, wherever Christianity had been preached, Roman authorities had come forward to restrain the evil forces seeking to destroy it.

The worst persecution of the Christians had been while Judaea was under the rule of a native prince. Everywhere the Jews had stirred up persecutions, and the imperial officials had interfered and protected the Apostle. And so both in this Epistle [Romans] and throughout his life St. Paul emphasizes the duty of obedience to civil government and the necessity of fulfilling our obligations to it. But also St. Paul was himself a Roman citizen. This privilege, not then so common as it became later, would naturally broaden the view and impress the imagination of a provincial; and it is significant that the first clear conception of the universal character inherent in Christianity, the first bold step to carry it out, and the capacity to realize the importance of the Roman Church should come from an Apostle who was not a Galilean peasant but a citizen of a universal empire.[40]

The conclusion of these studies of Paul has been anticipated at each critical juncture in Paul's ministry and has been stated in several different ways already. It should be clear by now that however far he was from attributing to state power any significant ability to perfect or reform society, and no matter how much he may have deprecated the frequent tendency of individual magistrates to exceed their just powers or to misuse them, Paul did rely on government to restrain the violent intentions of malicious people. He trusted the due process of law to conserve his civil rights, to protect his liberty against persecution and suppression by rival religious people to preach his message and to protect the infant churches which he founded. Though well aware of the limited number of benefits from government, the possible dangers of it, its numerous failings, and even intermittent persecutions, he was aware of no right of armed resistance to tyrants. He practiced neither resistance nor disobedience when at various times civil power gone awry might have impelled him to do so. Finally, he appreciated the help of orderly civil government, even in heathen hands, in pursuing "a tranquil and quiet life," thereby preserving normal Christian family, church, and community life with freedom to proclaim the gospel of God, "who would have all men to be saved, and come to the knowledge of the truth" (1 Ti 2:4).

18

THE TEACHINGS OF PAUL WITH REGARD TO CIVIL GOVERNMENT

THERE ARE FIVE PASSAGES in his epistles wherein Paul distinctly treats human government and Christian relation to it, and possibly a sixth passage. These five are 1 Corinthians 2:6-8; 6:1-10; Romans 13:1-7; 1 Timothy 2:1-4; and Titus 3:1-3. The possible sixth is 2 Thessalonians 2:7-12.

Scholars who make it their business to trace an alleged development of doctrine within the various authors' sections of the Bible have sought to correlate these expressions with the experience of each author. There is a limited validity to this approach. Yet there is little that might be labeled "advance" within the five or six sections noted above. If there were, then there should be initial skepticism regarding the positive value and allegiance claims of Roman government, then growing trust in it, followed by disillusionment. But such is not the case, for if it were, and granting that the blasphemous "lawless one" ("man of sin," KJV) of 2 Thessalonians 2:7-12—so like the fourth beast of Daniel 7 and the beast out of the sea of Revelation 13—may be the Roman emperor, then the man of sin should represent the final stage of Paul's thought. But he does not, for this passage is probably the very earliest of the six texts. The plain truth of the case is that Paul states his essential doctrine firmly, with more or less completeness, in two texts (Romans and Titus), while in the others he adduces tangential considerations. There is no important particular developmental clue within the passages or in the history of their author. The order of treatment that follows is to suit considerations of the interest of the subject of this section of this book.

1 CORINTHIANS 2:6-8

We speak wisdom, however, among them that are fullgrown: yet a wisdom not of this world, nor of the rulers of this world, who are coming to nought: but we speak God's wisdom in a mystery, even the wisdom that hath been hidden, which God foreordained before the worlds unto our glory: which none of the rulers of this world hath known: for had they known it, they would not have crucified the Lord of glory.

These lines fall in a somewhat ironic passage wherein to readers who conceived themselves as quite worldly-wise, Paul had disclaimed any worldly wisdom at all in his preaching. He had likewise disclaimed any of the customary rhetorical polish expected of public speakers in centers of culture such as Corinth, in his presentation (1 Co 2:1-5, cf. Ac 18:1-8; 1 Co 1:18-31). The "however" (Gr. *de*) indicates a contrast with these disclaimers. He is affirming that there is nevertheless a high Christian wisdom in the message of Christ and His death by crucifixion. It may be foolishness "to them that perish" (1:18). It may not even be fully understood by the common run of Christians (of which he suggests there are all too many at Corinth, 1 Co 3:1-4). But those who are mature understand the divine wisdom involved in the atoning death of Christ (2:6). The "rulers of this world" (2:6, *archontōn*, the word used generally for government officials in the New Testament) such as Paul had met in many of his travels, especially at the Areopagus court of Athens (Ac 17:16-34), have none of this wisdom. They do not truly understand man, much less God (1 Co 2:14). If any of these rulers had known the divine wisdom, "they would not have crucified the Lord of glory" (2:8). Peter had commented that the Jewish and Roman rulers responsible had acted in ignorance, yet they had carried out the "determinate counsel of God" (Ac 2:23, cf. 3:17), while Jesus prayed, "Father, forgive them; for they know not what they do" (Lk 23:34).

Thus Paul is indicating that in carrying out God's providence, the agents of government (at least the non-Christian ones) are ignorant of their place in that providence. It is only a Christian ruler who understands the doctrinal basis of being a ruler by the grace of God. Nebuchadnezzar, for example, had to be taught that God sets up kings part of the time and sets them down the rest of the time, even though he never knew that God called him "my servant" (Jer 25:9;

27:6).* Hence, though in texts which will soon be treated herein, Paul takes a very high view of government, his insistence on man's fallenness and his scorn of the supposed wisdom of the world's rulers and savants are such that these words might greatly anger a secularist humanitarian judge or cause a cynical opportunist politician to laugh. It represents a point of view that explains why a sophisticated lecturer on American history said, "It's a pity that Plymouth Rock did not land on the Pilgrims rather than they on the rock." There is no area where the Christian's biblical view of reality seems more foolish than in its insistence on man's fallenness and consequent spiritual blindness as well as intellectual dullness.

1 CORINTHIANS 6:1-8

Dare any of you, having a matter against his neighbor, go to law before the unrighteous, and not before the saints? Or know ye not that the saints shall judge the world? and if the world is judged by you, are ye unworthy to judge the smallest matters? Know ye not that we shall judge the angels? how much more, things that pertain to this life? If then ye have to judge things pertaining to this life, do ye set them to judge who are of no account in the church? I say this to move you to shame. What, cannot there be found among you one wise man who shall be able to decide between his brethren, but brother goeth to law with brother, and that before unbelievers? Nay, already it is altogether a defect in you, that ye have lawsuits one with another. Why not rather take wrong? why not rather be defrauded? Nay, but ye yourselves do wrong, and defraud, and that your brethren.

All except a very few interpreters, mainly of Anabaptist tradition, hold that this passage is not intended to forbid all use of secular law courts by Christians. It is to condemn the "litigious spirit" (as Calvin put it), in order to prevent believers from weakening the force of Christian witness before the pagan world. Paul does not mean to forbid the use of legal contracts. He does not even absolutely forbid, under every circumstance, a lawsuit with a professed believer. He does insist that believers live under the shadow of eternity and the im-

---

*In Daniel 4:17, Nebuchadnezzar's chastened pronouncement was, "The Most High ruleth in the kingdom of men, and giveth it to whomsoever he will, and setteth up over it the lowest of men."

minent end of the present order in the coming of Christ. As argument, he cites the fact that the secular courts are in the hands of those less just and less competent than themselves; for saints in the coming kingdom, what was promised especially to apostles—to "sit upon twelve thrones, judging the twelve tribes of Israel" (Mt 19:28)— shall be true in some degree of all believers. Perhaps his "know ye not" of verse two has reference to Daniel 7:18, 22, and 27 which says that the saints shall possess the coming kingdom of God. Paul himself had earlier appealed to public law in his own defense at Philippi (Ac 16:35-40), and would later appeal to Caesar's own judgment seat. So this is not an outright condemnation of use of secular courts by Christian believers; it was a warning not to expect too much from them, and it discourages unnecessary and hurtful use of them.

ROMANS 13:1-7

Let every soul be in subjection to the higher powers: for there is no power but of God: and the powers that be are ordained of God. Therefore he that resisteth the power, withstandeth the ordinance of God: and they that withstand shall receive to themselves judgment. For rulers are not a terror to the good work, but to the evil. And wouldest thou have no fear of the power? do that which is good, and thou shalt have praise from the same: for he is a minister of God to thee for good. But if thou do that which is evil, be afraid; for he beareth not the sword in vain: for he is a minister of God, an avenger for wrath to him that doeth evil. Wherefore ye must needs be in subjection, not only because of the wrath, but also for conscience' sake. For for this cause ye pay tribute also; for they are ministers of God's service, attending continually upon this very thing. Render to all their dues: tribute to whom tribute is due; custom to whom custom; fear to whom fear; honor to whom honor.

Nothing in the entire Bible is more important to the subject of the place of human civil government in the providence of God than is this text. Yet it is a very great mistake to consider it apart from the preceding context, the last verses of chapter 12, and to a lesser degree the following context.

The Christian lives in many spheres of relationship. The same man may be son to one, father to another, husband to another. Each sphere has its own kind of autonomy—the rules of action are special to each sphere. Now the immediate preceding context treats the Christian's private personal relationship to other equally private persons—that is, to other persons in their individual capacity. In such relationships the rules, in part, are: "Render to no man evil for evil . . . . If it be possible, as much as in you lieth, be at peace with all men. Avenge not yourselves, beloved, but give place unto the wrath of God: for it is written, Vengeance belongeth unto me, I will recompense, saith the Lord. But if thine enemy hunger, feed him; if he thirst, give him to drink: for in so doing thou shalt heap coals of fire upon his head. Be not overcome of evil, but overcome evil with good" (Ro 12:17-21).

While the passage speaks plainly, there are some minor obscurities due to translation and some links with other Scriptures which call for notice. Both the American Standard Version, cited above, and the Revised Standard Version, "so far as it depends upon you, live peaceably with all" (v. 18), show that the apostle means that any breach of peace must not come from the Christian believer. "Whether you actually live peaceably or not, will depend solely on how others behave toward you."[1] Paul's own life record shows that, if one is a witnessing Christian, others will not let him have constant peace.

"Give place unto wrath" (v. 19) is in the Greek "the wrath," which, as the following verse makes certain, is God's wrath, hence, "leave it to the wrath of God." Other explanations such as, Hold in your own wrath; Give place to the wrath of your enemy; or, Do not be hastily angry, but let your anger wait for a proper time; are all rendered incorrect by the connection with what immediately follows, "for it is written, Vengeance belongeth unto me . . . saith the Lord." God's vengeance goes forth sooner than one might think, as we shall see in connection with Romans 13:4. Paul is emphasizing a truth taught everywhere in the Bible: Personal vengeance has no proper place in the life of a godly man. As has been pointed out earlier, the maxim, "eye for eye, tooth for tooth" has reference to exact justice in execution of public law, having no immediate connection with private vengeance.

Misunderstanding in this regard is so widespread that the following verses are cited to enforce the point that everywhere in the Bible, taking personal revenge is against God's expressed will, and that reports of revenge taken by otherwise good men is not condoned. "Thou shalt not hate thy brother in thine heart. . . . Thou shalt not take vengeance, nor bear any grudge against the children of thy people; but thou shalt love thy neighbor as thyself: I am the Lord" (Lev 19:17-18). Paul's "for it is written" (Ro 12:19) is a quotation of Deuteronomy 32:35, "Say not thou, I will recompense evil: Wait for the Lord, and he shall save thee" (Pr 20:22), which puts the teaching succintly, as does Proverbs 25:21-22, which Paul quotes here in verse 20. 1 Samuel 25:31-33 and 2 Samuel 16:12 report incidents wherein it is made plain that this high standard for God's people was well understood among the children of Israel. So Jesus was not raising a new standard at all when He made His announcement about loving one's enemies (Mt 5:43-48). The doctrine leads straight back to Leviticus. Jesus was correcting not scriptural doctrine, but apostate elements in Judaism, or perhaps even plain common misunderstanding, for statements similar to Jesus' are not absent from the rabbis.

Exactly how caring for an enemy's physical needs of food and drink shall "heap coals of fire on his head" (Ro 12:20) is not quite so clear, though the following verse, "overcome evil with good," seems to explain it. Several views have been taken of the problem. Least satisfactory is that which finds its support in the admonition of the book of 2 Esdras, "Let not the sinner say that he hath not sinned: for God shall burn coals of fire upon his head" (2 Esd 16:53), that the Christian's kindness to his wrongful enemy will draw down God's wrath on him, though it has the support of several ancient, medieval, and modern writers. Against it is the fact that whereas the context in 2 Esdras does demand such a meaning of the figure, here the context is against it, and such an explanation is out of keeping with the spirit of the Christian religion, unless very guardedly set forth. A second view, advocated by three famous exegetes, Hodge, Alford, and Jowett, holds that the meaning is that such kindness is the most effective vengeance. A third view, similar to the second, would paraphrase the figure to say that you will, by treating your enemy kindly, prepare him for the pain of self-accusation, remorse, and perhaps even repentance. Thus there is an evangelistic force in Christian kindness to enemies. By far the greater number of interpreters have taken this viewt—and it is rendered close to certain by the connection with verse 21—"overcome evil with good." This is not to say that kindness to wicked enemies does not sometimes make their enmity more fierce, but this is not the way they ought to respond nor is it even the usual response.‡ It was by obeying these injunctions that the early Christians brought the Roman Empire around (following initial freedom to propagate and exercise their faith) from persecution, first to toleration, and finally, to acceptance throughout the empire.

It is against this background that Romans 13:1-7 must be understood. It is hardly possible to miss the meaning of this passage. Sanday and Hedlam summarized that meaning as follows.

> While we adhere to what has been said about the absence of a clearly-defined system or purpose in these chapters, we may notice that one main thread of thought which runs through them is the promotion of peace in all the relations of life. The idea of the civil power may have been suggested by verse 19 of the preceding chapter, as being one of the ministers of the Divine wrath and retribution (vs. 4): at

---

†Heinrich August Meyer names Jerome, Chrisostom, Theodoret, Oecumenius, Theophylact, Photius, Beza, Camerarius, Estius, Grotius, Wetstein, Koppe, Boehme, and Hengstenberg as proponents of this thought (*Critical and Exegetical Hand-Book of the Epistle to the Romans* [New York: Funk & Wagnalls, 1884], p. 481.)

‡The Roman historian Tacitus describes in his *Annals* the greatest fire of Rome which occurred in Nero's reign. A famous section of this report relates to the response the public made to the innocent suffering of the first century Christians. "So far, the precautions taken were suggested by human prudence: now means were sought for appeasing deity, and application was made to the Sibylline books; at the injunction of which public prayers were offered to Vulcan, Ceres, and Proserpine, while Juno was propitiated by the matrons, first in the Capitol, then at the nearest point of the seashore, where water was drawn for sprinkling the temple and the image of the goddess. Ritual banquets and all-night vigils were celebrated by women in the married state. But neither human help, nor all the methods of placating Heaven, could stifle scandal or dispel the belief that the fire had taken place by Nero's order. Therefore to scotch the rumour, Nero substituted as culprits and punished with the utmost refinements of cruelty, a class of men, loathed for their vices, whom the crowd styled Christians. Christus, the founder of the name, had undergone the death penalty in the reign of Tiberius, by sentence of the procurator Pontius Pilatus, and the pernicious superstition was checked for a moment, only to break out once more, not merely in Judaea, the home of the disease, but in the capital itself, where all things horrible or shameful in the world collect and find a vogue. First, then, the confessed members of the sect were arrested; next, on their disclosures, vast numbers were convicted, not so much on the count of arson as for hatred of the human race. And derision accompanied their end: they were covered with wild beasts' skins and torn to death by dogs; or they were fastened on crosses, and when daylight failed were burned to serve as lamps by night. Nero had offered his Gardens for the spectacle, and gave an exhibition in his Circus, mixing with the crowd in the habit of a charioteer, or mounted on his car. Hence in spite of a guilt which had earned the most exemplary punishment, there arose a sentiment of piety, due to the impression that they were being sacrificed not for the welfare of the state but to the ferocity of a single man" (Tacitus, *Annals*, XIII-XVI [Cambridge: Harvard U., 1962], pp. 283-85).

any rate the juxtaposition of the two passages would serve to remind St. Paul's readers that the condemnation of individual vengeance and retaliation does not apply to the action of the state in enforcing law; for the state is God's minister, and it is the just wrath of God which is acting through it.[2]

This passage then is a strong demand that every Christian must obey the *de facto* government (its law and magistrates) of the region where he lives.

This leads to a question that has often been discussed: Why is the doctrine of obedience to civil government and civil magistrates treated so emphatically in this particular epistle, to Christians at Rome? Why not the epistle to Philippians or Ephesians? Scholars have with good reason suggested at least two possible reasons—both or either of which might have called forth this expression of an important portion of the whole counsel of God at this particular juncture.

In the first place, while the church at Rome was mainly of Gentile constituency (1:13, cf. 15:15-16), there was also a strong Jewish element present. The Jews at Rome were notoriously turbulent. Whether this Jewish element in the church at Rome actually was being tempted to join in the growing Jewish nationalistic feeling against Rome or not, all the Christians were, because of their proximity to the capital of government, very apt to be associated in the public mind with the Jews, as a Jewish sect, and to reap any punishment meted out to Jews. This was Calvin's view.

Phillip Schaff has well written:

> This exhortation was probably occasioned by the turbulent spirit of the Jews in Rome, who had been on this account banished from the city by the Emperor Claudius (A.D. 51). Their messianic expectations assumed a carnal and political character, and were directed chiefly toward the external emancipation from the odious yoke of the heathen Romans. A few years after the date of the Epistle to the Romans, the spirit of revolt burst forth in open war, which ended in the destruction of Jerusalem (A.D. 70). The Jewish, and even the Gentile Christians, might readily be led away by this fanaticism, since the gospel proffered liberty, and they might not understand that it was mainly spiritual-moral freedom from the slavery of sin, out of which, by degrees, in the appointed way, a reformation and transformation of civil relations should proceed. Such mistakes have been common; e.g.,

the Peasant's war, the Anabaptist tumults in the time of the Reformation, and many revolutions since the latter part of the last [i.e., the eighteenth] century. The attitude of Christ, his Apostles, and his Church, down to the time of Constantine, toward the civil government is truly sublime. They recognized in it an ordinance of God, despite its degeneracy, yielding to it in all legitimate affairs a ready obedience, despite the fact that they were persecuted by it with fire and sword. It was . . . by just such Christian conduct in contrast with such cruelty that Christ's Church won the moral victory over the Roman Empire and heathendom. . . . Thus she was enabled to "overcome evil with good."[3]

Only very shortly before Paul wrote this epistle, the emperor Claudius in a moment of anti-Semitic exasperation had expelled all Jews from Rome, including their minority of Christians (see Ac 18:2). There is strong evidence of history and recent archaeology that a Jewish riot against Christians had been the cause.[4]

There was still possibility, as there had been even during the Lord's ministry, that some disciples might have a totally false outlook concerning Christ's kingdom message and program. From the time when certain of our Lord's disciples sought to take Jesus by force and make him king, to the Fifth Monarchy Men of the Civil War era in seventeenth century Britain, and on to the present, there have been sincere Christians who have not seen their duty in this regard. Since the first readers of this epistle lived in Rome, where every disturbance of the peace, real or alleged, quickly would be noticed, these Christians needed especially to be on guard against even the appearance of sedition.

Yet Paul's motives were more than prudential. He was speaking truth for the sake of the church in all ages and in every place. This is emphasized in two ways. First, the address of the demand, "Let every soul be subject unto the higher powers." "Every soul" means every man, "yet with reference to the life of the soul, whose emotions in relation to the government come into special consideration [Ac 2:43; 3:23; Rev 16:3]."[5] A specific reference to the soul as opposed to man's body is not to be eliminated. "The Hebraism suggests prominently the idea of individuality. These rules apply to all, however privileged, and the question is treated from the standpoint of individual duty."[6]

Second, the demand, "be in subjection," is an expression which in Greek means to subject oneself to another.§ Some indication of the sense is to be gained from the fact that in the New Testament it is used of proper subjection to the law of God (Ro 8:7), of Christian subjection to Christ (Eph 5:24), of younger believers to elder believers (1 Pe 5:5), of slaves to masters (1 Pe 2:18), of wives to husbands (Eph 5:22), of Jesus' submission to His own parents (Lk 2:51) as well as of citizens to their government—commanded|| not only in Romans 13:1, but also in Titus 3:1 and 1 Peter 2:13.

The "higher powers" (*exousiais huperechousais*, authorities which are over) is a clear reference to governmental officers.[7] Certain European writers, notably Karl Barth, a professional theologian, and Oscar Cullman, a New Testament specialist, have attempted to demonstrate, somewhat unsuccessfully, that these words in this context refer to demon or angelic spirits that are presumed to stand behind governments and their officers. That the Bible makes rare reference to such is not disputed; that *exousia*, especially in the plural, is sometimes used of supramundane spirits is well-known; that the two words together, the second qualifying the first (authorities which are over) ever has such a reference cannot be shown.[8]

It is significant that Cullman and Barth have not won over fellow German-speaking scholars to this point of view, though the prestige of their names, especially of Cullman's in this case, has won considerable acceptance of it and wider interest in it among English-speaking scholars. To most persons, this notion will seem bizarre and exceedingly strange when considered solely on the basis of its merits and the evidence for it. The thesis has been developed by Clinton D. Morrison.[9] John Reumann, while rejecting the position, provides a guide to the literature of the discussion.[10] A fair assessment will be found in Daniel B. Stevick, *Civil Disobedience and the Christian.*[11] It does not lend strength to the view that the article on *exousia* in *Theologisches Woerterbuch Zum Neuen Testament*, which asserts that "a special use of *exousia* in the New Testament is for supernatural powers, usually together with *archai, dunameis, kuriotetes.*"[12]

---

§*Hupotassesthō*, present, imperative middle of *hupotassō* used with dative.

||In view of this, it seems unlikely that apparent efforts to make Paul something of a parliamentary democrat in his theory of civil obedience are bound to fail. The lengthy argument advocated by C. E. B. Cranfield (*A Commentary on Romans 12-13* [Edinburgh: Oliver & Boyd, 1965], pp. 69-72) is an example of such an effort.

The entry does not include Romans 13:1, 3 among the exemplary passages.

It is noteworthy that the passage makes no distinction between good rulers and bad ones, between laws pleasant to obey and those unpleasant. This is not to say that the demand is made unconditionally, for it is not. There are certain conditions, but in every case they relate to abnormal circumstances. Normally, all men must obey their civil rulers and the civil laws—the ones they have, not the ones they wish they might have. No distinction is drawn between *de facto* and *de jure* government. And we will have to go elsewhere in Scripture to find guidance for the rare occasion when a person is called upon by competing governments for his obedience, or what one is to do when obedience to government requires disobedience to the moral laws of God. Let the reader not be distracted just yet by ruminations about the unusual and abnormal. There has rarely been a time in the life of most of us when we needed guidance for other than the normal.

Third, there are specific reasons for obedience to magistrates. In the first place, governments—all human governments—are such by divine appointment: "there is no power but of God; and the powers that be are ordained of God" (v. 1). This is the Old Testament biblical view. Here the teaching is given a strong moral bearing on the conscience. In an epoch such as ours, when democratic ideas of sovereignty prevail, it is something of a rebuke to read that "the Most High ruleth in the kingdom of men, and giveth it to whomsoever he will, and setteth up over it the lowest of men" (Dan 4:17, cf. Rev 17:17). The President of the United States, the premier of the Soviet Union, the mayor of Chicago, no less than Her Majesty, Queen Elizabeth II, are such by the grace of God.

In the second place, resistance to constituted government is resistance to God's ordinance. This is an inference drawn by the author of Romans from the first reason—"Therefore he that resisteth the power, withstandeth the ordinance of God" (v. 2a). To break the law by assaulting an officer of the law is an offense against the majesty of God. The policeman's authority, the president's, or the king's—whatever be the type of constitutional theory for it—is God's. Those who wish their thoughts and actions to be controlled by biblical considerations will be deeply moved by knowledge of this fact. David's horror at doing harm to King Saul, and the penalty of death for incorrigible disobedience to parents should be seen as aspects of this dread fact. It accounts likewise for the firm statute in the Pentateuch: "Thou shalt not revile the gods [*elohîm*], nor curse the ruler of thy people" (Ex 22:28, KJV). There is a divine order of authority which cannot be broken guiltlessly. This principle extends to the removal of unrighteous and oppressive governmental authority, and was a basic consideration of Christian leaders of the English Glorious Revolution of 1688 and the American Revolution of 1776. For, says a famous New Testament scholar, "To obtain, by lawful means [only], the removal or alteration of an unjust or unreasonable law, is another part of this duty; for all the powers among men must be in accord with the highest power, the moral sense."[13]

In the third place, those who resist this power will be punished. "And they who have opposed will receive condemnation upon themselves" (v. 2b, NASB). It may be a fine, imprisonment, beating, or even death. "The logical result of this theory as to the origin of human power is that resistance to it is resistance to the ordering of God; and hence those who resist will receive *krima*—a judgment of condemnation which is human, for it comes through human instruments, but Divine as having its origin and source in God. There is no reference here to eternal punishment."[14]

The next arguments proceed from the services of government—all human government—rather than from the divine source of it. So, fourth, rulers restrain evil. "For rulers are not a terror to the good work, but to the evil" (v. 3a). Here is a case where the Greek article appears to be used before the noun to indicate a class of things—good works as a class, evil works as a class. If rulers are a terror to the evil work, then they must be able to recognize evil works. It has already been observed that men do not need biblical revelation to have, within limits, knowledge of good and evil. The prophets proclaimed the responsibility of heathen magistracies to enforce these universally known standards. Any reading of the classical authors of ancient Greece and Rome will support this. Falling far short of God's glory as the goal of right action, the classical pagan moralists knew a good deal about basic righteousness. Just how pagans of any age know—whether by right reason, natural law, natural light, general revelation, common grace, or whatever—is a matter of some legitimate difference of opinion. It is a fact, nevertheless, that without written standards, there is a divine morality which rulers everywhere know and enforce, and which the public acknowledges in spite of perverse denials among certain members of society. If this were not so, human life as a society could not exist. This is part basis for the statement that "law is not made for a righteous man, but for the lawless and unruly, for the ungodly and sinners, for the unholy and profane, for murderers of fathers, and murderers of mothers, for manslayers, for fornicators, for abusers of themselves with men, for menstealers, for liars, for false swearers, and if there be any other thing that is contrary to sound doctrine" (1 Ti 1:9-10). Law here is anarthrous—that is, not *the* law, but "law in general, including of course the Mosaic Law. It is doubtful whether 'law' when anarthrous is ever used by St. Paul for the law of Moses exclusively, though it may be, when that law is in his mind the most prominent."[15] It is quite remarkable and provides cause for reflection that rulers, in many lands untouched by the light of the Bible, do better in restraining violent evil works than professedly Christian rulers do in some parts of Christendom. The streets of Peking under Maoist Communist rule, for example, are acknowledged to be much safer and freer from violence than is Hong Kong, which has had "Christian" (British) rule since its founding.

Another service of government, a fifth argument for civil obedience, is that rulers promote good things for their people. "Wilt thou then not be afraid of the power? do that which is good, and thou shalt have praise of the same: For he is the minister of God to thee for good" (vv. 3b-4a). Many writers, especially in the Lutheran tradition, are inclined to assign a wholly negative function to government. And no doubt the government's service of restraint—as policeman—is primary. It seems, however, that there is a positive side, not to be overemphasized, for it is a minor element in Scripture. It is not necessary to endorse secular socialism and the welfare state idea to acknowledge that government is "a minister of God to thee for good."# There is a negative overtone even in this

---

#The word translated "minister" is *diakonos* (deacon). But there is no religious connotation. It is the Greek word for any male household servant who performs menial tasks.

Pauline assertion, for protection from thieves and murderers is a "good." But insofar as is consistent with men's true good—not bondage to a cradle-to-grave physical security that would substitute "big brother" for personal effort and servile dependence on state edicts for private decision, as in all forms of totalitarianism where men trade their manhood for false security—insofar as is consistent with true good, governments may do just that. Again, there are recognized dangers in government "do good." Recently, for example, it is reported that a hundred thousand doctors have quit smoking cigarettes, but only after a United States federal government report declared what any thoughtful person has always known about the deleterious effect of smoke in the lungs and pulmonary tract, and what scientific experiments have been rendering specific for many years. Do even our medical scientists now lean on government as a big brother to do their private thinking for them? The general substitution of government edict for private responsible decision has come a long way indeed! Yet government has a legitimate sphere in which to operate for the positive good of citizenry. Only thus can the factory owner's freedom, for example, be prevented from pouring smoke from his stacks so thick that another man has no freedom to breath clean air. Even here, it must be admitted, there is frequently more negative than positive coercive quality to the good. Modern communities will never correct environmental pollution, as only one example, on a purely voluntary basis. There must be governmental coercion.

A further service, and thereby a sixth argument for civil obedience, is that rulers are empowered by God to inflict God's temporal punishments on evildoers. "But if thou do that which is evil, be afraid; for he beareth not the sword in vain: for he is a minister of God, an avenger for wrath to him that doeth evil" (v. 4b). There never has existed for any extended time an extensive society of men wherein someone did not have power to enforce laws. In enforcement, penalties for infractions are necessary. The power of government to take away the life of offenders is an ultimate and necessary instrument for enforcement of civil order.

Many years later, Paul, the author of these words, confirmed his own belief in them under most significant circumstances. He was in danger of losing his life to a Jerusalem riot stirred up against him by Jewish fanatics from Asia, whereupon the Roman military tribune intervened when they wanted to kill him (Ac 21:27-33). Even in the local prison, with the military custody, he was not safe (23:12-35). Paul had reason to be grateful for Rome's power of the sword, not borne in vain, for that power had saved his life. It was in circumstances such as these that two years later, after enduring the two years of the governor Felix' petty malingering (23:25-30) that Paul had opportunity to defend himself before Festus, Felix's successor, who suggested a return to Jerusalem for trial (25:6-9). This was the end of Paul's patience with the officials of the provincial government and, apparently having made up his mind previously, he responded: "I am standing before Caesar's judgment-seat, where I ought to be judged: to the Jews have I done no wrong, as thou also very well knowest. If then I am a wrong-doer, and have committed anything worthy of death, I refuse not to die; but if none of the things is true whereof these accuse me, no man can give me up to them. I appeal unto Caesar. Then Festus, when he had conferred with the council, answered, Thou hast appealed unto Caesar: unto Caesar shalt thou go" (Ac 25:10-12).

This forthright speech by the prisoner in the dock reminded Festus, the present custodian and officer of Caesar's judgment-seat, that he was neglecting justice. But if right judgment should discover Paul to be guilty, he claimed to be ready to die for his crimes. Paul was prepared to eat his own words of Romans 13, which he had written some years previously, if he could be proven wrong. Nevertheless he trusted that Caesar's laws would not condemn him, that he would be freed.

After a few years of release, sometime in the later years of Nero, Paul was arrested again. New Testament indications and tradition unite in affirming that Nero then condemned and executed him.

The biblical incidents in this connection show that the just power of human government is not always justly employed. Our Lord was executed unjustly either because the government, in the person of Pilate, did not make sufficient inquiry to ascertain the true facts of the case, or because of insufficient courage on the part of the government officer. In any case, the death penalty itself was not wherein the injustice lay. In Paul's case, as with persecution of religion for perverted patriotic purposes always, the injustice lay in an inevitable collision between the righteous *total* claims of God on the one hand with the unrighteous *totalitarian* claims of some ruler on the other. Government is not wrong, for it is divinely ordained and established. Being in the custody, however, of fallible, sinful men, it is frequently much less than perfectly just.

What must not be lost sight of is that unpleasant as is the task of the jailor and the use of the whip, the cell, the noose, the guillotine, these things stand behind the stability of civilized society, and they stand there necessarily, for God has declared it so, in harmony with reality, rather than with apostate sociological opinion. Government, with its coercive powers is a social necessity, but one determined by the Creator, not by the statistical tables of some university social research staff! No society can successfully vote fines, imprisonment, corporeal and capital punishment away permanently. The society which tries has lost touch with realities of man (his fallen sinful state), realities of the world, and the truth of divine revelation in nature, man's conscience, and the Bible.

In the context of Romans 12 and 13, then, that vengeance which is forbidden the individual is committed by God, to whom as Creator all vengeance belongs, to the civil minister of God to execute. It is then the duty of private persons to support rulers obediently, and for rulers to lead justly and decisively.

The seventh and last of Paul's reasons for Christian obedience to civil officers is conscience—"for conscience' sake" (v. 5). Since God is the creator and enlightener of conscience (in the case of Christians, by this particular passage of Scripture), "for conscience' sake" is not materially different from Peter's maxim, "Be subject to every ordinance of man for the Lord's sake" (1 Pe 2:13). The Christian serves his country, obeys its laws, and supports its rulers so far as a biblically informed conscience lets him, not out of servile fear or out of rigid dogmatic necessity, but because he knows it is right.

Right (understood as expression of the will of the Creator-God) is ultimately the ground of all righteous action. Ethics, with the essentially secular notion of custom, usual, natural, is not a true synonym for righteousness. Right, rather, is ultimately the reason for being righteous. "Children, obey your parents in the Lord; for this is right" (Eph 6:1). "Shall not the Judge of all the earth do right?" (Gen 18:25).

19

THE TEACHINGS OF PAUL AND PETER WITH REGARD TO CIVIL GOVERNMENT

Areas in Which Obedience Is Rendered to Rulers

"He is a minister of God to thee for good. But if thou do that which is evil, be afraid; for he beareth not the sword in vain: for he is a minister of God, an avenger for wrath to him that doeth evil" (Ro 13:4). These words continue Paul's discussion of civil government.

The rulers are characterized as ministers of God's service. The language is that of service rendered to God, not to man. This is truly an exalted notion of the state. What the Christian in one realm does in service to God, the officers of government do in still another, though in either case imperfectly. Such doctrine certainly puts a high value on the civil service and has always been accepted where the Bible has been read and understood.

In such a case, however, the strict limits of this service must be recognized. Caesar may claim Caesar's things, but not God's. When Caesar claims that which belongs to God, then he must be refused, even if life is forfeited on that account. The Scriptures soberly demand no less from those who truly know Jesus as Lord.

Paul's list of areas of civil obedience is not long, and leaves unmentioned a number of areas in which Christians ever since have had questions, with no invariable Christian answer. We are to pay tribute (v. 6). This may be understood simply as taxes, for ancient categories of money payment to government are not strictly parallel with modern ones, especially in modern democratic countries.

There is a dispute over whether the duty of paying taxes is to be connected with "wrath" and "conscience" in the verse immediately

257

preceding, or with the services of government mentioned earlier. Commentators have discussed it since the time of Calvin or earlier.[1] Recent textual science has eliminated the "therefore" (Gr. *oun)* from verse seven. Even so, it appears that each of verses 5, 6, and 7 is a separate inferential conclusion based on verses 1-4, indicated in the first two cases by "wherefore" (Gr. *dia touto gar*), "for this cause" (Gr. *dio*), and in the last by "therefore" (Gr. *oun*). If the "therefore" be omitted, then only verses 5 and 6 are parallel inferential conclusions while verse 7, though a conclusion also, is not formally so.[2] Robert Haldane, a widely respected authority whose great work on Romans continues to be distributed and read throughout the English-speaking world, asks:

> Is it on account of conscience, or on account of civil government's being an appointment of God? The latter is the true answer. The reason why the thing is a matter of conscience is, because government is a divine appointment. Taxes are to be paid to government for the good of society, and this is the argument that is immediately added. For they are God's ministers. They are public officers whom God himself, as the ruler of the world, has appointed to this business. Here, in order to impress the truth, that "the powers that be are ordained of God," and that they are "of God," it is for the third time repeated that they are "God's ministers," attending continually on this very thing; that is, civil governors are devoted to the affairs of the public, and they should be adequately remunerated. . . . The "very thing," to which they constantly attend . . . is the ministry of God in the things of government . . . their duty as ministers of God in civil things.[2]

"Render to all their dues: tribute to whom tribute is due, custom to whom custom; fear to whom fear; honor to whom honor" (Ro 13:7). This is a comprehensive statement, as indicated by "to all their dues," evidently intended to cover all positive duties toward government and perhaps toward all men. Tribute has been mentioned in verse 6, and now custom is considered. Lexical authorities seem unable to distinguish precisely between these two. If there is a distinction, it is between taxes on one's person (tribute) and indirect taxes on commerce (custom). Burdensome as taxes are and misused as they often may be, it is within the rights of government to collect them. If so, it is wrong to avoid payment. On the assumption that the wider interpretation of "to all [men] their dues" is correct, then honor is that which is due magistrates and others over us, and fear is that which is due our peers.

A further observation, drawn from the subsequent context, must be made. The Pauline texts thus far considered all have a context of last things. The "princes of this world" are coming "to nought" (1 Co 2:6), and a grand assize wherein the saints shall judge angels is going to supersede the civil courts of Corinth (1 Co 6:1-4). Likewise, the thought of Romans in the immediately subsequent context, connected without break from verses one through 14 (after which a break does occur), is eschatological. The present age is held already to be an advanced season upon which the day of the coming of Christ is to break immediately: "Knowing the season, that already it is time for you to awake out of sleep: for now is our salvation nearer to us than when we first believed. The night is far spent, and the day is at hand" (vv. 11-12). We are thus reminded that human government as now constituted is temporary and has no value in itself. "The kingdom of the world [will] become the kingdom of our Lord, and of his Christ; and he shall reign for ever and ever" (Rev 11:15)—and we with him. Christians should not become deeply attached to this present order of things. If they do not, they will neither resent civil government nor become too dependent upon it.

The Christian belongs to a heavenly commonwealth. "For our citizenship [literally, commonwealth] is in heaven; whence also we wait for a Saviour" (Phil 3:20). We must not be surprised therefore if the citizens and magistrates of this present evil world do not treat us well. They do not understand us, our ideals, or our motives. In Paul's time, when lack of Roman citizenship and the disabilities thereby were widely experienced, Paul's metaphor was fully understood. E. A. Judge has written, "Lack of citizenship was a humiliating barrier to social acceptance in many cases. The New Testament writers frequently reflect the feelings of the disqualified in their metaphors for the ideal moral alienation from the world. The familiar group of terms: 'strangers,' 'foreigners,' 'aliens,' 'pilgrims,' 'sojourners,' (e.g., Eph. 2:19; Heb. 11:13; I Pet. 1:1; 17; 2:11) are all drawn from the technical vocabulary of republican exclusiveness. Addressed to persons who were undoubtedly often under civil disabilities in their own communities, they must have added peculiar points to the demand for moral detachment."[3]

The context of the seventh chapter of 1 Corinthians is that of worldly involvement of a different sort. Christians simply do not have free time to use the world to the full. All human relationships of this life are of short duration "for the fashion of this world passeth away" (v. 31). Thus the believer's personal eschatology with prospect of heaven above after a short life here on earth, as well as the eschatological second advent of Christ, argue for much less than total involvement in the world's course.

The apostle, anxious that his spiritual sons and daughters live out their lives in proper involvement and disengagement, as regards the world, put it this way (the specific problem was marriage, with its poignant mixture of joy with care):

> "Art thou bound unto a wife? seek not to be loosed. Art thou loosed from a wife? seek not a wife. But shouldest thou marry, thou hast not sinned; and if a virgin marry, she hath not sinned. Yet such shall have tribulation in the flesh: and I would spare you. But this I say, brethren, the time is shortened, that henceforth both those that have wives may be as though they had none; and those that weep, as though they wept not; and those that rejoice, as though they rejoiced not; and those that buy, as though they possessed not; and those that use the world, as not using it to the full; for the fashion of this world passeth away. But I would have you free from cares" (1 Co 7:27-32).

This runs counter to much that is being said today by some who want the church to be less heavenly minded and more earthly focused (referring to social improvement). They have lost the spirit of the New Testament, which does not present this outlook, even though the social interest element is certainly present. Balance will always be something of a *desideratum* in this regard, for it is precisely those whose heavenly vision is clear who see the earthly human needs truly, because they see them in their connection with eternal things.

1 TIMOTHY 2:1-4

I exhort therefore, first of all, that supplications, prayers, intercessions, thanksgivings, be made for all men; for the kings and all that are in high place; that we may lead a tranquil and quiet life in all godliness and gravity. This is good and acceptable in the sight of

God our Saviour; who would have all men to be saved, and come to the knowledge of the truth.

Oscar Cullmann refers to this passage as "one which speaks of an unreservedly positive relationship between Christians and the State: the prayer for the State and those who stand at its head. This holds true even at the point where the state reveals itself as the beast from the abyss [Rev 13:1-7]. . . . Even in times when the Christians were being cruelly persecuted by the State this prayer did not cease to be voiced. Because the Christian never renounces the State as an institution, he will always pray for it."[4]

This is true, but it is only part of the great body of truth that lies in germ herein, for it contains a whole philosophy of state relations for the Christian.

Chapter one of Paul's first epistle to Timothy sets the stage: one of primary concern for right belief and good church order at Ephesus where Paul had urged Timothy to work for a while. This was during the early resumption of Paul's missionary travels after release from his first Roman imprisonment. The text quoted is his first specific charge to Timothy in this Ephesian ministry. Being only recently released from prison, and knowing thereby how truly helpless the Christians were to remain free from civil disability except the emperor and his minions allow it, he is driven to emphasize the one channel open whereby humble citizens of the kingdom of heaven may affect the counsels of kings.

THE PRIMACY OF PRAYER FOR RULERS (1-2a)

"First of all" (v. 1) is not merely rhetorical, nor does it merely indicate first in order of instruction, for the apostle does not customarily enumerate his sentences; it means first in importance. Importance of prayer is likewise indicated by the piling up of synonyms—"supplications, prayers, intercessions, thanksgivings"—not in poetic fashion, as in Hebrew poetry, but for emphasis as in forensic speech—like Lincoln's "dedicate . . . consecrate . . . hallow this ground." Practically speaking, this is the one avenue whereby the simple earthly citizen of heaven's kingdom can affect both the counsels of the mighty and the actions of the masses. It is a method despised in days of spiritual lassitude, but nevertheless the only basis on which the church has ever advanced. Churchmen whose Christian activism has taken mainly to placarding, marching, protesting, and shouting might well observe the author of these verses first at prayer, then in counsel with his friends, and *after that* preaching in the homes and market places. When Paul came to be heard by the mighty, it was to defend his action as a preacher (albeit in the streets) of a way to heaven (see Ac 26:1-32; Ro 1:9-10). It is notable that while Paul's planning did not get him to Rome, his prayers did—but not in the way he had planned. There is biblical support for missionary strategy as well as for active labor till arms and feet, mind and soul are exhausted, but not apart from spiritual forces accompanying (2 Co 10:3-6).

The church and the kings and potentates with which she must deal are much like women and men in marital diplomacy. The woman who stands up with brute force to her husband will lose her case, for she is stepping out of her feminine role. She may state her case—but always within the framework of her position—if she wishes to succeed. So the church may stand up to government to gain proper ends—but always as a church, not as a political party. Christians may form or join parties, but churches should not.

The Goal of Prayer for Rulers (2b-3)

This may be briefly: that the Christian community may have civil peace and legal toleration in order to carry on its own internal activity of Christian nurture and its external work of saving men through preaching the gospel.

Of special importance in our time is that Christians in their homes and churches, as well as in the market place, exemplify the tranquil and quiet life. This was held in high regard by Paul, and he pressed it upon his readers many times. To the Thessalonians, very early in his ministry, he once wrote: "But we exhort you, brethren . . . that ye be ambitious to be quiet, and to do your own business, and to work with your hands, even as we charged you; that ye walk becomingly toward them that are without, and may have need of nothing" (1 Th 4:10-13). The spirit of Peter's admonition to the Christian women is quite the same (1 Pe 3:1-4).

Thus evangelism in times of civil quiet is to be accomplished not only by words, but also by deeds. These are not specifically deeds of charity toward "them that are without," but rather the manifestation of a manner of life—family, personal, community—which in the long run verifies itself to reflective people. This was the method of the church of the early centuries.

True, it arouses initial envy and misunderstanding, as is noticed in the entire fourth chapter of 1 Peter. This kind of testimony is especially effective in times of persecution.

At the present, outside of the totalitarian Communist countries (and recently also Nazi and fascist countries) there is little real persecution on account of any kind of Christian separation, social or otherwise. However, as total statewide integration of life progresses in the democracies now moving toward socialism, we may see something of a return to the situation of the first three centuries. There is thus a certain sinister aspect of the movement toward mutuality in social concerns today. Rome itself was a *polis,* something like a modern state, as were most of the great urban centers of the empire. Thus: "If we would picture to ourselves the true notion which the Greeks embodied in the word *polis,* we must lay aside all modern [these words are pre-Marxian] ideas respecting the nature and object of a state. With us, practically, if not in theory, the object of a state hardly embraces more than the protection of life and property. The Greeks, on the other hand, had the most vivid conception of the state as a whole, every part of which was to co-operate to some great end to which all other duties were considered subordinate. . . . In all governments the endeavor was to draw the social union as close as possible."[5]

W. M. Ramsay has accurately written of the interplay of pagan religion with patriotism in the ancient Greco-Roman world: "A citizen who was not active and interested in his own State was disliked and condemned in general opinion; and the unwillingness of the early Christian to perform the religious acts required in all religious duties, and their consequent abstention from politics, intensified the disapproval which the pagan mob felt for them."[6]

It is not surprising, then, that the Roman historian, Tacitus, reported of the Neroian persecution that it was for political as well as seemingly religious reasons.[7]

E. M. Blaiklock comments: "In such words, the Christians enter history, tormented, scorned, misrepresented. They reaped, from Nero's crime, the bitter harvest of unpopularity whose seeds they had already sown by their abstention from common social life. It was maliciously alleged that they hated the human race. An uncompromising conscience had, in fact, withdrawn the followers of Christ from many of the activities of a society much more communal in habits and more closely knit than that of the modern democratic world. The crowds commonly react towards minorities which provoke dislike by difference."[8]

There is thus a great deal of danger in being the light of the world, for "men love darkness rather than light" (Jn 3:19). It is even more dangerous to claim to be salt and to have lost the savor, for it is then "good for nothing, but to be cast out and trodden under foot of men" (Mt 5:13). Luke adds: "It is fit neither for the land nor for the dunghill" (Lk 14:5). The judgment of God in the form of the ferocity of violent men and mobs has fallen heavily on more than one community of moribund Christians. Witness, for example, the scourge of Islam in the Levant and in northern Africa.

TITUS 3:1-2, 8b

Put them in mind to be in subjection to rulers, to authorities, to be obedient, to be ready unto every good work, to speak evil of no man, not to be contentious, to be gentle, showing all meekness toward all men. . . . To the end that they who have believed God may be careful to maintain good works.

These words do little more than reaffirm near the end of their author's ministry what he had said much earlier in his ministry, before he had suffered so much from government power gone astray. There is no essential change of view.

There is a duty affirmed many times in Scripture, here placed in the context of "subjection to rulers, to authorities," namely, good works of a general sort. He says it twice. Christians have a right to claim that throughout the ages it has been they who have taught good works to other men. Christianity, for example, taught the ancient world to love all its children and to care for them. Abortion and exposure of unwanted babies was the scandal of antiquity.* Orphanages

---

*The following extract in brief fashion summarizes the situation in ancient society. "How far [abortion] was considered a crime among the civilized nations of antiquity

and hospitals are both essentially Christian inventions. Generally speaking, the present effort at social betterment through government has been the secularizing of a Christian ideal. It was noι the idea of either Plato or Aristotle, though both wrote extensively on politics and the state. Neither Robert Owen, nor Karl Marx, nor August Comte would have had the idea if Christianity had not disseminated the Christian idea in the social soil wherein those men's notions arose.

Paul wrote nothing at all of the Christians' sitting back and leaving good works to Caesar and his minions. In medieval and Reformation times, the religious-political unity of the various communities in Christendom provided care, such as was available (and it was much better than is sometimes nowadays smugly supposed), for the indigent, sick, orphaned, and abandoned. Ordinarily it was under church sponsorship, but at government expense. This is to say, it was paid for by taxes, which in turn were not clearly distinguishable from tithes. In any case, the inspiration was Christian. With

---

has long been debated. Those who maintain the impunity of the practice rely for their authority upon certain passages of the classical authors, while, bitterly lamenting the frequency of this enormity, never allude to any laws by which it might be suppressed. For example, in one of Plato's dialogues (*Theat.*), Socrates is made to speak of artificial abortion as a practice, not only common but allowable; and Plato himself authorizes it in his *Republic* (lib. v). Aristotle (*Polit.* lib. vii c.17) gives it as his opinion that no child ought to be suffered to come into the world, the mother being above forty or the father above fifty-five years of age. Lysias maintained, in one of his pleadings quoted by Harpocration, that forced abortion could not be considered homicide, because a child *in uter* was not an animal, and had no separate existence. Among the Romans, Ovid (*Amor.* lib. ii) Juvenal (*Sat.* vi. 594) and Seneca (*Consol. ad Hel.* 16) mention the frequency of the offence, but maintain silence as to any laws for punishing it. On the other hand, it is argued that the authority of Galen and Cicero (*pro Cluentio*) place it beyond a doubt that far from being allowed to pass with impunity, the offence in question was sometimes punished by death; that the authority of Lysias is of doubtful authenticity; and that the speculative reasonings of Plato and Aristotle, in matters of legislation, ought not to be confounded with the actual state of the laws. Moreover Sobacus (*Serm.* 73) has preserved a passage from Musonius in which that philosopher expressly states that the ancient law-givers inflicted punishments on females who caused themselves to abort. After the spread of Christianity among the Romans, however, foeticide became equally criminal with the murder of an adult, and the barbarian hordes which afterwards overran the empire also treated the offence as a crime punishable with death. This severe penalty remained in force in all the countries of Europe until the middle ages. With medieval times came also a reversal of opinion as to the magnitude of the crime in killing a child not yet born. But the exact period of transition is not clearly marked" (*Encyclopedia Britannica*, 11th ed., 1910, s.v. "Abortion").

Current literature on the subject of abortion is mountainous in size, with more being published every day. A very recent book which promises to present a dependable discussion, giving proper place to biblical and Christian teaching, is F. F. R. Gardner, *Abortion, the Personal Dilemma* (Exeter, England: Paternoster, 1972). In addition to being an evangelical Christian, the author is an obstetrician and gynecologist.

the rise of political and social liberalism over the past two and a half centuries, these responsibilities have been progressively shifted to government expense, government control, and purely secular-social-humanitarian inspiration. Some Christians seem to have acknowledged less and less responsibility, so much so that now they sometimes seem opposed to any involvement at all. Others, who appear to be correct, are reminding us that God has not relieved us of our responsibilities in these regards. Whether coming generations will be inclined to look to Caesar to care for these matters is unknown, but it seems likely, according to present trends. Whatever the issue of that, it is clearly the privilege and duty of Christians in any society and economic system to maintain good works in the context of obedience to civil authorities. This is not to say that the need and ability may not vary greatly accordingly to the times and the economic-political system. If the government confiscates salary by taxes and regiments time, obviously Christian good works will have to wait for better times.

1 PETER 2:11-17

Beloved, I beseech you as sojourners and pilgrims, to abstain from fleshly lusts, which war against the soul; having your behavior seemly among the Gentiles; that, wherein they speak against you as evil-doers, they may by your good works, which they behold, glorify God in the day of visitation. Be subject to every ordinance of man for the Lord's sake: whether to the king, as supreme; or unto governors, as sent by him for vengeance on evil-doers and for praise to them that do well. For so is the will of God, that by well-doing ye should put to silence the ignorance of foolish men: as free, and not using your freedom for a cloak of wickedness, but as bondservants of God. Honor all men. Love the brotherhood. Fear God. Honor the king.

The early contacts between Roman government and the Christians were not unfriendly. But in the late 50's, things began to change. "The Christians had separated from Judaism and were becoming recognized as a different group. Their firm adherence to belief in an invisible God and in a risen Christ excited the suspicion and the contempt of the public, while their talk of a coming judgment and overthrow of the existing world created misunderstanding and hatred.

The reaction against them in Rome under Nero was the product of this popular dislike. . . . The close of the Pastoral Epistles shows that Paul's death marked a turn in the policy of the government from casual tolerance to hostile criticism."[9]

Though it does not seem that systematic persecution of Christians had yet taken place in the provinces (see 1 Pe 2:1), news of events in Rome under Nero had reached there, and since they were already experiencing locally inspired persecutions, Christians wondered about their future. Peter's first epistle is distinctly designed to assure and to guide Christians of the provinces at that juncture and into the future when, as Pliny's *Letters*† show, the provincial officials were

---

†Pliny the Younger (nephew of Pliny the Elder and adoptive son), already a famous literateur, was appointed governor of Bithynia (to the south of the Black Sea in present Turkey) about A.D. 111. He seems to have died two or three years later in that office. During those years, he dispatched many letters to the emperor, Trajan. Modern interest is mainly in letters 96 and 97 of that collection, both relating to his problems with Christians. Nothing coming from antiquity is quite so candid on the point of worship of the emperor and empire as are these letters. In letter 96, Pliny writes:

"Sire, it is my custom to refer to you all matters about which I am doubtful: for who is better able to direct my hesitation or instruct my ignorance? At trials of Christians I have never been present and I am therefore ignorant of the usual practice in regard to the matter and the limits of punishment or inquiry. I have had also no little difficulty as to whether some distinction of age should be made, or if persons of the most tender age stand on the same footing as the more adult; whether the penitent is to be pardoned or if a person who has once been a Christian shall have no benefit of ceasing to be one. Whether the mere name of Christian, apart from crime, is punishable, or only crime coupled with the name. Meanwhile in the case of those reported to me as Christians I have followed this procedure. I asked themselves whether they were Christians. If they admitted it, I put the question a second time and a third, with threats of punishment. If they persisted in their confession, I ordered them to be led to execution; for I had no doubt that whatever the nature of that which they confessed, in any case their pertinacity and inflexible obstinacy deserved to be punished. There were others of a similar delusion whom, as they were Roman citizens, I noted for remission to Rome.

"Presently the mere handling of the matter produced the usual result of spreading the crime, and more varieties occurred. There was published an anonymous pamphlet containing many names. Those who denied that they were Christians or ever had been, when, after me, they invoked the gods and worshipped with incense and wine your statue which I had ordered to be brought for that purpose along with the images of the gods, and, further reviled Christ—things which it is said that no real Christian will do under any compulsion—I consider this should be dismissed. Others who were named by the informer admitted that they had ceased to be, some several years before, some even twenty. All these likewise did homage to your statue and to the images of the gods and reviled Christ. They affirmed moreover that the sum of their crime or error was that they had been wont to meet together on a fixed day before daybreak and to repeat among themselves in turn a hymn to Christ as to a god and to bind themselves by an oath (sacramentum), not for some wickedness but not to commit theft, not to commit robbery, not to commit adultery, not to break their word, not to deny a deposit when demanded; these things duly done, it had been their custom to disperse and to meet again to take food—of an ordinary and harmless kind. Even this they had ceased to do after my edict by which, in accordance with your instructions, I had forbidden the existence of societies (hetaeriae). For these reasons I deemed it all the more necessary to find out the truth by the ex-

asking for instructions on how to handle the numerous Christian persons who simply would not acknowledge Caesar or any pagan deity as God. The message of Peter is heart-touching against such a background and in such circumstances.

As various scholars acknowledge, Peter's message about Christians and their response to persecution is obviously indebted to the sayings of Jesus and the epistles of Paul, and it makes no important advance upon them. We present Peter's words here as commentary and application of Jesus' and Paul's words. Some of the people who first read and carried out these admonitions doubtless were also among the first martyrs whose blood became the seed of the church.

First the Christians are reminded of their heavenly commonwealth, of their alien status in the world of the heathen (for such is the sense of "Gentiles," v. 12), and of how they should live in such a way as to represent well their heavenly Sovereign while on an essentially foreign mission, as seen in verses 11 and 12.

Persecution brought no change of instruction regarding their relation to laws and rulers (vv. 13-17). And the passing of nineteen centuries has not altered the message. The Christian message to its own is still the same: "Honor all men. Love the brotherhood. Fear God. Honor the king."

---

amination—even with torture—of two maids who were called deaconesses (ministrae-*diakonoi*). I found nothing but a perverse and extravagant superstition.

"I have therefore adjourned the inquiry and have had recourse to consulting you. For the matter seemed to me one deserving a consultation, especially in view of the number of these imperilled. For many persons of every age, of every rank, of both sexes even, are daily involved and will be, since not in the cities only, but in villages and country districts as well, has spread the contagion of that superstition—which it seems possible to check and correct. At any rate it is certain that temples which were already almost deserted have begun to be frequented; the customary religious rites, long intermitted, are being restored; and fodder for sacrificial victims—for which hitherto it was rare to find a purchaser—now finds a market. Whence it is easy to infer what a mass of men might be reformed, if penitence were recognized" (as quoted in *Encyclopedia Britannica*, 1953, s.v. "Pliny the Younger").

Trajan's reply discloses a firm but enlightened humanitarianism according to the pagan standard of the time. He approved of Pliny's procedures and leaned toward what, on the presuppositions of imperial paganism, was the mildest possible treatment of sincere but stubborn dissidents. "No formula capable of universal application can be laid down. The Christians are not to be sought out; if reported and convicted, they are to be punished, with this reservation that any person who denies that he is a Christian and confirms his testimony by overt act, that is, by worshipping our gods, however suspect he may have been in the past, shall obtain pardon by penitence. Anonymous publications ought to have no place in a criminal charge. It is a thing of the worst example and unworthy of our age (*et pessimi exempli nec nostri saeculi est*)" (ibid.).

20

NEW TESTAMENT WARNINGS AND PREDICTIONS WITH REGARD TO CIVIL GOVERNMENT

SCATTERED THROUGHOUT the New Testament are many sayings and precedents having bearing on Christian behavior toward civil government in particular and society in general.

The Christian is not ignorant regarding the future. He knows that the kingdom of God shall come. In the meantime, whatever the hopes of utopian planners or the promises of ambitious politicians, the world will always be the world, society always a depraved society of fallen men. Whatever the divine ideal regarding governments, with attendant Christian duties and attitudes, government will fall short of the ideal. However divinely ordered the government may be, the Christian knows things about the future which an essentially pagan government does not know; hence he has other fish to fry than those of the ruling political party. His interests can never be merely the popular preoccupation of the moment.

New Testament predictions of religious persecution by civil authorities begin at Matthew and end with Revelation. Jesus' disciples are sent forth as sheep in the midst of wolves. Some of them will be haled before governors and kings (Mt 10:16-18). The Christian faith will drive wedges between members of many families, resulting in betrayal to death (v. 21). In some circumstances "ye shall be hated of all men for my name's sake," said Jesus (v. 22). In this sense, the purpose of Jesus' first advent was "not to send peace, but a sword" (v. 34). The very early chapters of the book of Acts report harassment of the church by Jewish authorities, and in chapter 12 the beheading of James and the imprisonment of Peter by Herod are recorded. The book of Revelation predicts a final season of restrictions, disabilities, and atrocities without previous parallel (Rev 13-18, cf. 2 Th 1:6-12). Christians in every epoch of severe persecution have viewed their experiences as fulfillments of these sad warnings. Hence Peter is quite explicit that persecution should take no Christian believer by surprise (1 Pe 4:11-19).

The Christian response in regard to government persecution is to be quite flexible. Christians are to be assured that if they are faithful in witnessing, God will be as faithful to them as He was to His Son (Mt 10:24-27). Therefore, they need not fear men, but God alone (Mt 10:28-33). They are warned not to take arms against government, as the Zealots of Jesus' time were doing (Mt 26:52), though they may seek to avoid persecution. If persecuted, they may flee to another locality (Mt 10:23). One is reminded of the frantic migrations of the Reformation era, and of the population of Georgia by Huguenots from France. Yet, in response to dangers from robbers and brigands, or peril from the civil disorder, a degree of weapon-carrying and of self defense is authorized by Jesus. A comparison of Luke 22:35-36 with 9:3-6 and parallels makes this interpretation of Jesus' words about buying a sword hardly avoidable.[1] The presence of two swords already among the apostolic company, who, presumably as other Jews, bore arms as they made the paschal journey through dangerous districts, hardly warrants the strict defenseless pacifism frequently attributed to Jesus' doctrine. Also, as put by J. J. Van Oosterzee, "The Lord would certainly have avoided the expression as to buying a sword for threatening danger if he had willed that his disciples in no case should think of self-defense with outward weapons."[2] This is quite consistent with everything said elsewhere about obedience to authorities of law.

Warnings and exhortations concerning proper Christian attitudes are set forth in a number of texts. A certain shunning of intimacy with heathen and publicans is presupposed by the words of Jesus concerning church discipline (Mt 18:17), but this does not mean that under proper conditions one may not eat with them (Mk 2:13-20). As long as they are in this world, Christians are bid to do business as necessary even with fornicators, extortioners, and idolators (1 Co 5:11). Bitter anger, even when the majesty of God has been outraged, is not warranted, nor should the believer imprecate God against wicked men (Lk 9:51-56). One may show up corrupt officials for what they are (Lk 13:31-32), but he should not deliberately treat them with disrespect (Ac 23:3-5). If commanded to give to a ruler that which belongs only to God, they must refuse, whatever the consequences, obeying God rather than man (Ac 4:19-20, cf. 5:29), and knowing that God will deliver them from their tormentors even if it be through death (Dan 3:17). When unnecessary violence and bloodshed is perpetrated by rulers, Christians are to understand that there is a divine judgment of sin in it, for all men are deserving of judgment, that unless men will repent, they shall all perish by the hand of God (Lk 13:1-9). There is a grim fierceness about Jesus' declarations concerning future punishment, for He said more than any other biblical person about hell and its torments.

The New Testament affirms a certain unearthliness in connection with the motions of power toward the church and Christians. This feature of the doctrine of civil government will seem curious and totally unacceptable by all who reject a biblical world view. As discussed earlier, the Christian warfare is in part against mysterious spiritual beings and powers whose forces can be overcome only by spiritual weaponry. For some reason, though God holds them all in leash, these powers are granted some freedom to attack us. Paul felt himself a mark for their efforts. His words, "For, I think, God hath set forth us the apostles last of all, as men doomed to death: for we are made a spectacle unto the world, both to angels and men" (1 Co 4:9) so indicate. The supernatural principalities and powers would learn through the church something of the wisdom of God (Eph 3:10). Elsewhere, the unearthly quality of our struggle is set forth in more detail (Eph 6:10-12).

This strong element of despair of ever ultimately winning the world fully from its ways gives the Christian good reason for adopting realistic goals and expectations regarding the Christianizing of society. Satan is not about to be converted. The present world will always be an evil one. Our hope must be consistent with what we know of man, atonement, the doctrine of the world, and the doctrine of last things. Until the second advent, the time will never come when the warnings of Scripture against the world will cease to be in force. Only at His advent will our Lord "strike through kings in the day of his wrath" and "judge among the nations" (Ps 110:2, 5-6). The idea of some sort of ultimate conquest of the world by Christian reconstruction of society short of the *parousia* of Christ is not a biblical hope—it is neither taught directly in the Scriptures, nor to be inferred from the present kingly reign of Christ. He is "preached *among* the nations, believed on *in* the world" (1 Ti 3:16), not *by* the nations and *by* the world. Nations have experienced great betterment through the percolation of biblical faith among their peoples, as a fair assessment of Christendom will substantiate. There is, however, flow and ebb as well as ebb and flow in the tides of Christian life and loyalty among the nations. Nothing is much more emphatic, in the realm of biblical prediction, than that the period of the end of this age will be one of ebb. Satan has already been deposed from heaven—but he goes about as a roaring lion nevertheless. The victory wrought at Calvary put a chain upon his power, but he moves about dragging that chain, roaring as a lion, blinding the eyes of those who believe not. He, himself, is not yet bound, even though he be judged (Jn 16:11) and fallen from heaven (Lk 10:18). Rather, he is free to exercise great power, furious because he knows his time is short, for shortly "the kingdom of this world [will] become the kingdom of our Lord, and of his Christ" (Rev 11:15). Meanwhile the church does not cease to suffer. She fills up that which is lacking of the sufferings of Christ. She expects suffering and persecution, knowing how to behave under them because her Lord left an example and specific instructions thereto (1 Pe 2:11-17; 3:13-17; 4:12-19).*

---

*There is a document, coming from the first Christian centuries, called "The Epistle to Diognetus," which shows clearly how seriously and how successfully the first generations of Christians took the manner of life toward pagan government and pagan society outlined in these texts. This document was first published in modern times in 1592. The fifth chapter is herewith cited in full, plus a small portion of chapter six next following.

"Christians are not different from the rest of men in nationality, speech, or customs; they do not live in states of their own, nor do they use a special language, nor adopt a peculiar way of life. Their teaching is not the kind of thing that could be discovered by the wisdom or reflection of mere active-minded men; indeed, they are not outstanding in human learning as others are. Whether fortune has given them a home in a Greek or foreign city, they follow the local custom in the matter of dress, food, and way of life; yet the character of the culture they reveal is marvellous and, it must be admitted, unusual. They live, each in his native land—but as though they were not really at home there. They share in all duties like citizens and suffer all hardships like strangers. Every foreign land is for them a fatherland and every fatherland a foreign land. They marry like the rest of men and beget children, but they do not abandon the babies that are born. They share a common board, but not a common bed. In the flesh as they are, they do not live according to the flesh. They obey the laws that men make, but their lives are better than the laws. They love all men, but are persecuted by all. They are unknown, and yet they are condemned. They are put to death, yet are more alive than ever. They are paupers, but they make many rich. They lack all things, yet in all things they abound. They are dishonored, yet glory in their dishonor. They are maligned, and yet are vindicated. They are reviled, and yet they bless. They suffer insult, yet pay respect. They do good, yet are punished with the wicked. When they are punished, they rejoice, as though they were getting more of life. They are attacked by the Jews as Gentiles and are persecuted by the Greeks, yet those who hate them can give no reason for their hatred.

"In a word, what the soul is to the body Christians are to the world. The soul is distributed to every member of the body, and Christians are scattered in every city of the world. The soul dwells in the body, and yet is not of the body. So Christians live in the world, but they are not of the world. The soul which is guarded in the visible body is not itself visible. And so, Christians who are in the world are known, but their worship remains unseen. The flesh hates the soul and acts like an unjust aggressor, because it is forbidden to indulge in pleasures. The world hates Christians— not that they have done it wrong, but because they oppose its pleasures. The soul loves the body and its members in spite of the hatred. So Christians love those who hate them. The soul is locked up in the body, yet it holds the body together. And so Christians are held in the world as in a prison, yet it is they who hold the world together. The immortal soul dwells in a mortal tabernacle. So Christians sojourn among perishable things, but their souls are set on immortality in heaven. When the soul is ill-treated in the matter of food and drink it is improved. So when Christians are persecuted their numbers daily increase. Such is the assignment to which God has called them, and they have no right to shirk it" (as quoted in *The Fathers of the Church, A New Translation,* [Washington: Catholic University of America, 1962] 1:260-62).

Philip Schaff states: "The community of Christians thus from the first felt itself, in distinction from Judaism and heathenism the salt of the earth, the light of the world, the city of God set on a hill, the immortal soul in a dying body; and this its impression respecting itself was no proud conceit, but truth and reality, acting in life and in death, and opening the way through hatred and persecution even to an outward victory over the world. . . . In relation to the secular power, the ante-Nicene church is simply the continuation of the apostolic period, and has nothing in common either with the hierarchical, or with the Erastian systems. It was not opposed to the secular government in its proper sphere, but the secular heathenism of the government was opposed to Christianity. The church was altogether based upon the voluntary principle, as a self-supporting and self-governing body. In this respect it may be compared to the church in the United States, but with this essential differ- ence that in America the secular government, instead of persecuting Christianity, recognizes and protects it by law, and secures to it full freedom of public wor- ship and in all its activities at home and abroad" (*History of the Christian Church* [Grand Rapids: Eerdmans, 1963], 2:10-11).

EPILOGUE

A POINT HAS NOW BEEN REACHED where an extensive organization and application of the results of this study of civil government in the Bible might reasonably be developed into a systematic theology of civil government. I have, however, already registered a good many conclusions and recommendations of this sort in connection with various aspects of the study as it developed. Perhaps we can allow the example of Ernst Troeltsch to guide us, for in writing a history of Christian social teaching extending to over a thousand pages, he allowed himself only twenty-one pages at the end to state his final conclusions.[1] At any rate, I shall omit much more that might be said at this point of final pause than readers in this hasty age of the world are apt to allow me to say.

As I have emphasized several times, though the natural man, as Paul calls him, may know nothing of the things of the Spirit of God, he is not totally ignorant of ethical matters involved in good civil government. If this were not true, effective civil government would not exist at all. The biblically informed Christian, on the other hand, knows a good many things about reality in general and about human society in particular which nonbelievers do not know and would not willingly accept if they did know. That there is a distinctly Christian world-and-life-view, a thesis expressed and defended persuasively over seventy years ago by James Orr in his great book, *The Christian View of God and the World,* that was developed early in the present study and related specifically to five areas in the first section. The teachings of Scripture in these five areas—man, sin, the world (cosmology), redemption, and the demonic—refine the Christian outlook so that one need never commit himself to the erroneous social medicines and political panaceas which have from time to time captured the mind of a generation or a nation. Those Christians who have permitted themselves to be led astray did so because they did not understand the doctrines of their own religion. Many of these errors and their Christian antidotes in these aspects of doctrine have been

274

suggested in the first eight chapters of this book. I wish now to carry this a little further.

Because man is God's child, created as a person with distinct permanent conscious identity and (if we may resist the momentary theological fashion) with a never-to-be-extinguished soul, and of permanent value to God, man must be treated by "man," that is civil government, with care and regard. Governmental policy is thereby automatically settled for the informed Christian on a host of questions, namely, men may never be treated merely as things to be manipulated by state mind control. Divine righteousness (not what the social theorists of the moment deem to be socially desirable, or perhaps official state policies) must be the primary standard and norm, ever true basis of judgment. As rational beings, men are also responsible beings. The state is not to shape their opinions. Nor should the state forgive their crimes. This is God's prerogative. Judges are not chaplains, nor are juries churches. The creation ordinances are to be honored: the distinctions between the sexes, the sanctity of the home, the value of honest work, the need for a weekly sabbath of rest will be protected. Certain crimes against persons, such as abortion and euthanasia, will not be matters of debate among informed believers, for God's rights to justice to the persons involved will not be balanced against supposed prudential of purely social considerations. Because man bears the divine image, and because of the biblical implication drawn thereby (Gen 9:6; Ro 13:4), believers will hardly be numerous among those advocating less than capital punishment for capital crimes. Furthermore, the individuality of man in his motives (not all prompted internally and externally by the same things) and in the differences of gifts and abilities will be honored. A strictly conformist society, or totalitarian government claims, will not therefore be advocated, however much tolerated of necessity.

Because each man as sinner is a member of a ruined race, living in an evil world dominated by its deceitful prince, the biblically informed man on the one hand will not expect too much of civil government, nor on the other will he expect too little. Civil government by itself cannot reform individuals. Though it may witlessly conspire to destroy both men's self-esteem and their personal initiative, government cannot make them industrious, wise, or good, for government powers cannot touch the heart of man wherein lie the springs of emotion, and hence of action. The state, therefore, should never be in direct charge of moral instruction, nor should it be expected to care directly for matters which, under the conditions of creation and fall, are the duties of parents and other societal organs such as church, family, industry, and labor. It is too much to expect that states should function directly as reformatory agents for criminals, in addition to restraining and punishing them. Government is not competent for such things in the hands of even the most able administrators. Furthermore, the hearts of lawbreakers are not amenable to state manipulation. Yet the Christian will expect government to restrain violent men, providing also the decencies of civilized community living. He will demand, where he can, protection for the church in doing her divinely appointed works of evangelizing, instructing (thereby reforming repentant lawbreakers), civilizing, refining her own and others. Where he cannot yet demand it (as in Maoist China), he will pray for it (1 Ti 2:1-3).

Because he understands that the world is not a friend to God and that it is, in the providence of God, temporarily under satanic control, the Christian believer will not set out for utopia—be it the original one of Sir Thomas More (whose notions lost him his head to the axeman of King Henry VIII) or the more recent ones—socialistic, communistic, humanitarian, democratic, papal, capitalist, Townsendite, Calvinist-Puritan or otherwise. There is no biblical promise that either the world or Satan, its god, will ever be converted. While supporting every genuine social improvement, the Christian will not succumb to the reformist temper; though supporting constructive change, he will hardly be a revolutionary—at least not in the violent sense of that term.

There is a temper of mind, apparently present in every generation, which feels that society, being corrupt, must be overthrown, rooted out, and reconstructed into the shape of some social ideal. This opinion may be held by some sincere liberal like Robert Owen, one of the fathers of modern socialism who wanted to be as peaceful as possible about the change; by a convinced revolutionary atheist, committed to violence, such as Karl Marx; or by a crusading evangelist, usually vague about the method of accomplishment (of which there are numerous historical examples). This temper of mind may sometimes seize a large segment of the Christian population, as it did in seventeenth century Britain. English-speaking Calvinists, the Puritans in particular, periodically have been captured by the utopian delusion, which, convinced as they are of the exceeding sinfulness of sin and of the doctrine of original sin, really is difficult to explain. Twice in the seventeenth century, the Puritans attempted to establish a kind of biblical theocratic utopia—one in Britain, another in America—both times failing, though not without some moral victories and a valuable testament to their posterity in both lands in spite of the encumbering utopianism.

The Puritans of Britain provide an illustrative example. On May 12, 1912, there was preached to the University of Cambridge a sermon entitled, "The Moral of a Great Failure."[2] Why, the author asked, after less than twenty years of Puritan rule, did the English people, Puritans included, in the year 1660 restore the dynasty, calling Charles II, son of the deposed and executed Charles I, to the throne? Why did they also two years later quietly accede to the establishment of Anglicanism and a hated prayer book accompanied by the turning out of two thousand Puritan pastors of churches who chose lifelong penury rather than to accept the Anglican form of worship?

In answer, asserts H. Hensley Henson, whose sermon I am citing, "Perhaps it would not be untrue to say that the error of the Puritans has more to teach us now than that of their opponents. For in truth it was a more generous error, and it belongs to the type of error which is never obsolete, whereas the gross error of the Anglicans is little likely to be defended or repeated in any recognizable form. Religious persecutors bid fare to become an extinct species, but social reformers are always with us; and while the Anglican of the Restoration was a religious persecutor inspired by political panic, the Puritan of the Commonwealth was a persecuting social reformer inspired by religious fervour. It will be worth our while to appreciate his error, and endeavor to trace its modern forms."[3]

Henson points out several errors of the seventeenth century British Puritans as instigators of reform (really a revolution) on the wholesale scale. First, they had a political creed which was weak in that "it assumed in a nation the ethical standards and ideals of a Church, and applied the coercive methods proper to the first in the interests of the latter." Second, they failed to build their social legislation on the general will (a large segment of the population being excluded entirely from the legislative process). Third, they failed "to respect the essential condition of moral health, namely individual liberty. By a process which was really inevitable, Puritanism in politics sank quickly into hypocritical tyranny, equally feeble and irritating. Never were ideals loftier, or the self-dedication of men to them more complete and sincere, or the courage with which they were striven for more amazing, yet never was defeat more absolute and humiliating."[4]

The author goes on to draw the lesson: "The enthusiastic Puritan, aflame with his dream of a Kingdom of God on earth, could not by the purity and fervour of his zeal extricate himself from the conditions under which all men, saints and reformers as well as the rest, must needs act in such a world as this. Nor was it only in the political sphere that his attempt to transcend the limits of normal humanity was made, and defeated. Within the narrower sphere of his private life he made the same mistake, and was overtaken by the same failure. He could not permanently maintain himself at the level to which his occasional ecstasies uplifted him. The prosaic claims of ordinary existence laid hands on him also, and, though his fervent modes of speech and fantastic disciplines of habit, might disguise from himself the humbling fact, yet it was plain enough to his neighbors that, save for some personal affectations, which were not attractive or intelligible to common folk, he was really swayed by the familiar motives, and in bondage to the conventional desires. He seemed, therefore, to his critics and victims less the exponent of virtue, than a dour shrewd man who 'made the best of both worlds.' When the crash came at the Restoration, and the whole edifice of Puritan legislation lay in ruins, none cased to remember the lofty ideal which had inspired it in the joy of release from its actual burden."[5]

This is not to say that item by item, the values of Puritanism were discredited and have therefore disappeared—far from it. It is specifically and solely the "heresy of utopia" which is discredited. The English Puritans would have been horrified at the charge of heresy, but they did not fully appreciate their own doctrines of the chronic sinfulness of the world and of original sin in mankind, or they would never have tried what they did. They were inconsistently orthodox.

I have put "heresy of utopia" above, in quotation marks, indicating in part that the Puritans were not heretics. More specifically I am referring to a 1967 book by a Roman Catholic writer, entitled *Utopia, the Perennial Heresy*.[6] Written entirely from an orthodox viewpoint, author Molnar says in the preface,

> From time to time the belief spreads among men that it is possible to construct an ideal society. Then the call is sounded for all to gather and built it—the city of God on earth. Despite its attractiveness, this is a delirious ideal stamped with the madness of logic.
>
> The truth is that society is always unfinished, always in motion, and its key problems can never be solved by social engineering. Yet, man must conquer, again and again, the freedom to see this truth. In the intervals he succumbs to the dream of a mankind frozen and final in its planetary pride. The dream—utopia—leads to the denial of God and self-divinization—the heresy.
>
> I wrote this book to show the reader the truth about utopia and heresy, and the link between them. I cannot hope to rid the world of the utopian temptation; this would be itself utopian. But the book may help some of my more lucid contemporaries to undo their commitment to the grotesquerie of the perfect society of imperfect men.

In a real sense, Molnar has written the sort of a book, dealing with the history of ideas and of movements, which might be written as a sequel to the present essentially biblical study—a book which would never need to have been written if Christians had truly followed out their beliefs in the doctrines of creation, fall, the world, the demonic, and redemption.*

---

*Carl Becker, in a book of 1932, now in several dozen printings, has traced the utopian tendencies of the eighteenth-century philosophers, showing their confidence that man could make his future marvelously better than the past had been. He shows that the Marxists of this century have taken over the "democratic faith of the eighteenth century." Modern political expectation is generally utopian. (*The Heavenly City of the Eighteenth Century Philosophers* [New Haven, Connecticut U., 1932]). Becker did not see, however, as the researches of Alan Heimert (*Religion and the American Mind from the Great Awakening to the Revolution* [Cambridge: Harvard U., 1966]) show decisively, that the political hopes of the Americans, prior to their War of Independence, were rooted far more in a misconceived millennialism than in utopianism. They were, after all, informed religiously by a Bible and ministry, of the profound, imperfectable depravity of men, Americans included. Another highly regarded writer (Irving Kristol, *On the Democratic Idea in America* [New York: Harper & Row, 1972]) asserts, quite correctly, that though Americans have forgotten the ideals on which their democratic governmental machinery was based and wonder why it does not work anymore, are still thoroughly utopian. A few sentences may serve to summarize and give the flavor of this book by this distinguished writer: "It is not only in foreign affairs that our government proceeds by utopian promises

Furthermore, though he will be criticized unmercifully by unbelievers for it and, to a lesser degree, by some believers, the biblically
informed Christian will never forget that the present world is not
man's permanent home. Men should hope for a heavenly country
(Heb 11:13-16) and societally look forward to the consummation.
This attitude—as certainly ought to be well known—can be traced
back to Jesus and to His apostles. Jesus taught His disciples to live
ever as if in the very shadow of an imminent consummation of all
wordly affairs in the visible appearance of the kingdom of God. Yet
this did not mean for Jesus' immediate followers a withdrawal from
the world's field of battle. The world is precisely the scene of their
proclamation of the gospel of deliverance from sin, of their ministra-
tions to their neighbors and of their salting, seasoning, brightening
effect on society—by action or by their enemies' reaction, by acceptance or persecution, as the case might turn out to be. Oscar Cullmann
has furnished the faithful saying that "The world as a place of action
affirmed by Jesus . . . must . . . be distinguished from the world as a
norm of action denied by him." He questions "whether this hope does
not above all provide for him [the Christian] the impulse to strive
for justice in a world destined to perish, as long as it still endures,
and indeed within all groups."[7]

Because he is aware of the indispensable services of civil government in the providence and plan of God, as well as the divine purposes of it, he will have a constructive attitude toward government. His Christian world-and-life-view has a definite place for both
the citizen and the magistrate. Since the Bible says so little about
church and state relations, there will be little uniformity of Christian
convictions relating thereto. But such will not be the case with regard
to civil government itself. (I am thinking of all times and places.)
What are some of the political, economic, and social ideas which
an understanding of the biblical world-and-life-view in general and
the teachings of Scripture on society and government in particular
will produce in the Christian?

---

of future benefits and hypocritical explanations of actual performances. Our entire
domestic policy is suffused with this self-defeating duality. Thus as a domestic 'war
to end all wars' we have . . . launched a 'war to end poverty.' The very title of that
crusade reveals a mindless enthusiasm which could lead only to bitter disillusionment" (p. 139). See also S. I. Hayakawa's discerning review of Kristols' book under
the title, "The Twin Pillars of Democracy" (*Chicago Tribune*, July 30, 1972).

It will not be news to readers of the preceding pages of this book that one will learn very little, indeed, of social or political theory and only a little of economic theory from the Bible. This is not to say that Christianity does not seem to flourish better in certain social-political-economic climates than in others. Neither do I mean to say that particular integral features of certain systems of social life are not contrary to godliness. It is also quite true that particular integral features of several systems find specific uncensured precedent in the Scriptures.

Two examples illustrate this. The doctrine that personal property is a sacred right is clearly evident in Scripture. "Thou shalt not steal," the eighth commandment, and "Thou shalt not covet . . . ought that is thy neighbour's," the tenth commandment (Ex 20:15, 17) seem to be decisive on that point. I have already devoted several pages to this idea in the Old Testament laws. The instructions of the New Testament on supporting Christian work by private donations (1 Co 16:1; 2 Co 8-9), Jesus' evident approval of private property and interest taking (Mt 25:14-31; Lk 19:12-26), James' words on buying, selling, and profit taking (Ja 4:13-16) clearly imply many familiar features of capitalism. No disapproval of the rich because they are rich nor of the poor because they are poor ever appears in Scripture. Yet the Bible reports that under the Mosaic system, land was held by families rather than persons and was inalienable on any permanent basis. Furthermore, wealth is proclaimed by the Old Testament prophets, by Jesus, and by the New Testament writers to be a sacred trust, a stewardship for God (e.g., 1 Ti 6:17-19; Ja 5:1-6). Yet there is nothing doctrinaire about all this. Many features of capitalism are there (if my informants are correct) but not capitalism per se, for much that seems contrary to the formal theory is also there. Many of the criticisms against capitalism (e.g., that it is morally wrong to buy an sell with profit as motive) are specifically rejected by Scripture. Yet it is perfectly possible for a Christian man to live in a socialist country and submit to the socialist economic system. I dare say, the same man will be freer to invest his life and substance in Christian missions, evangelism, and benevolences as features of private enterprise and free competition are reintroduced into the socialist system. The problem is that until the individual is able to gather to himself some monetary or other substantial surplus not allowed in a strict socialism, he has nothing at all to give away on a personal basis. Thus, though the system of private enterprise and free competition (which is what most of us really mean when we speak of capitalism) is in certain respects more congenial to Christianity than is strict socialism, one does not find the Bible forbidding him to practice socialism. Furthermore, the Bible itself furnishes examples of limitation on private enterprise and furnishes a number of examples of voluntary poverty and even of voluntary communism, mixed with wealth and private property holding. In fact, as everyone knows, a form of voluntary communism existed for awhile in the earliest age of the church. All this is far from any doctrinaire economic system.

Another example is the manner in which the Bible treats the human appointment of magistrates (human government officers). James I of England thought he could prove that hereditary monarchy alone is endorsed by Scripture and wrote a book to prove it. In our own day, not only the secular multitude but apparently millions of Christians assume that laws should always be made and enforced by representatives chosen by democratic processes—that if government is not democratic, it is certainly inferior and probably wrong. Yet, as we have had occasion to note earlier, the Bible endorses neither monarchy nor democratic republic, though it repeatedly proclaims, in a variety of ways, that magistrates of civil government have their power given them by God Himself. The officers (no division between officers who legislate, others who execute laws, and others who preside in courts of justice is found in Scripture) make the laws, execute them, and superintend justice, but as God's representatives, not the people's. Hence in times of "divine right of kings," biblical Christians have not been democratic; in the period of Anglo-Saxon democracy, they have not been royalist. Nor in the socialist countries of today are they solidly antisocialist. This is not to say that in given times and places one form of government is not preferable to another; rather that considerations which dictate the form of government cannot arise from directly relevant biblical injunctions. The considerations will be practical, historical, pragmatic—biblical only in the sense that biblical religion and ethical teachings be honored in principle always.

But the biblical Christian knows many things about government which others can only suppose, surmise, hope, or not know at all. Let us call attention to some of them.

The Christian revelation witnesses to the permanent necessity of government in sinful society. (According to the narrative of Genesis chapter nine, a state of anarchy has never long existed in any society since God first ordered that the violent impulses of sinful men be held in check by man.) A paradise of anarchy in the past as envisioned by philosophers, has never existed; and the supposed anarchy of the future when, in the Marxist paradise, government shall have withered away, shall never come to pass. Quite to the contrary, the kingdom of this world shall become the kingdom of the Lord and of His Christ; and He shall reign forever.

Within the world of present reality—the human race created by God, fallen in sin, redeemed by Christ—there are many autonomous spheres of social activity, of which government is one. Some of these, such as sexuality, marriage, home and family, labor, art, science, education, philosophy, religion, though involved in the fall and to a degree affected by it (and certainly to be supported and protected by civil government) exist before and apart from civil government. Of this list—and it could be considerably extended—only government appears to be a distinct sphere coming into existence subsequent to and as a result of the primitive fall of man.

What is important to recognize is that all of these have received their authority to exist from God. For example, the right to marry, bear children, rear a family and to educate them is a divinely-given right, not a privilege to be granted or withdrawn by civil authority. Artistic expression likewise grows out of man's endowments by God. His privilege and duty of labor is by divine provision and command— thus labor (as an act of men), for example, is not truly the business of government. When labor deals with science or industry, however, government may want to see that both sides keep the same rules—as policeman for the whole of society.

This leads to the truth that as the force for maintenance of order and peace among men, government should police the "spheres" to provide a favorable civil climate for each individual, to insure that they do not infringe upon one another, and to see that personal rights are protected. Marriage is thus a right of people as people, not a privilege offered to men by civil law. Civil laws and magistrates should provide that the rights of all within the institution be protected. It should provide a setting of civil peace and order, including, according to many Bible interpreters, such restraints on public immorality as are dangerous to the integrity of the family and the nurture of children. If this last be debatable, this much is certain: wherever biblical views have come to prevail in a populace, some effort has been made at civil enforcement of all the Decalogue by public law. Of course the futile project of demanding faith by law has seldom if ever been tried, but restraint of blasphemy, punishment of known violation of the command against sexual impurity, a legal sabbath day, and so on have all been tried. Throughout the Christian centuries, sumptuary laws to enforce public conformity to Decalogue standards have been the rule. There were as many before the Reformation in Catholic Europe as afterward. To what extent government may—perhaps *must*—coerce the "orders" or "spheres" will inevitably reflect the convictions of the public the government serves. At just what point, for example, the sphere of art has moved from legitimate autonomous expression to pornographic invasion of the rights of the sphere of family in the protection of its members from unnecessary temptation is a sticky problem for government. Apparently it has no direction to go except to respond, in a democratic society, to majority opinion, though at present it sometimes seems to be more responsive to well-financed publishers and noisy propagandists of corruption. But now that the public school is frequently in the charge of anti-Christian teachers, and seems to be increasingly possessive of the children's social life, influential on their ethical views and moral behavior as well, Christian people rightly take action to recover their own from the authority of a public school system that is not merely a *state* school but a *statist* school. So the spheres are not *absolutely* autonomous. This is why there will always be conflicts of views as to limits of government sponsorship and regulation.

The Christian insights based on understanding of the Scriptures must be passed on to the state by whatever means can be devised, wherever Christian influence can be expressed and wherever men will listen. Primarily the message must be communicated of what man is by creation and fall and what he can become by redemption. This is, in part, evangelism. It is also education and persuasion. All the spiritual resources of the church of Christ must be thrown into the effort to carry off such a project if in the providence of God it is to succeed.

As noted early in this study, the prevailing view of men today takes no notice of man's God-relatedness, of his proper destiny in eternal life, of his responsibility therefore to God, to himself, to other men in all civil relation. The simple determinism of cause-effect relationship observed in physical science is applied to the understanding of human affairs with deadening effect, as Christian sociologists and legal writers have been observing for some time. Let me cite results only in one area. One Christian sociologist, William L. Kalb, observes, "Our political institutions, our legal institutions . . . are largely based upon the presupposition that man is not totally determined in his behavior. These assumptions are related in such a way that if you develop a society which explains human behavior in terms of cause and effect, and this comes to be applied in the courts, then tension arises between the old legal assumption of freedom of responsibility and the social scientific assumption that human behavior is determined by causal factors."[8] Hence courts seem reluctant to punish any offender in proportion to his crime, and the most vicious of convicted law-breakers are paroled, only to repeat their past bad performances. Because God's interest is not only in civil justice, but also in the man's true worth as a responsible free being, the punishment that justice calls for has not been administered, offenders are not reformed, and society is not protected.

The believer can protest this low view of man through every avenue open to him, but the secular-minded jurists (a product of the social sciencism of the university), the legislators and citizens, likewise caught up in the *Zeitgeist*, will not likely understand what he is talking about and would deeply resent it if they did. It is hard for people whose God is not in their thinking, the Creator's primary rights in all human justice being unknown to them, to conceive of any criterion or purpose of judgment other than protection of society or correction of offenders. Permanent help will come only through restoration of better views. This will come about only by Christian evangelism and instruction. Christian social action is necessary, but there must be Christians present where such action is taken, and they must be aware of the teachings of their own religion. Social changes undertaken under Christian inspiration tend to be short-lived where there is no public understanding of the Christian reasons for them—witness the Eighteenth Amendment to the United States Constitution. These views, in the present state of things, will not be propagated by the professors at the university's social science division!† They must come, as always, from the Bible and thereby through the teachers whom God sets in the church (1 Co 12:28).

As to the precise stance which believers should take toward the social order in general and toward civil government in particular, it can be said that though the Bible has given them a consensus on many matters—with exception, of course—there has been variety of response to critical situations. The Scriptures do not speak directly or distinctly to every human situation. The present search of the Scriptures has, for example, turned up no texts which tell believers exactly what to do if, as happened in Virginia about two hundred years ago, the authorities in the local area (Virginia House of Burgesses) declare the area out of the jurisdiction of the central authorities (king and parliament). Quite aside from the question of enlisting in the revolutionary armies, whom should they obey? Further, there is no specific text on what church authorities in, say, Antioch of Syria should do if the chief magistrate of the realm should do as Constantine did, when he ordered the local bishop to appear with other bishops (A.D. 325) at Nicea in Asia Minor to consult and decide on a theological problem. If he had been a Baptist, he would have had a king-sized problem of conscience! Again, what text speaks specifically on how much public welfare is sufficient to absolve the civil structure

---

†A paragraph from Emil Brunner's *Christianity and Civilization* will lend weight to the argument. "There is always a certain tendency in cultural humanity to understand spirit and culture in such a way that so-called 'higher' culture becomes detached from everyday life, from marriage and family, from civic order and from social obligations. Such a humanism is inclined to forget that the soundness of family life is the basis of all true civilization, that justice and freedom in public life are necessary presuppositions of all higher culture. There is a certain aristocracy of spirit which has little interest in popular education, or in the task of giving a real meaning to the work of the ordinary man, and which focuses all its interest in popular education, or in the task of giving a real meaning to the work of the ordinary man, and which focuses all its interest on science, art and so-called higher culture. Such an attitude proves detrimental to real culture. It is at this point that the importance of the Christian view of life becomes particularly obvious. All this makes the question of the relations between historical Christianity and civilization so complicated that it is hardly possible to reach a final judgment. On one point, however, we can speak without reserve: the history of civilization during the last hundred years has made clear beyond all doubt that the progressive decline of Christian influence has caused a progressive decay of civilization. But even that may remain doubtful to one who personally has no understanding of what Christian faith means" (as quoted in *Religion in Contemporary Western Culture*, ed. Edward Cell [Nashville: Abingdon, 1967], p. 75).

of its obligation to the honest poor, yet not so much as to degrade those poor to the point that they give up efforts at helping themselves? Though the most thoroughly Christian elements in every state have always tried to work constructively within the social order, depending on the times, the place and the circumstances, as well as particular Christian theological tradition, they have not always made the same response to the state's claims upon them.‡

The reflections up to this point have related to the general doctrinal background of biblical history of civil governments, and to precedents and teachings related thereto. As for the rest, the Christian's position will inevitably be that of witness to what God has said. All that biblical history, Mosaic legislation, prophetic proclamation, Messianic expectation, and Old Testament wisdom yielded to him by way of harvest of teaching, joined to precedents and teachings of our Lord and His apostles must be communicated—first to the church; then through its facilities and members to the communities of men in which they live, work, and have their civic being.

This will be an ongoing, never-to-be-completed task as long as the present order of the world continues. Human nature being what it is, the Christian witness will be advised always to be a hopeful, prayerful realist rather than a utopian enthusiast. The natural man does not love light; he does not take naturally to it; rather he fights shy of it wherever it touches his self-serving impulses.

‡This author knows of no adequate treatment which discusses precisely the varieties of Christian responses to civil government. The subject has been treated, however, in connection with the larger subject of the Christian response to the social order, of which a chief feature is the various civil governments which have prevailed through Christian history. There was considerable interest in the relation of church and society near the beginning of the present century, issuing in several important books in several languages. The most important of these, published in 1911 and still read in fresh editions today, is Ernst Troeltsch, *The Social Teachings of Christian Churches* (New York: Harper & Row). It is an historical survey of very impressive completeness. His factual reporting, if not all his conclusions, are dependable and well worth reading today. The immense literature of the subject prior to date of Troeltsch's publication is noted and sifted in hundreds of pages of notes. More recently in a book of a different type, H. Richard Niebuhr in *Christ and Culture* (Goucester, Mass.: Peter Smith, 1951), gives an analysis, finding five main types of Christian response to society's culture, including civil government. Another superior work from a Roman Catholic who wrote before Vatican II, but a very progressive work nonetheless, which traces the response of church to state and state to church from earliest time is Luigi Sturzo, *Church and State* (Notre Dame: Notre Dame Press). Appearing first in Italian in 1939, but not issued in English until 1962, it was written by one who, having participated in the political developments growing out of the political unification of Italy in the late nineteenth century, lived to see those developments through to climax. This work focuses more directly on the specific subject of Christian response to civil government than does either Troeltsch or Niebuhr.

Furthermore, the task will proceed necessarily in spite of inevitable subversion of the Christian witness by those who, often quite sincerely, sieze upon some facet of the message only to substitute it for the whole, thus making it ultimately an instrument of evil rather than good. Only the Spirit of God can enable men to see truth in its wholeness.

It is not difficult for certain elements of the world to see value in the "justice" and human good elements of the prophetic teaching, but joined to a pagan notion of society and humanist-secularist view of man it inevitably ends up in perversion. From Western liberal thought and accompanying secular socialism, whether overt or subvert, dependent for its valid insights upon a first rejected and now forgotten set of Christian presuppositions, a godlessness in society has developed which threatens all that is honestly good, beautiful, and true. Christian truth teaches that there never has been and never can be authentic goodness, particular beauty, or specific truth, apart from Him who is goodness, beauty, and truth. It is inevitable that gospel light thus perverted should only deepen the darkness, precisely as Jesus said it would.

There have been epochs when the social stability factor of the biblical message on civil government has been perverted by the politically favored and economically secure to the defrauding and enslavement of the politically disenfranchised and economically disinherited. Ironically, this has occasionally occurred with the supine concurrence of the victims. This is the religion which Marx, with a true insight, called the opiate of the people. It provides the negative inspiration for moving poetry such as Heinrich Heine's "The Silesian Weavers." Written in 1844, shortly after an abortive rebellion of the Silesian weavers against horrible conditions of labor and life, it was published in Marx's newspaper *Vorwärtz*. It is perhaps the greatest piece of social protest in world literature.

THE SILESIAN WEAVERS

> Not a tear in their dim eyes,
> They sit at the loom and gnash their teeth.
> Germany, we are weaving your shroud,
> We weave into it the triple curse—
> We weave, we weave!

A curse for the God, to whom we prayed
In winter's cold and hunger's distress;
We have hoped and waited in vain,
He has aped, mocked and fooled us—
    We weave, we weave!

A curse for the king, the king of the rich,
Whom our misery could not soften,
Who squeezes the last dime out of us
And has us shot down like dogs—
    We weave, we weave!

A curse for the false fatherland,
Where thrive only shame and disgrace,
Where every flower is early nipped,
Where rottenness and mould nourish the worm—
    We weave, we weave!

The shuttle flies, the loom groans,
We weave busily day and night—
Old Germany we are weaving your shroud,
We weave therein the triple curse,
    We weave, we weave!

Trans. ROBERT CULVER

Older people can recall how persuasively certain vocal elements of the community of nations transmuted the peace to the nations' aspect of biblical teaching and prediction, using it as a lever to bring peace (they told themselves) without either God or His righteousness. An agreement among sinful men of a world quite alien to God was to inaugurate peace in our time half a generation before Chamberlain's ill-starred mission to Munich. Tennyson expressed this perversion of the true Christian vision in *Locksley Hall*.

For I dipt into the future, far as human eye
    could see,
Saw the vision of the world, and all the wonder
    that would be;
Saw the heavens filled commerce, argosies of
    magic sails,
Pilots of the purple twilight, dropping down with
    costly bales;

> Heard the heavens fill with shouting, and there
>   rained a ghastly dew
> From the nations' airy navies grappling in the
>   central blue;
> Far along the world-wide whisper of the south-
>   wind rushing warm,
> With the standards of the peoples plunging
>   through the thunder-storm;
> Till the war-drum throbbed no longer, and the
>   battle-flags were furled
> In the parliament of man, the federation of
>   the world.
> There the common sense of most shall hold a
>   fretful realm in awe,
> And the kindly earth shall slumber, lapt in uni-
>   versal law.
>
> (lines 119-130)

Alfred, Lord Tennyson (died 1892) did indeed look over time's shoulder to capture a glimpse of the air age in commerce and warfare, yet his Christian heart, overwhelmed by the humanistic optimism of his epoch, perverted the biblical ideal, destined ultimately to be accomplished by the regeneration of the world by God himself, into an heretical human perfectionist triumph.

There are many further implications. In closing, here is one. If Christian influence on government is to be successful in promotion of durable improvements, then the church must be effective in performing its own distinct God-given commission, making disciples— hopefully very many of them (Mt 28:19-20)—who shall in turn honor Jesus Christ as Lord in every sphere of their own lives and who will understand the meaning for the nations of all that Christ in the Scriptures has taught them to observe (Mt 28:20).

These pages are issued forth with the prayer that they faithfully represent the voice of God in the Scriptures, beckoning distinctly toward a Christian understanding of civil government.

NOTES

NOTES

CHAPTER ONE

1. See G. P. Spurrell, *Notes on the Hebrew Text of the Book of Genesis* (New York: Oxford, 1887), pp. 20-21; and P. J. Wisemann, *New Discoveries in Babylonia About Genesis* (London: Marshall, Morgan, & Scott, 1946), pp. 45-57.
2. See John Murray, *Principles of Conduct, Aspects of Biblical Ethics* (Grand Rapids: Eerdmans, 1964), pp. 30-39, 82-106.
3. Ibid., p. 36.
4. Ibid., pp. 30-35.
5. See J. B. Heard, *The Tripartite Nature of Man* (Edinburgh: T. & T. Clark, 1868).
6. Reinhold Niebuhr, *The Nature and Destiny of Man* (New York: Charles Scribner's Sons, 1964).
7. G. C. Berkouwer, *Man: The Image of God,* trans. Dirk W. Jellema (Grand Rapids: Eerdmans, 1962).
8. Quoted by Niebuhr, *Nature and Destiny of Man,* 1:265.
9. Niebuhr, 1:265.
10. Ibid., 1:267-69.
11. Emil Brunner, "The Christian Doctrine of Creation and Redemption," in *Dogmatics,* trans. Olive Wyon (Philadelphia: Westminster, 1952), 2:103.
12. See ibid., 2:103-4.
13. Ibid., p. 101; also Emil Brunner, *The Mediator,* trans. Olive Wyon (Philadelphia: Westminster, 1947), pp. 377-96.
14. Brunner, p. 378.
15. *A New Catechism* (New York: Herder & Herder, 1967), p. 261.
16. Ibid., p. 262, italics added.
17. Pascal *Pensees* 434 (Brunschvicg).

CHAPTER TWO

1. Abraham Kuyper, *Lectures on Calvinism* (Grand Rapids: Eerdmans, 1931), p. 92.

CHAPTER THREE

1. Gerhard von Rad, *Genesis, a Commentary,* trans. John H. Marks (Philadelphia: Westminster, 1961), p. 90; and F. Delitzsch, *New Commentary on Genesis,* trans. Sophia Taylor (Edinburgh: T. & T. Clark, 1888), 1:3:17-19.
2. Robert Haldane, *Expositions of the Epistle to the Romans,* Fifth Edinburgh ed. (New York: Robert Carter, 1847), p. 378.
3. G. Elson Ruff, *The Dilemma of Church and State* (Philadelphia: Muhlenberg, 1954), pp. 67-68.
4. See John Calvin, *Institutes of the Christian Religion,* III. xix. 9.
5. *Luther's Works,* ed. J. Pelikan and D. E. Poellot (St. Louis: Concordia), 1:104; 46:237.
6. Helmut Thielicke, *Theological Ethics,* ed. W. H. Lazareth (Philadelphia: Fortress, 1969), 2:17.

CHAPTER FOUR

1. Rienhold Niebuhr, *The Nature and Destiny of Man,* 1:3.
2. W. F. Arndt and F. W. Gingrich, *Greek-English Lexicon of the New Testament and Other Early Christian Literature* (Chicago: U. of Chicago, 1967), s.v. "World."

3. Niebuhr, pp. 134-35.
4. Ibid., p. 135.
5. Henry Liddel and Robert Scott, *A Greek-English Lexicon* (Oxford: Oxford U., 1869, 1940). Also *Theological Dictionary of the New Testament,* ed. Gerhard Kittel, trans. Geoffrey W. Bromiley (Grand Rapids: Eerdmans, 1964), 3:868-95.
6. *Theological Dictionary of the New Testament,* 3:868-95.
7. Ibid.
8. Ibid.
9. Ibid., 5:157.
10. Ibid.

CHAPTER FIVE

1. Abraham Kuyper, *Lectures on Calvinism,* p. 84.
2. Ibid.
3. Ibid., p. 85.
4. *Encyclopedia Britannica,* 11th ed., s.v. "King."
5. *Myth, Ritual, and Kingship: Essays on the Theory and Practice of Kingship in the Ancient Near East and Israel,* ed. Samuel Henry Hooke (Oxford: Clarendon, 1958), p. 23.
6. *Smith's Dictionary of Greek and Roman Antiquities* (London: John Murray, 1882, s.v. "Apotheosis."
7. G. Currey, *The Holy Bible with Commentary,* ed. F. C. Cook (London: John Murray, 1900), 6:123-24.
8. See, for example, Oscar Cullmann, *The State in the New Testament* (London: SCM, 1963), p. 77.
9. See ibid., pp. 70-88.

CHAPTER SIX

1. A good discussion with bibliographical elaboration is found in Paul van Imshoot, *Theology of the Old Testament,* trans. Kathryn Sullivan and Fidelis Buck (New York: Desclee, 1954), pp. 101-6.
2. Martin H. Scharlemann, "Scriptural Concepts of Church and State," *Church and State Under God,* ed. Albert G. Huegli (St. Louis: Concordia, 1964), p. 16.
3. John Calvin, *Institutes of the Christian Religion,* III. xiv. 4.
4. Ibid.
5. Georg Wilhelm Friedrich Hegel, *Philosophy of Right,* 3:257-340, summarized in B. A. G. Fuller, *A History of Philosophy* (New York: Henry Holt, 1945), 2:321-24.
6. John H. Hallowell, *Main Currents in Modern Political Thought* (New York: Holt, Rinehart, Winston, 1950), p. 263.
7. E. L. Hebden Taylor, *The Philosophy of Law, Politics and the State* (Nutley, N.J.: Craig, 1966), pp. 157-58.
8. Herman Dooyeweerd, *The Christian Idea of the State,* trans. John Kraay (Nutley, N.J.: Craig, 1968), p. 8.
9. Abraham Kuyper, *Lectures on Calvinism,* p. 79.
10. See Carl Friedrich Keil, *Manual of Biblical Archaeology* (Edinburgh: T. & T. Clark, 1888), 2:290-92.
11. *Luther's Works,* ed. Jaroslav Pelikan and Daniel E. Poellat, II. vi-xiv.
12. Ibid.
13. John Calvin, *Commentary on the First Book of Moses Called Genesis,* trans. John King (Grand Rapids: Eerdmans, 1948), comments on 9:6.
14. See, for example, Gerhard von Rad, *Genesis, A Commentary,* comments on 9:6.
15. Carl Friedrick Keil, *Commentary on the Pentateuch,* trans. James Martin (Edinburgh: T. & T. Clark, 1887), F. Delitzsch, *New Commentary on Genesis,* trans. Sophia Taylor (Edinburgh: T. & T. Clark, 1888), J. G. Murphy, *Commentary on the Book of Genesis* (Andover: Draper, 1866); *Exposition of Genesis* (Columbus, Ohio: Wartburg, 1942); Erich Sauer, *The Dawn of World Redemption* (Grand Rapids: Eerdmans, 1951), pp. 71-72; and Alva J. McClain, *The Greatness of the Kingdom* (Chicago: Moody, 1968), pp. 46-47.
16. Alva J. McClain, pp. 46-47.

17. *Lange's Commentary on the Holy Scriptures* (Grand Rapids: Eerdmans, 1951), comments on Genesis 9:12.
18. C. J. Elliott, *The Bible Commentary* (London: Murray, 1892), p. 382.
19. Franz Delitzsch, *Biblical Commentary on the Psalms,* trans. Francis Bolton, (Edinburgh: T. & T. Clark, 1871), 3:73.
20. John Murray, *Principles of Conduct* (Grand Rapids: Eerdmans, 1957), p. 112.
21. Ibid., pp. 107-22.
22. For a survey of the various views on the subject of justice, see Otto A. Bird, *The Idea of Justice* (New York: Praeger, 1967). For a guide to Christian literature on the subject, especially to the thought of the Dooyeweerdian school, see "The Christian Philosophy of Law" in E. L. Hebden Taylor, *The Philosophy of Law, Politics and the State* (Nutley, N.J.: Craig, 1966).
23.. A good discussion of these words is found in Leon Morris, *The Biblical Doctrine of Judgment* (London: Tyndale, 1960), pp. 7-43.
24. R. J. Rushdoony, *The Foundations of Social Order* (Nutley, N.J.: Presbyterian & Reformed, 1968), p. 219.
25. McClain, p. 46.
26. Kuyper, pp. 79-80.
27. An introduction to this subject, including basic bibliography, will be found in Jack Finegan, *Light from the Ancient Past,* 2d ed. (Princeton: U. Press, 1959), pp. 253-63.

CHAPTER SEVEN

1. John Calvin, *Institutes of the Christian Religion,* Battles trans., 2 vols. (Philadelphia: Westminster, 1960), 1:43-69.
2. Ibid.
3. Franz Delitzsch, *Biblical Commentary on the Prophecies of Isaiah,* trans. James Martin (Edinburgh: T. & T. Clark, 1889), 1:262-63.
4. See Robert Culver, *Daniel and the Latter Days* (Chicago: Moody, 1964), pp. 50-52.
5. C. Von Orelli, *The Prophecies of Isaiah,* trans. J. S. Banks (Edinburgh: T. & T. Clark, 1889), pp. 140-41, cf. 151-52.
6. Delitzsch, p. 427.
7. Robert Ottley, *Aspects of the Old Testament,* The Bampton Lectures, 1897 (London: Longmans, 1898), pp. 430-31.

CHAPTER EIGHT

1. Franz Delitzsch, *Biblical Commentary on the Psalms,* 2:288-300.
2. As quoted by Will Herberg, *Community, State and Church* (Garden City, N.Y.: Doubleday, 1960), p. 29.
3. Herberg, pp. 27-28.
4. Alva J. McClain, *The Greatness of the Kingdom,* p. 207.
5. Herman Dooyeweerd, *A New Critique of Theoretical Thought,* 4 vols. (Philadelphia: Presbyterian & Reformed, 1954-58).
6. E. L. Hebden Taylor, *The Philosophy of Law, Politics and the State.*
7. McClain, p. 209.
8. Dietrich Bonhoeffer, *Ethics,* trans. N. H. Smith (New York: Macmillan, 1965), pp. 328-29.
9. Abraham Kuyper, *Lectures on Calvinism,* p. 87.
10. Alan Heimert, *Religion and the American Mind from the Great Awakening to the Revolution* (Cambridge: Harvard U., 1966), pp. x, 668.
11. William G. McLoughlin, "The American Revolution as a Religious Revival," *New England Quarterly* 40 (March 1967):99-110.
12. Ibid., p. 110.
13. Talbot W. Chambers in *Lange's Commentary on the Minor Prophets* (New York: Charles Scribners' Sons, 1874), s.v. "Zechariah."

CHAPTER NINE

1. See Josephus, *Antiquities of the Jews,* IV. viii. 40.

2. Edwin Cone Bissell, *Biblical Antiquities,* 9th ed. (Philadelphia: American Sunday School Union, 1892), p. 214.
3. *Encyclopedia Britannica,* 11th ed., s.v. "State."
4. Ibid.
5. Pierre de Vaux, *Ancient Israel: Its Life and Institutions* (New York: McGraw-Hill, 1961), pp. 98-99.
6. Ibid., p. 99.
7. *Webster's New World Dictionary of the American Language,* College ed., s.v. "Nation."
8. Carl Friederich Keil, *Manual of Biblical Archaeology,* 2:338.
9. Ibid., 2:293.
10. Carl Friederich Keil, *Commentary on the Pentateuch,* 1:311, 319, 371.
11. Ibid., 1:371.
12. John Bright, *A History of Israel* (Philadelphia: Westminster, 1959), p. 145.
13. See W. F. Albright, *Archaeology and the Religion of Israel* (Baltimore: Johns Hopkins, 1953).
14. *Smith's Dictionary of Greek and Latin Antiquities,* p. 80.
15. O. T. Allis, *Prophecy and the Church* (Philadelphia: Presbyterian & Reformed, 1945), p. 59.
16. Alva J. McClain, *The Greatness of the Kingdom,* p. 57.
17. *International Standard Bible Encyclopedia* (Grand Rapids: Eerdmans, 1943), s.v. "Moses."

CHAPTER TEN

1. A. N. Whitehead.
2. H. Frankfort, H. A. Frankfort, John A. Wilson, Thorkild Jacobsen, William A. Irwin, *The Intellectual Adventure of Ancient Man: An Essay on Speculative Thought in the Ancient Near East* (Chicago: U. Press, 1946).
3. Whitehead.
4. See Henry Van Til, *The Calvinistic Concept of Culture* (Nutley, N.J.: Presbyterian and Reformed, 1959), p. 59.
5. See, for example, J. H. Nichols, *Democracy and the Churches* (Philadelphia: Westminster, 1941).
6. This is ably set forth by Rousas J. Rushdoony, *The Foundations of Social Order* (Nutley, N.J.: Presbyterian & Reformed, 1968), pp. 219-26.
7. Will Herberg, *Community, State, and Church: Three Essays by Karl Barth* (Garden City, N.Y.: Anchor Books, Doubleday ed.; 1960), pp. 24-25.
8. Ibid., pp. 27-29.
9. *International Standard Bible Encyclopedia,* s.v. "King, Kingdom."
10. As quoted in *Religion and Contemporary Western Culture,* ed. Edward Cell (Nashville: Abingdon, 1967), pp. 74-75.

CHAPTER ELEVEN

1. J. Barton Payne, *The Theology of the Older Testament* (Grand Rapids: Zondervan, 1964), pp. 182-83.
2. See W. Kay, *The Holy Bible, Commentary* (London: John Murray, 1898), s.v. "Isaiah."
3. E. W. Hengstenberg, as quoted in C. F. Keil, *Commentary on the Pentateuch,* p. 382.
4. Keil, p. 340.
5. See, e.g., Josephus, *Antiquities of the Jews,* IV. viii. 14; *Wars of the Jews,* II. xx. 5; Talmudists, *Sanhedrin,* i. 6.
6. Keil, pp. 344-45.
7. See 1 Mac 1:10; 4:44; 11:27; also Josephus, *Antiquities of the Jews,* XII. iii. 3; XIII. v. 8; XIV. ix. 4.
8. See Edwin Cone Bissell, *Biblical Antiquities,* p. 191; and Pierre de Vaux, *Ancient Israel: Its Life and Institutions,* p. 155; cf. 1 Ch. 23:4; 26:29. They were not the same as the scribes, Heb., *sopherim* (2 Ch 34:13).
9. Bissell, pp. 319-20.
10. Ibid., pp. 218-19.

11. de Vaux, p. 156.
12. John M'Clintock and James Strong, *Cyclopedia of Biblical, Theological, and Ecclesiastical Literature,* (New York: Arno ,1969), 5:291.
13. Ibid., 5:289-90.
14. Carl Friederich Keil, *Manual of Biblical Archaeology,* 2:53-54.
15. Bissell, p. 226.

CHAPTER TWELVE

1. Edwin Cone Bissell, *Biblical Antiquities,* p. 228.
2. Carl Friederich Keil, *Manual of Biblical Archaeology,* 2:364.
3. Denis Baly, *The Geography of the Bible* (New York: Harper, 1957), p. 227.
4. Ibid., p. 47.
5. See C. F. Keil, *Commentary on the Pentateuch,* pp. 307ff.
6. See, e.g., de Vaux, *Ancient Israel: Its Life and Institutions,* pp. 175-77; and *Hastings Dictionary of the Bible,* s.v. "Sabbatical Year."
7. Jacques Ellul, *The Theological Foundations of Law,* trans. Marguerite Wieser (New York: Seabury, 1969), p. 107.
8. Alva J. McClain, *The Greatness of the Kingdom,* p. 76.
9. See *Nave's Topical Bible* (Chicago: Moody, 1970), s.v. "Poor."
10. See C. F. Keil, *Commentary on the Pentateuch* 3:369-71; also *Hastings Dictionary of the Bible,* s.v. "Sabbatical Year."
11. Robert Culver, *The Sufferings and the Glory of the Lord's Righteous Servant* (Moline, Ill.: Christian Service Foundation, 1958), p. 23.
12. Josephus, *Antiquities of the Jews,* XVI. i. 1.
13. Ibid.
14. *Smith's Dictionary of the Bible,* s.v. "Slave;" see also de Vaux, pp. 85-88; and Bissell, pp. 55-58.
15. de Vaux, p. 86.

CHAPTER THIRTEEN

1. Otto Eissfeldt, *The Old Testament: An Introduction,* trans Peter B. Ackroyd (New York: Harper & Row, 1965), p. 476.
2. J. Barton Payne, *The Theology of the Older Testament* (Grand Rapids: Zondervan, 1962), pp. 339-40 has a helpful discussion of this matter.
3. See Eissfeldt, pp. 474-75 for advocacy of Egyptian borrowing and basic bibliography of that point of view; and Gleason L. Archer, Jr., *A Survey of Old Testament Introduction* (Chicago: Moody, 1964), pp. 457-58 for advocacy and basic bibliography of the opposing view.
4. E. H. Plumptre, *Commentary by Bishops and Other Clergy of the Anglican Church* (London: John Murray, 1892), s.v. "Proverbs."
5. F. Delitzsch, *Commentary on Proverbs,* comments on 8:14-15.
6. F. Brown, S. R. Driver, C. A. Briggs, *A Hebrew and English Lexicon of the Old Testament* (Oxford: Clarendon, 1955), s.v. *"Māshal."*
7. For a contrary construction of the text and different interpretation, see C. H. Toy in *International Critical Commentary* (New York: Scribner, 1903), p. 298.
8. Toy, p. 323.
9. Delitzsch, p. 340.
10. Moses Stuart, *Commentary on the Book of Proverbs* (New York: M. W. Dodd, 1852), pp. 290-91.
11. Delitzsch, p. 222.
12. Plumptre, p. 606.
13. Ibid., p. 596.
14. Toy, p. 450.
15. Ibid.
16. Delitzsch, comments on 29:8.
17. See Stuart, p. 498.
18. Gordon Spyerman in a bulletin of the National Association for Christian Political Action, Sioux Center, Ia. (an address to the first congress of that organization, July, 1971).

CHAPTER FOURTEEN

1. See Oscar Cullmann, *The Kingship of Christ and the Church in the New Testament* (London: SCM, 1966), p. 105; and G. C. H. Berkouwer, *The Work of Christ,* trans. C. Lambregtse, (Grand Rapids: Eerdmans, 1965), pp. 202-41.
2. Oscar Cullmann, *The State in the New Testament* (London: SCM, 1963), pp. 28-29.
3. Ibid., pp. 36-41.
4. M'Clintock and Strong, *Cyclopedia of Biblical, Theological, and Ecclesiastical Literature,* s.v. "Jesus Christ."
5. Meyer.
6. W. F. Arndt and F. W. Gingrich, *Greek-English Lexicon of the New Testament and Other Early Christian Literature* (Grand Rapids: Zondervan, 1963).

CHAPTER FIFTEEN

1. Josephus, *Wars of the Jews,* VII. vi. 6.
2. Alfred Edersheim, *The Life and Times of Jesus the Messiah* (New York: Longmans, 1907), 1:241-42, 2:385.
3. Oscar Cullman, *The State in the New Testament,* p. 15.
4. Edersheim, 2:385.
5. Ibid., 2:386.
6. Ibid.
7. Abraham Kuyper, *Lectures on Calvinism,* pp. 78-109.
8. Cullman, pp. 32-33.
9. Quoted in Charles Norris Cochrane, *Christianity and Classical Cultures* (London: Oxford, 1944), p. 228.
10. Cullmann, p. 33.

CHAPTER SIXTEEN

1. A. N. Sherwin-White, *Roman Law and Society in the New Testament* (London: Oxford, 1965), p. 122; see also Frederick John Foakes Jackson and Kirsopp Lake, eds., *The Beginnings of Christianity* (London: Macmillan, 1933), 5:277-333.
2. Cf. e.g., Sherwin-White, pp. 120-43.
3. Sherwin-White, p. 145.
4. W. M. Ramsay, *Cities of St. Paul* (London: Hodder & Stoughton, 1897), p. 115; see also his *Pauline and Other Studies in Early Christian History* (Grand Rapids: Baker, 1970), pp. 59-62.
5. Josephus, *Antiquities of the Jews,* XII. iii. 2.
6. Emil Schuerer in *Hastings Dictionary of the Bible,* rev. ed. (New York: Scribner, 1927), s.v. "Diaspora."
7. Ramsay, pp. 177-78.
8. Sherwin-White, pp. 100-101.
9. Josephus, XIV. vii. 2.
10. *Smith's Dictionary of Greek and Roman Antiquities,* p. 964.
11. Henry J. Cadbury, *The Beginnings of Christianity* (London: Macmillan, 1933), 5:270.
12. W. M. Ramsay, *St. Paul the Traveller and the Roman Citizen* (London: Hodder & Stoughton, 1897), p. 119; cf. Ac 14:11.

CHAPTER SEVENTEEN

1. W. M. Ramsay, *St. Paul the Traveller and the Roman Citizen,* pp. 214-15.
2. Cf. Josephus, *Antiquities of the Jews,* XIX, x. 1-26.
3. Salo Wittmayer Baron, *A Social and Religious History of the Jews* (New York: Columbia U., 1956), 1:239-41.
4. Ibid., 1:188-91; 3:271-72.
5. A. N. Sherwin-White, *Roman Law and Society in the New Testament,* p. 95.
6. Ramsay, p. 218.
7. See *Smith's Dictionary of Greek and Roman Antiquities,* s.v. "Fasces;" "Lictors."
8. See Sherwin-White, pp. 71-75 for a good discussion of these terms.

9. See Ramsay, pp. 224-25, comments on "uncondemned."

10. W. D. Conybeare and J. S. Howson, *The Life, Times, and Travels of St. Paul* (New York: E. B. Treat, 1869), pp. 333-34.

11. Ramsay, pp. 230-31.

12. Sherwin-White, p. 100.

13. Josephus, XIV. vii. 2; xix. v. 2.

14. Sherwin-White, p. 100.

15. Josephus XIV. x. 1-26.

16. Ibid., XIX. vi. 3.

17. A reading of Judah Goddin fully supports and extensively illustrates the assertions expressed in these pages concerning the legal status and social position of Jews in the Roman Empire at the time of Paul's mission to Corinth (*The Jews, Their History, Culture and Religion,* ed. Luis Finkelstein [New York: Harper & Row], pp. 126-46; see also Salo Wittmayer Baron, *A Social and Religious History of the Jews* [New York: Columbia U., 1956], 1:188, 191, 239, 240).

18. Ramsay, p. 256.

19. Ibid., p. 258; also W. F. Arndt and F. W. Gingrich, *Greek-English Lexicon of the New Testament and Other Early Christian Literature,* s.v. "Corinth."

20. See *Smith's Dictionary of Greek and Roman Biography and Mythology,* s.v. "Gallio, L. Junius;" also *Holy Bible with Commentary by Bishops and Other Clergy of the Anglican Church,* comments on Ac 18:12.

21. Conybeare and Howson, 4:181.

22. See Sherwin-White, pp. 1-23 for details on the Latin terms relating to the judicial powers in Roman law with excellent explanations, placing all in the setting of about A.D. 50, the period when the incidents of Ac 18 took place.

23. Ibid., p. 5.

24. Ibid., p. 13.

25. Ibid., p. 79.

26. Ramsay, pp. 259-60.

27. F. F. Bruce, *The Book of Acts, New International Commentary on the New Testament* (Grand Rapids: Eerdmans, 1954), p. 373.

28. Sherwin-White, p. 92.

29. Ramsay, pp. 270-72.

30. Ibid., p. 277.

31. Ramsay, pp. 134-35.

32. Sherwin-White, pp. 83-87.

33. Ramsay, pp. 281-82.

34. Ibid.

35. W. M. Ramsay in *Hastings Dictionary of the Bible,* s.v. "Ephesus."

36. Conybeare and Howson, 2:440.

37. See Robert Culver, *Daniel and the Latter Days,* pp. 64-68.

38. Henry Alford, *The Greek Testament,* 2d ed. (London: Rivingstons, 1857), 3:56ff.

39. William Sanday and Arthur Hedlam in *International Critical Commentary,* "Romans," 5th ed. (Edinburgh: T. & T. Clark, 1902), p. xiv.

40. Ibid., pp. xiii-xiv; see also E. R. Goodenough, *The Church in the Roman Empire* New York: Cooper Square, 1970), pp. 60, 70, 147-48, 158 note; also J. B. Lightfoot, *Biblical Essays* (London: Macmillan, 1893), pp. 202-5.

CHAPTER EIGHTEEN

1. Henry Alford, *New Testament for English Readers* (Chicago: Moody, n.d.).

2. William Sanday and Arthur Hedlam in *International Critical Commentary,* "Romans," p. 366.

3. *Lange's Commentary,* p. 398 note.

4. See E. M. Blaiklock, *The Century of the New Testament* (Downer's Grove, Ill.: Inter-Varsity, 1962), pp. 41-43; and *Out of the Earth* (London: Intervarsity, 1962), pp. 42-49.

5. M. B. Riddle in *Lange's Commentary,* comments on Romans 13:1.

6. Sanday and Hedlam, comments on Romans 13:1.

7. See W. F. Arndt and F. W. Gingrich, *Greek-English Lexicon of the New Testament and Other Early Christian Literature,* s.v. "Huperecho."

8. See Oscar Cullmann, *The State in the New Testament,* pp. 50-56.

9. C. D. Morrison, *The Powers that Be* (London: SCM, 1960).
10. John Reumann and William Lazareth, *Righteousness and Society* (Philadelphia: Fortress, 1967), p. 101.
11. D. B. Stevick, *Civil Disobedience and The Christian* (New York: Seabury, 1969), pp. 28-30.
12. *Theological Dictionary of the New Testament,* s.v. "Exestin," "Exousia," "Exousiadzo," "Katexousiadzo."
13. Alford, comments on Ro 13:1-2.
14. Sanday and Hedlam, comments on Romans 13:2.
15. The (Anglican) Bishop of London in *Holy Bible with Commentary, The New Testament,* Vol. 3, comments on 1 Timothy 1:9.

CHAPTER NINETEEN

1. See *Lange's Commentary;* also *Meyer's Commentary on the New Testament* (Edinburgh: T. & T. Clark, 1882), comments on Ro 13:6.
2. Robert Haldane, *Exposition of the Epistle to the Romans,* 5th Edinburgh ed. (New York: Robert Carter, 1847), pp. 559-60.
3. E. A. Judge, *The Social Pattern of Christian Groups in the First Century* (London: Tyndale, 1960), p. 28.
4. Oscar Cullmann, *The State in the New Testament,* p. 65.
5. Ibid.
6. W. M. Ramsay, *Cities of St. Paul,* p. 90; see also pp. 89-93.
7. For more information, see footnote on p. 247.
8. E. M. Blaiklock, *The Century of the New Testament,* p. 48.
9. Merrill C. Tenney, *New Testament Survey* (Grand Rapids: Eerdmans, 1953), p. 344.

CHAPTER TWENTY

1. See Oscar Cullmann, *The State in the New Testament,* pp. 29-30.
2. J. J. Van Oosterzee in *Lange's Commentary,* p. 344.

EPILOGUE

1. Ernst Troeltsch, *The Social Teaching of the Churches* (New York: Harper Torchbook, 1960).
2. H. Hensley Henson, *Puritanism in England* (London: Hodder & Stoughton, 1912).
3. Ibid., p. 282.
4. Ibid., p. 283.
5. Ibid., pp. 283-85.
6. Thomas Molnar, *Utopia, the Perennial Heresy* (New York: Sheed & Ward, 1967).
7. Oscar Cullmann, *Jesus and the Revolutionaries,* trans. Gareth Putnam (New York: Harper & Row, 1970), pp. 53-54.
8. William L. Kalb, in *Religion and Contemporary Western Culture,* p. 361.
9. Alfred, Lord Tennyson, *Locksley Hall,* lines 119-30.

GENERAL INDEX

Abortion, 264n, 275
Albright, W. F., 122
Alford, Henry, 212fn, 239, 245n.1, 246, 252n.13
Allis, O. T., 124n.15
Angels, 56, 65, 67
Aquinas, 65-67, 68fn
Archer, G. L., 166n.3
Aristotle, 67, 68, 113, 265
Arndt, W. F., 224fn
Atonement, 36
Augustine, 14, 17, 67, 113

Babylon, 88-89, 136, 137
Bainton, Roland, 207fn
Balance of power, 104, 105, 130, 138
Baly, Denis, 152nn.3, 4
Baron, Salo, 222, 228n.17, 230fn
Barth, Karl, 37, 57, 250
Barton, G. A., 98fn
Becker, Carl, 279fn
Berkouwer, G. C., 14, 189n.1
Bird, Otto, 78fn
Bissell, E. C., 140n.8; 142nn.9, 10, 146n.15, 151n.1, 163n.14
Blaiklock, E. M., 216fn, 249n.4, 263-64
Bonhoeffer, Dietrich, 107-8, 169fn, 186, 207
Bourke, V. A., 184fn
Brandon, S. G. F., 200fn
Breasted, J. H., 55fn
Bright, John, 98fn, 122
Bruce, F. F., 231
Brunner, Emil, 17, 18, 105fn, 134, 286fn
Bultmann, R., 17
Buswell, J. O., 85fn

Cadbury, H. J., 217fn
Calvin, John, 34n.4, 35, 65, 73, 87, 104, 105, 111fn, 112fn, 113, 116fn, 130, 180fn, 236-37, 243, 248, 258
Capitalism, 111fn, 155-56, 179, 281-82
Capital punishment, 72-74, 77-78, 80, 142, 143, 148, 254, 256, 275
Chambers, Talbot, 115
Citizenship, 174-78, 206-7, 259-60
Civilization, 25, 27-28, 45

Cochrane, C. N., 204n.9
Coneybeare, W. D., 225n.10, 229, 237n.36
Cosmological outlook, 126-31
Covenants, 25, 72-74, 117, 123, 131, 132, 135
Creation, 40-42, 43-45, 47, 129, 275, 279
Cullman, Oscar, 37, 56n.8, 57, 189n.1, 191, 200, 201, 202, 203, 204, 207, 250, 261, 263n.5, 270n.1, 280
Culver, R. D., 95n.4, 161n.11, 238n.37
Currey, G., 55n.7

Deism, 41
Delitzsch, F., 73, 76-77, 91, 95-96, 102, 169n.5, 171, 172n.11, 177n.16
Democracy. See Government, civil, democratic
Demons, 37, 51, 56
deVaux, Pierre, 118-19, 140n.8, 143n.11, 154n.6, 163n.14, 164n.15
Dibelius, Martin, 56, 57
Dooyeweerd, H., 67, 78fn, 105, 207

Edersheim, Alfred, 201, 202, 203
Egypt, 55, 89, 114, 121, 126
Eissfeldt, Otto, 165n.1, 166n.3
Elert, Werner, 105fn
Elliott, C. J., 75n.18
Ellul, Jacques, 78fn, 155
Evil, problem of, 31

Fall, 13, 15-18, 20, 24, 25, 28, 29, 32, 33, 37, 68fn, 71, 279, 283
Family, 20-24, 28, 29, 143, 157fn, 164, 165, 178-79
Fate, 45, 62
Frankfort, H., 127
Freedom, 108-110

Gardner, F. F. L., 265fn
God
  doctrine of, 26, 34, 41, 42, 43, 207
  preservation by, 129-30
  providence of, 41, 62-64, 85fn, 87, 88, 173, 176, 178, 207
  sovereignty of, 41, 44, 47, 53, 74-76, 87, 88, 123, 251

Goddin, Judah, 228 n.17
Government, civil
  aristocracy, 111, 112
  basis, 65-71, 74-80
  in biblical history, 61-83
  in biblical legislation, 116-25
  in biblical prophecy, OT, 84-101
  in biblical wisdom, 165-81
  Christian's relation to, 39, 47, 48, 64,
    182, 184, 225, 227, 244, 248, 251-
    90
  Christian view of, 8, 18-19, 24, 28-29,
    38-39, 43, 47, 48, 74, 225-27, 244,
    248-90
  democratic, 47, 53, 70, 130, 131 fn,
    168, 282
  establishment of, 72-80
  Jesus' view of, 182-207, 249
  Messianic, 102-115, 187
  monarchical, 47, 53, 54, 55, 111, 119,
    123, 130, 282
  Mosaic, 126-64
  New Testament warnings and predic-
    tions with regard to, 269-73
  patriarchal, 29, 65, 121, 122, 123
  Paul's view of, 208-266
  Peter's view of, 266-68
  and providence, 62-64
  and religion, 126-31, 133
  republican, 130
  responsibility of, 88-101
  and Satan, 49-52, 55-57, 225, 231,
    271-72, 276
  theocratic, 53, 76, 77, 119, 125, 130,
    132, 134, 144, 145, 202
Green, Robert, W., 111 fn, 112 fn
Grounds, Vernon, 109 fn, 201 fn

Haldane, Robert, 33, 258
Hallowell, John, 7 fn, 66 n.6
Hamilton, Alexander, 103, 109
Hayakawa, S. I., 280 fn
Heard, J. B., 14 n.5
Hegel, Georg, 65, 66, 74
Heimert, Alan, 109, 112 fn, 279 fn
Heine, Heinrich, 288-89
Hengstenberg, E. W., 137 n.3
Henson, H. H., 277-78
Herberg, Will, 103-4, 129-30
Herschberger, Guy F., 207 fn
Hobbes, Thomas, 74
Hodge, C., 246
Hohner, H. W., 201 fn
Hooke, S. H., 54-55
Hoyt, Herman, 207 fn
Hudson, Winthrop, 112 fn
Hyma, Albert, 112 fn

Irwin, W. A., 128
Israel, 82, 85, 92, 119, 121, 122, 125,
  126, 138

Jesus
  and political power, 186-96
  practice & example of, with regard to
    civil government, 182-96,
  teachings of, with regard to civil
    government, 197-207
Johnson, A. R., 54 fn
Josephus, 76; 116 n.1; 134; 135;
  140 nn.5, 7; 162 nn.12, 13; 198 n.1;
  200; 214; 216; 220 fn; 221 n.2; 222;
  228
Jowett, J. H., 246
Judge, E. A., 216 fn, 259
Judges, 139-41
Justice, 78, 79, 89-91, 105-8, 139, 141-
  50, 169, 205, 206, 245-46, 255-56,
  285

Kalb, William, 285
Kant, Immanuel, 66
Kay, W., 136 n.2
Keil, C. F., 70 n.10; 73; 93 fn; 121;
  122 nn.10, 11; 140; 145 n.14; 148 fn;
  151 n.2; 154 n.5; 159 n.10
King, 171, 173, 176, 282
Kristol, Irving, 279 fn
Kuyper, Abraham, 28 n.1, 52, 54, 68, 81,
  109, 180, 203 n.7, 207
Kyle, M. J., 125

Labor, 12-13, 24, 35, 283
Law
  moral, 86, 87, 92, 96, 252
  Mosaic, 86, 87, 89, 91-93, 116-19,
    121, 131-32, 144-45, 147, 149, 155,
    160, 161, 167, 173, 230
  natural, 69, 85, 86, 92, 95-96, 129,
    252
  Roman, 207-15, 222, 224, 225, 227-
    28, 229, 230
Leupold, H. C., 73
Lewis, C. S., 73
Lex Talionis, 142, 205-6, 245-46
Lightfoot, J. B., 217, 240 n.40
Littel, Franklin, 207 fn
Locke, John, 74
Luther, Martin, 38, 72, 73, 105, 111 n,
  112 fn, 180 fn

M'Clintock, John, 144 nn.12, 13; 192 n.4
McLain, A. J., 73, 74 n.16, 79 n.25,
  105 n.4, 107 n.7, 124, 156
McLaughlin, W. G., 109
Madison, James, 103
Man
  as created being, 11-16, 28, 34, 68,
    69, 70
  doctrine of, 7, 274, 275
  as fallen being, 15-25, 28, 29, 32, 33,
    35, 103, 104, 256, 274, 275
  as image of God, 11, 12, 14, 28, 34,
    74, 77, 78, 80, 275

Manson, T. W., 191fn
Marlowe, Christopher, 49
Marriage, 12, 21, 22, 28, 165, 178-79, 283-84
Marx, Karl, 265fn, 276, 288
Mercy and justice, 105-8
Messiah, 102, 106, 110, 187, 188
Meyer, H. A., 247fn
Milton, John, 57
Molnar, Ferenc, 279
Mommsen, Theodor, 216fn
Monarchy. *See* Government, civil, monarchical
Monotheism, 120-28
Morris, Leon, 79n.23
Morrison, C. D., 250
Moses, 123, 124, 135
Mowinckel, Sigmund, 54
Murphy, J. G., 73
Murray, John, 13, 73, 77-78

Nation, concept of, 119-21
Nichols, J. H., 67fn, 128n.5
Niebuhr, Reinhold, 14, 15, 40, 43, 287fn
North, Robert, 157
Noth, Martin, 98fn

Occult, 44, 117, 118
Orr, James, 274
Ottley, R. L., 100-101
Owen, Robert, 276

Pacifism, 207fn, 270
Pantheism, 41, 42, 43, 62, 66
Pascal, Blaise, 15, 18
Paul
   practice & example of, with regard to civil government, 208-40
   as Roman citizen, 211-15, 223
   teaching of, with regard to civil government, 241-66
Payne, J. B., 134, 166n.2
Penner, Archie, 50
Plato, 113, 265
Pliny, 267-68
Plumptre, E. H., 166n.4, 172n.12, 176n.13
Poor, 91, 97, 99, 100, 118, 156-65, 172-75, 180-81, 265, 281
Preservation. *See* God, preservation by
Press, S. D., 132
Property, 68fn, 145, 151-60, 165, 175, 179, 180, 281, 282
Providence, see God, providence of
Puritans, 277, 278

Rachfall, F., 111-12fn
Ramsey, W. M., 213; 214; 215; 218; 220fn; 221n.1; 223; 224nn.6, 9; 227n.11; 229; 230-31; 232n.29; 233n.30; 234n.31; 235; 236; 263

Religion, 24-27, 128-31
Reumann, John, 250
Revelation, natural, 87, 93, 94, 95, 96
Revolution, 108-11, 172, 176-77, 180, 276
Rich, 99, 100, 156-58, 165, 173, 174, 281
Riddle, M. B., 249n.5
Robertson, H. M., 112fn
Rome, 209, 211, 212, 239, 248, 263
Rousseau, J. J., 74
Ruff, G. E., 34n.3
Rulers
   functions of, 168-73, 206
   responsibility of, 88-99, 117, 141, 167, 169, 172, 173, 257
   terms for, 167-68
Rushdoony, R. J., 78fn, 79, 129n.6, 131fn, 207

Sabbath, 12, 13
Salvation, doctrine of, 27
Sanday, William, 239-40, 247, 249n.6, 252n.14
Satan, 7, 37, 49-52, 55, 56, 57, 272, 274, 279
Sauer, Erich, 73
Schaff, Phillip, 248, 273fn
Scharlemann, M. H., 64n.2
Schuerer, A. N., 214, 215, 216fn
Seneca, 229, 236, 237, 265fn
Sherwin-White, A. N., 208; 209n.2; 212n.3; 216n.8; 223n.5; 224fn; 227; 228; 231; 234n.32; 229nn.22, 23; 230nn.24, 25
Sin
   and civil government, 68-71, 102, 103, 104, 256
   original, 16-18, 104, 130, 277
Singer, Gregg, 109fn
Slavery, 68n, 89, 151, 160-64, 211
Socialism, 99, 155, 186, 276, 281-82
Sombart, Werner, 111fn, 112fn
Sovereignty
   of God. *See* God, sovereignty of
   of government, 52-55, 75, 76, 123, 129, 169-70
   spheres of, 105, 203, 245, 283-84
Spurrell, G. P., 11n.1
Spyerman, Gordon, 180n.18
State, concept of, 118-19, 121, 129
Stevick, Daniel B., 250
Stuart, Moses, 171n.10, 179n.17
Sturzo, Luigi, 287fn

Tacitus, 220fn, 247fn, 263
Tawney, R. H., 111fn
Taxes, 197-204, 257-59
Taylor, E. L. H., 66fn, 67n.7, 78fn
Tenney, M. C., 267n.9
Tennyson, A. L., 289, 290
Tertullian, 204

Theocracy. *See* government, civil, theo-
    cratic
Thielicke, Helmut, 38, 105fn
Tillich, Paul, 78fn
Totalitarianism, 66, 75, 204, 254, 275
Toy, C. H., 167fn, 170n.7, 171, 176-77
Troeltsche, Ernst, 66fn, 68fn, 111fn,
    112fn, 207fn, 274, 287fn
Trojan, 268fn

Utopia, 276-80, 288

Van Imshoot, Paul, 64n.1
Van Oosterzee, J. J., 270
Van Til, Henry, 128n.4
Von Orelli, C., 95
von Rad, Gerhard, 33n.1, 73n.14

Weber, Max, 111fn, 112fn
Werner, Karl, 68fn

Whitehead, A. N., 127
Wilson, W. R., 201fn
Wisemann, P. J., 11n.1
Woman, 20-24, 71
World
    biblical statements about, 30-38, 50
    biblical words for, 40-42, 45-49
    Christian's relation to, 31, 38, 42, 43,
        47, 48
    as controlled by Satan, 49, 50, 51,
        271-72, 276
    doctrine of, 7, 30-49, 274, 279
    as evil, 36, 38
    as governed by God, 41, 42, 44, 47
    redeemed by Christ, 36-38, 129

Yoder, John, 50, 207fn

Zealots, 200-204, 270

SCRIPTURE INDEX

OLD TESTAMENT

GENESIS

1-4	11
1-11	18
1:4	31
1:27	14, 69
1:28	12, 20, 70
1:31	31
2	13
2:3	41
2:4	12
2:7	32 fn, 95
2:15	12
2:21-22	68 fn
2:24	70
3	16, 17
3:7-19	32
3:16	20-21, 23, 71
3:17-24	24, 33
3:20	68 n
4	25
4:1-2	25
4:1-16	71
4:3	26
4:6-15	27
4:16	26
4:16-24	27
4:19-24	71
5-9	28
5:3-4	25
6-9	29
6:13	71
8:21-22	72
9	38, 75, 283
9:1-7	97
9:4-6	72, 74, 95
9:5	74
9:6	74, 275
9:12	73
10	65, 81
10:5, 10	65
10:32	81
11	136
11:1-9	81
12	18, 82
12:2	121, 125 fn
12:3	138
14	65
15:2-5	123
15:12-15	121
15:12-18	94
15:14	125 fn
15:16	137
17:20	125
18:25	75, 256
25:31-34	154
35:29—36:8	136
37:25	152
47:1, 6	153
47:8, 21	122
47:27	153
48:20-22	154
49:3-4	154

EXODUS

3:1—5:18	135
3:6-7	131
4:1-9	135
4:22-23, 25	132
4:29-31	123
5:6, 14-16	140
7:4	134
8:19	135
9:16	123
11:1-3	153
12:29-31	123
12:35-36	153
12:41	134
12:44	164
14:14	134
15:1	134
15:18	77
15:20	24
16:22-30	13, 26
17:14, 16	137
18:13-25	124, 139
18:16, 22	134
20	13, 132
20:10	164
20:12	182
20:12-17	94
20:15-17	281
21-22	89
21:2	163
21:6	139, 163
21:7-11	145, 162
21:12-25	148
21:15	140
21:16	162
21:20	163
21:22-25	205
21:23	142
21:23-36	151
21:27-28	163
21:28-36	145, 162
22:1-3	151
22:1-4	162
22:4	143, 151
22:6-14	151
22:8	139
22:11	143
22:21	136, 158
22:22-25	158
22:25	179
22:28	252
23:1	186
23:1-9	145
23:2-3	99
23:9	136, 158
23:11	159
23:12	164
23:22	134
23:27-33	137
24:1-11	124
24:4	122
28:30	135
28:36	115
30:13	198
31:1	123

31:18	135
34:10-29	137
38:26	198

LEVITICUS

6:1-7	152
8:8	135
10	143
10:10-11	141
18	137
18:1-23	148
18:7, 15	92
18:24-28	94, 149
19	132
19:15-16	99
19:17-18	206, 246
19:18	145
19:36	171
20:10	140
20:11	92
20:22-27	149
20:28	137
22:10-11	164
24:10-23	124, 205
24:17-18	142, 151
24:17-21	148
24:21	145
24:22	205
25-26	149
25:6	159
25:23-28	153-54, 162
25:25-46	151
25:39	162
25:39-46	163

NUMBERS

5:6-7	143
10:35	134
11:16-30	124, 137
12:6	43
12:8	135
15:32-36	124
16	123, 124
16:3	169
16:18-19	141
16:28-30	124
17:21	122
21:14	134
24:11	140
24:20	137
25	137
26:28	122
26:52-56	153
26:57	122
27:4	154
27:21	135
27:36	154
30:1-16	23
31:16	137
31:25-54	153
33:54	153
34:12-29	137
35:9-34	148
35:30	143

DEUTERONOMY

1:13	139
1:17-18	123
2:4-19	137
2:10-22	145
4:25-40	138
5	132
6	137
6-9	145
6:4-13	145
6:5-6	132
7:1-5	137
8:3	135
8:7-10	152
8:17-18	123
9:1-5	148
9:10	135
10	132
10:12-13	131
10:17-19	131, 136
12:12, 18	164
13:1-11	140
13:10	143
14:28-29	160
15:1-12	89, 159
15:11	156
15:14-18	163
16:11, 14	164
16:18	140
16:18-20	139, 141
17:5	140
17:6	143, 186
17:7	143
17:8-13	139, 140
17:13	147 fn
17:14-20	119, 123
17:15, 18	124
18:9-22	117, 118, 135
19:10-13	148
19:15	143, 186
19:15-20	206
19:16	139
19:18	143
19:19	139, 143
19:19-21	146, 147 fn
19:21	142, 205
20:5, 8-9	140
20:10-18	137
21:1-9	148
21:5	141
21:15	93 fn
21:15-17	154
21:18	146
21:18-21	183
22:1-4	145
23:5	77
23:7-8	136
23:15, 19-20	158
23:24-25	151
24:6	147 fn
24:7	162
24:14-15	158
24:16	142
25:1-3	142
25:11-12	146
25:13-16	171
25:17-19	137
26:12-13	160
27:19	158
32:15-18	44
32:17	129
32:35	206, 246
33:1-5	123
33:5	124, 134
33:8	135

JOSHUA

1:10	140
3:2	140
4:2	122
7:16-18	139
13:7, 14, 33	122
16:1, 14, 17	122
17:3	154

JUDGES

2:6-23	132
4:4-24	24
4:15	141
5:8	44, 129

RUTH

2:3, 20	63
4:3	154
4:11	123

1 SAMUEL

1:27	123
6:9	63
8:5	119, 168
8:7-9	119
8:10-20	170
8:11-18	119
8:19-20	168
10:25	119
25:9-38	206
25:31-33	246
28:6	135

2 SAMUEL

7:14	146
8:18	134
14:2-20	24
16:12	246
18:6-8	152
24:1	31

1 KINGS

3:26	143
16:9	174
21	154
21:10	143
21:10-16	144

2 KINGS

4:1	151, 162
8:3	154
21	157
23:30, 31-33	90

1 CHRONICLES

2:34-35	164
3:15	90
5:1	154
21:1	31

2 CHRONICLES

6:32-33	113
17:7-9	141
19:4-7, 8-11	141
34:22-28	24
36:11-21	96
36:14-16	133
36:21	154

EZRA

2:63	135

NEHEMIAH

5:5	151, 162
7:65	135
9:6	42
9:13-14	13, 26

JOB

10:12	62
12:18-25	88
13:1-11	136
13:15	45
19:25	45
20:19	159
24:3-4	159
24:9	151
24:9-14	159
29:12-16	159
31:13-15	164
31:17	159
38-39	40

[PSALMS]

38:4	45
41:33	45

PSALMS

2:1-5	170
2:7-9	107
8	13
8:4	7, 40
10:9-10	107
17:14	100
19:1-7	43
23	98
24:1-2	31
33:11	62
36:6	42
50	132
55:25	73
72	100
72:1-2	79, 100, 170
72:4	100
72:7	112
72:12-14	100
73:1-16	107
74	132
75:7	88
83:18	123
89:14	106
90:2	94
92-99	75
92:8	75
93:1-2	75
94	149, 150
94:1-2, 10	75
95:3-6	75
96:3-4	75
96:5, 7-10, 12-13	76
97:1-6	76
98:2, 6-7, 9	76
99:4	76
99:6	135
103:7	135
103:19	31
104	42, 43
105:26-43	135
106	135
110:1-2	189
110:2, 5-6	271
113:9	123
114:1-2	121
115:6	12
126	123, 136
127	123
148:11	167 fn
149:8	170

PROVERBS

2:17	178
3:16	179
3:27-28	180
5:15-19, 20	178
6:20	179
8:6	168
8:12-15	170
8:15-16	63, 167-69
9:13	178
10:1, 4	179
10:15	180
11:4	180
11:10-11	174
11:28	180
12:4	178
12:9	179
12:24	169 fn
13:4, 8, 11	179
13:24	146
14:1	178
14:20, 23, 26	179
14:28	97, 170
14:31	180
14:34	174
15-16	180
15:20	179
16:10-15	170-172

16:33	63	16:5	172	18:12-17	159		
17:1	180	16:12	114	18:20	142		
17:2	169 fn	17:5-8	114	20	132		
17:26	172	18:6-7	114	22:29	159		
18:3	172	19:21, 22-25	114	25-32	84		
18:13	186	23:8	168	26-28	89		
18:22	178	24:4	94	27:17	152		
19:4	180	24:5	95	28:2	55, 89		
19:5, 9	172	24:13	94	28:4-7, 12	89		
19:10	174	24:21-23	95	29:3	55		
19:13	178	26:4-6	91	33:1-9	217		
19:14	178-79	26:9	107	34:2, 5, 7-10, 12, 23	99		
19:18	146	32:1, 5, 8	112	35	84		
19:26	179	33:17-22	104	37:24	99		
20:10, 11, 20	179	33:22	134	38-39	84		
20:22	206, 246	34	136	46:16	154		
21:1	63	35:4	29				
21:3	180	40:9-11	106	**DANIEL**			
21:6	179	42:14	102	1:2	87		
21:9	178	44:28	88, 98	2	63		
21:14	180	44:28—45:7	91	2:1-30	87		
21:19	178	45:13	88	2:19-23	43		
21:20	179	48:47	114	3-4	84		
21:28	172	49:6, 7-22, 39	114	3:17	271		
21:31	174	52:13	177	4:17	63, 88, 242, 251		
22:1-2	173, 180	52:13—53:12	161	4:25-27	89		
22:4	173	53	184	4:35	31, 87		
22:6	179	55:8-9	62	4:37	89		
22:7	169 fn, 179	59:14	107	5	84		
22:15	179, 183	63:1-6	136	5:1-30	89		
22:20	169 fn			5:21	88		
22:22-23	158, 172	**JEREMIAH**		6	84, 89		
22:28	175	1:9-10	85	6:26	88		
22:29	176	2:1-37	129	6:28	84		
23:1-2	176	2:8	98	7	63, 95, 241		
23:10-11	175-76	2:32	23	7:13	102, 103		
23:13	146, 179	2:34-37	148	7:17-18	112		
24:3	179	5:1, 4-8	99	7:18	103, 244		
24:21-22	176-77	5:7-17	94	7:21-27	112		
24:27	178	5:28	159	7:22	103, 244		
25:2-7, 15	176	5:30-31	92	7:27	88, 103, 244		
25:21-22	206, 246	6:13	99	8:5-8	84		
27:15	178	6:16-21	132	8:16	56		
28:2-3	158, 172	8:22	152	8:20-22	84		
28:8	179	10:21	99	9	132		
28:15-16	173	12:10	99	9:21	56		
28:16	168	21:1-7	96	9:26	102		
28:20-22	179	21:11-12	97	10:2, 11-13	31		
29-31	173	21:12	96	10:13, 21	56, 168		
29:2	173	22:2-3	97	11:2	84		
29:3	179	22:6	152	13:62	143		
29:4	173	22:10-17	96				
29:8	177	22:13-17	90, 159	**HOSEA**			
29:12-14	173	22:18-19	91, 96	1:4	148		
29:25-26	177	22:22	99	4:1-5	148		
30:1-10	178	22:24-29	96				
30:24-28	69	23:1, 2, 4	99	**JOEL**			
30:29-31	174	23:5-6	105-6, 110	2:20	84		
31:1-7	174	25	96	3:1-21	84		
31:1-9	178	25:9	242				
31:9	169	25:34-36	99	**AMOS**			
31:10-31	23, 178	27:5	123	1:3—2:3	84		
31:16	178	27:6	242	1:3-5	91		
		29:7	39	1:6-8, 9-10	92		
ECCLESIASTES		32:7	154	1:11	136		
8:9	88	33:15	102, 110	1:11-12	92		
		34:8-22	89-90	1:13-15	92		
ISAIAH		36:30	91	2:1-3, 4-5	92		
1:2-31	132	37:6	90	2:6-7	92, 97, 159		
1:4-7	94	39:10	99	2:8	92		
2:1-5	113	40-44	99	3:2	138		
5:19	62	46	89	4:1	97		
8:2	143	46-51	84	4:4	160		
8:19	43, 44	46:11	152	5:11-12	97		
9:6-7	102, 195, 196	50:6, 44	99	8:6	97		
10:1-2	91, 159	50:15-18	88	9:12	113		
11:1-5	110						
11:1-2	102	**LAMENTATIONS**		**OBADIAH**			
11:4	97	3:27	80	1-21	84		
12:14-17	114						
13-24	84, 94	**EZEKIEL**		**JONAH**			
13:1—14:23	136	7:12-13	154	1:2	93		
13:9-11	89	16:1-14	23				
14:4-6, 11-14	89						

MICAH

4:1-13	113
5:5	99
6:11	171

NAHUM

3:18	99

HABAKKUK

1:1-17	107

ZEPHANIAH

2:4-15	84

HAGGAI

2:7	84

ZECHARIAH

2:6-13	84
6:1-15	84
7:9-10	159
8:23	84
9:1-8	84
10:2-3	99
10:10	152
11:3, 5, 8, 15-16	99
12:1-14	84
14:1-21	115
14:9	103
14:9-21	84
14:20	115, 134

MALACHI

3:9-11	160

NEW TESTAMENT

MATTHEW

2:1	82
3:11	163
4:8-9	49, 57
5	100
5:5	91
5:13	264
5:38-39	205
5:43-48	246
6:24	203
8:5-13	186
9:34	56
10:14	217
10:16-18	185, 269
10:18	64
10:21-22	269
10:23, 24-27, 28-33	270
10:34	269
12:1	151
12:24, 27	56
15:1-8	34
15:16-20	35
16:21	190, 198
16:22-27	198
17:24-27	197-99
18:6	199
18:17	185, 270
18:23-25	162
19:28	244
20:17-19	186, 190, 191
20:25	185
21:31	185
21:33-41	187
22:1-14	188
22:15-22	197, 199-204
23	184-85
24:14	46
25:14-31	281
25:19	194
26:50-54	192
26:52	193, 270
26:59-68	143-44
26:63-66	190, 191
27:20-26	190
28:19-20	290

MARK

2:13-20	270
2:27	13
5:30-31	198
7:1-4	34
8:31	190
9:1	187
10:6	41
10:17-25	186
10:32-34	186, 190, 191
1:15-16, 27-33	187
12:13-17	197, 199-204
13:19	41
14:47-50	192
14:61-65	190
15:10	195
16:15	46
16:19	189

LUKE

1:5	82
1:32-33	187
1:52	88
2:1-7	83
2:2	82
2:51	183, 250
3:12-13, 14	186
4:6	49, 57
5:27-32	186
6:15	200
7:1-10	186
9:3-6	270
9:22, 51	190
9:51-56	270
10:18	272
12:13-14	189
13:1-3	185
13:1-9	271
13:22-35	190
13:31-32	185, 271
14:5	264
14:8-10	176
16:9-13	203
16:19-31	186
18:18, 31-33	186
18:32	190
19:1-10	186
19:11	194
19:12-26	281
19:38, 40	187
20:9-18	186
20:20-26	197, 199-204
22:30	188
22:35-36	270
22:66-71	191
23:2	201
23:34	242

JOHN

1:17	183
1:29	26
3:16	31
3:19	264
3:36	16
7:3-7	35
7:45-51	186
8:7	143
9:11	170
12:31	50
13:8	163
14:30	31, 50
16:11	50, 272
18:10-11	192-93
18:33-37	193-94
18:36	195
19:10-11	192

ACTS

1:6-8	195
1:13	200
2:23	192, 242
2:29-36	194, 207
2:34	189

2:43	249
3:17	242
3:23	249
4:19-20	271
5:29	271
5:31	189
6:8—7:60	144
7:35	124
7:54-60	215 fn
7:55	189
7:57—8:1	215
8:3-4	216
9:1-9	216
9:2	216 fn, 227
9:3	216 fn
9:30	210
10:1-22	221
11:22-26	210
12	269
13-20	236
13:28	209-10
13:5-12	210, 219
13:13-52	210
13:14, 44	218
13:51	217, 218
14	210, 217
14:1-5, 19-20	218
15:22, 26	218
16	210
16:11-40	222-25
16:14-15	221
16:35-40	244
17	210
17:1-9	222
17:5	226
17:6, 8	82
17:16-34	242
17:22-31	221
17:26	68 fn
17:28	42
18	211
18:1-8	242
18:1-17	222, 228-31
18:2	24, 249
18:3	232
18:6	217
18:12-16	216 fn
18:21-22	233
18:26	24
19	211
19:1-20	232-36
19:5	226
19:21	239
19:23-41	222, 226-27
19:31	234
20	211
20:31, 34	232
21:27-33	255
21-28	211, 222, 236-38
21:39	213 fn, 214
22-28	86
22:1-19	216
22:5	216 fn, 228
22:19	216 fn
22:20	215 fn
22:23	217
22:24-25	238
22:28	212 fn, 238
23:1	239
23:1-3	186
23:3-5	271
23:11	239
23:12-35	255
24:2	62
25:6-9	255
25:9-10	238
25:10-12	255
25:13	82
26:1-32	262
26:9-20	216
26:11	216 fn
26:12	227-28

ROMANS

1:1	161
1:9-10	262
1:13	248
1:18	92
1:18—2:16	150
1:20	41
1:21-23	26
1:28	92
2:14-15	86, 95
3:29	113
5:12	17
5:12-20	16, 18
6:16	55
8:7	250
8:19-22	33, 41
8:19-25	37
8:34	189
8:38	56
9:3	215
9:13	136
10:17	27
11:36	41
12	244
12:17-21	245, 246, 247
12:17—13:14	166
12:19—13:5	77
13	103, 129
13:1	47, 51, 76, 88, 170, 238
13:1-7	57, 241, 244-59
13:1-14	259
13:3	225
13:4	275
13:5	95, 171
13:8-9	74
14:1	199
15:15-16	248
15:24, 28	233
16:1	24
16:3	232
16:7-21	215

1 CORINTHIANS

1:18-31	242
1:24	169 fn
2:1-5	242
2:6	57, 259
2:6-8	241-43
2:8	51, 57, 259
2:14	242
3:1-4	242
4:9	271
4:11-12	232
5:11	270
6:1-10	241, 243-44, 259
7	260
7:17	123
7:21-23	161
7:25	23
7:27-32	260
7:36	23
8:4-5	51, 56
8:5-6	44
10:19-20	56
10:20-21	51
11:3	23
12:28	286
14:33	69
14:34	23, 118
15:9	216
15:25	189
15:32	233
16:1	281
16:19	232

2 CORINTHIANS

4:3-4	51
4:18	42
8-9	281
10:3-5	190
10:3-6	262
11:13-15	51

11:24	216 fn
11:32	82

GALATIANS

1:4	35
1:13, 22-24	216
4:3	56
4:4	138
4:9	56

EPHESIANS

1:11	31
1:20	189
2:2	47, 50
2:3	17
2:8-9	27
2:19	239, 259
3:9	41
3:10	271
5:1	31
5:22	250
5:24	250
5:24-25	23
6:1	256
6:5	161
6:10-12	271
6:12	50, 56

PHILIPPIANS

1:14, 20, 24	237
1:27	239
2:6-10	56, 189
2:10-11	37
2:12-13	27
2:19-24	237
3:6	216
3:20	239, 259

COLOSSIANS

1:14	36
1:17	42
1:18	36
1:19-23	36-37
1:20	56
2:15	56
3:1	189
3:11	231
3:22	161

1 THESSALONIANS

2:18	226
3:1-3	226
4:10-13	262

2 THESSALONIANS

2	225, 231 fn, 238-39
2:3	239
2:6-7	238-39
2:7-12	241
2:8	231 fn
3:6-10	13

1 TIMOTHY

1	261
1:3	237
1:8-9	193
1:9	225
1:9-10	253
1:13	216
2:1-4	241, 260-64, 276
2:1-5	39
2:4	240
3:16	272
4:3	34
5:8-16	13
6:17-19	281

2 TIMOTHY

1:16-17	237
3:16	118

4	238
4:6-8, 20	237

TITUS

1:5	237
2:3-5	23
2:12	183
3:1	250
3:1-3	241, 264-66
3:12	237

HEBREWS

1:1-2	42
1:3	189
2:5	45
4:10	41
8:1	189
9:22	26
10:12-13	189
10:25	26
10:28	143
11:4	25-27
11:13	259
11:13-16	280
11:16	48
12:16-17	136

JAMES

4:13-16	281
5:1-6	281

1 PETER

1:1, 17	259
1:19, 20	192
1:23-25	27
2:1	267
2:11	184, 259
2:11-17	266-68, 272
2:12	184, 259
2:13	250, 256
2:13-14	184
2:17	184
2:18	250
2:21-23	184
3:1	23
3:1-4	262
3:5-6	23
3:13-17	272
3:22	56, 189
4	263
4:11-19	270, 272
5:5	250

2 PETER

3:4	41

1 JOHN

2:15	31
2:17	42
3:10-11	27
3:11-12	25
4:4	51
5:19	51

2 JOHN

10-11	13

JUDE

11	25

REVELATION

1:9	190
3:14	41
3:21	189
4-20	95
6:9	190
11:15	194, 259, 272
12:11	190
13	241
13-18	269
13:1-7	261
14:8	136
16:3	249

16:19	136	18:2, 10, 21	136	21:24	114
17:5	136	19:11—20:4	195	22:17	38
17:17	251	20:3, 8, 10	51